INVISIBLE NO MORE

Latino men and boys in the United States are confronted with a wide variety of hardships that are not easily explained or understood. They are populating prisons, dropping out of high school, and over-represented in the service industry at alarming degrees. Young Latino men, especially, have among the lowest wages earned in the country, a rapidly growing rate of HIV/AIDS, and one of the highest mortality rates due to homicide. Although there has been growing interest in the status of men in American society, there is a glaring lack of research and scholarly work available on Latino men and boys.

This groundbreaking interdisciplinary volume, edited by renowned scholars Pedro Noguera, Aída Hurtado and Edward Fergus, addresses the dearth of scholarship and information about Latino men and boys to further our understanding of the unique challenges and obstacles that they confront during this historical moment. The contributors represent a cross section of disciplines from health, criminal justice, education, literature, psychology, economics, labor, sociology and more. By drawing attention to the sweeping issues facing this segment of the population, this volume offers research and policy a set of principles and overarching guidelines for decreasing the invisibility and thus the disenfranchisement of Latino men and boys.

Pedro Noguera is Peter L. Agnew Professor of Education in the Steinhardt School of Culture, Education, and Human Development at New York University.

Aída Hurtado is Professor and Luis Leal Endowed Chair in the Chicana and Chicano Studies Department at the University of California, Santa Barbara.

Edward Fergus is Deputy Director of the Metropolitan Center for Urban Education at New York University.

INVISIBLE NO MORE

Understanding the
Disenfranchisement of
Latino Men and Boys

Edited by
Pedro Noguera
Aída Hurtado
Edward Fergus

Routledge
Taylor & Francis Group

NEW YORK AND LONDON

First published 2012
by Routledge
711 Third Avenue, New York, NY 10017

Simultaneously published in the UK
by Routledge
2 Park Square, Milton Park, Abingdon, Oxon OX14 4RN

Routledge is an imprint of the Taylor & Francis Group, an informa business

Library of Congress Cataloging in Publication Data
    Understanding the disenfranchisement of Latino men and boys:
    invisible no more/edited by Pedro Noguera, Aída Hurtado,
    Edward Fergus.
    p. cm.
    1. Hispanic American men—Social conditions. 2. Hispanic American
    men—Economic conditions. 3. Hispanic American men—Psychology.
    4. Hispanic American boys—Social conditions. 5. Hispanic American
    boys—Economic conditions. 6. Hispanic American boys—Psychology.
    7. Alienation (Social psychology)—United States. I. Noguera, Pedro.
    II. Hurtado, Aída. III. Fergus, Edward, 1974–
    E184.S75U44 2011
    305.38′868073--dc22
    2011015112

ISBN: 978–0–415–87778–7 (hbk)
ISBN: 978–0–415–87779–4 (pbk)
ISBN: 978–0–203–81349–2 (ebk)

Typeset in Bembo
by Florence Production Ltd, Stoodleigh, Devon
Printed and bound in the United States of America on acid-free paper
by Edwards Brothers, Inc.

SUSTAINABLE FORESTRY INITIATIVE   Certified Fiber Sourcing   www.sfiprogram.org

CONTENTS

ILLUSTRATIONS

Figures

Tables

1

INVISIBLE NO MORE

The Status and Experience of Latino Males from Multidisciplinary Perspectives

Pedro A. Noguera
Aída Hurtado

Many working-class Latino men living in the United States are visible when they are of utility to the economy, but more often their talents and vulnerabilities are invisible to the larger society. In this volume we attempt to make them "invisible no more" through a multidisciplinary set of analyses of the issues and challenges they face at the beginning of the twenty-first century in North America. We begin by describing a common scene that is being played out in urban and rural communities across the United States.

As is true most mornings, the intersection of Highway 27 and Majors Path is lined with Latino men. On this particular morning, about forty to fifty men are gathered in clusters, waiting patiently along the side of the road. By their attire—beat-up work clothes and a wide variety of t-shirts—they seem out of place in Long Island's Southampton, one of the wealthiest communities in the United States. But today, few of the people in the cars that pass by seem to notice their presence; they blend in and are largely ignored, as though they were part of the landscape.

To even the casual observer, it is clear that these men are here for a purpose. They may seem idle but actually they are waiting, waiting for work. Waiting to be picked up to fix a roof, to paint a wall, to cut a lawn, or move some furniture. Some are skilled craftsmen who can perform complex tasks such as masonry, drywall, plumbing, or electrical work on new homes and mansions. Others are there simply to sell their labor, willing to take on any job, no matter how dirty or laborious.

Although gatherings such as this one may seem haphazard and unorganized, these men, and thousands of others like them across the United States, are part of an informal, unregulated labor market that has become vital to the economy of the nation. Without their labor, important economic sectors such as construction, tourism, food processing, and agriculture could not function (Valenzuela et al., 2006). Aside from the occasional protester, the presence of these Latino men in Southampton does not evoke a response from most passers-by. This early-morning ritual of waiting for work at this intersection has gone on for years so those who have no need for the men's services casually ignore them. The tacit acceptance of their presence is perhaps the most poignant evidence of how marginal they are to the larger social scene in this affluent community.

Although not representative of Latino men as a whole, the social positioning of the day laborers in Southampton serves as a metaphor and as a useful starting point for an investigation into the lives of Latino men and the challenges they face in the United States. These men lining the streets may appear insignificant, yet they are in fact essential and integral to the economic well-being of this affluent subdivision. They are quiet, unassuming, and unobtrusive, but their numbers and presence also make them impossible to ignore. On some days while they are out waiting, a small group of angry protesters do their best to call attention to the fact that their presence, and the transaction to contract their labor, is illegal. That is because most, if not all, of these men are undocumented immigrants— who else would wait for these low-wage, dirty jobs in the hot sun? Hiring them is a federal offense and a violation of U.S. immigration laws. However, the legality of their status does not seem to matter to most individuals.

The day laborers in Southampton are not representative of the Latino population as a group in the United States; however, their plight and status are directly relevant to the experience of many Latino men. Latinos hold a variety of occupations, professions, and positions in U.S. society, but their role as a source of cheap, exploitable labor largely defines them in the media and increasingly in the popular imagination (Chavez, 2008; Children Now, 2003). The absence of serious scholarly investigations and alternate portrayals of Latino men provides flimsy protection from harassment, scrutiny, and distortion of the image of who they are and, in the case of day laborers, why they have come to the United States. To the degree that Latino men are perceived as an undifferentiated mass of low-wage workers, non-Latinos are prevented from appreciating and under-standing the vast diversity and complexity that characterizes their lives. A more nuanced and precise understanding of who Latino men are and why they are here might humanize them, so that they are no longer simply seen as undocu-mented workers, outsiders, and illegal scabs taking jobs. Such negative and simplistic characterizations create an enabling caricature, one that allows men like these to be used and exploited, disregarding their hardships and commitment to work.

A closer examination reveals that even this group of day laborers is not as monolithic as they might appear. One of the editors of this volume (Noguera) has spoken with the men informally over the past few years and has learned that they come from a variety of countries and have a wide range of experiences and stories to tell. Most are from Mexico (many from the Chiapas region and several from Oaxaca and Puebla), but some are from Guatemala, Honduras, El Salvador, and Ecuador. Most have families and are part of vast social networks of immigrants who live and work in eastern Long Island. Some are unskilled, with little formal education, while others—for example, Manuel and Hector, two brothers from the suburbs of Guadalajara, Mexico—are highly skilled carpenters. José, a man in his late 50s and one of the oldest on the block, is well known in the town as a master plumber. Diego, Miguel, and Ernesto, two brothers and a cousin, are known for their skill and speed with drywall. Some of the younger men—Jorge and Enrique, in this case—have had run-ins with employers who tried to cheat them out of a day's wage. Despite such encounters, these men return to the street each morning because they have no other options and need the work to support themselves and their families. They are not the same in background, needs, or aspirations; however, to those who employ their labor, who protest their presence, or who simply ignore them, they are all the same—Latino men looking for work.

How is it possible that Latino men like these (particularly those who are undocumented), who are so *integral* and *essential* to the economy, can also be regarded as a threat to the social and economic order by anti-immigration activists and their political supporters? Why is it that these Latino men with varying backgrounds, skills, and experiences are perceived as simply cheap, undifferen-tiated, and even fungible labor? What might we learn if their individuality were not obscured and their presence not treated as irrelevant to the life of this community? If the diversity in the backgrounds of these day laborers is obfuscated by the obvious characteristics they seem to share—undocumented, Latino, male—what else about them might be unknown?

The Project at Hand

The purpose of this book is to humanize and illuminate the complexities in the lives of Latino men. Drawing on the expertise of scholars from a broad range of disciplines and fields—health, criminal justice, education, literature, psychology, economics, labor, sociology—we have compiled this volume to draw attention to the unique challenges confronting men of Latino heritage in the United States. We do so not because we believe that Latino men are more disadvantaged than Latina women[1] or that they are at greater risk than other subgroups within the U.S. population (though in some areas they are). Rather, we have undertaken this project to address the dearth of scholarship and information about Latino men and to further our understanding of the unique challenges and obstacles they confront during this historical moment.

Although there has been growing interest in the status of men in American society (particularly African-American men and boys in recent years), there is a glaring lack of research and scholarly work available on Latino men. A search for scholarly studies on Latino men yields surprisingly few reports (other than those studies done by the scholars who have contributed to this volume), and a wider scan that includes more popular publications provides only a few more accounts. This book has been undertaken in part to fill that void. A secondary goal is to spark other researchers to pick up from where we have left off, to include what has invariably been left out.

In the 1980s and 1990s, feminist scholars such as Cherríe Moraga and Gloria Anzaldúa (1983) and Norma Alarcón (1990) called attention to the fact that the experiences of Latinas were unique and could not be subsumed under the rubric of a broader discourse on feminism or simply included as a footnote within the larger master narrative on American womanhood. Their work shed light on the unique experiences of Latina women whose opportunities and life chances are shaped by the intersection of oppression based on race, class, gender, and sexuality. The scholarship of Latina feminist writers focused on the manifestations and expressions of oppression in the workplace, the academy, the media, and their communities. Latino men show up in this work as well, but rarely as central to the analysis. For good reason, the purpose of this scholarship was to place the experiences of Latina women at the center of scholarly production, something that had rarely happened before. From a Latina feminist perspective, Latino men emerge largely as a source of oppression and hardship for women, often as overbearing and dominating fathers, incestuous uncles, and brothers who benefit from the deeply ingrained ideology of male privilege (Méndez-Negrete, 2006; The Latina Feminist Group, 2001). Although such portraits of some Latino men are not inaccurate, they are far from complete. Latino men are more than the benefactors of unquestioned male privilege; they can also be loving fathers and husbands who dedicate their lives to serving their families, among many other life trajectories. Others are teachers, doctors, plumbers, and electricians—that is, men who work hard most of their lives to support their families. To understand Latino men, the broader expression of Latino masculinities must be uncovered and analyzed—in other words, made visible.

Increasingly, writers who have focused on Latina feminism have come to recognize the detrimental aspects of patriarchy for men and have urged an expansion of the scope of gender-based inquiry to include men (Hurtado & Cervantez, 2009). Now some writers within the Latina feminist tradition are advocating that we should address the absence of knowledge about the lives and experiences of Latino men (Baca Zinn, 1982; Hurtado & Sinha, 2006, 2008). This volume responds to that call for inclusion by placing Latino men at the center of investigation.

Similar omissions and distortions can be found in the growing body of research on African-American men and boys. While books, articles, and empirical studies on this segment of the population have proliferated in recent years (Laubscher, 2005; Rashid, 2009), largely in reaction to an increasing awareness about the tremendous hardships facing Black men and boys, there has not been a similar outpouring of research focused on the challenges confronting Latino men. Even though Black and Latino boys frequently encounter similar disadvantages in educational settings—more likely to be suspended or expelled, to be placed in special education, or to drop out—most of the studies available have focused on Black men exclusively or have aggregated both groups in ways that render the experiences of Latino men less visible than those of Blacks. In these studies Latino men are not given the same focus as African-American men, minimizing the diversity of experiences among men of Color. While in many cases there are important parallels between African American and Latino men, in many cases there are significant divergences, which merit further exploration.

While our goal in this book is to place the experiences of Latino men at the center of analysis, we look through a lens that does not deny the privileges that patriarchy bestows on all men, regardless of class and ethnicity; simultaneously, however, we also recognize the hardships of class and racialized oppression on Latino masculinities (Connell, 1995). To a large degree, the vulnerabilities of Latino men, like the day laborers in Southampton, have been rendered invisible. To the extent that Latino men are known outside their communities in U.S. society, this is largely through the media, where their images are systematically distorted through stereotypes that often cast them as macho chauvinists, docile but reliable workers willing to accept even the dirtiest jobs at the lowest wages, or gangsters and drug traffickers wreaking havoc on inner-city streets. The complexity, and normalcy, of Latino men's lives is rarely addressed in media portrayals and is missing in much of the existing scholarship.

A Larger Sociodemographic Picture of Latino Men

According to the U.S. Census (2010), Latino men constitute fewer than 6 percent of the U.S. population. Of course, the percentage is actually higher because large numbers of undocumented Latino men reside in this country and are systematically undercounted by the census. Latino men differ significantly from other subgroups of men and these variations need to be examined. For example, in several states (California, New York, Illinois, Arizona) Latino men are over-represented among the ranks of the incarcerated and under-represented among the ranks of college and university students (Harris & Walter, 2005). Nationally, Latino men are less likely than White or Black men to be unemployed, but they are also more likely to be over-represented among low-wage workers (Borjas, 2007). Compared to African American and White men, Latino men are more likely to be married and to have children (more than two) and least likely to live alone (U.S. Census, 2010). In some cities (New York and Los Angeles), Latino men have homicide rates that are as high as, and occasionally higher than, those of Black men (Earls, 2000). In North Carolina, Georgia, and Kansas, three of the states with the fastest growing Latino populations, Latino men are less likely than any other demographic group to vote (Southwest Voter Education Project, 2008). A broad array of demographic and economic trends associated with Latino males are analyzed in greater depth in Chapter 2 (Torres & Fergus). We examine these patterns to reinforce the point that the stereotypical images of Latino men do not capture the full picture of these men's lives.

The Changing Status of Men: The End of Patriarchy?

A preponderance of evidence suggests that men and boys are increasingly in trouble. On a broad array of social and economic indicators, men fare significantly less well than women. In the United States, this is not just the case for men of Color—Black, Latino, Asian, and Native American—though the trends for men in these groups have more serious economic, political, and social consequences because they start already with many vulnerabilities (Kimmel, 1996). National data suggest that on several important quality-of-life measures, men and boys are faring less well with respect to health, education, and employment than they have in the recent past. Interestingly, there is growing evidence that this is an international phenomenon. In several nations, men on average live shorter lives than women and are more likely to be murdered (and to do the murdering), less likely to complete secondary school or enroll in universities, more likely to commit crimes, and less likely to use the money they earn to benefit their families (Giele & Holst, 2004). In the United States, there are now more women than men enrolled in colleges and universities in most states (Aud et al., 2010). This is truly a remarkable development because for years boys outperformed girls in education (Sadker & Sadker, 1994); the primary concerns about the relationship between gender and education were the lack of equity in funding for women's sports and the lagging performance of girls in science and math (Sadker & Sadker, 1994). The advances by women in education are perhaps the clearest evidence that the political mobilization generated by the women's movement changed the status of girls and women in U.S. society.

Similar trends of upheaval in traditional gender patterns and roles are evident among Latinos in the United States as well. As Nancy López (Chapter 14 in this volume) explains in her chapter on education, Latino males are significantly more likely to drop out of high school, to be suspended or expelled from school, and to underachieve on most academic tests than their female counterparts. As Rodríguez, Argeros, and Miyawaki (Chapter 12 in this volume) show in their chapter on the labor market, while Latino males have higher employment rates than most other subgroups, they are more likely to be concentrated and trapped in low-wage, blue-collar occupations. Latino men are also vastly under-represented in professional roles and occupations and are even less likely than Latinas to be employed in white-collar, service sector jobs. Latino men are still far more likely than Latina women to hold top leadership positions in politics, business, and religious organizations (most notably, the Catholic Church). This suggests that patriarchy remains largely intact as a cultural norm, reinforcing power and dominance at the highest levels. However, male dominance in certain areas should not be taken as a sign that nothing has changed in Latino gender relations. In other areas—the family, education, grassroots leadership, and so on—the rise of women is pervasive and merits serious scholarly attention.

The assertion that we are witnessing the end of patriarchy or the decline of men as the dominant gender, as recently proposed by Hanna Rosin (2010) in *The Atlantic*, may be an overstatement, but there are nonetheless clear signs that we are in the midst of dramatic changes in gender roles, in the structure and role of families, and in conceptions of masculinity. These trends seem unlikely to reverse themselves any time soon. Sociologists Janet Giele and Elke Holst (2004) attributed the declining fortunes of men to what sociologist Talcott Parsons (1966) termed "adaptive upgrading"—modifications and improvements that occur in social roles and norms as a result of broader economic and social changes occurring in society. As argued by Rosin (2010), women may be gaining advantages over men because they are better suited for the work and leadership roles that will be in demand in the twenty-first century. Rosin argued further that, by being socialized to multitask, work collaboratively, and acquire high levels of social and emotional intelligence, women have advanced in part due to their ability to adapt to the demands of the global economy and to take advantage of the new opportunities that are being created. The skills required by the new global economy are also the skills that women are predominantly taught as part of their gender socialization.

Giele and Holst (2004) claimed that as Western nations and increasingly major sectors of the global economy have shifted the focal point of economic activity away from manufacturing and industrial production to services and trade, the status of men as workers has become increasingly less important. In the United States and Western Europe, the displacement of male blue-collar workers began with the onset of de-industrialization and subsequent transfer of manufacturing jobs from the urban centers of the North to the industrial centers of the South in the 1970s, and has proceeded at an advanced pace ever since (Reich, 1992). In fact, in the current recession, men have been considerably more likely to lose their jobs than women (Rampell, 2010).

In three groundbreaking studies, sociologist William Julius Wilson (1978, 1987, 1996) documented how de-industrialization in cities such as Chicago, Detroit, Cleveland, and Buffalo contributed to the emergence of impoverished ghettos. In neighborhoods where poverty was concentrated and racial isolation the norm, Wilson (1987) argued, a Black underclass emerged, characterized by large numbers of permanently unemployed Black men. Unlike the Black middle class, which was able to take advantage of the opportunities for social mobility created by the Civil Rights movement, the "truly disadvantaged" were marginalized by spatial separation and the lack of blue-collar, industrial jobs, which in turn were compounded by lack of education and employer bias. Wilson (1996) suggested that as the unemployed were unable to adapt to the demands of the new economy on their own, new social policies were needed to prevent mass incarceration from becoming the exclusive social policy solution to address the problems associated with this troubled population. Interestingly, while Wilson's analysis focused largely on the impact these structural changes had upon urban Blacks, and men in particular, in many parts of the country—Chicago, Los Angeles, and Miami—Latino men experienced similar hardships and dislocations related to these macro-level economic trends.

As important and compelling as structural explanations might be to understanding the declining status of men, the plight of Latino men cannot be reduced to their status in the economy, their presence or lack thereof in educational institutions, or their location within the criminal justice system. As is true for most ethnic groups in the United States, the Latino family unit has historically played an important role in socializing children into gender roles and reinforcing male dominance through patriarchal cultural practices, values, and norms (Hochshild, 1989; Segura & Zavella, 2007). In recent years, there has been growing evidence of flux in the structure and values of Latino families, which will undoubtedly have tremendous bearing on the status of men. According to a recent study by the Center for American Progress (Halpin & Teixiera, 2010), Latino men are more likely than any other group of men in American society to report that they take primary responsibility for child care within their household (32 percent of Latino men claimed to take primary child care responsibility compared to 15 percent of men generally). In the same survey, Latino men reported that they were more likely to view the rise of women in the workforce as a positive development and more likely than other men to express progressive attitudes about the role of women in politics. Perhaps because they work longer hours on average (Guzmán & McConnell, 2002), Latino men were also more likely to express a desire for greater balance between work and family than other men in the survey. Reports such as these provide further evidence that the attitudes and status of Latino men are changing as the role of women, the nature of families, and the entire society changes. Understanding how Latino men change in reaction to these broader patterns of economic and social change is a central focus of this book.

In addition to the changes in the economy, Giele and Holst (2004) also argued that a decline in the power and status of men has occurred as a result of the women's movement, which produced significant changes in gender relations and subsequently began to transform men's roles in the family and society. As more women began working outside the home in the 1960s, as divorce became more prevalent and socially acceptable, and as greater numbers of women enrolled in colleges and universities and entered professions, a new power dynamic in gender roles emerged (Collins, 2009). By the 1970s women were less likely to overtly concede power to men or to accept subservient roles in many public or private spheres. Similarly, with the support and encouragement of increasingly enlightened institutional representatives like teachers, coaches, and family members, many girls began questioning and expanding traditional gender roles and occupations.

Over time, girls began to show clear signs that gender roles were changing and that traditional female-gendered occupations were not the only options (Collins, 2009). The question that many of the authors in this book address is, how have Latino men reacted to these massive changes resulting from women's struggle for personal civil rights? Of equal importance is that the feminist movement for civil rights has also taken on the cause of men to help make their vulnerabilities visible. Instead of abandoning men as they fall in many indicators and increase their presence in the criminal justice system, the authors in this volume propose innovative solutions and policy recommendations to address the decreasing status of Latino men.

While changes in the economy and in gender relations are important to understanding the decline in the status of men, these narratives fail to fully explain the experience of Latino males. Certainly, macro-level changes such as the restructuring of the economy and the advent of the women's movement have affected the status of Latino men, but there are other findings to consider. For example, there is ample evidence that immigrants are generally not affected by economic and cultural trends in the same way as U.S.-born groups and individuals. According to the 2010 U.S. Census, as many as 40 percent of Latinos are either new immigrants or the children of immigrants. Economic restructuring has not had the same impact on immigrant Latinos as it has had on U.S.-born workers because most immigrants were never able to secure well-paid union jobs in the manufacturing sector. Even as Latinos have been recruited to jobs in construction and the service sector, higher wages and benefits are typically not part of the deal in the "new economy" where jobs are contracted out and labor is largely non-unionized (Greenhouse, 2010). Similarly, while cultural norms related to gender are changing throughout the world including Latin America, there is considerable evidence that Latino immigrants are more socially conservative than most people born in the United States, including other Latinos; for example, they are less likely to smoke, consume illicit drugs, or have abortions (Hayes-Bautista, 2002). These findings do not mean that change in gender roles among Latino immigrants is not occurring, but they do suggest that there is much more to the study of Latino men than what is covered in large-scale studies of men in general. Our aim is to fill in the many missing details relevant to Latino men and boys.

Machismo and the "Male Crisis": Redefining Latino Masculinity

To the degree that there is a Latino male crisis (a notion that is analyzed at length by Way, Santos, & Cordero, as well as by other authors in this volume), it must be examined within the context of the severe and persistent structural inequalities in American society. Social and economic inequalities shape the education, employment opportunities, health, and overall life chances of poor children throughout the United States. While not all Latinos are poor, nearly one third (27 percent) of Latino children come from households with incomes that fall below the poverty line. Likewise, median incomes for Puerto Ricans ($21,056), Mexicans ($23,694), and Central and South Americans ($29,803, on average the highest paid Latinos), all fall below $30,000 per year (Center for Reproductive Health and Research Policy et al., 2002). National data on wealth, wages, and household income suggest that, although Latinos are the fastest growing minority in the United States and many have experienced upward mobility in recent years, a disproportionate number of Latinos are poor (one out of three Latinos are impoverished compared to one out of nine White Americans (ibid). The vast majority of Latinos have incomes that place them just a few notches above the poverty level, and like many Americans, they live close to the edge of financial ruin. Because of the high concentration of poverty in many Latino communities, Latino children are more likely than any other group of children to attend schools that are segregated on the basis of race and class (Orfield & Eaton, 1996). For these reasons and many others, understanding how social class, inequality, and economic uncertainty have influenced gender relations must be integral to a study on the status of Latino men.

Intersectionality and Latino Men

To examine the many inequalities faced by Latino men, the collection of studies in this book utilizes a theoretical framework that places the intersection of race, class, and gender at the center of all empirical and theoretical analysis. Several of the chapters also consider differences in national origin, neighborhood, sexuality, education, and phenotype (particularly skin color) of Latino men. By contextualizing the analysis of the status of Latino males in this way, the authors acknowledge that understanding the many diversities among Latino men is essential. As we have seen in other studies, focusing too heavily on any particular aspect of identity (e.g., race or gender) at the expense of others can lead to broad generalizations and a distorted analysis of the population under study.

While masculinity and the culture of machismo among Latinos is a central theme of several of the chapters in this book, in none of the chapters do these ideas stand alone as a focal point in the study of Latino men. Male socialization patterns, child rearing practices, and the subjective conceptions of masculinity, which influence everything from the attitudes of Latino boys toward school to the willingness of Latino fathers to care for their children, must be understood within a social context. Quite obviously, middle-class fourth-generation Cuban men in Miami are likely to have different experiences with gender relations and masculinity than recent Mexican male immigrants working in poultry farms in Iowa or Salvadoran war refugees living in central Los Angeles. A contextual analysis of Latino men within the schools, communities, labor market, and families they belong to is one of the major goals of this book.

Differences in educational achievement between Latino girls and boys are apparent throughout the educational pipeline, even though the trend of girls outperforming boys is not as dramatic among Latinos as it is among African Americans (Sáenz & Ponjuan, 2009). There has been no social movement initiated to address the disproportionate academic failure of Latino boys or men. Perhaps one reason an initiative aimed at the issues of Latino men, men of Color, or poor men in general has yet to emerge is because White men have not felt the need for it, and White men still comprise the majority of men in the United States. Wealthy White men continue to wield most of the power in American society, and while there is evidence that many poor and working-class White males are struggling (Kimmel, 1996), there is also considerable evidence that affluent White youths are thriving. Even among poor men and males of Color, the lack of a movement to address the obstacles they face can be attributed to the continued belief that males are inherently privileged over females. There is no doubt that, both structurally and inter-personally, men still hold gender privilege over women; there is also increasing evidence that low-income men, especially Blacks and Latinos, are at tremendous risk of being marginalized and disenfranchised in American society.

In addition, a men's social movement may be lacking because these trends of relative disadvantage among poor men of Color are a very recent phenomenon. Men of Color are just beginning to gain a political consciousness about their own role in mobilizing on "men's issues" within certain arenas. For example, there is the recent work of Frank De Jesus Acosta (2007) who has written about men of Color working with young men to keep them out of the criminal justice system. Another area of mobilization has been the rise of non-profits to help men of Color re-enter society after incarceration. Men as a group, regardless of class and race, have not been socialized to care for one another or to take a politically nurturing role that is outside the hegemonic structures of corporate and political power. In the coming years, it will be interesting to see whether a significant critical men's movement emerges that is similar to the one generated on behalf of women when society failed to respond to their needs.

Masculinity and its accompanying privileges are not the only dimensions of identity that Latino men use to negotiate society. Class, sexuality, ethnicity, and race also shape and influence the way Latino men are treated and their perceptions of social reality. In a study of Latino young men, Hurtado & Sinha (2008) applied an intersectional theoretical framework to explore definitions of masculinity within this group. One of the major findings from the study is that the views of young Latino men on gender relations are directly affected by their subjective understanding of their social identities (social class, phenotype, and sexual orientation). Individuals who identify as working class while growing up are more likely to experience discrimination and to be critical of the disadvantages that the women in their lives experience as a result of their gender. They also found that young, working-class Latino males are more likely to experience harassment by the police and to have male friends and relatives who are incarcerated (Hurtado & Sinha, 2012a and b).

Such research exemplifies the nuanced approach to the study of Latino men employed by the chapter authors in this book. By placing Latino men at the intersections of race, class, and gender and going to great lengths to contextualize empirical research, the authors ground their analyses in the social reality of the men they study. In this way, this interdisciplinary book on Latino men aims to provide readers with as broad and multifaceted picture of the experiences of Latino men as is currently possible.

Among the questions that the authors of this volume and hopefully future scholarship will explore are: What are the versions of masculinity that have been embraced by Latino families and that infuse the socialization of Latino men and boys as factors that are contributing to the disenfranchisement of so many? How would a social movement go about redefining masculinity and how would it be organized? Would Latino men be willing to give up the privileges that are associated with their gender in exchange for a less constrained, more egalitarian experience? Questions such as these are central to several of the chapters in this book. It is our hope that the approach we pursue—emphasizing a comprehensive study of Latino diversity—will facilitate bringing Latino men, like the day laborers we encountered in Southampton, from the obscurity of stereotypes into the light of human understanding.

An Overview of the Book

This book is divided into four sections: (1) The State of Latino Males, (2) The Construction of Masculinity, (3) Race, Gender, and Skin Color in Constructing Identification, and (4) Environmental Factors and Violence. The final chapter proposes policy recommendations and future directions for research. These sections are not meant to be mutually exclusive; we organized the book into sections to provide overviews for pedagogical use and to orient the reader. Certainly the chapters may be recombined in a variety of clusters based on the reader's purpose with the book.

The first section presents a demographic snapshot of the status of Latino men, providing the empirical foundation for the sections that follow. In their chapter, Torres and Fergus examine the social, economic, and educational attainment within and across the Latino population, which illustrates a complex portrait of Latino men's experiences by national origin. The balance of the chapters in this section focus on: the mental health status of Latinos, with particular attention to Latino adolescents (Roberts & Roberts), the sexual and reproductive health status of Latino men (Muñoz-Laboy & Perry), and the participation of Latino immigrants in the labor market (Valenzuela & Olivares Pasillas).

The second section of this edited volume explores the ways in which Latino men and their masculinities are constructed in the United States. The chapters address the influence that masculinity has on men's vulnerabilities in social interactions (Hurtado et al.), the media representations of Latino masculinities (Casillas), problematizing mainstream measures of the concept of machismo (Felix-Ortiz et al.), the construction of masculinity in children's books (Serrato), the struggles undocumented Latino youth negotiate while pursuing higher education (Diaz-Strong et al.), and the contribution of immigrant, queer masculinities to the definition of cultural citizenship (Roque Ramírez).

The third section, Race, Gender, and Skin Color in Constructing Identification, explores the influence of race and national origin on Latino men's wages (Rodríguez et al.), the influence of phenotype on Mexican and Puerto Rican men's life chances (Fergus), the influence of racialized masculinities on young Latinos' educational opportunities (López), and the influence of gender on young Latinos' friendships with peers (Way et al.).

The final section, Environmental Factors and Violence, explores the issue of Latinos and violence: its effect on young Latinos' psychosocial development (Vigil) and the overall patterns of violence among Latino men in the United States (Martinez & Stowell).

The last chapter on policy and research directions proposes application and changes to policy based on the lessons learned from the empirical studies and theoretical propositions in this book. We feel that the dire status of Latino men requires that we, at the very least, offer partial solutions that could be applied in policy arenas. In addition, as stressed throughout this book, the status of Latino men continues to be understudied, with vast areas of research yet to be explored. Many of the authors in this volume end their chapters calling for action as well as outlining areas for future study. Our last chapter summarizes those concerns and provides a roadmap for future research, as well as for potential solutions in ending the current trend of disenfranchising Latino men and boys in society.

Note

1   Throughout this book we use the term *Latino men* in order to reduce the likelihood of confusion on the part of non-Spanish speaking readers who may be unaware that the term *Latinos* can be used to refer either to men and women collectively or to men alone. We use the terms *Latinas* and *Latina women* interchangeably.

References

Alarcón, N. (1990). The theoretical subject(s) of this bridge called my back and Anglo-American feminism. In G. Anzaldúa (Ed.), *Making face, making soul: Haciendo caras*, (356–369). San Francisco: Aunt Lute Foundation Books.

Aud, S., Hussar, W., Planty, M., Snyder, T., Bianco, K., Fox, M., . . . Drake, L. (2010). *The condition of education 2010* (NCES 2010–028). Washington, DC: National Center for Education Statistics, Institute of Education Sciences, U.S. Department of Education.

Baca Zinn, M. (1982). Chicano men and masculinity. *Journal of Ethnic Studies*, 10(2), 29–44.

Borjas, G. (2007, January). *The new face of the low-wage workforce.* Policy brief #8. Ann Arbor: National Poverty Center.

Chavez, L. (2008). *The Latino threat: Constructing immigrants, citizens and the nation.* Stanford, CA: Stanford University Press.

Center for Reproductive Health and Research Policy, Department of Obstetrics, Gynecology and Reproductive Sciences & The Institute for Health Policy Studies. (2002, November). Fact Sheet on Latino youth: Income and poverty. San Francisco, CA: University of California. Retrieved from http://bixbycenter.ucsf.edu/publications/files/LatinoYouth_Income_2002.pdf

Children Now. (2003, May). *Fall colors: Prime time diversity report 2003–04.* Retrieved from www.childrennow.org/uploads/documents/fall_colors_2003.pdf

Collins, G. (2009). *When everything changed. The amazing journey of American women from 1960 to the present.* New York: Little, Brown.

Connell, R. (1995). *Masculinities.* Berkeley, CA: University of California Press.

De Jesus Acosta, F. (2007). *The history of Barrios Unidos: Healing community violence.* Houston: Arte Público Press.

Earls, F. (2000). Urban poverty: Scientific and ethical considerations. *Annals of the American Academy of Political and Social Science,* 572(1), 53–65.

Giele, J. Z., & Holst, E. (2004). New life patterns and changing gender roles. In J. Z. Giele and E. Holst (Eds.), *Changing life patterns in western industrial societies* (3–22). Amsterdam: Elsevier.

Greenhouse, S. (2010, January 23). Most U.S. union members are working for the government, new data shows. *The New York Times,* p. B1.

Guzmán, B., & McConnell, E. D. (2002). The Hispanic population: 1990–2000 growth and change. *Population Research and Policy Review,* 21(1–2), 109–128.

Halpin, J., and Teixiera, R. (2010, July). *Latino attitudes about women and society.* Washington DC: Center for American Progress. Retrieved from www.americanprogress.org/issues/2010/07/latino_attitudes.html

Harris, A., & Walter, A. (2005). Lest we forget thee . . . .The under- and over-representation of Black and Latino youth in the California higher education and juvenile justice institutions. *Race and Society,* 6(2), 99–123.

Hayes-Bautista, D. (2002). The Latino health research agenda for the twenty-first century. In M. Suarez-Orozco and M. M. Paez (Eds.), *Latinos: Remaking America.* Berkeley: University of California Press.

Hochshild, A. (1989). *The second shift.* New York: Penguin Books.

Hurtado, A., & Cervantez, K. (2009). A view from within and from without: The development of Latina feminist psychology. In F. A. Villarruel, G. Carlo, J. Grau, M. Azmitia, N. Cabrera & T. J. Chahin (Eds.), *The handbook of US Latino psychology: Developmental and community based perspectives* (171–190). Thousand Oaks, CA: Sage Publications.

Hurtado, A., & Sinha, M. (2006). Differences and similarities: Latina and Latino doctoral students navigating the gender divide. In J. Castellanos, A. M. Gloria, & M. Kamimura (Eds.), *The Latina/o pathway to the Ph.D.: Abriendo Caminos* (149–168). Sterling, VA: Stylus.

Hurtado, A., & Sinha, M. (2008). More than men: Latino feminist masculinities and intersectionality. *Sex Roles,* 59(5–6), 337–349.

Hurtado, A., & Sinha, M. (2012a). Beyond machismo: An intersectional analysis of young Latinos' definitions of manhoods. Manuscript in preparation.

Hurtado, A., & Sinha, M. (2012b). Getting educated while brown: Young educated Latinos' experiences with the criminal justice system. Manuscript in preparation.

Kimmel, M. (1996). *Manhood in America*. New York: Free Press.

Laubscher, L. (2005). Toward a (de)constructive psychology of African-American men. *The Journal of Black Psychology*, 31(2), 111–129.

Méndez-Negrete, J. (2006). *Las hijas de Juan: Daughters betrayed*. Durham, NC: Duke University Press.

Moraga, C., & Anzaldúa, G. (Eds.). (1983). *This bridge called my back: Writings by radical women of color*. Watertown, MA: Persephone Press.

Orfield, G., & Eaton, S. (1996). *Dismantling desegregation*. New York: New Press.

Parsons, T. (1966). *Societies: Evolutionary and Comparative Perspectives*. NJ: Prentice Hall.

Rampell, C. (2010, February 6). Women now a majority in American workplaces. *The New York Times*, p. A10.

Rashid, H. M. (2009). From brilliant baby to child placed at risk: The perilous path of African American boys in early childhood education. *The Journal of Negro Education*, 78(3), 347–355.

Reich, R. (1992). *The work of nations: Preparing ourselves for 21st century capitalism*. New York: Vintage Books.

Rosin, H. (2010, August). The end of men. *The Atlantic Magazine*, 16–25.

Sadker, M., and Sadker, D. (1994). *Failing at fairness: How schools shortchange girls*. New York: Touchstone.

Sáenz, V. B., & Ponjuan, L. (2009). The vanishing Latino male in higher education. *Journal of Higher Education*, 8, 54–89. doi: 10.1177/1538192708326995

Segura, D., & Zavella, P. (Eds.). (2007). *Women and migration in the U.S.-Mexico borderlands: A reader*. Durham, NC: Duke University Press.

Southwest Voter Education Project, President's Report #1 (2008): The Latino Voter Registration Surge in 2008. Los Angeles, CA.

The Latina Feminist Group. (2001). *Telling to live: Latina feminist testimonios*. Durham, NC: Duke University Press.

Valenzuela, A., Theodore, N., Melendez, E., & Gonzalez, A. (2006). *On the corner: Day labor in the United States*. Retrieved from www.sscnet.ucla.edu/issr/csup/index.php

Wilson, W. (1978). *The declining significance of race*. Chicago: University of Chicago Press.

Wilson, W. (1987). *The truly disadvantaged*. Chicago: University of Chicago Press.

Wilson, W. (1996). *When work disappears*. New York: Alfred Knopf.

PART 1
The State of Latino Males

2

SOCIAL MOBILITY AND THE COMPLEX STATUS OF LATINO MALES

Education, Employment, and Incarceration Patterns from 2000–2009

Mellie Torres
Edward Fergus

The education, employment/labor, and incarceration status of Latino males in the United States is a complex one. Although the conditions of this population mirror those of other vulnerable populations, their status is far less explored and understood. There are many possible reasons for this lack of focus on Latino males. First, Latinos are by definition an extraordinarily diverse group, comprised of individuals from a variety of countries and racial and ethnic backgrounds, and these regional variations result in significantly different Latino experiences. Second, because of the diversity within the Latino population, many of the challenges that are specific to Latino males often go unrecognized and, therefore, do not receive the attention they deserve. When Latinos are disaggregated by national origin, social class, or region, it becomes clear that certain groups are particularly vulnerable to hardships and challenges (e.g., Puerto Rican males are more likely to drop out of school, Mexican American males in California are more likely to be incarcerated) while other groups (e.g., Cubans and South Americans) are less so.

The absence of scholarship and concern for this group has resulted in few descriptive studies of the state of Latino males. By and large, this lack of concentrated examination has made Latino men an invisible group. This chapter focuses on framing the status of this diverse group across three domains—education, employment/labor, and incarceration—in an effort to highlight the issues and make the group no longer invisible. Although there are other outcomes in which Latino boys and men do not perform well, our attention to education, employment, and incarceration is intentional because these areas represent important levers of mobility and project future patterns for this population. In addition, understanding the distribution of Latino boys and men in these areas provides a landscape within which to contextualize the mental health and health disparities discussed in Chapters 3 and 4; the labor market participation discussed in Chapter 5; the significance of gender role construction in research and media in Chapters 6–9; the impact of race and national origin boundaries as discussed in Chapters 12, 13, and 15; and the educational and violence terrain surrounding this population, as presented in Chapters 14, 16, and 17.

In this chapter we outline the status of Latino males across these domains over the past 10 years (2000–2010). Our intention is not to be exhaustive but rather to establish a terrain of significant outcome markers within these various domains. This chapter is divided into four sections. First, we provide the composition of the Latino population, which includes outlining national groups, nativity status, and age; these markers are used to further describe the other sections when the data are available. The second section provides educational attainment of Latino males, including school enrollment patterns, achievement in grades K–12, and educational attainment among Latino males over 18 years old. In the third section, we provide the labor/employment patterns found among Latino males, including employment rates and industry distribution. Incarceration patterns are the focus of the fourth section. Lastly, we turn to policy interventions and summarize recommendations for the future.

Composition of the Latino Population

It is important to first establish the population of Latino males within the context of the demographic growth of Latinos within the United States, particularly given its exponential growth during the 1990 to 2008 period. In the 1990 Census, 21.9 million Latinos were counted, and in 2000 the number grew to 35.2 million and in 2008 to over 46 million (U.S. Census Bureau, n.d.). This dramatic growth is adding significantly to a booming U.S. population that was noted by the Population Reference Bureau as getting "bigger, older and more diverse" (Congressional Research Service, 2005). However this growth is not occurring among all Latino national groups. Figure 2.1 illustrates the percentage of Latinos by national origin during 1990, 2000, and 2008. In general, the Latino population disaggregates as follows: Mexican (65.5 percent), Puerto Rican (9 percent), Cuban (3.4 percent), Central American (8.3 percent), South American (5.8 percent), and other Latinos (8 percent) (U.S. Census Bureau, n.d.). These percentages are reflective of the approximately 46.9 million Latinos in the United States as of 2008. There are 30.7 million Mexicans, 4.2 million Puerto Ricans, 3.9 million Central Americans, 2.7 million South Americans, and 3.7 million other Latinos (U.S. Census Bureau, n.d.). As Figure 2.1 also illustrates, although Mexicans comprise the largest percentage of Latinos in the United States during these three periods, the percentage of Central and South Americans comprising

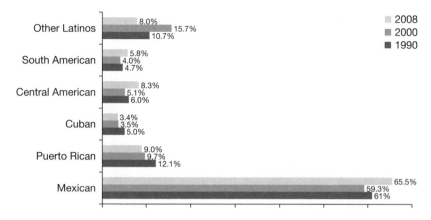

FIGURE 2.1 Percentage of Latinos living in the United States by national origin: 1990, 2000, 2008

the overall Latino population has increased during the past two periods. Meanwhile the percentage of Cubans has decreased over this time period.

Figure 2.2 illustrates the gender distribution during 1990, 2000, and 2008. Apparent in this analysis is the relatively even distribution of Latino males to females (51 percent to 49 percent), with a slightly greater difference in 2008 (52 percent Latino males to 48 percent females) (U.S. Census Bureau, n.d.).

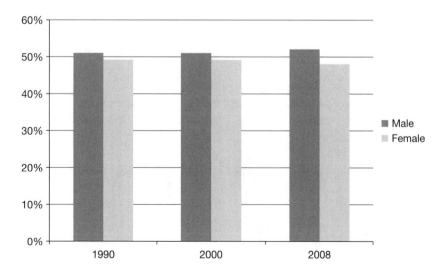

FIGURE 2.2 Male and female distribution of Latino population: 1990, 2000, 2008

What is the age distribution of Latino men?

Although the male and female populations among the different Latino groups are relatively even, the Latino male population is comprised mostly of men under the age of 35. Figure 2.3 demonstrates the age percentages of the various Latino national groups in 2000, 2006, and 2008. In 2000, among the 20 million Latino males counted in the United States, 68 percent were under 35 years of age; by 2008 among 24 million Latino males, 64 percent were under 35 (U.S. Census Bureau, n.d.). This translates into a mean age of 21.7 in 2006, rising to 27.3 by 2008. Although a significant proportion of the Latino male population is under 35 years of age, the distribution varied across the different Latino national groups. In 2008, among Mexican males, 66.8 percent were under 35 years of age, similar to Puerto Ricans (60.8 percent) and Central Americans (63.3 percent). On the other hand, Cuban and South American males under 35 years of age comprised only 40.7 percent and 52.9 percent of the population, respectively, in 2008 (U.S. Census Bureau, n.d.). However, it is also important to note the steady decline in the percentage of males in each national group under age 35 over this eight-year period.

Where were Latino men born?

Given the frequent use of legal status as a political sword in public and policy debate, as well as a tool for mobility, examining nativity status is another critical dimension in describing the Latino male population. The Latino male population in the United States is mostly native-born (59.6 percent) (U.S. Census Bureau, 2008). Similar to the age group distribution, nativity status differs across national

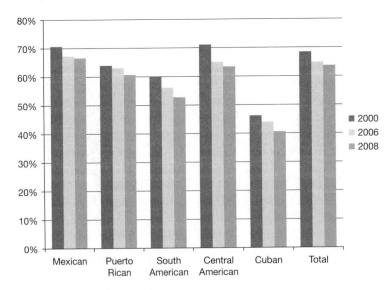

FIGURE 2.3 Percentage of Latino males under 35 years of age by national group

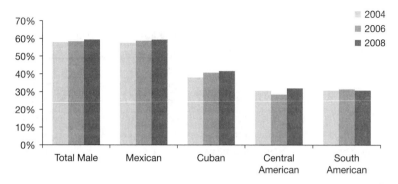

FIGURE 2.4 Percentage of native-born Latino males by national group: 2004, 2006, 2008

groups; much of this difference is probably due to the immigration history and the current status of the various national groups (Figure 2.4). From 2004 to 2008, the majority of Mexican males were native born (59.6 percent) (U.S. Census Bureau, 2004, 2006, 2008). Meanwhile, a lesser percentage of Cuban (41.7 percent), Central American (31.9 percent), and South American males (31 percent) were native-born (U.S. Census Bureau, 2008).

Although Mexican males maintain the largest percentage of native-borns, they also comprise the highest number of recent arrivals. Among foreign-born Latino males, the majority migrated to the United States during the past three decades, with over 60 percent arriving in 1990 or later (Table 2.1). While the migration patterns are similar for all foreign-born males across national groups, Mexican and South and Central American men are the groups most recent to immigrate; over 60 percent of foreign-born males in these national groups arrived after 1990 (U.S. Census Bureau, 2008).

TABLE 2.1 Year of Entry of Foreign-born Male Population by National Origin, 2008

	Total male		Mexican		Cuban		Central American		South American	
	N	%	N	%	N	%	N	%	N	%
Total	9,581	100	6,355	100	479	100	1,284	100	860	100
2000–2008	3,232	33.7	2,128	33.5	129	27	495	38.5	326	37.9
1990–1999	2,904	30.3	2,014	31.7	101	21.1	366	28.5	222	25.8
1980–1989	1,955	20.4	1,290	20.3	72	15	291	22.7	170	19.8
1970–1979	905	9.4	612	9.6	43	8.9	100	7.8	78	9.1
Before 1970	585	6.1	311	4.9	134	28	33	2.6	64	7.4

Figures in thousands; civil non-institutional population.

Source: U.S. Census Bureau, Current Population Survey, Annual Social and Economic Supplement, 2008

Where do Latino men live?

The regional geographical distribution of the Latino male population parallels the residential patterns of the Latino population (Figure 2.5). Over the course of 2002 to 2008, the majority of the Latino male population shifted from having a significant presence in the U.S. Midwest, West, and Northeast to primarily being located in the South and West. By 2008, the majority of Latino males resided in the West (42.2 percent) or the South (36.2 percent), the remainder being located in the Northeast (13 percent) and Midwest (8.5 percent) (U.S. Census Bureau, 2008). In comparison to previous years of regional data, the Latino male population has grown exponentially in the West and decreased significantly in the Midwest. Another unique dynamic is that the distribution within these various regions is not uniform. Of the Latino males in the Northeast, over one third (36.6 percent) are Puerto Rican and approximately two-fifths are South American (14.2), Mexican (12.8 percent), or Central American (11 percent), with only 3 percent Cuban. On the other hand, in the West, Midwest, and South, Mexican men constitute the majority of the Latino males (U.S. Census Bureau, 2008).

Overall, Latino males over a 10-year period (2000–2010) tend to be mostly Mexicans, Central and South Americans, and Puerto Ricans who are native-born and under the age of 35. A majority (59.7 percent) are native-born, with Mexicans having the highest percentage of males born in the United States. Additionally, among the foreign-born population nearly two thirds entered the United States in 1990 or later. Finally, the largest concentrations of Latinos are in western and southern states. These demographic patterns demonstrate a relatively young and native-born population of Latino males living in the western and southern regions of the country.

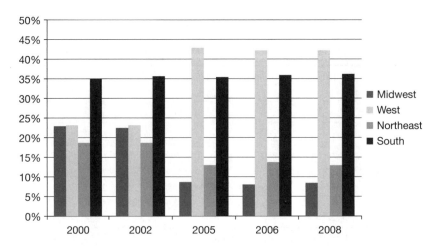

FIGURE 2.5 Regional distribution of the Latino male population: 2000, 2002, 2006, 2008

Educational Attainment

How many Latino children are attending U.S. schools?

In 2008, Latino children represented the second largest group of public school children after Whites; over 14.2 million Latino children were enrolled in kindergarten through twelfth grade (Aud et al., 2010). From 1998 to 2008, the percentage of Latinos representing the student enrollment doubled from 11 to 22 percent (ibid). This dramatic growth in the Latino student population was experienced throughout the United States. The regional differences in the proportion of Latino students enrolled in public schools are detailed in Figure 2.6. All regions saw a nearly two-fold increase in Latino student enrollment from 1998 to 2008. During this 10-year period, the West and South were the two regions with the fastest growing proportion of Latino students. The Latino student population increased in the West from 23 percent in 1998 to 40 percent in 2008. In the South, Latino enrollment increased from 10 to 19 percent (Aud et al., 2010).

What are the school experiences of Latino boys?

The school experiences of Latino boys differed from those of their White counterparts. Table 2.2 illustrates the percentages of the Latino, White, and Black male populations that were suspended, classified with a learning disability, and enrolled in a talented and gifted program in 2000 and 2006 (U.S. Department of Education, n.d.). Apparent in these findings are the slightly higher percentages

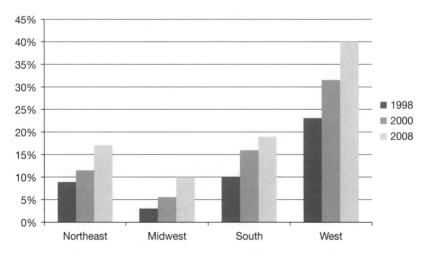

FIGURE 2.6 Percentage of Latino student enrollment in public school system by region: 1998, 2000, 2008

TABLE 2.2 Suspension, Special Education Classification, and Talented and Gifted Programs: 2000 and 2006

	2000			2006		
	Latino male (%)	White male (%)	Black male (%)	Latino male (%)	White male (%)	Black male (%)
Suspended from school	8.7	7.4	17.3	9.1	6.6	18.6
Learning disability classification	8.2	8	8.7	7	6.6	8.2
Talented and gifted programs	3.5	7.3	2.6	4	8	3

Source: U.S. Department of Education, Office for Civil Rights Elementary and Secondary School Survey, 2000 and 2006

of Latino males than White males being suspended and classified with a learning disability in 2000 and 2006 (U.S. Department of Education, n.d.). However, most troubling is the nearly double percentage of White males in talented and gifted programs compared to Latino males; this finding is of course significant because participation in such programs provides a student with greater access to rigorous curricula and college-track courses in high school (U.S. Department of Education, n.d.).

What is the achievement level of Latino boys and men?

While Latino students are a growing presence in the K-12 public school system across the United States, they maintain limited successful academic performance and attainment compared to their White counterparts. The achievement story of Latinos, and Latino males in particular, includes a performance distance with other racial/ethnic groups, primarily with Whites but also with Asians (U.S. Department of Education, n.d.). At the elementary school level, the fourth and eighth grade 2009 National Assessment of Educational Progress (NAEP) mean reading and math scores of Latino males were at least 20 points below those of their White peers (Figures 2.7 and 2.8). While Latino male elementary school students have made some gains since 2000 in reading and math, score gaps persist between Latino males and Asian and White males. From 2000 to 2008, the average fourth grade reading scores for Latino males increased from 207 to 228. However, average reading scores for eighth graders remained relatively flat between 2002 and 2009. In math, while Latino male students continued to make progress in fourth and eighth grade scores since 2000, racial and ethnic gaps persist (U.S. Department of Education, n.d.).

Unfortunately, by the time Latino males are in high school, only about one in every two (49 percent) graduates (Winters & Greene, 2006). This figure is comparable to that of Black males (48 percent). However, it is much lower than

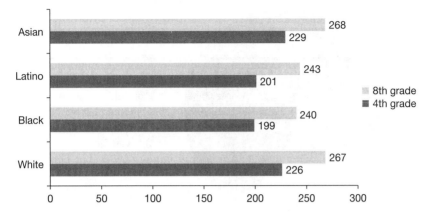

FIGURE 2.7 Fourth and eighth grade NAEP mean reading scores of males by race and Latino origin, 2009

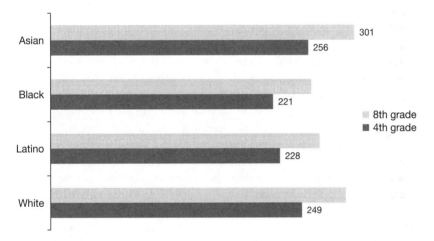

FIGURE 2.8 Fourth and eighth grade NAEP mean math scores of males by race and Latino origin, 2009

that of White males (74 percent). Latino males graduate at lower rates than Latina females (58 percent) (Winters & Greene, 2006). In New York City, the largest urban school district in the United States, only 28 percent of Latino males in the 2007 cohort graduated with a Regents diploma (Meade et al., 2009).

These patterns of limited academic performance and attainment result in few Latino males over 18 years of age achieving educational distinction and, in turn, positive mobility. According to the 2009 Current Population survey of 16 million Latino males 18 years and over, only about 30 percent were high school graduates and less than 10 percent were college graduates (Figure 2.9) (U.S. Census Bureau, 2009).

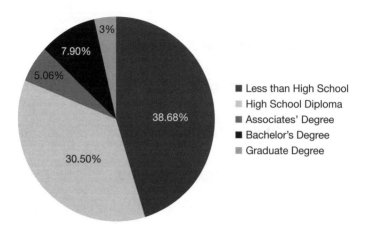

FIGURE 2.9 Educational attainment of Latino males 18 years and older, 2009

The aggregate of the educational statistics suggest that Latino males are not attaining academic proficiency and that a significant percentage are not graduating high school nor enrolling in college. Such patterns of educational attainment not only challenge the social mobility of this population, they may partially explain the pattern of labor market participation, which is discussed in the following section. The research on why these patterns exist and persist varies. For example, some argue that Latino children continue to be woefully underserved in the early years of childhood as they are less likely than their White and Black peers to attend a preschool program due in part to limited access to programs, low socioeconomic status, language barriers, and maternal educational levels (Bainbridge et al., 2005; Buysse et al., 2004; Laosa & Ainsworth, 2007; Magnuson & Waldfogel, 2005). Mother-to-child book reading in Latino families is low compared to that in White families (Barrueco et al., 2007; Brooks-Gunn & Markman, 2005), and as parental book reading has been linked to a child's school readiness, there is decreased "readiness" for school.

Cultural as well as environmental factors are also theorized to explain the school experiences and outcomes of Latinos (Delgado-Gaitan & Trueba, 1991; Noguera, 2003; Ogbu, 1992; Rumbaut & Portes, 2001; Trueba, 1989). Some studies have explored the role of social networks in and out of the school setting, including teachers and guidance counselors who would explain educational opportunities (Stanton-Salazar, 2001; Valenzuela, 1999). Still other studies have investigated gender differences in Latino school achievement and attainment (Ibañez et al., 2004; Jordan et al., 1996; Kao & Tienda, 1998; Rodriguez, 2002, 2003; Sánchez et al., 2005; Zarate & Gillmore, 2005). Additional explanations for this uneven educational progress have invariably focused on school factors, such as school structure (tracking, testing, teacher quality, curriculum, instruction, equitable access), and district/school resources and other cultural factors, such as immigrant status/

nativity, language barriers, home-school culture compatibility, teacher expectations, location (urban, suburban, and rural; region of the United States), academic and racial/ethnic identity compatibility, as well as racial/ethnic identification (Carter & Segura, 1979; Delgado-Gaitan & Trueba, 1991; Flores-González, 2002; Matute-Bianchi, 1986; Ogbu, 1978; Suárez-Orozco,1991; Suárez-Orozco & Suárez-Orozco, 1995; Trueba, 1987; Valenzuela, 1999). Although the exploration of these factors is varied and incomplete, it is clear that the educational outcomes of Latino students are tied to their social-cultural environments, as well as the structural conditions that construct and/or reinforce their current social conditions.

Labor Market Participation

What jobs do Latino men hold?

The employment and unemployment rates among Latino males reflect unique patterns. Specifically, the Latino male population in the workforce in 2009 were concentrated in three industries (Figure 2.10): production and transportation (22.2 percent), construction and maintenance (26.6 percent), and services (21.2 percent) (Bureau of Labor Statistics, n.d., a). The remaining employed Latinos work in management and professional (15.9 percent) and sales/office occupations (14.2 percent) (Bureau of Labor Statistics, n.d., a). On the other hand, of the total male population in the United States, about half are in management and professional (34.5 percent) and service (14.3 percent) occupations, the balance somewhat equally split between the construction/maintenance and production/transportation industries (Bureau of Labor Statistics, n.d., a). Except for a noticeable

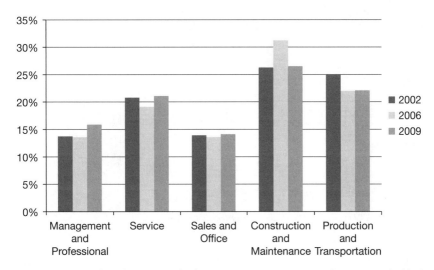

FIGURE 2.10 Employed Latino males by occupation, 2002–2009 (16 years and older)

TABLE 2.3 Occupation of the Civilian Employed Latino Male Population by National Origin, 2008

Occupation	Latino (%)	Mexican (%)	Puerto Rican (%)	Cuban (%)	Central American (%)	South American (%)
Management and professional	14.3	10.9	24.0	30.3	11.2	24.7
Service	19.2	19.5	21.2	19.4	19.1	15.5
Sales and office	14.1	12.7	20.0	18.5	10.9	19.7
Construction and maintenance	27.5	30.0	14.5	13.5	35.6	20.7
Production and transportation	22.3	23.1	19.4	18.0	22.0	19.3

Age 16 years and older

Source: U.S. Bureau of Labor Statistics, Current Population Survey

drop in the proportion of Latinos in the construction industry from 2006 to 2009, which may be due to the housing bubble of 2006 and 2007, Latinos' participation in these respective occupations has remained relatively stable since 2002 (Bureau of Labor Statistics, n.d., b, c and d).

Not surprisingly, the occupation distribution of Latino males differs greatly by national origin. As shown in Table 2.3, in 2008 over half of Mexican and Central American male workers were employed in the construction/maintenance and production/transportation industries. On the other hand, over 40 percent of Cubans (48.8 percent), South Americans (44.4 percent), and Puerto Ricans (44 percent) are in white collar professional occupations such as management and sales (U.S. Census Bureau, 2008).

Another unique pattern found among Latino males is their over-representation among employed dropouts (Borjas, 2006). Figure 2.11 provides the percentage of employed Black, White, and Latino males lacking a high school diploma. Apparent is the high percentage of Latino males who are employed despite their

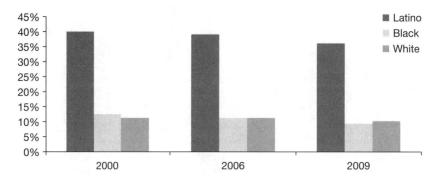

FIGURE 2.11 Employed males (25 years and older) with less than a high school diploma by race and Latino origin: 2000, 2006, 2009

lack of a high school diploma. This pattern should be examined in relation to not only the employment patterns among this population, but also in relation to the desirability of this population versus other groups. Some researchers note preferential hiring practices towards Latino and Caribbean males over African American males in low-skilled industries (Neckerman & Kirschenman, 1991; Wilson, 2009). Thus, our interpretation of relatively high employment rates of Latino males without high school diplomas must also reflect the non-desirability of hiring Black males who lack high school diplomas.

These statistics confirm that Latino males are not only occupying mostly blue-collar jobs but also they are becoming the "new face of the low wage industry" (National Poverty Center, 2007). Such labor market participation may well explain the median earnings of this population. Figure 2.12 illustrates the median weekly earnings of employed full-time male workers by race and Latino origin. Latino males earn the least (about $569 per week in 2009) compared to their Asian, White (non-Hispanic), Pacific Islander, or Black (non-Hispanic) counterparts (Bureau of Labor Statistics, n.d., e, f, g and h).

Although Latino males have maintained high employment patterns since 2002, even among those lacking a high school diploma, they also have the second highest unemployment rates. In 2009, of the Latino males in the civilian labor force (approximately 13 million), 87.5 percent were employed, while 12.5 percent were unemployed (Table 2.4). Between 2002 and 2009, Latino males of 16 years or older have generally maintained high unemployment rates (Bureau of Labor Statistics, n.d., i). Overall, the 2009 unemployment rates of Latino males is higher than that of White males (9.4 percent compared to 12.5 percent); however, it is significantly lower than that of Black males (17.5 percent unemployed),

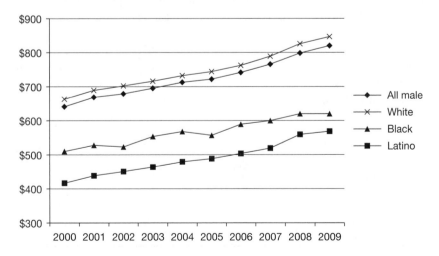

FIGURE 2.12 Median weekly earnings of employed full-time wage and salary workers for males by race and Latino origin: 2000–2009

TABLE 2.4 Unemployment Rate for Males by Race and Latino Origin, 2002–2009

	2002	2006	2008	2009
Asian	6.1	3.0	4.1	7.9
Black	10.7	9.5	11.4	17.5
Latino	7.2	4.8	7.6	12.5
White	5.3	4.0	5.5	9.4

Age 16 years and older; civilian non-institutional population

Source: U.S. Bureau of Labor Statistics, Current Population Survey

and notably unemployment is much more pronounced among Mexican and Puerto Rican males.

These rates also differ across national groups (Table 2.5). Until 2009, Mexicans and Cubans had similar percentages of unemployment rates. The unemployment rate of Puerto Rican males, on the other hand, reached double digits in 2008 and grew in 2009 (Bureau of Labor Statistics, n.d., i, j and k)

Various studies have examined the factors that impact the workforce partici-pation and earnings of Latino males. These studies have focused on a multitude of individual and structural forces such as English proficiency, acculturation, nationality, phenotype, discrimination, self-identity, and residential location (Espino & Franz, 2002; Farley, 1987; Greene & Hoffnar, 1994; Mason, 2004; Mora & Dávila, 2006; Reimers, 1984; Tienda, 1983). Differences in labor market performance as a function of phenotypic variations have been found across Latino ethnic backgrounds. For Mexican and Cuban Americans, darker skin color appeared to hamper hourly wages and annual earnings (Espino & Franz, 2002; Mason, 2004). Human capital characteristics such as educational attainment, English language proficiency, and job experience have also been posited as impacting wage differentials and labor market participation (Farley, 1987; Mason, 2004; Reimers, 1984; Tienda, 1983; Tienda & Niedert, 1984). For example, greater English language fluency accounted for a positive impact on earnings for Latino men com-pared to that of White men (Mason, 2004; Stolzenberg & Tienda, 1997).

TABLE 2.5 Unemployment Rate by National Origin, 2002–2009

	2002	2006	2008	2009
Latino	7.2	4.8	7.6	12.5
Cuban	6.5	3.3	7.0	8.4
Mexican	7.1	4.7	7.5	12.5
Puerto Rican	9.4	7.2	11.6	15.0

Age 16 years and older; civilian non-institutional population

Source: U.S. Bureau of Labor Statistics, Current Population Survey

Various studies point to structural forces—minority concentration, central city residence, and local market conditions—as impacting the earnings of Latino males (Farley, 1987; Tienda, 1983; Tienda & Lii, 1987). In accordance with the spatial mismatch theory, Farley (1987) traced increased Latino male unemployment to their residence in inner cities, while employment opportunities were located in suburbs. A high concentration of Latino males in the labor market also appeared to negatively impact earnings for Latino males (Tienda, 1983). Thus, the research undertaken documents the patterns of labor market participation among Latino males not solely regarding who is employed/unemployed but also what confounding cultural and structural factors are influencing these patterns.

Incarceration Rates

Latino males have a 17 percent chance of serving time in prison at some point in their lives

As noted in the section on age demographics, the age range most represented among the Latino male population is males under 35, which is the age group over-represented in prisons. Table 2.6 documents the Latino male prison population. In 2009, one in twenty-five Latino males aged 25–29 was incarcerated (The Sentencing Project, n.d.). Not surprisingly, when examining the incarceration rates among Latino males, over half (55 percent) of the Latino men imprisoned in 2008 were between the ages of 20 and 34 (Sabol et al., 2009). According to the Bureau of Justice Statistics, at year-end 2008 about one-fifth of the males sentenced under state or federal jurisdiction, with sentences of more than one year, were Latino (approximately 295,800), the third highest percentage compared to that of their White (33.2 percent) and Black (39.2 percent) counterparts

TABLE 2.6 Latino Male Prisoners Under State or Federal Jurisdiction, 2000–2008

Year	Total Latino male prisoners	Age 20–34	Latino male prison population (% of total)
2000	206,900	120,000	57.9
2003	251,900	148,800	59
2004	260,600	151,200	58
2005	279,000	161,100	58
2006	290,500	159,800	55
2007	301,200	166,400	55
2008	295,800	162,800	55

Source: Beck, A. J. & Harrison, P. M. (2001), Prisoners in 2000. Harrison, P. M. & Beck, A. J. (2004), Prisoners in 2003. Harrison, P. M. & Beck, A. J. (2005), Prisoners in 2004. Harrison, P. M. & Beck, A. J. (2006), Prisoners in 2005. Sabol, W. J., Couture, H. & Harrison, P. M. (2007), Prisoners in 2006. West, H. C. & Sabol, W. J. (2008), Prisoners in 2007. Sabol, W. J., West, H. C. & Cooper, M. (2009), Prisoners in 2008

(Sabol et al., 2009). The Latino male prison population grew 42 percent between 2000 and 2008; over 47 percent of this growth is comprised of the increase among the 20- to 34-year-old group. Within this period, the incarceration rate of Latino males ages 20–34 grew 35 percent (Sabol et al., 2009). Thus, the participation of Latino males under 35 years of age in the prison system is of significant concern, particularly in light of the current prevalence of limited educational attainment and labor/employment beyond low-skilled industries.

While the number of imprisoned Latino male offenders has risen since 2000, the incarceration rate has remained relatively steady at about 1,200 per 100,000 of the U.S. resident population during this period (Figure 2.13). On the other hand, the incarceration rate for Black men has decreased and for White men increased between 2000 and 2008 (Sabol et al., 2009).

While the data for types of offenses disaggregated by gender and Latino origin are not available, it can be inferred that the available data reflect Latino male prisoners because Latinas account for only 5 percent of the total percentage of Latino sentenced prisoners in 2008 (Table 2.7). Much of the increase in the incarceration rates of Latino males in state prisons is due to involvement in violent crimes, with over half of prisoners in 2006 and 2000 having committed serious offenses (Sabol et al., 2009). While Latino males have one of the fastest growing incarceration rates in the United States (Morín, 2008; The Sentencing Project, n.d.), they are largely absent from the theoretical and empirical discussions in the criminology literature (Schuck et al., 2004). Generally, research in this area has focused on the trends and differentials of Blacks and Whites (Aguirre & Baker, 2000). Public-use data that use race as a primary descriptor and do not include ethnicity (Hispanic, non-Hispanic, or unknown ethnicity) to categorize Latinos contribute to the serious paucity of research on Latinos in the prison system.

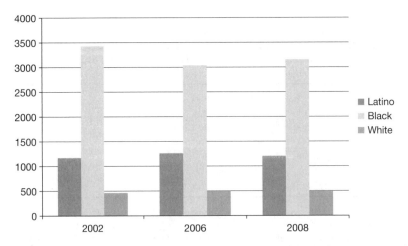

FIGURE 2.13 Incarceration rate for Latino, Black, and White males in U.S. resident population, 2002–2008

TABLE 2.7 Number of Latino Inmates in State Prisons by Type of Offense: 2000–2006

	Prisoners in 2006	Prisoners in 2000	% Change
Total	248,900	202,100	23.2
Violent	145,300	93,800	55.0
Property	25,000	34,100	−26.7
Drug	55,700	52,100	6.9
Other★	22,900	22,000	4.1

★Includes public disorder and other unspecified offenses

Source: Beck, A. J. & Harrison, P. M. (2001), Prisoners in 2000. Harrison, P. M. & Beck, A. J. (2004), Prisoners in 2003. Harrison, P. M. & Beck, A. J. (2005), Prisoners in 2004. Harrison, P. M. & Beck, A. J. (2006), Prisoners in 2005. Sabol, W. J., Couture, H. & Harrison, P. M. (2007), Prisoners in 2006. West, H. C. & Sabol, W. J. (2008), Prisoners in 2007. Sabol, W. J., West, H. C. & Cooper, M. (2009), Prisoners in 2008

A few studies have examined the factors contributing to the rise in Latino prisoners in the United States (Díaz-Cotto, 2000; Martinez, 1996; Morín, 2008; Oboler, 2009; Rios, 2006; Walker et al., 2004). According to this research, social and economic inequality (e.g., poverty, segregation), mass imprisonment, racialization, and illegal immigration, as well as the increased enforcement of immigration, are among the factors that impact Latino imprisonment (López & Light, 2009; Morín, 2008). Although empirical exploration is limited, the available data and studies suggest that social and structural barriers play an important role in the disenfranchisement of Latinos via the prison system.

Conclusion

The plight of Latino males across social, economic, and educational outcome indicators is formidable: nearly half of the Latino male population is not graduating from high school, the majority of Latino men above 18 are involved in the construction/services side of the labor market, and Latino males in their twenties and early thirties represent nearly half of the growth in the Latino prison population. Together, such alarming patterns point to the pervasive nature of disenfranchisement among Latino males aged 15 to 35 in the United States and raise substantive questions about the opportunities for greater social and economic mobility.

As detailed in this chapter, Latino males as a whole constitute an extraordinarily diverse group. It is important to keep in mind such heterogeneity when considering public policies and programs to attempt to ameliorate the social and educational risks and hardships commonly associated with Latino males. We know that not all Latino males are at risk. However, limitations in the current data collection strategies do not allow for disaggregation of statistics about Latinos by gender and by ethnic origin, preventing a detailed understanding and analysis.

Furthermore, conceptual tools must account for the intersectionality of gender, race, class, national origin, and immigration status, among other variables.

Nonetheless, the patterns of limited education, over-representation in low-wage industries, and increased imprisonment that Latino males face necessitate a call for understanding how such patterns emerged and how to begin to formulate a remedy from a national and local policy perspective. This also entails understanding the degree to which interventions conducted in Latino communities are reversing negative trends and creating access and opportunity for social and economic mobility. It is crucial that these interventions be reviewed and assessed for effectiveness, that they be conceptualized and formulated with clearly defined goals, that they be carried out in partnerships with communities, particularly families subject to intervention, and that they be based on building capacity through the inclusion of multi-sector collaboration.

In sum, this descriptive study of the state of Latino males across education, employment/labor, and incarceration over the past ten years provides an initial exploration of the patterns and factors that impact the long-term life chances of young and adult Latino males, and the overall Latino community. These data collectively underscore the complexity of this vulnerable and under-examined population. It is our hope that this chapter is an effective call to scholars, policy makers, and funders for the need to engage in and support on-going research on the status of Latino males in the three domains presented here—education, employment/labor, and incarceration—as well as directing focus to other areas, such as health and poverty and the development of targeted interventions for this population.

References

Aguirre, A., Jr., & Baker, D. V. (2000). Latinos and the United States criminal justice system: Introduction. *Criminal Justice Studies*, 13(1), 3–6.

Aud, S., Hussar, W., Planty, M., Snyder, T., Bianco, K., Fox, M., . . . Drake, L. (2010). The condition of education 2010 (NCES 2010–028). National Center for Education Statistics, Institute for Education Sciences. Washington, DC: U.S. Department of Education.

Bainbridge, J., Meyers, M. K., Tanaka, S., & Waldfogel, J. (2005). Who gets an early education? Family income and the enrollment of three- to five-year-olds from 1968 to 2000. *Social Science Quarterly*, 86(3), 724–745.

Barrueco, S., López, M. L., & Miles, J. C. (2007). Parenting behaviors in the first year of life: A national comparison of Latinos and other communities. *Journal of Latinos and Education*, 6(3), 253–265.

Beck, A. J., & Harrison, P. M. (2001). Prisoners in 2000. Washington, D.C.: Bureau of Justice Statistics. Retrieved from http://bjs.ojp.usdoj.gov/content/pub/pdf/p00.pdf

Borjas, G. J. (2006). Wage trends among disadvantaged minorities. In R. M. Blank, S. H. Danzinger, and R. F. Shoeni (Eds.), *Working and poor: How economic and policy changes are affecting low-wage workers* (59–86). New York: Russell Stage Foundation.

Brooks-Gunn, J., & Markman, L. B. (2005). The contribution of parenting to ethnic and racial gaps in school readiness. *The Future of Children*, 15(1), 139–168.

Bureau of Labor Statistics. (n.d., a). *Employed persons by occupation, race, Hispanic or Latino ethnicity, and sex, 2009 and 2010.* Retrieved from www.bls.gov/cps/cpsaat10.pdf

Bureau of Labor Statistics. (n.d., b). *Employed persons by occupation, race, Hispanic or Latino ethnicity, and sex, 2006 and 2007.* Retrieved from ftp://ftp.bls.gov/pub/special.requests/lf/aa2007/pdf/cpsaat10.pdf

Bureau of Labor Statistics. (n.d., c). *Employed persons by occupation, race, Hispanic or Latino ethnicity, and sex, 2004 and 2005.* Retrieved from ftp://ftp.bls.gov/pub/special.requests/lf/aa2005/pdf/cpsaat10.pdf

Bureau of Labor Statistics. (n.d., d). *Employed persons by occupation, race, Hispanic or Latino ethnicity, and sex, 2002 and 2003.* Retrieved from ftp://ftp.bls.gov/pub/special.requests/lf/aa2003/pdf/cpsaat10.pdf

Bureau of Labor Statistics. (n.d., e). *Median weekly earnings of full-time wage and salary workers by selected characteristics, 2009 and 2010.* Retrieved from www.bls.gov/cps/cpsaat37.pdf

Bureau of Labor Statistics. (n.d., f). *Median weekly earnings of full-time wage and salary workers by selected characteristics, 2006 and 2007.* Retrieved from ftp://ftp.bls.gov/pub/special.requests/lf/aa2007/pdf/cpsaat37.pdf

Bureau of Labor Statistics. (n.d., g). *Median weekly earnings of full-time wage and salary workers by selected characteristics, 2004 and 2005.* Retrieved from ftp://ftp.bls.gov/pub/special.requests/lf/aa2005/pdf/cpsaat37.pdf

Bureau of Labor Statistics. (n.d., h). *Median weekly earnings of full-time wage and salary workers by selected characteristics, 2003 and 2004.* Retrieved from ftp://ftp.bls.gov/pub/special.requests/lf/aa2004/pdf/cpsaat37.pdf

Bureau of Labor Statistics. (n.d., i). *Employment status of the Hispanic or Latino population by sex, age, and detailed ethnic group, 2008 and 2009.* Retrieved from ftp://ftp.bls.gov/pub/special.requests/lf/aa2009/pdf

Bureau of Labor Statistics. (n.d., j). *Employment status of the Hispanic or Latino population by sex, age, and detailed ethnic group, 2005 and 2006.* Retrieved from ftp://ftp.bls.gov/pub/special.requests/lf/aa2006/pdf/cpsaat6.pdf

Bureau of Labor Statistics. (n.d., k). *Employment status of the Hispanic or Latino population by sex, age, and detailed ethnic group, 2002 and 2003.* Retrieved from ftp://ftp.bls.gov/pub/special.requests/lf/aa2003/pdf/cpsaat6.pdf

Buysse, V., Castro, D. C., West, T., & Skinner, M. (2005). *Addressing the needs of Latino children: A national survey of state administrators of early childhood programs.* Chapel Hill, NC: University of North Carolina, FPG Child Development Institute.

Carter, T. P., & Segura, R. D. (1979). *Mexican Americans in school: A decade of change.* Princeton, NJ: College Board.

Congressional Research Service. (2005). The changing demographic profile of the United States. Retrieved from www.fas.org/sgp/crs/misc/RL32701.pdf

Delgado-Gaitan, C., & Trueba, H. (1991). *Crossing cultural borders: Education for immigrant families in America.* London: Falmer.

Díaz-Cotto, J. (2000). The criminal justice system and its impact on Latinas (OS) in the United States. *Criminal Justice Studies*, 13(1), 49–67.

Espino, R., & Franz, M. M. (2002). Latino phenotypic discrimination revisited: The impact of skin color on occupational status. *Social Science Quarterly*, 83(2), 612–623.

Farley, J. E. (1987). Disproportionate Black and Hispanic unemployment in U.S. metropolitan areas: The roles of racial inequality, segregation, and discrimination in male joblessness. *American Journal of Economics and Sociology*, 46(2), 129–150.

Flores-González, N. (2002). *School kids/street kids: Identity development in Latino students.* New York: Teachers College Press.

Greene, M., & Hoffnar, E. (1994). Residential location and the earnings of White and Hispanic men. *Applied Economics Letters,* 1(8), 127–131.

Harrison, P. M., & Beck, A. J. (2004). Prisoners in 2003. Washington, DC: Bureau of Justice Statistics. Retrieved from http://bjs.ojp.usdoj.gov/content/pub/pdf/p03.pdf

Harrison, P. M. & Beck, A. J. (2005). Prisoners in 2004. Washington, DC: Bureau of Justice Statistics. Retrieved from http://bjs.ojp.usdoj.gov/content/pub/pdf/p04.pdf

Harrison, P. M. & Beck, A. J. (2006). Prisoners in 2005. Washington, DC: Bureau of Justice.

Ibañez, G. E., Kuperminc, G. P., Jurkovic, G., & Perilla, J. (2004). Cultural attributes and adaptations linked to achievement motivation among Latino adolescents. *Journal of Youth and Adolescence,* 33(6), 559–568.

Jordan, W. J., Lara, J., & McPartland, J. M. (1996). Exploring the causes of early dropout among race-ethnic and gender groups. *Youth & Society,* 28(1), 62–94.

Kao, G., & Tienda, M. (1998). Educational aspirations of minority youth. *American Journal of Education,* 106(3), 349–384.

Laosa, L. M., & Ainsworth, P. (2007). *Is public pre-K preparing Hispanic children to succeed in school?* New Brunswick, NJ: National Institute for Early Education Research.

López, M. H., & Light, M. T. (2009). *A rising share: Hispanics and federal crime.* Washington, DC: Pew Hispanic Center.

Magnuson, K. A., & Waldfogel, J. (2005). Early childhood care and education: Effects on ethnic and racial gaps in school readiness. *The Future of Children,* 15(1), 169–196.

Martinez, R., Jr. (1996). Latinos and lethal violence: The impact of poverty and inequality. *Social Problems,* 43(2), 131–146.

Mason, P.L. (2004). Annual income, hourly wages, and identity formation among Mexican-Americans and other Latinos. *Industrial Relations,* 43(4), 817–834.

Matute-Bianchi, M. E. (1986). Ethnic identities and patterns of school success and failure among Mexican-descent and Japanese-American students in a California high school: An ethnographic analysis. *American Journal of Education,* 95(1), 233–255.

Meade, B., Gaytan, F., Fergus, E., & Noguera, P. (2009). A close look at the dropout crisis among Black and Latino males. New York: Metropolitan Center for Urban Education.

Mora, M. T., & Dávila, A. (2006). A note on the changes in the relative wages of LEP Hispanic men between 1980 and 2000. *Industrial Relations: A Journal of Economy and Society,* 45(2), 169–172.

Morín, J. L. (2008). Latinas/os and US prisons: Trends and challenges. *Latino Studies,* 6(1–2), 11–34.

National Poverty Center. (2007). The new face of the low-wage workforce. Ann Arbor: University of Michigan.

Neckerman, K. M., & Kirschenman, J. (1991). Hiring strategies, racial bias and inner-city workers. *Social Problems,* 38(4), 433–447.

Noguera, P. (2003). *City schools and the American dream.* New York: Teachers College Press.

Oboler, S. (Ed.). (2009). *Behind bars: Latino/as and prison in the United States.* New York: Palgrave Macmillan.

Ogbu, J. U. (1978). *Minority education and caste: The American system in cross-cultural perspective.* New York: Academic Press.

Ogbu, J. U. (1992). Understanding cultural diversity and learning. *Educational Researcher,* 21(8), 5–14.

Reimers, C. (1984). The wage structure of Hispanic men: Implications for policy. *Social Science Quarterly,* 65(2), 401–416.

Rios, V. M. (2006). The hyper-criminalization of Black and Latino male youth in the era of mass incarceration. *Souls*, 8(2), 40–54.

Rodriguez, T. D. (2002). Oppositional culture and academic performance among children of immigrants in the USA. *Race Ethnicity and Education*, 5(2), 199–215.

Rodriguez, T. D. (2003). School social context effects on gender differences in academic achievement among second-generation Latinos. *Journal of Hispanic Higher Education*, 2(1), 30–45.

Rumbaut, R. G., & Portes, A. (2001). *Ethnicities: Children of immigrants in America*. Berkeley: University of California Press.

Sabol, W. J., West, H. C., & Cooper, M. (2009). *Prisoners in 2008*. Washington, DC: Bureau of Justice Statistics. Retrieved from http://bjs.ojp.usdoj.gov/index.cfm?ty=pbdetail& iid=1763

Sánchez, B., Colón, Y., & Esparza, P. (2005). The role of sense of school belonging and gender in the academic adjustment of Latino adolescents. *Journal of Youth and Adolescence*, 34(6), 619–628.

Schuck, A. M., Lersch, K. M., & Verrill, S. W. (2004). The invisible "Hispanic"? The representation of Hispanics in criminal justice research: What we know and where should we go? *Journal of Ethnicity in Criminal Justice*, 2(3), 5–22.

The Sentencing Project. (n.d.). *Hispanic prisoners in the United States*. Retrieved from www.sentencingproject.org/doc/publications/publications/inc_factsAboutPrisons_ Jul2010.pdf

Stanton-Salazar, R. (2001). *Manufacturing hope and despair: The school and kin support networks of U.S.-Mexican youth*. New York: Teachers College Press.

Stolzenberg, R. M., & Tienda, M. (1997). English proficiency, education, and the conditional economic assimilation of Hispanic and Asian origin men. *Social Science Quarterly*, 26(1), 25–51.

Suárez-Orozco, C., & Suárez-Orozco, M. (1995). *Transformations: Migration, family life, and achievement motivation among Latino adolescents*. Stanford, CA: Stanford University Press.

Suárez-Orozco, M. (1991). Immigrant adaptation to schooling: A Hispanic case. In M. A. Gibson & J. U. Ogbu (Eds.), *Minority status and schooling: A comparative study of immigrant and involuntary minorities*. New York/London: Garland Publishing.

Tienda, M. (1983). Nationality and income attainment among native and immigrant Hispanic men in the United States. *The Sociological Quarterly*, 24(2), 253–272.

Tienda, M., & Lii, D. (1987). Minority concentration and earnings inequality: Blacks, Hispanics, and Asians compared. *The American Journal of Sociology*, 93(1), 141–165.

Tienda, M., & Niedert, L. (1984). Language, education, and the socioeconomic achievement of Hispanic origin men. *Social Science Quarterly*, 65(2), 519–536.

Trueba, H. T. (1987). *Success or failure: Learning and the language minority student*. Cambridge, MA: Newbury House.

Trueba, H. T. (1989). *Raising silent voices: Educating the linguistic minorities for the 21st century*. New York: Newbury House.

U.S. Census Bureau. (n.d.). Available from http://factfinder.census.gov/servlet/Dataset MainPageServlet?_program=ACS&_submenuId=&_lang=en&_ds_name=ACS_2008_ 3YR_G00_&ts

U.S. Census Bureau. (2004). *The Hispanic Population in the United States: 2004 Detailed Tables*. Available from www.census.gov/population/www/socdemo/hispanic/cps2004.html

U.S. Census Bureau. (2006). *The Hispanic Population in the United States: 2006 Detailed Tables*. Available from www.census.gov/population/www/socdemo/hispanic/cps2006.html

U.S. Census Bureau. (2008). *The Hispanic Population in the United States: 2008 Detailed Tables.* Available from www.census.gov/population/www/socdemo/hispanic/cps2008.html

U.S. Census Bureau. (2009). *Educational Attainment in the United States: 2009 Detailed Tables.* Available from www.census.gov/hhes/socdemo/education/data/cps/2009/tables.html

U.S. Department of Education. (n.d.). Institute of Educational Sciences, National Center for Education Statistics, National Assessment of Educational Progress (NAEP). Available from http://nces.ed.gov/nationsreportcard/naepdata/dataset.aspx

U.S. Department of Education. (n.d.). Office for Civil Rights Elementary and Secondary School Survey. Available from http://ocrdata.ed.gov/

Valenzuela, A. (1999). *Subtractive schooling: U.S.-Mexican youth and the politics of caring.* Albany, NY: State University of New York Press.

Walker, N. E., Senger, J. M., Villarruel, F. A., & Arboleda, A. M. (2004). *Lost opportunities: The reality of Latinos in the U.S. criminal justice system.* Washington, DC: National Council of La Raza.

West, H. C., & Sabol, W. J. (2008). Prisoners in 2007. Washington, DC: Bureau of Justice Statistics. Retrieved from http://bjs.ojp.usdoj.gov/content/pub/pdf/p07.pdf

Wilson, W. J. (2009). *More than just race: Being Black and poor in the inner city.* New York: W.W. Norton.

Winters, J., & Greene, M. (2006). *Leaving boys behind: Public high school graduation rates.* New York: Manhattan Institute.

Zarate, M. E., & Gillmore, R. (2005). Gendered differences in factors leading to college enrollment: A longitudinal analysis of Latina and Latino students. *Harvard Educational Review,* 75(4), 383–408.

3

ADOLESCENT MEXICAN AMERICAN MALES

No Increased Risk of Mental Health Problems[1]

Robert E. Roberts
Catherine Ramsay Roberts

We cannot say with any degree of confidence which males from different ethnic groups are at greater or lesser risk for psychological distress broadly defined. For example, we do not know either the prevalence or incidence of diagnosable psychiatric disorders for adolescent males or females among most ethnic groups in the United States. Because we do not have data on incidence and prevalence, it follows that we do not understand the etiology or consequences of psychiatric disorders among youths in the many ethnocultural groups that make up American society. In particular, our review of the limited evidence available demonstrates that we know little about Mexican American males.

Rates of psychological dysfunction may be similar or different across ethnocultural groups. In the latter case, such differentials may be due to (1) different (unique) risk and protective factors in the groups, (2) the same (generic) risk and protective factors operating differentially across groups, or (3) the effects of both generic and unique factors across groups (Roberts, 2000; Roberts & Roberts, 2007). Lincoln et al. (2003) note that there is little information about the role of generic risk and protective factors in the mental health of minorities. Wu et al. (2003) point out that factors may operate differently within specific subgroups. Further, there is some evidence that general stress–diathesis models do not predict mental health outcomes as well among African Americans, for example, as among Euro-Americans (Lincoln et al., 2003).

How might ethnicity affect risk for psychological distress (if, indeed, it does)? Studies of the relationship between ethnicity and psychological distress or psychiatric disorder implicitly examine two competing hypotheses, one of which argues that observed ethnic differences are due primarily to disadvantaged social status (particularly social class) and the other that there are ethnic effects (both positive and negative) on mental health over and above social status effects (Roberts, 2000). Mirowsky and Ross (1980) have labeled these two arguments, respectively, the minority status perspective and the ethnic culture perspective. Essentially these two arguments turn on a single question of fact: Are the rates of disorder in ethnic minority populations different than the rates in the dominant ethnic populations, when social class is controlled? If so, then the ethnic culture hypothesis is supported; if not, the minority status hypothesis is sustained (Roberts, 2000).

There are a myriad of review articles and empirical studies that have addressed the role of risk and protective factors in the epidemiology of psychological dysfunction among children and adolescents. The theme emanating from this body of literature is that risk and protective factors can be subsumed under four broad domains: family history of disorder, status attributes, personal and social resources, and stressors.

What is the role of ethnicity in this conceptual framework? By extension, given a particular family history constellation and given a particular combination of status factors such as age, gender, and ethnic status: to the extent ethnic experience reduces stressors and enhances resources, its impact on mental health should be positive, and to the extent ethnicity increases stressors and decreases resources, its impact on mental health should be negative.

Given the relatively few studies of adolescents to date, and the even greater paucity of data on prevalence of clinical disorders among adolescent males from different ethnocultural groups, we re-examine this question using data from our study, Teen Health 2000 (TH2K), a large, community-based study, which used a structured interview schedule to generate DSM-IV diagnoses according to the Diagnostic and Statistical Manual of Mental Disorders, Fourth Edition (DSM-IV, American Psychiatric Association, 2000). TH2K is the largest study of psychopathology among adolescents ever conducted in the United States that incorporates these procedures. We selected a sample designed to permit comparisons of Euro, African, and Mexican American youths. We focus specifically on adolescent Mexican American males.

Drawing upon our research to date, we examine prevalence of DSM-IV disorders, suicidal thoughts and behavior, and insomnia, as well as other important indicators of psychological dysfunction and well-being such as happiness, life satisfaction, and perceived mental health.

Methods

The sample was selected from households in the Houston metropolitan area enrolled in the two largest local health maintenance organizations (combined enrollment, 600,000). One youth, aged 11–17 years, was randomly sampled from each eligible household, oversampling for African American and Mexican

American households. If more than one youth 11–17 resided in a household, one was selected using Kish procedures. As ethnic status was not available, a sampling strategy was developed to achieve approximately equal numbers in each of the three ethnic groups. Because there were proportionately fewer minority subscriber households encountered, we developed sample weights, which were adjusted by poststratification using 2000 census data respectively to reflect the age, ethnicity, and gender distribution of the five-county Houston metropolitan area in 2000. The precision of estimates is thereby improved and sample selection bias reduced to the extent that it is related to demographic composition (Andrews & Morgan, 1973).

Data were collected at baseline on sample youths and one adult caregiver by trained lay interviewers using computer-assisted personal interviews and self-administered questionnaires. Interviews and questionnaires were completed with 4,175 youths—1,475 Euro American, 1,479 Afro American, and 857 Mexican American youths. Another 364 youths were of various ethnic backgrounds. Interviews were completed in 66 percent of the eligible households. There were no significant differences among ethnic groups in completion rates. All youths and parents gave written informed consent prior to participation in this study. All study forms and procedures were approved by the University of Texas Health Sciences Center Committee for Protection of Human Subjects.

Psychiatric disorders among youths were assessed with the Diagnostic Interview Schedule for children, Version 4 (DISC-IV) a highly structured instrument (Shaffer et al., 2000) designed to be administered by lay interviewers. Here, we include anxiety disorders (agoraphobia, generalized anxiety, panic, social phobia, post-traumatic stress disorder), affective disorders (major depression, dysthymia, mania, hypomania), disruptive disorders (conduct and oppositional defiant), attention-deficit hyperactivity disorders, and substance use (alcohol, marijuana and other substances) disorders. Our measure of presence of mental or behavioral problems is a DSM-IV disorder in the previous 12 months.

Insomnia was measured approximating DSM-IV criteria. Suicidal indicators were taken from the major depression module and include thoughts, plans, and attempts in the past year.

Happiness was assessed with a single item inquiring whether youths were very happy to very unhappy. Life satisfaction was assessed by asking, overall, whether youths were very satisfied to very dissatisfied. Perceived mental health was assessed by asking youths whether they thought their mental health was excellent to very poor.

Controlling for the effects of status differentials, if observed differences are diminished, provides support for the social status hypothesis. If not, then by definition, there is support, at least implicitly, for the ethnic culture hypothesis. For generation of the confidence interval for the odds ratio, we employed survey mean (svymean) and survey logistic regression (svylogit) procedure in STATA V8.2 (StataCorp., 2006). This procedure uses Taylor series approximation to compute the standard error of the odds ratio. Lepkowski and Bowles (1996) indicate that the difference in computing standard error between this method and other repeated replication methods such as the jackknife is very small.

Results

Table 3.1 reports prevalence rates by ethnicity and gender for past year DSM-IV disorders. There are few differences. The two male minority groups have higher rates of anxiety disorders and African American males have lower rates of substance abuse, as do African American females. The male–female gender ratio is also much more dramatic for African Americans. Rates of attention deficit hyperactivity disorder are much lower among minority females and the gender ratios much larger than for the majority group. We then focus on males, adjusting for age, family income, and stressors. Mexican American males are at greater risk of anxiety disorders than Euro-American males, and similar to Afro American males. Mexican American males are at greater risk for attention deficit hyperactivity disorder than African American males and for substance abuse (data not shown).

Table 3.2 presents prevalences of insomnia by ethnicity and gender. There are essentially no differences among males or among females. In general, the rates for the three different indicators of insomnia are higher for females than males in all ethnic groups. Focusing on males, after adjustment, the only difference noted is a lower risk for Mexican American versus African American males for symptoms of insomnia with daytime fatigue or sleepiness.

Table 3.3 presents suicidal indicators by gender and ethnicity. Again, few differences are evident. The only differences noted are the higher rates for suicidal thoughts and plans for Euro and Mexican American females. Some of the differences between male groups and females groups are large, but due to the low frequency and small sample sizes, statistical power is substantially reduced. With larger sample sizes, some of these differences no doubt would be significant. There are no ethnic differences for males, after adjustment for covariates.

As can be seen in Table 3.4, there are no ethnic–gender differences in prevalence of happiness, life satisfaction or perceived mental health. There is a trend for males to be happier, more satisfied with life and to report better perceived mental health, but there are no male–ethnicity differences that are significant. For males, none of the odds ratios were significant after adjustments for age, family income and stressors.

Discussion

Our findings on the mental health of Mexican American adolescent males further extend our earlier work in which we found few ethnic differences for DSM-IV psychiatric disorders (Roberts et al., 2006), suicidal behaviors (Roberts et al., 2007),

TABLE 3.1 Prevalence of Psychiatric Disorders by Gender and Ethnicity (Wave 1)

N, %

	Male			Female		
	Euro American	African American	Mexican American	Euro American	African American	Mexican American
Any anxiety (1)	3.42★ (2.15–4.69)	6.09 (4.34–7.83)	6.11 (3.87–8.35)	7.97 (5.95–10.00)	10.09 (7.94–12.25)	10.84 (7.84–13.85)
Any mood (2)	2.66 (1.54–3.79)	2.07 (1.03–3.12)	2.71 (1.19–4.24)	3.91 (2.46–5.36)	2.12 (1.09–3.16)	3.61 (1.81–5.42)
Any disruptive(3)	7.48 (5.64–9.32)	6.50 (4.70–8.30)	6.56 (4.24–8.88)	2.75 (1.53–3.98)	3.45 (2.15–4.76)	3.37 (1.63–5.12)
Attention-deficit hyperactivity disorder	3.30 (2.05–4.54)	1.80 (0.83–2.77)	1.81 (0.56–3.06)	2.90★(1.64–4.15)	0.66 (0.08–1.25)	0.72 (0.00–1.55)
Any substance(4)	7.86★ (5.98–9.74)	3.18 (1.90–4.46)	6.56 (4.24–8.88)	4.06★(2.58–5.53)	0.80 (0.16–1.43)	4.82 (2.75–6.89)
Any disorder	18.25 (15.55–20.95)	15.35 (12.72–17.99)	16.74 (13.25–20.24)	16.09 (13.34–18.84)	14.61 (12.08–17.14)	18.55 (14.80–22.31)

★ Significant difference by ethnicity within each gender (p<0.05)

(1) Agoraphobia, Generalized Anxiety, Panic Disorder, Social Phobia, and Post-Traumatic Stress
(2) Mania, Hypomania, Major Depression, and Dysthymic Disorder
(3) Conduct Disorder and Oppositional Defiant
(4) Alcohol Abuse, Marijuana Abuse, Other Substance Abuse, Alcohol Dependence, Marijuana Dependence, and Other Substance Dependence

TABLE 3.2 Prevalence of Insomnia by Gender and Ethnicity (Wave 1)

	N, %					
	Male			*Female*		
	Euro American	*African American*	*Mexican American*	*Euro American*	*African American*	*Mexican American*
P1	22.93 (19.98–25.88)	25.18 (21.98–28.37)	24.26 (20.22–28.29)	30.31 (26.85–33.76)	29.55 (26.27–32.82)	28.75 (24.33–33.16)
P2	5.48 (3.88–7.07)	5.77 (4.05–7.48)	2.97 (1.38–4.57)	10.25 (7.97–12.53)	7.62 (5.71–9.53)	10.07 (7.14–13.01)
P3	4.44 (3.00–5.88)	4.70 (3.16–6.25)	2.26 (0.87–3.65)	7.39 (5.43–9.35)	5.98 (4.28–7.67)	6.02 (3.73–8.32)

*No significance by ethnicity within each gender

P1: One or more symptoms of insomnia
P2: At least one symptom plus Daytime Fatigue or Sleepiness or Both
P3: P2 plus Exclusion for Mood, Anxiety, and Substance Use Disorders

TABLE 3.3 Prevalence of Suicidal Behaviors by Gender and Ethnicity (Wave 1)

Past Year	N, %					
	Male			Female		
	Euro American	African American	Mexican American	Euro American	African American	Mexican American
Suicide thought	3.93 (2.57–5.29)	2.21 (1.14–3.29)	2.71 (1.19–4.24)	5.80 (4.05–7.55)	2.26 (1.20–3.33)	4.59 (2.57–6.61)
Suicide plan	1.27 (0.49–2.05)	0.83 (0.17–1.49)	1.13 (0.14–2.12)	2.17 (1.08–3.26)	0.40 (0.00–0.85)	1.69 (0.44–2.94)
Suicide attempt	0.63 (0.08–1.19)	0.28 (0.00–0.66)	1.36 (0.27–2.44)	2.46 (1.30–3.62)	0.93 (0.24–1.62)	2.17 (0.76–3.58)

* Suicide thought and Suicide plan were significantly different by ethnicity in females ($p<0.05$)

TABLE 3.4 Prevalence of Unhappiness, Life Dissatisfaction, and Poor Perceived Mental Health by Gender and Ethnicity (Wave 1)

	N, %					
	Male			Female		
	Euro American	African American	Mexican American	Euro American	African American	Mexican American
Unhappiness (1)	15.05 (12.54–17.56)	16.17 (13.46–18.89)	14.06 (10.77–17.34)	19.53 (16.55–22.52)	18.95 (16.13–21.77)	16.79 (13.13–20.45)
Life dissatisfaction (2)	16.09 (13.5–18.68)	16.31 (13.58–19.05)	15.96 (12.47–19.45)	20.12 (17.09–23.15)	22.54 (19.52–25.55)	19.95 (16.02–23.88)
Poor perceived mental health (3)	15.36 (12.83–17.9)	15.94 (13.24–18.64)	14.85 (11.48–18.22)	19.65 (16.65–22.65)	20.43 (17.53–23.33)	19.65 (15.75–23.55)

* No significant difference by ethnicity within each gender (p>0.05)

(1) Neither happy or unhappy, pretty unhappy, or very unhappy
(2) About equally satisfied or dissatisfied, pretty dissatisfied, or very dissatisfied
(3) Fair, poor, or very poor

insomnia (Roberts et al., 2006), and other general measures of mental health functioning such as happiness, life satisfaction or perceived mental health (Roberts et al., 2005a).

The most noteworthy finding is regarding anxiety and substance abuse disorders. Mexican American males were at greater risk of anxiety disorders than majority youths, as were African American youths. Mexican American males had higher risk of substance use disorders than African American males, but no greater risk than Euro American youths. This finding of lower risk for substance use disorders among African American youths is not new. However, the findings for anxiety have not been reported elsewhere and need to be explored further. Clearly the data do not support the emotional contradiction hypothesis that Mexican culture engenders lower risk for anxiety and greater risk for depression (Mirowsky & Ross, 1984).

One possible hypothesis for higher rates of anxiety among minority youths is differential exposure to stress. Minority youths are disproportionately lower status and differentially exposed to life stress from the social and physical environment (see Thoits, 2010; Williams & Sternthal, 2010), which may increase risk for psychiatric disorders, in particular anxiety disorders.

These results are from only one study sampling youths from one metropolitan area, and thus results need to be replicated in other Latino groups such as Puerto Ricans and Cuban Americans as well as Asian subgroups. The same is true for African Americans born in the United States, Africa, or the Caribbean.

Our finding at this point, however, is that neither ethnic status nor nativity probably will take us very far in understanding the etiology and natural history of mental health problems among adolescent Latino males.

In a recent paper (Roberts & Roberts, 2007), we found that there was little unique risk associated with ethnic status. When we examined the role of a broad array of generic versus ethnic specific risk factors, two general patterns were noted. First, among generic indicators of status factors, personal and social resources, and stressors, many more of the indicators were significantly associated with prevalence of DSM-IV disorders for Euro American youths than for either African American and Mexican American youths. In fact, what was striking is that the role of risk and protective factors extant in the literature are indeed associated with risk of disorder among Euro American youths, but not African American and Mexican American youths. This should come as no surprise, as most of the research presented in the literature is based on samples of Euro American youths or samples for which data for different ethnic groups were not disaggregated. When data were disaggregated, markedly fewer of these generic factors were related to prevalence of psychiatric disorders among African American or Mexican American youths. In fact, on average, only a third to half as many associations were significant. The good news is that, for those that were significant, the associations were in the same direction as for Euro American youths. The most surprising finding, in some respects, was the lack of association between indicators of ethnic experience. There was essentially none, after controls for generic risk and protective factors. There were only four out of seventy-two significant odds ratios, and these were limited to African American youths. The results, limited as they were, suggest stronger ethnic identity and higher salience of ethnicity are protective for African American youths (but not for Mexican American youths).

The results reported by us thus far, and those from other studies cited, albeit limited in number and scope, clearly suggest that the developmental epidemiology of psychiatric disorders may differ in different ethnic groups, as the literature from developmental psychopathology would predict (Cicchetti & Cohen, 1995; Costello & Angold, 1995; Rutter & Sroufe, 2000; Sroufe & Rutter, 1984). That is, ethnicity appears to influence differences in symptom presentation at different developmental periods as well as the association of risk and protective factors with symptom manifestation and disorder (Boyce et al., 1998; Cicchetti & Toth, 1998; Costello et al., 2006).

Our data also support the contention by Wu et al. (2003) that factors may operate differently within specific ethnic subgroups. The results also support the argument by Lincoln et al. (2003) that stress-diathesis models predict mental health outcomes less well among African Americans, and extend this to the case of Mexican Americans.

The question arises that, if there are few differences in prevalence rates between ethnic groups among adolescents generally, or males particularly—and that appears to be the case—but the risk factor profiles are considerably different across groups, then what forces might be involved in the etiology of the disorders? The answer to this question, we submit, will require more extensive and systematic examination of the role of risk and protective factors within different ethnic groups. However, no study examines the full range of potential explanatory variables for any particular outcome, and TH2K is no exception. In particular, our study did not include many of the measures suggested in recent papers on correlates of mental health in minority populations (Brown, 2003; Lincoln et al., 2003; Ryff et al., 2003; Wu et al., 2003). This relates both to outcomes and predictors. In terms of the former, Brown (2003) has suggested that we examine outcomes such as nihilism, suppressed anger, delusional denial, and racial paranoia. Others (Ryan & Deci, 2001; Ryff et al., 2003) have argued that constructs such as hedonic and eudaimonic well-being should be examined in regard to ethnicity and mental health.

In terms of predictors, we have not examined the role of personality traits although some authors suggest that this may account for variance in risk across adolescent ethnic groups (Blumentritt et al., 2004). Lincoln et al. (2003) find negative interaction, which we did not examine, operates differentially across ethnic groups in terms of risk for psychological distress. Beyond generic coping skills (which we examined), there may be ethnic-specific coping strategies in response to stress related to ethnic experiences (Noh et al., 1999; Williams et al., 1992).

The answer to this question will also require prospective data, because factors associated with prevalence may be factors related both to incidence and duration of disorders, when the key epidemiologic question is whether and how the etiology (incidence) of mental health problems differs across groups, including Mexican American adolescent males. In particular, the apparent increased risk for anxiety disorders merits further examination.

Conclusions

Beyond the data on anxiety disorders, based on our findings thus far, we conclude overall that there is little to suggest that Mexican American adolescent males are noteworthy either for increased or decreased risk of psychological dysfunction compared to their majority group counterparts. Given the dearth of data on mental health of Mexican American adolescent males thus far, and our consequent lack of understanding concerning issues of etiology and natural history, it is difficult to discuss implications regarding policy. From a public health perspective, prevention and early detection are the keys to reducing the burden of mental health problems among all adolescents. Even though Mexican American adolescent males do not appear at greater risk in general, their burden is still substantial. A number of strategies for detecting and preventing mental health problems have been outlined (see Goldsmith et al., 2002; Mrazek & Haggerty, 1994; Romer, 2003). However, there is little evidence of the efficacy of such interventions specifically for Mexican American adolescent males. But, then again, there are few data to suggest whether such programs would benefit from the available evidence base in terms of identification of ethnic- and gender-specific risk and protective factors, which might be the target for intervention efforts.

To reiterate, we found few differences in indicators of mental health functioning to indicate Mexican American adolescent males are disadvantaged in terms of mental health status. However, even if Mexican American adolescents in general, and males in particular, manifest mental health problems at rates comparable to other groups, including majority youths, this is not the whole story. Once youths have developed symptoms or episodes of psychiatric disorder, receipt of mental health treatment or interventions can reduce the burden of such dysfunction and alter the subsequent natural history of the disorders. Therein lies a key element relating to the mental health of Mexican and other Latino adolescents. These youths do not receive services commensurate with their needs.

In almost every area of health services examined by the Institute of Medicine Report (Institute of Medicine, 2002), minority youths were found more likely to receive inferior health care services compared to their non-Hispanic White counterparts, a finding that has been confirmed by widespread findings on both access to and the type of care (Beal, 2004). Latino youths exhibit lower rates of mental health service use compared to non-Hispanic Whites (Kataoka et al., 2002;

Yeh et al., 2003; Zahner & Daskalakis, 1997). Both Latino youths with attention-deficit hyperactivity disorders and those with depression make fewer office visits for these conditions (Olfson et al., 2003a, b), and Latino adolescents with psychiatric disorders enter care later and make fewer specialty mental health visits, compared to non-Hispanic Whites (Hough et al., 2002).

Combined with lower access to and use of mental health services, there is also scarce empirical research identifying appropriate issues to focus on in mental health services for Latino youths and a dearth of data on effective treatments for Latino youths. A number of barriers including language, cultural attitudes about help-seeking, and stigma about mental illness no doubt contribute to Latino youths' lack of access to care (Alegria, 2004). For example, lack of parental recognition of youth mental health problems is also an important factor in explaining under-utilization of mental health services in minority and immigrant youths (Roberts et al., 2005a). Several studies (Gleser et al., 1980; Roberts et al., 2005b; Wachtel et al., 1994; Walton et al., 1999) suggest that minority parents are less likely than majority parents to recognize and/or label their children's behavior as a mental health problem requiring intervention.

Health insurance coverage is one area clearly contributing to disparities in receipt of mental health services for Mexican American and other Latino youths. Employer insurance coverage of both children and adults has declined (Kaiser Family Foundation, 2008), eroding the coverage of the near poor, who are less likely to qualify for public insurance. These coverage gaps can contribute to disparities in health service delivery for minority youths because minorities are over-represented among the under- and uninsured (Bodenheimer, 2005; Rylko-Bauer & Farmer, 2002). As an example of the importance of insurance coverage, Medicaid-eligible youths are nearly five times more likely than non-Medicaid youths to use mental health services (Deck & Levy, 2006).

Minority youths face a number of barriers to effective mental health care that result in mental health service disparities. These include *sociodemographic* barriers such as socioeconomic disadvantage, stigma, poor health education, and lack of activism; *provider factors* including deficits in culturally competent care, youth-orientation, and youth/provider interaction; and *systemic factors* such as location of services, availability of linguistic appropriate services, and policy restrictions that reduce access to services (Pumariega et al., 2005). Drawing from these barriers, Alegria et al. (2009) posit six main mechanisms tied to these service disparities:

(1) failure of healthcare markets, institutional bias and limited financing leading to decreased access to and utilization of behavioral healthcare services;

(2) differential pathways into behavioral healthcare and educational services leading to differential experiences of service, no services or inadequate services;

(3) poor youth–teacher interaction leading to miscommunication, dispro-portional in-school referrals for behavioral problems, low school retention, elevated rates of suspensions, and expulsions;

(4) mismatches between behavioral health and educational service offerings, minorities' services needs and their living circumstances, leading to low or no service use;

(5) lack of community trust and erroneous expectations of services leading to disengagement and poor collaboration in the educational and behavioral service systems; and

(6) limited workforce availability and training of service providers to treat ethnic and racial minority youth, especially immigrant youth that are non-English speakers, leading to reliance on informal or poorly trained service providers.

(Alegria et al., 2009)

Based on their extensive review, Alegria et al. (2009) make three recom-mendations that could improve knowledge of the mental health of Latino youths and their use of mental health services: (1) Designing research studies that allow for subgroup comparisons within the Latino youth population, including nativity, language proficiency, and ethnic subgroups. For example, Mexican Americans report the lowest rates of past-year service and Puerto Ricans report some of the highest (Alegria, Mulvaney-Day, et al., 2007a); (2) Research to further disentangle contextual effects for risk of mental disorders and access to mental health services as well as to develop interventions to prevent development of dysfunction; (3) Research on the effect of cultural factors on mental health outcomes, including social networks and family support, focusing on the effects of bolstering social support systems and social networks as well as resolving family conflict in addition to other cultural and linguistic factors.

There is a growing body of research on the mental health of Latino adolescents, in particular Mexican American youths. As yet, however, our knowledge base specific to Latino adolescent males is rudimentary. Clearly more research is needed, both on the etiology and natural history of mental health problems and interventions to prevent and treat such problems.

Note

1 This research was supported, in part, by Grants No. 49764 and No. 65606, both awarded to Robert E. Roberts, Ph.D., by the National Institutes of Health.

References

Alegria, M. (2004). Outreach to youth living in underserved communities: Challenges and recommendations. *NAMI Beginnings* 4, 3–6.

Alegria, M., Canino, G., & Pescosolido, B. (2009). A socio-cultural framework for mental health and substance abuse service disparities. In B. J. Sadock, B. A. Sadock, & P. Ruiz

(Eds.), *Comprehensive textbook of psychiatry*. Baltimore: Wolters Kluwer Health, Lippincott Williams & Wilkins.

Alegria, M., Mulvaney-Day, N., Torres, M., Polo, A., Cao, Z., & Canino, G. (2007a). Prevalence of psychiatric disorders across Latino subgroups in the United States. *American Journal of Public Health* 97, 68–75.

Alegria, M., Shrout, P., Woo, M., Guarnaccia, P., Sribney, W., Vila, D., Polo, A., Cao, Z., Mulvaney-Day, N., Torres, M., & Canino, G. (2007b). Understanding differences in past year psychiatric disorders for Latinos living in the US. *Social Science & Medicine* 65 (2), 214–230.

American Psychiatric Association (2000). *Diagnostic and statistical manual of mental disorders* (4th edition, text revision). Washington, D.C.: American Psychiatric Association.

Andrews, F. F. & Morgan, J. N. (Eds.) (1973). *Multiple classification analysis* (2nd edition). Ann Arbor: Institute for Social Research, University of Michigan.

Beal, A. C. (2004). Policies to reduce racial and ethnic disparities in child health and health care. *Health Affairs* 23, 171–179.

Blumentritt, T. L., Angle, R. L., & Brown, J. M. (2004). MACI personality patterns and DSM-IV symptomology in a sample of troubled Mexican-American adolescents. *Journal of Child and Family Studies* 13, 163–178.

Bodenheimer, T. (2005). High and rising health care costs Part 1: Seeking an explanation. *Annals of Internal Medicine* 142 (10), 847–854.

Boyce, W. T., Frank, E., Jensen, P. S., Kessler, R. C., Nelson, C. A., & Steinberg, L. (1998). MacArthur Foundation Research Network on Psychopathology and Development, Social context in developmental psychopathology: Recommendations for future research from the MacArthur Network on Psycholopathology and Development. *Development and Psychopathology* 10, 143–164.

Brown, T. (2003). Critical race theory speaks to the sociology of mental health: Mental health problems produced by racial stratification. *Journal of Health and Social Behavior* 44, 292–301.

Cicchetti, D. & Cohen, D. J. (Eds.) (1995). Perspectives on developmental psycho-pathology. In D. Cicchetti & D. J. Cohen, *Developmental psychopathology 1, theory and methods*, New York: John Wiley & Sons, 3–20.

Cicchetti, D., & Toth, S. (1998). The development of depression in children and adolescents. *American Psychologist* 53, 221–241.

Costello, E. J., & Angold, A. (1995). Developmental epidemiology. In D. Cicchetti & D. J. Cohen (Eds.), *Developmental psychopathology 1, theory and methods*, New York: John Wiley & Sons, 23–56.

Costello, E. J., Foley, D. L., & Angold, A. (2006). 10-year research update review: The epidemiology of child and adolescent psychiatric disorders: II. Developmental epidemiology. *Journal of the American Academy of Child and Adolescent Psychiatry* 45, 8–25.

Deck, D., & Levy, K. V. (2006). Medicaid eligibility and access to mental health services among adolescents in substance abuse treatment. *Psychiatric Services* 57 (2), 263–265.

Gleser, G. C., Seligman, R., Winget, C. & Raugh, J. L. (1980). Parents view their adolescents' mental health. *Journal of Adolescent Health Care* 1 (1), 30–36.

Goldsmith, S. K., Pellmar, T. C., Kleinman, A. M., & Bunney, W. E. (Eds.). (2002). *Reducing suicide: A national imperative*. Washington, D.C.: The National Academies, Press.

Hough, R. L., Hazen, A. L., Soriano, F. I., Wood, P., McCabe, K., & Yeh, M. (2002). Mental health services for Latino adolescents with psychiatric disorders. *Psychiatric Services* 53 (12), 1556–1562.

Institute of Medicine. (2002).*Unequal treatment: Confronting racial and ethnic disparities in health care*. Smedley, B. D., Stitl, A. Y., & Nelson, A. R. (Eds.) Washington, D.C.: National Academy Press.

Kaiser Family Foundation. (2008). *About the health care marketplace project*. Retrieved November 20, 2008, from www.kff.org/about/marketpalce.cfm

Kataoka, S. H., Zhang, L., & Wells, K. B. (2002). Unmet need for mental health care among U.S. children: Variation by ethnicity and insurance status. *American Journal of Psychiatry* 159 (9), 1548–1555.

Lepkowski, J. & Bowles, L. (1996). Sampling error software for personal computers. *Survey Statistician* 35, 10–17.

Lincoln, K. D., Chatters, L. M., & Taylor, R. J. (2003). Psychological distress among Black and White Americans: Differential effects of social support, negative interaction and personal control. *Journal of Health and Social Behavior* 44, 390–407.

Mirowsky, J. & Ross, C. E. (1980). Minority status, ethnic culture and distress: A comparison of Blacks, Whites, Mexicans and Mexican Americans. *American Journal of Sociology* 86, 479–495.

Mirowsky, J. & Ross, C. E. (1984). Mexican culture and its emotional contradictions. *Journal of Health and Social Behavior* 25 (1), 2–13.

Mrazek, P. J. and Haggerty, R. J. (Eds.) (1994). *Reducing risk for mental disorders: Frontiers for preventive intervention research*. Washington, D.C.: National Academy Press.

Noh, S., Beiser, B., Kasper, V., Hou, F., & Rummens, J. (1999). Perceived racial discrimination, depression, and coping: A study of Southeast Asian refugees in Canada. *Journal of Health and Social Behavior* 40, 193–207.

Olfson, M., Gameroff, M., Marcus, S., & Jensen, P. (2003a). National trends in the treatment of attention deficit hyperactivity disorder. *American Journal of Psychiatry* 160 (6), 1071–1077.

Olfson, M., Gameroff, M., Marcus, S., & Waslick, B. (2003b). Outpatient treatment of child and adolescent depression in the United States. *Archives of General Psychiatry* 60 (12), 1236–1242.

Pumariega, A. J., Rogers, K., & Rothe, E. (2005). Culturally competent systems of care for children's mental health: Advances and challenge. *Community Mental Health Journal* 41 (5), 539–555.

Roberts, E. & Roberts, R. E. (2000). Depression and suicidal behaviors among adolescents: The role of ethnicity. In I. Cuellar & F. H. Pariagua (Eds.), *Handbook of multicultural mental health*. San Diego: Academic Press, 360–380.

Roberts, R. E., Alegria, M., Roberts, C. R., & Chen, I. G. (2005a). Concordance of reports of mental health functioning by adolescents and their caregivers: a comparison of European, African and Latino Americans. *The Journal of Nervous and Mental Disease* 193, 528–534.

Roberts, R. E., Alegria, M., Roberts, C. R., & Chen, I. G. (2005b). Mental health problems of adolescents as reported by their caregivers: A comparison of European, African and Latino Americans. *The Journal of Behavioral Health Services & Research* 32 (1), 1.

Roberts R. E., & Roberts C. R. (2007). Ethnicity and risk of psychiatric disorder among adolescents. *Research in Human Development* 4, 89–117.

Roberts, R. E., Roberts, C. R., & Chan, W. (2006). Ethnic differences in symptoms of insomnia among adolescents. *Sleep* 29, 359–365.

Roberts, R. E., Roberts, C. R., & Xing, Y. (2006). Prevalence of youth-reported DSM-IV psychiatric disorders among African American, European and Mexican

American adolescents. *Journal of the American Academy of Child and Adolescent Psychiatry* 45, 1329–1337.

Roberts, R. E., Roberts, C. R., & Xing, Y. (2007). Are Mexican American adolescents at greater risk of suicidal behaviors? *Suicide & Life-Threatening Behaviors* 37, 10–21.

Romer, D. (Ed.) (2003). *Reducing adolescent risk: Toward an integrated approach.* Thousand Oaks, CA: Sage Publications.

Rutter, M. & Sroufe, L. A. (2000). Developmental psychopathology: Concepts and challenges. *Development and Psychopathology* 12, 265–296.

Ryan, R. M. & Deci, E. L. (2001). On happiness and human potentials: A review of research on hedonic and eudaimonic well-being. *Annual Review of Psychology* 52, 141–166.

Ryff, C., Keyes, C., & Hughes, D. (2003). Status inequalities, perceived discrimination, and eudaimonic well-being: Do the challenges of minority life hone purpose and growth. *Journal of Health and Social Behavior* 44, 275–291.

Rylko-Bauer, B. & Farmer, P. (2002). Managed care or managed inequality? A call for critiques of market-based medicine. *Medical Anthropology Quarterly* 16 (4), 476–502.

Shaffer, D., Fisher, P., Lucas, C. P., Dulcan, M. K., & Schwab-Stone, M. E. (2000). The NIMH diagnostic interview schedule for children version IV (NIMH DISC-IV): Description, differences from previous versions, and reliability of some common diagnoses. *Journal of American Academy of Child Adolescent Psychiatry* 39, 28–38.

Sroufe, L. A. & Rutter, M. (1984). The domain of developmental psychopathology. *Child Development* 55, 17–29.

StataCorp. (2006). Stata Statistical Software: Release 9.0. College Station, TX: Stata Corporation.

Thoits, P. A. (2010). Stress and health: Major findings and policy implications. *Journal of Health and Social Behavior* 51, S41–S53.

Wachtel, J., Rodrigue, J. R., Geffken, G., Graham-Pole, J., & Turner, C. (1994). Children awaiting invasive medical procedures: Do children and their mothers agree on child's level of anxiety? *Journal of Pediatric Psychology* 19, 723–735.

Walton, W, J., Johnson, S. B. & Algina, J. (1999). Mother and child perceptions of child anxiety: Effects of race, health status and stress. *Journal of Pediatric Psychology* 24 (1), 29–39.

Williams, D. R., & Sternthal, M. (2010). Understanding racial-ethnic disparities in health: Sociological contributions. *Journal of Health and Social Behavior* 51, S15–S27.

Williams, D. R., Takeuchi, D. T. & Adair, R. K. (1992). Socioeconomic status and psychiatric disorder among Blacks and Whites. *Social Forces* 71, 179–194.

Wu, Z., Noh, S., Kaspar, V., & Schimmele, C. M. (2003). Race, ethnicity, and depression in Canadian society. *Journal of Health & Social Behavior* 44, 426–441.

Yeh, M., McCabe, K., Hough, R. L., Dupuis, D., & Hazen, A. (2003). Racial/ethnic differences in parental endorsement of barriers to mental health services for youth. *Mental Health Services Research* 5 (2), 65–77.

Zahner, G.E., & Daskalakis, C. (1997). Factors associated with mental health, general health, and school-based service use for child psychopathology. *American Journal of Public Health* 87 (9), 1440–1448.

4

REDUCING SEXUAL AND REPRODUCTIVE HEALTH DISPARITIES AMONG LATINO MEN

Exploring Solutions in the Boundaries of Masculinity

Miguel Muñoz-Laboy
Ashley Perry

Conceptions of Sexual and Reproductive Health Disparities Among Latino Men

Since the introduction of the U.S. Department of Health and Human Services' Healthy People 2010 initiative, the overall health of Americans has improved significantly. However, not all populations have benefited equally from these improvements. Men of Color in the United States continue to experience significant health disparities relative to their White counterparts. These disparities include access to care, unequal treatment, language barriers, lack of diversity among health care staff and providers, and low levels of health education and knowledge (Gornick, 2000).

Similar to other ethnic minority men in the United States, Latino men are less likely to see a doctor, even when in poor health, less likely to have employer-based health insurance, and more likely to receive less aggressive treatments compared to their White counterparts (Tewari et al., 2005; Williams, 2001). Latino men are second only to African-American men with respect to the burden of sexually transmitted infections, particularly HIV, gonorrhea, and syphilis (Centers for Disease Control and Prevention [CDC], 2000b, c). AIDS is a leading cause of death among Latino men ages 18 to 45 (Espinoza et al., 2007; Hall et al., 2006; Hunt et al., 2002; Lanting et al., 2005; Lavery et al., 1997; Wong et al., 2005).

Despite the need for effective health promotion programs among this population, most interventions targeting Latino men have failed. This is because these interventions: (1) treat culture as a static variable; (2) do not recognize critical within-group differences among the diverse population of Latino men; and (3) focus on individual-level determinants of risk instead of taking a more expansive view that also accounts for sociocultural determinants. In the following sections, we will examine each of these shortcomings in further detail.

Moving beyond Machismo: Cultural and Structural Determinants of Health Disparities

Sexual and reproductive health disparities experienced by Latino men are often conceptualized as the outcome of behavioral characteristics and sociocultural norms, particularly those pertaining to Latino ideologies of masculinity. The literature on masculinity as a sexual risk factor among Latino men concentrates on *machismo* as the predominant sociocultural model of hypermasculinity. Machismo is a social construct that refers to an amalgamation of male traits characterized by extreme aggression and intransigence in male–male relationships, as well as by sexual aggression and contempt in male–female relationships (Ramirez et al., 2004). The female complement to the notion of machismo is *marianismo*, which refers to attempts to emulate the behavior of the Christian religious figure, the Virgin Mary, including abstaining from premarital sex, not expressing sexual desire, and demonstrating submissive behavior. Marianismo has been used to explain sexual risk among Latinas, although the literature on this topic is limited (Amaro et al., 2001; Asencio, 2002).

Previous studies on machismo have highlighted significant limitations with the conceptualization of culture in sexual and reproductive health research. Much of this work treats culture as a static variable, a series of beliefs and practices that are isolated from the broader social structures within which epidemics, such as HIV, occur. The interactive processes of gender relations or of adapting, resisting, or rejecting a new culture are often overlooked in the measurement of constructs such as machismo and marianismo.

Sexual and reproductive health disparities observed among Latino men have also been associated with structural inequalities, including economic exclusion and institutionalized racism. In recent years, there has been growing interest among public health researchers and practitioners in developing and implementing structural interventions to prevent the spread of HIV and other STIs, as well as to increase access to sexual and reproductive health services and promote adherence to treatment. A limitation of this work, however, is that it has focused on aspects of social organization that are outside the traditional purview of public health, with the exception, perhaps, of structural approaches that focus on reducing stigma or enhancing sexual rights (National Institutes of Health [NIH], 2001; Parker & Aggleton, 2003). Proponents of structural approaches to disease prevention have tended to overlook lessons learned about culture, creating a false dichotomy between culture and structure (Parker et al., 2000). Considering culture in relation to structure, however, forces us to move beyond a static model of culture. From this perspective, culture is a set of symbolic resources from which people draw differentially, depending on the other resources available to them. Thus, a more robust analysis of Latino men's sexual health requires that we position the social causes of disparities (both proximal and distal predictors) at the intersection of structure and culture.

Cultural Divisions and Within-group Gradients in Sexual and Reproductive Health Risk

Adopting a more nuanced approach to examining the determinants of health disparities among Latino men—one that incorporates dynamic sociocultural factors, as well as structural factors—also serves to highlight important within-group differences that exist between subgroups of Latino men. Comparisons of absolute differences in health disparities between men of Latino ancestry and men of other ethnicities, in contrast, overlook these critical within-group differences. Latino men are not equally vulnerable to sexual and reproductive health disparities, and those who reside at the boundaries of cultural and structural spaces are among the most vulnerable.

American society is organized in hierarchies of social and economic power driven by structures surrounding class, gender, sexual orientation, and race/ethnicity. For example, women frequently occupy a lower social status than men due to the institutionalized gendered division of power and labor (Connell, 1987). Similarly, racial and ethnic groups are organized along structures of power through which dominant ethnic groups hold more power and disproportionately control access to societal resources. Taking these factors into account, the hierarchy of social power in the United States can be viewed as strata, in which White, upper-class, heterosexual men are at the top and ethnic minority, low-income, non-heterosexual women are at the bottom. If this is indeed the case, it follows that all Latino men do not occupy the same position within this strata, and therefore do not face the same sexual and reproductive health risks. For example, light-skinned, middle-class, heterosexual Latino men will likely confront fewer sexual and reproductive health risks than dark-skinned, homosexual men from economically disadvantaged backgrounds. Thus, we propose employing a more nuanced approach to examining sexual and reproductive health disparities among Latino men, one that accounts for gradients in class, gender identity, and sexual orientation (see Table 4.1).

Research on social class has demonstrated that each class has its own culture, customs, and practices. Cultural variations among Latino men, therefore, are not only the product of differences in nationality, but also are the result of cultural differences stemming from the intersection of class, sexual orientation, and gender

TABLE 4.1 Heuristic Model of Sexual and Reproductive Health Outcomes Across Subgroups of Latino Men

Social class/position in the labor market	Sexual orientation and gender identity			
	Heterosexual, straight	Homosexual, gay	Bisexual, queer, questioning	Male-to-female transgender
Upper class	Optimal			
Middle class				
Working class	Average			
Informal economy				
Illicit economy	Below average			Worst

identity. For example, upper-class Mexican and Puerto Rican gay men may share more cultural similarities with each other than they do with working-class, heterosexual men from their respective countries.

Cultural divisions based on differences in class, sexual orientation, and gender identity are not isolated, bound units. They exist within exchanges that radiate up and down class, sexual orientation, and gender identity structures, and they are engaged in a constant cultural exchange with other groups present in shared social spaces. Such divisions, however, play an important role in determining how subgroups of Latino men construct ideologies surrounding sexuality and masculinity.

Overview of the Case Studies: Identifying Unique Vulnerabilities Facing Subpopulations

In this chapter, we do not present evidence proving that cultural divisions stemming from variations in class, sexual orientation, and gender identity produce a gradient in the distribution of sexual and reproductive health disparities among Latino men. We do, however, identify three subgroups of Latino men that exhibit greater sexual and reproductive health vulnerability than others: (1) prisoners and formerly incarcerated men; (2) urban migrant workers; and (3) behaviorally bisexual men. We then present case studies drawn from these subpopulations that support our thesis that a sexual and reproductive health gradient exists within the larger population of Latino men living in the United States.

The first case study focuses on formerly incarcerated Latino men and stems from a sexual and reproductive health promotion intervention that we piloted among a group of these men in collaboration with the Misión San Juan Bautista and La Asociación Pro Derechos del Confinado Ñeta in the South Bronx, New York (n = 15, 2007–2008). The second case study examines sexual and reproductive health risks among urban migrant workers based on a mixed-methods study of the social context of sexual risk among married Mexican migrant workers in Queens, New York (2005–2007). Findings from ethnographic observations, structured surveys (n = 50), and life history interviews (n = 10) are presented. The final case study focuses on behaviorally bisexual Latino men and is based on data collected from bisexually active youths and adults in New York City (1998–2008). Key findings from all three studies are presented, as well as relevant findings from related studies, including an ethnographic study of sexuality and masculinity among bisexually active Latino men (n = 18, 1998–2001); a community-based survey on HIV risk behavior and HIV optimism among Latino men who have sex with men (n = 395, 2002–2004); and a qualitative study on gender and power dynamics among bisexual teens (n = 30, 2007–2008).

Finally, in the latter part of the chapter, we present a series of research questions that need to be answered to inform future policy aimed at reducing sexual and reproductive health disparities among Latino men. We also provide a list of preliminary policy recommendations, based on the information currently available, for each of the subpopulations examined in the case studies.

Case study 1: Formerly incarcerated Latino men in the South Bronx, New York

Latinos and African Americans comprise the vast majority of prison inmates in the United States (Bureau of Justice Statistics, 2009). Ethnic minority men are disproportionately arrested and sentenced to prison, serve longer sentences, and have higher rates of recidivism than their White counterparts (Bureau of Justice Statistics, 2005a, b, 2006). Based on the most recent data available, nine out of ten non-violent (i.e., burglary, drug possession, drug trafficking, or larceny) offenders discharged from prison are male and two-thirds are racial and ethnic minorities (47.9 percent Black and 24.7 percent Latino) (Freudenberg et al., 2005).

Imprisonment constitutes a major risk to men's sexual and reproductive health. Even though it has been widely documented that sexual activity occurs between inmates, condoms are not distributed in the penitentiary system (Khan et al., 2005; Kushel et al., 2005; MacNeil et al., 2005). In 2008, the U.S. Department of Justice reported that 1.5 percent of male federal and state prison inmates (20,075 men) were HIV positive or had confirmed AIDS (Bureau of Justice Statistics, 2010). These reported rates, however, may represent a significant underestimate of actual infection rates, as less than half of all state prison systems routinely test inmates for HIV (Bureau of Justice Statistics, 2010).

Blood transmission of hepatitis B and C through tattooing during incarceration is another health risk that has not been adequately addressed. Although the hepatitis B vaccine is available and has been included in the treatment policies of more than 1,000 correctional facilities, the vaccine is not routinely administered by prison health systems (Bureau of Justice Statistics, 2004). Similarly, nearly 70 percent of state correctional facilities report that they have a policy in place to screen and treat inmates for hepatitis C; however, the current hepatitis C screening criteria—self-reported injection drug use—has led to a consistent underestimate of the number of infected inmates (Binswanger et al., 2005). As a result, many prisoners continue to go untested and untreated.

Looking beyond HIV and hepatitis B and C, a variety of chronic diseases are also known to affect the sexual and reproductive health of incarcerated men, including cancer and diabetes. Currently, state and federal prison systems do not have an adequate mechanism for tracking cancer and diabetes among prisoner populations (American Diabetes Association, 2006). It is estimated that over 80,000 inmates have diabetes—a prevalence of 4.8 percent—yet diabetes care in correctional facilities is not currently delivered in accordance with the recommendations of the American Diabetes Association.

The majority of health promotion interventions targeting inmates in the United States have focused on HIV prevention, neglecting other areas of men's sexual and reproductive health (Braithwaite et al., 2005; Bryan et al., 2006; Ehrmann, 2002; El-Bassel et al., 1995; Grinstead et al., 2001; Ross et al., 2006). Some important lessons, however, can be gleaned from the limited experience of these interventions and applied to broader health promotion initiatives targeting prisoners and formerly incarcerated Latino men.

There is limited understanding of the impact of prison-based interventions post-release. Presumably, prison-based interventions are intended to reduce HIV risk both during incarceration and post-release; however, a recent review of the literature identified only a handful of programs that evaluated the impact of the intervention on HIV risk behaviors post-release. Of these, most were ineffective in sustaining behavior change (Ehrmann, 2002; El-Bassel et al., 1995; Ross et al., 2006). The failure of prison-based HIV prevention interventions to influence risk behaviors post-release is likely due to constraints associated with prison settings (e.g., condom distribution is prohibited, sex is often not consensual). These conditions make it difficult, if not impossible, for inmates to practice preventative behaviors and skills promoted by the intervention during incarceration, making it unlikely that they will retain the information for use after their release (Braithwaite et al., 2005; Grinstead et al., 2001; Ross et al., 2006).

Interventions with prison populations must move beyond disease-specific programming. The literature on the health status of prison populations clearly indicates that increased HIV risk is not the only public health problem affecting this population (Braithwaite et al., 2005; Bryan et al., 2006; Ehrmann, 2002; El-Bassel et al., 1995; Grinstead et al., 2001; Ross et al., 2006). Yet, very few interventions take a holistic approach to prisoner health. Singer and colleagues used the term *syndemic* to refer to populations that are affected by the intersection of multiple epidemics (Baer et al., 1998; Freudenberg et al., 2006; Singer, 1998; Singer & Clair, 2003).

In the United States, no population embodies the notion of a syndemic better than the male prison population, which is simultaneously affected by the epidemics of HIV, STIs, drug addiction, and poverty, as well as chronic diseases such as diabetes and cancer (Freudenberg et al., 2006; Romero-Daza et al., 2003). *Health promotion interventions targeting prison populations must be culturally sensitive.* In a study of 196 inmates in Connecticut (90 percent male, 28 percent Latino), an HIV prevention program was found to be effective among all inmates *except* Latinos, for whom it resulted in decreases in both condom-use self-efficacy and positive attitudes toward not sharing needles and tattooing equipment (Bryan et al., 2006). In a subsequent process evaluation, evaluators determined that materials used in the intervention did not have cultural relevance and were not appropriate for Latinos (Bryan et al., 2006).

In an effort to address some of the issues described above, the pro-prisoners' rights organization, La Asociación Ñeta; an Episcopalian church, Misión San Juan Bautista in the South Bronx; and the Center for Gender, Sexuality and Health at the Mailman School of Public Health at Columbia University developed a theoretically based intervention to promote healthy behaviors among formerly incarcerated Latino men. *Sin Rodeos* (pronounced seen roe-day-oce; literal translation "without fences") was developed between December 2006 and March 2007 and implemented among a group of 12 formerly incarcerated Latino men in April 2007. Findings from this pilot intervention indicated that prevention programs focusing on masculinity and critical reflection can be effective in reducing sexual health risks among formerly incarcerated Latino men (see Table 4.2).

This pilot intervention highlighted significant gaps regarding sexual and reproductive health for formerly incarcerated Latino men and the complexities of behavior modification. Developing an intervention specifically for formerly incarcerated Latino men, as opposed to one for men from diverse ethnic backgrounds, could prove to be an effective strategy for addressing sociocultural determinants of sexual and reproductive health risks that are unique to this population.

If we revisit our initial conceptual model, formerly incarcerated heterosexual Latino men, similar to the ones in this case study, often fall within the boundaries of the working class and informal economy, most having participated in the illegal economy. From the needs assessment we conducted prior to implementing our pilot intervention, it was clear that these men had limited knowledge of HIV and STI prevention strategies or contraceptive methods. Reflecting on and initiating actions pertaining to issues of structural violence (i.e., social-economic exclusion, institutionalized racism), masculinity, fatherhood, sexual-emotional relations, sexual communication, and social mobilization were fundamental to the men who participated in this intervention. The fact that the intervention itself was created in equal collaboration with leaders of the pro-prisoners' rights organization, La Asociación Ñeta, underscores the urgency of developing effective sexual and reproductive health programming for this underserved population.

TABLE 4.2 Selected Findings from Process Evaluation of a Pilot Intervention for Formerly Incarcerated Latino Men (South Bronx, 2007)

- *Participants stated that they learned a lot.* Topics about which they felt they learned the most included: testicular exams; female anatomy; infectivity during HIV window period; death due to AIDS, meaning that death is actually the result of an opportunistic infection; non-sexual intimacy between males; non-sexual intimacy with females; and communication, family, and fatherhood. A participant mentioned becoming much more open-minded; specifically, it was a new experience to become more comfortable talking with other men about sex rather than just making comments about passing women ("she's got a big ass," for example). Another topic mentioned repeatedly had to do with becoming less homophobic.

- *Participants expressed fear about their daughters' sexuality.* All but one of the participants had daughters, and they spoke about their fears, which had been expressed in getting angry when a daughter tells her father she has begun to menstruate; getting angry when asked to change a baby girl's diaper because they don't want to confront her genitals; not knowing how to help their daughters "not end up always choosing the wrong guy, not just once, but all the time"; and not knowing how or whether to educate their daughters about sex.

- *Participants revealed anger about absent father.* Several participants noted that growing up with a father who was either physically or emotionally absent had left them with a lot of anger and made it difficult for them to communicate with their own children. The majority also mentioned the importance of what they will take from the workshops and use when raising their own children. All but one of the participants had children. "We can teach our sons they don't have to be the tough guy," commented one participant. The men also spoke about how the program helped them realize that they can teach their sons to express their emotions and that they should be more affectionate with their sons. This topic was obviously still a difficult one for many participants; when they talked about it, the conversation often devolved into jokes about letting their sons be sentimental, sensitive, or feminine.

Nonetheless, with the exception of drug rehabilitation and re-entry programs for formerly incarcerated Latino men, there are virtually no interventions directed at addressing the basic health needs of this group, which is a major barrier to reducing the burden of health disparities experienced by this population.

Case study 2: Mexican migrant workers in Queens, New York

Mexican migrant men in the United States are more likely to be infected with HIV than their counterparts who remain in Mexico (Bronfman et al., 1998). When Mexican workers migrate to the United States, they learn new sexual practices and modify their behavioral norms to reflect those of their new social environment, which includes practices and norms that are associated with increased HIV risk (Bronfman et al., 1998; Bronfman & Minello, 1995; Ferreira-Pinto et al., 1996; Gonzalez-Lopez, 2006; Hirsch, 2003; Hirsch et al., 2002; Simon & Gagnon, 1999).

Studies suggest that Mexican migrant workers have a limited perception of HIV risk, associate a high degree of stigma with talking about sex or sexually transmitted diseases, demonstrate a lack of knowledge regarding condom use, and use condoms inconsistently with sexual partners in the United States and Mexico (Bronfman et al., 1998; Ferreira-Pinto et al., 1996; Gonzalez-Lopez, 2006; Hirsch, 2003; Hirsch et al., 2002; Perez & Fennelley, 1996). Mexican migrant workers in the United States also live in social environments that are characterized by extreme inequality, which has been shown to be associated with increased HIV risk. Social inequalities encountered by this population include: class and racial/ethnic discrimination; lack of legal rights; inability to work legally due to lack of documentation; and limited access to health care services, including HIV and STI testing and treatment (Farmer, 1999; Hirsch et al., 2002; Magaña et al., 1996; Parker et al., 2000; Smith, 2006).

In an effort to understand how migration experiences influence the sexual and reproductive health vulnerabilities of migrant workers, we conducted a mixed-methods study of Mexican migrant workers in Queens, New York (2005–2007). We found that loneliness (measured by an adapted version of the UCLA loneliness scale) was the strongest predictor of unprotected sex. Loneliness was also found to be a central component of the migration experience. Feelings of loneliness often started when men crossed the border into the United States; almost half of the men in the study made this journey alone. Men in the study also had limited access to material resources, and this, combined with the isolating social conditions associated with migrant work, created a context of institutionalized loneliness that resulted in increased HIV risk.

Men in the study reported that having sex helped them feel better and forget about their problems for a period of time, beliefs that are associated with an increased likelihood of engaging in unprotected sex. This finding supports the thesis that sex serves as an escape mechanism that migrant workers use to deal with stress in their lives, which is consistent with findings from the literature on men's sexualities and escapist behavior (Torres & Gore-Felton, 2007).

In addition to migrating to a new country only to occupy a lower position in the local workforce hierarchy (e.g., many said that they do jobs that "no one wants to do"), the men in this study also reported experiencing a lack of power in other aspects of their lives. Mexicans are a "minority" within the larger Latino ethnic population in New York, unlike many states in the South and West where they are the dominant ethnic minority. Mexican men in New York are exposed to prejudice and discrimination not only from non-Latinos, but also from more established migrant groups, creating an additional layer of isolation from community-level systems of support (Schultz & Moore, 1986). Feeling sexually powerful is one way of feeling in control, in spite of the isolation and stressors of the migrant experience (Bourgois, 2003). We found that stronger feelings of loneliness were reported among those who felt a sense of superiority and power during sex. In other words, in the context of loneliness, sex served as a mechanism that enabled the married Mexican migrant workers in this study to regain a sense of power and control.

In our study, we identified two key social spaces that married Mexican migrant men frequented to counteract loneliness: table dance clubs and Catholic churches. Table dance clubs served as a source of entertainment, camaraderie, and national identification, as well as a way of getting close to women and experiencing heteroerotic interactions. From a public health perspective, the problem was that men frequenting these establishments tended to consume large volumes of alcohol while there and—as demonstrated in this study and many others in the literature—alcohol use is associated with increased sexual risk (MacNeil et al., 2005).

Active participation in the Catholic Church was also found to facilitate sexual risk among the men in our study. Participation in religious services and church-sponsored social activities provided a buffer that helped men cope with loneliness. The Catholic Church's prohibition on condom use, however, increased the likelihood that men would not use condoms and mediated any positive effect that church participation had on loneliness and sexual risk.

Mexican migrant workers like the men in this case study are particularly vulnerable to HIV and STIs. Currently, there are no surveillance mechanisms in place to track HIV and STI rates among migrant workers in the United States (CDC, 2004; Schedlin & Shulman, 2004). Migrant workers are typically men from low-income backgrounds with limited education, factors that have been documented to increase the risk of HIV infection (Mishra et al.,1996; Singer, 1998).

The two case studies presented above—formerly incarcerated Latino men and Mexican migrant workers—provide an overview of the sexual and reproductive health vulnerabilities of subpopulations of heterosexual Latino men who reside at the bottom of the social class and labor market structure. In both cases, the members of these subpopulations vacillate between two worlds: prison and the free community, or Mexico and the United States (and in some instances, perhaps, all four of these worlds). In the third case study, we move from the heterosexual column of our conceptual framework to a group of Latino men who are characterized by the fluidity of their sexual desires and repertories—behaviorally bisexual men.

Case study 3: Behaviorally bisexual Latino men in New York City

The disproportionate impact of the HIV epidemic on Latino men is evident in the high infection rates documented among youth, men who have sex with men (MSM), injection drug users (IDUs), and heterosexual men (Amaro et al., 2001; CDC, 2000, 2002, 2003, 2007; Carter-Pokras & Zambrana, 2001; Monina-Klevens et al., 1999). Behaviorally bisexual Latino men often reside at the intersections of these groups; however, they are seldom defined as the specific target of HIV prevention research or interventions.

For over a decade, researchers have suggested that Latina women are more likely than White women to be infected with HIV by bisexually active male partners, raising questions about the role of bisexual behavior in the transmission of HIV (Chu et al., 1992; Diaz et al., 1993; Maguen, 1998). Scientific evidence substantiating the role of bisexually active men as an epidemiological "bridge" to HIV, however, remains inconclusive (Rodríguez-Rust, 2000). A limited number of studies have focused specifically on HIV risk among behaviorally bisexual Latino men; most of the previous research in this area has collapsed bisexual men and MSM into a single category.

To examine differences within this combined MSM population, we conducted a secondary data analysis of a study of 395 gay and bisexual men in New York City. We found that Latino MSM who reported having sex with women—rather than those who subscribed to any particular identity or configuration of identity and behavior—were most likely to engage in high-risk sexual behaviors with male partners. This relationship may be explained by the commonality between high-risk sex with male and female partners, which has to do with the insertive nature of the interaction. Sex with female partners is, for the most part, insertive, and our findings indicate that it is a predictor of insertive unprotected anal intercourse with men.

The literature on bisexuality in Latin America supports the finding that the gender of the object of sexual desire is less significant than the role performed (i.e., insertive or receptive) in sexual interactions with both male and female partners (Carrier, 1995; de Moya & Garcia, 1996; Exner et al., 1999; Lancaster, 1992; Liguori et al., 1996; Parker, 1985, 1991; Schifter, 2000). Thus, it is possible that in this study the men who had sex with women mostly engaged in insertive roles during sex with men, and that these men were "transferring" habits formed during sex with women—namely, infrequent condom use—to their sexual encounters with men (Exner et al., 1999; Hoffman et al., 2000).

The transference of sexual habits between male and female partners is a phenomenon that we observed in earlier ethnographic work with bisexually active Latino men, in which two main patterns of sexual organization were noted: "compartmentalized" sexual repertoires and "fluid" sexual repertoires (Muñoz-Laboy & Dodge, 2005). The first pattern included men who had distinct sexual repertoires for male and female partners, with limited exchange between them. Men following this pattern organized their sexual repertoires with male and female partners into separate spheres. For these men, maintaining two distinct dimensions was extremely important, although the reasons behind this were not articulated in the interviews. The second pattern included men who transferred what they learned during sexual encounters with one partner to other partners, regardless of any particular partner's gender. Men who fit into this category viewed both men and women as erotic bodies with differences and similarities, but with the constant possibility of transferring what is learned during sex with one partner to future partners, regardless of gender. Among this group of men, sexual repertoires and courtship codes were used interchangeably with potential partners of both genders to maximize the likelihood of engaging in a sexual encounter or the pleasure derived from that encounter. Some of the men following this pattern also expressed fluidity in the sexual imagery they employed, fantasizing about having sex with a partner of one gender while having sex with someone of another gender, suggesting that imagery and fantasy may be critical aspects of the sexual practices of some bisexual men.

In the public health research on sexuality, it is often assumed that the sexual behaviors of groups are standard and have little variation. A central finding from our earlier ethnographic study was that, far from having a monolithic set of sexual scripts, the sexual repertoires of bisexual Latino men are characterized by a plurality of configurations across the life course. At least four lifetime patterns of sexual desire were found among the bisexual Latino men interviewed: (1) "homoerotic desire"—sexual, erotic, and emotional interactions mostly with other men, and meaningless occasional sex with women; (2) "technical desire"—sex with men in exchange for money with strong sexual, erotic, and emotional interactions with female partners; (3) "transsexual desire"—men with close erotic, emotional, and sexual ties to both male-to-female transgender and biological women; and (4) "bi-erotic desire"—men who throughout their lives have had contiguous sexual and emotional relationships with both men and women (Muñoz-Laboy & Dodge, 2005).

Regardless of the pattern of sexual desire, sexual encounters with women were critical to bisexual Latino men's construction of masculinity (Muñoz-Laboy & Dodge, 2005). *Hacerse hombre* (becoming a man), the result of having penetrative sex with a woman was consistently viewed as an important developmental milestone, even though many of the research participants had already had sexual experiences (including intercourse) with male partners. This associative statement was found across the narratives. In addition, the desire to "have a family" and "protect the family's honor" (often by keeping bisexual behavior separate from family life) were frequently expressed in the narratives of bisexual men.

Bisexual Latino men face greater sexual and reproductive health risks as a result of their position with respect to multiple social boundaries. These men do not conform to: (1) sexual identity politics (i.e., they are neither gay nor straight); (2) the social institution of monogamy; (3) traditional heteronormative marriages; and (4) static sexual and gender scripts. Bisexual men are at risk of being infected with HIV and STIs from both male and female partners and through multiple transmission routes. As a result, these men face more complex sexual and reproductive health risks than their exclusively heterosexual or homosexual counterparts. In addition, as was also true in the previous two case studies, institutionalized and internalized stigmas may preclude bisexual Latino men from accessing preventative care, screening, and treatment services pertaining to sexual and reproductive health. Additional research is needed to examine the sexual and reproductive health status of this critical bridge population, as well as to identify personal and external determinants of risk and effective solutions to reduce these vulnerabilities.

Discussion: Finding Solutions in the Borders

One of the factors contributing to the health disparities experienced by men of Color in the United States is the failure of most health promotion programs. Most prevention programs fail because they are driven by tradition, instincts, or politics rather than by evidence and theory (Bartholomew et al., 1998). This situation is exacerbated by an overemphasis on interventions that focus exclusively on the individual (i.e., behavioral) level rather than contextualized programs that also address sociocultural and structural factors contributing to sexual and reproductive health vulnerabilities.

In an effort to increase effective programming for Latino men, we must first conceptualize determinants of sexual and reproductive health that recognize the fluid social context of this diverse population. Among structural determinants, there are two areas that have been insufficiently studied with respect to Latino men's sexual and reproductive health: sexual markets and sexual acculturation.

To understand the intersection between sexual risk practices and contextual-structural factors, we propose using the concept of a *sex market* as both an individual and external level determinant of risk. Edward Laumann and colleagues demonstrated that to effectively understand individuals' sexual behaviors, the behaviors must be studied in relation to a broader system of sexual partnering, which they refer to as a "sex market" (Laumann et al., 2004). Applying this concept to Latino men, systems of sexual partnering among this population consist of four main factors: social networks, masculine ideologies, physical place, and institutional spheres.

Social networks influence the flow of information and control patterns of partnership formation within sexual markets. Third parties within social networks (e.g., parents, friends, coworkers) often act as stakeholders influencing the kind of person an individual chooses as a sex partner and interfering with relationships of which they disapprove (Laumann et al., 2004). Social networks also provide information about possible venues to meet sex partners (Laumann et al., 2004). Thus, information and control mechanisms stemming from social networks constrain the potential pool of sexual partners for Latino men.

Masculine ideologies are representations of larger gendered cultural scripts (Simon & Gagnon, 1984; Weeks, 1986). Masculine ideologies operate at three levels: (1) cultural—masculine ideologies that dominate the social contexts where Latino men live and work; (2) inter-personal—men's perceptions and belief systems regarding their sexual and social interactions with other men and women; and (3) intrapsychic—men's private world of wishes and desires, which are experienced as originating in the deepest sense of the self.

Physical space delineates the geographic boundaries of the market and organizes specific "sexual market places," that is, places in the city where one can go to meet potential sexual partners (e.g., bars, dance clubs, sporting events)

(Laumann et al., 2004). The structuring of neighborhoods fosters different sexual partnering processes (e.g., housing segregation, number of individuals per household, income, access to public spaces). For example, studies have documented that, among unmarried Latino men living in strict homes, the lack of private space leads them to have sex outside their house (e.g., in cars or parks) (Diaz, 2000).

The *institutional spheres* through which Latino men navigate further shape possibilities for sexual partnering. For example, for Latino men in the Bronx, salient institutional spheres include religious organizations, the educational system, and the local and national security system. Although these institutions' primary concern is not sexuality, each institution implements policies to regulate sexual behavior. Thus, these institutions actively participate in the creation of social norms and in determining what is "good" and "bad" behavior. At the local level, such institutions vary in their implementation of policies, promulgation of morality, and tolerance for behavioral differences.

The goal of some sex markets is to establish long-term relationships, while others focus on fostering short-term relationships or facilitating transactional sex. Regardless of the particular goal, each sex market is regulated by inter-personal and structural forces that determine the relationship between supply and demand. For example, in certain spaces, Latino men may be in high demand because of their marriage potential or because of stereotypes regarding their perceived sexual attributes. Latino men participate in diverse sex markets, and as a result do not always occupy the same market position. Formerly incarcerated Latino men often participate in markets that are very different from those of recent immigrants living in the same general geographic area. Distinctions between markets are often the result of class and ethnic differences. From a public health perspective, however, different markets may also provide differential access to HIV and STI prevention services, testing, and treatment (e.g., access to information, contextual co-risk factors in places of sexual interactions, inter-personal scripts embedded in risk ideologies).

The sex market perspective described by Laumann et al. (2004) incorporates individual, cultural, and structural factors in the analysis of sexual partnering and sexual risk. As a result, the elements that comprise sex markets can themselves be conceptualized as intervention variables. Once these variables are empirically examined through need assessment studies of the various sex markets in which Latino men participate, they can be used to design behavioral and environmental change objectives capable of reducing multilevel risks within these markets.

Culture is also a critical aspect in defining sex markets and determining sexual and reproductive health risks. Drawing on the acculturation framework, the second conceptual tool that we see emerging from the social boundaries of Latino men's sexualities is "sexual acculturation." Latino men are active participants in the construction of their own masculinity. They navigate through multiple sex markets consisting of diverse sexual cultures. In the literature, it has been documented that Latin American societies have different sets of values and cultures with regard to sexual and gendered behavior. After migrating to the United States, these customs are maintained, adapted, or rejected. Similarly, new sexual practices, gendered behavior, and roles are learned, integrated, or resisted from the "old" immigrant groups or the dominant ethnic group in the new cultural environment. Within this theoretical standing, sexually acculturated Latinos are able to navigate ethnic-specific environments (e.g., a Dominican neighborhood) to socialize and meet sexual partners, as well as other ethnic minority and non-minority social environments (e.g., African American and White social clubs).

In the case of non-heterosexual behavior, processes of sexual acculturation are critical. For example, because bisexuality is not an accepted form of sexual expression, bisexual Latino men have to negotiate, adapt to, or reject the norms regarding sexuality and masculinity in many of the social spaces they inhabit. Sexually acculturated bisexuals are able to navigate both heterosexual and homosexual environments. Distinct from the concept of "passing" (in the stigma literature), sexual acculturation stresses cultural competence without judging the stigma attached to those practices. However, being sexually acculturated does not imply safer sexual practice. That is an empirical question that requires examination.

TABLE 4.3 Research Agenda to Reduce Sexual and Reproductive Health Disparities Among Vulnerable Subpopulations of Latino Men

---

Prisoners and formerly incarcerated Latino men

Collect data on HIV, hepatitis B, hepatitis C, and STI rates among all state and federal prison inmates annually.

Identify sociocultural and environmental determinants of sexual and reproductive health risks for prisoners and formerly incarcerated men; develop and pilot-test culturally competent interventions to address those determinants.

Migrant workers

Develop systems for tracking HIV and STI rates among migrant worker populations that are acceptable to migrant workers.

Identify sociocultural and environmental determinants of sexual and reproductive health risks for urban migrant workers; develop and pilot-test interventions to address those determinants.

Behaviorally bisexual Latino men

Examine reproductive needs and desires among bisexual men, as well as their impact on sexual and reproductive health risk behaviors.

Identify sociocultural and environmental determinants of sexual and reproductive health risks for bisexual men; develop and pilot-test interventions to address those determinants.

TABLE 4.4 Initial Policy Recommendations to Reduce Sexual and Reproductive Health Disparities Among Vulnerable Subpopulations of Latino Men

---

Prisoners and formerly incarcerated Latino men

Implement law enforcement policies and reform sentencing guidelines to reduce the number of non-violent offenders incarcerated in state and federal prison systems.

Eliminate mandatory minimum sentences for drug possession offenses and expand sentencing options, such as treatment and re-entry programs, that offer an alternative to long-term incarceration.

Implement routine screening and treatment programs for HIV, hepatitis B, hepatitis C, and STIs for all state and federal prison inmates.

Create labor re-entry programs—in addition to existing community re-entry programs—that enable formerly incarcerated Latino men to secure employment in the formal economy post-release.

Migrant workers

Create a national guest worker program that would allow seasonal migrant workers to travel between the United States and Mexico legally and in groups, as opposed to illegally and alone.

Fund and support social spaces and events where migrant workers can congregate and socialize, such as sports leagues and social clubs, that will provide alternatives to the alcohol-driven table dance clubs and the conservative doctrine associated with church-based services and social events.

Behaviorally bisexual Latino men

Prioritize research proposals focusing specifically on behaviorally bisexual Latino men; examine the methodology of research proposals involving Latino men to ensure that bisexual men are not collapsed into a single category with men who have sex with men.

Adopt sexual and reproductive health screening protocols that involve routine HIV and STI testing for all populations; encourage health care providers to take detailed sexual histories for all patients and not make assumptions about risk (e.g., not discussing HIV and STI screening with married patients, etc.).

Research Questions and Initial Policy Solutions

Most health promotion interventions targeting Latino men have failed for the reasons we have described above—they treat culture as a static variable, they do not recognize critical within-group differences among the diverse population of Latino men, they focus on individual-level determinants of risk instead of taking a more expansive view offered by the sex-market perspective. Reducing sexual and reproductive health disparities among Latino men will require addressing these problems. Before this can be done, however, additional data must be collected and critical research questions must be answered (see Table 4.3).

The gaps in the data and research detailed in Table 4.3 must be addressed to reduce sexual and reproductive health disparities in the subpopulations of Latino men represented by the case studies presented in this chapter. However, there are other subgroups of Latino men—such as men who have sex with transgender women (MSTW)—that also warrant further study. To truly reduce sexual and reproductive health disparities among Latino men, public health researchers and practitioners should: (1) continue to identify vulnerable subpopulations of Latino men; (2) conduct formative research on the sociocultural and environmental determinants of sexual and reproductive health risks for each subpopulation; and (3) design, pilot-test, and implement evidence-based interventions to address these determinants.

Although a great deal of additional research must be conducted before comprehensive policy solutions can be identified and implemented, there are some initial policy solutions that can be implemented immediately based on what is already known about the three subpopulations discussed in this chapter (see Table 4.4). Taken together, the research agenda and policy recommendations outlined in this chapter provide a roadmap for reducing sexual and reproductive health disparities among Latino men. It is now up to public health researchers, practitioners, and funders to come together to put this plan into action.

References

Amaro, H., Vega, R., & Valencia, D. (2001). Gender, context, and HIV prevention among Latinos. In M. Aguirre-Molina, C. Molina, & R. Zambrana (Eds.), *Health issues in the Latino community* (301–324). San Francisco: Jossey-Bass.

American Diabetes Association (2006). Diabetes management in correctional institutions. *Diabetes Care*, 29, S59–S66.

Asencio, M. (2002). *Sex and sexuality among New York's Puerto Rican youth*. Boulder, CO: Lynn Rienner.

Baer, H., Singer, M., & Susser, I. (1998). *Medical anthropology and the world system*. Westport, CT: Bergin and Garvey.

Bartholomew, L., Parcel, G., & Kok, G. (1998). Intervention mapping: A process for developing theory- and evidence-based health education programs. *Health Education & Behavior*, 25, 545–563.

Binswanger, I. A., White, M. C., Pérez-Stable, E. J., Goldenson, J., & Tulsky, J. P. (2005). Cancer screening among jail inmates: Frequency, knowledge and willingness. *American Journal of Public Health*, 95, 1781–1787.

Bourgois, P. (2003). *In search of respect: Selling crack in El Barrio (structural analysis in the social sciences)*. New York: Cambridge University Press.

Braithwaite, R., Stephens, T. T., Treadwell, H., Braithwaite, K., & Conerly, R. (2005). Short-term impact of an HIV risk reduction intervention for soon-to-be-released inmates in Georgia. *Journal of Health Care for the Poor and Underserved*, 16, 130–139.

Bronfman, M., & Minello, N. (1995). Habitos sexuales de los migrantes temporales Mexicanos a los Estados Unidos: Practicas de riego para la infeccion por VIH [Sexual habits of temporary Mexican migrants to the United States: HIV risk practices]. In M. Bronfman & A. Amuchastegui (Eds.), *SIDA en Mexico* [AIDS in Mexico] (19–89). Mexico City: Camara Nacional de la Industria Editorial.

Bronfman, M., Sejenovich, G., & Uribe, P. (1998). *Migracion y SIDA en Mexico y America* [Central Migration and AIDS in Mexico and Central America]. Mexico City: Conasida.

Bryan, A., Robbins, R. N., Ruiz, M. S., & O'Neill, D. (2006). Effectiveness of an HIV prevention intervention in prison among African Americans, Hispanics, and Caucasians. *Health Education & Behavior*, 33, 154–177.

Bureau of Justice Statistics (2004). *Special report: Hepatitis testing and treatment in state prisons.* Retrieved from www.ojp.usdoj.gov/bjs/

Bureau of Justice Statistics (2005a). *HIV in prisons, 2003.* Retrieved from www.ojp.usdoj. gov/bjs/

Bureau of Justice Statistics (2005b). *Prisoners and jail inmates at midyear 2004.* Retrieved from www.ojp.usdoj.gov/bjs/

Bureau of Justice Statistics (2006). *Mental health problems of prison and jail inmates.* Retrieved from www.ojp.usdoj.gov/bjs/

Bureau of Justice Statistics (2009). *Prisoners in 2008.* Retrieved from http://bjs.ojp.usdoj. gov/content/pub/pdf/p08.pdf

Bureau of Justice Statistics (2010). *HIV in Prisons, 2007–08.* Retrieved from http://bjs.ojp.usdoj.gov/content/pub/pdf/hivp08.pdf

Carrier, J. (1995). *De los otros: Intimacy and homosexuality among Mexican men.* New York: Columbia University Press.

Carter-Pokras, O., & Zambrana, R. (2001). Latino health status. In M. Aguirre-Molina, C. Molina, & R. Zambrana (Eds.), *Health issues in the Latino community* (23–54). San Francisco: Jossey-Bass.

Centers for Disease Control and Prevention (2000a). *Health, United States, 1999.* Hyattsville, MD: U.S. Department of Health and Human Services.

Centers for Disease Control and Prevention (2000b). HIV/AIDS among men who have sex with men and inject drugs, 1985–1998. *Morbidity and Mortality Weekly Report*, 49, 465–470.

Centers for Disease Control and Prevention (2000c). HIV/AIDS among racial/ethnic minority men who have sex with men, 1989–1998. *Morbidity and Mortality Weekly Report*, 49, 5–11.

Centers for Disease Control and Prevention (2002). Cases of HIV infection and AIDS in the United States, 2002, *HIV/AIDS Surveillance Report*, 14.

Centers for Disease Control and Prevention (2003). *Tracking the hidden epidemics 2000: Trends in STDs in the United States.* Retrieved from www.cdc.gov/STD/stats03/2003 SurveillanceSummary.pdf

Centers for Disease Control (2004). *HIV AIDS Surveillance Reports* (reports from 1982 to the present). Retrieved from www.cdc.gov/hiv/stats/hasrlink.HTM

Centers for Disease Control and Prevention (2007). Cases of HIV infection and AIDS in the United States and dependent areas, 2005. *HIV/AIDS Surveillance Report*, 17.

Chu, S., Peterman, T., Doll, L., Buehler, W., & Curran, J. (1992). AIDS in bisexual men in the United States: Epidemiology and transmission to women. *American Journal of Public Health*, 82, 220–224.

Connell, R. W. (1987). *Gender and power.* Palo Alto: Stanford University Press.

Diaz, R. (2000). Cultural regulation, self-regulation, and sexuality: A psycho-cultural model of HIV risk in Latino gay men. In R. Parker, R. Barbosa, & P. Aggleton. (Eds.), *Framing the sexual subject: The politics of gender, sexuality, and power.* Berkeley: University of California Press.

Diaz, T., Chu, S., Frederick, M., Herman, P., Levy, A., & Mokotoff, E. (1993). Sociodemographics and HIV risk behaviors of bisexual men with AIDS: Results from a multistate interview project. *AIDS,* 7, 1227–1232.

Ehrmann, T. (2002). Community-based organizations and HIV prevention for incarcerated populations: Three HIV prevention program models. *AIDS Education & Prevention,* 14, 75–84.

El-Bassel, N., Ivanoff, A., Schilling, R., Gilbert, L., Borne, D., & Chen, D. R. (1995). Preventing HIV/AIDS in drug-abusing incarcerated women through skills building and social support enhancement: Preliminary outcomes. *Social Work Research,* 19, 131–141.

Espinoza, L., Hall, H. I., Hardnett, F., Selik, R. M., Ling, Q., & Lee, L. M. (2007). Characteristics of persons with heterosexually acquired HIV infection, United States, 1999–2004. *American Journal of Public Health,* 97, 144–149.

Exner, T., Gardos, S., Seal, D., & Ehrhardt, A. A. (1999). HIV sexual risk reduction interventions with heterosexual men: The forgotten group. *AIDS and Behavior,* 3, 347–358.

Farmer, P. (1999). *Infections and inequalities: The modern plagues.* Berkeley: Unversity of California Press.

Ferreira-Pinto, J., Ramos, R., & Schedlin, M. (1996). Mexican men, female sex workers and HIV/AIDS in the U.S.-Mexico border. In S. Mishra, R. Conner, & R. Magaña (Eds.), *AIDS crossing borders: The spread of HIV among migrant Latinos* (113–136). Boulder, CO: Westview Press.

Freudenberg, N., Daniels, J., Crum, M., Perkins, T., & Richie, B. (2005). Coming home from jail: The social and health consequences of community reentry for women, male adolescents, and their families and communities. *American Journal of Public Health,* 95, 1725–1736.

Freudenberg, N., Fahs, M., Galea, S., & Greenberg, A. (2006). The impact of New York City's 1975 fiscal crisis on the tuberculosis, HIV, and homicide syndemic. *American Journal of Public Health,* 96, 424–434.

Gonzalez-Lopez, G. (2006). Heterosexual fronteras: Immigrant Mexicanos, sexual vulnerabilities, and survival. *Sexuality Research & Social Policy: A Journal of the NSRC,* 3, 67–81.

Gornick, M. E. (2000). *Vulnerable populations and Medicare services: Why do disparities exist?* New York: The Century Foundation Press.

Grinstead, O., Zack, B., & Faigeles, B. (2001). Reducing postrelease risk behavior among HIV seropositive prison inmates: The health promotion program. *AIDS Education and Prevention,* 13, 109–119.

Hall, H. I., McDavid, K., Ling, Q., & Sloggett, A. (2006). Determinants of progression to AIDS or death after HIV diagnosis, United States, 1996 to 2001. *Annals of Epidemiology,* 16, 824–833.

Hirsch, J. (2003). *A courtship after marriage.* Berkeley: University of California Press.

Hirsch, J., Higgins, J., Bentley, M., & Nathanson, C. (2002). The social constructions of sexuality: Marital infidelity and sexually transmitted disease-HIV risk in a Mexican migrant community. *American Journal of Public Health,* 92, 1227–1237.

Hoffman, S., Koslofsky, S., Exner, T., Yingling, S., & Ehrhardt, A. A. (2000). At risk or not? Susceptibility of women using family planning services in an AIDS epicenter. *AIDS and Behavior*, 4, 389–398.

Hunt, K. J., Williams, K., Resendez, R. G., Hazuda, H. P., Haffner, S. M., & Stern, M. P. (2002). All-cause and cardiovascular mortality among diabetic participants in the San Antonio Heart Study: Evidence against the "Hispanic Paradox." *Diabetes Care*, 25, 1557–1563.

Khan, A., Simard, E., Bower, W., Wurtzel, H., Khristova, M., Wagner, K., . . . Bell, B. P. (2005). Ongoing transmission of Hepatitis B virus infection among inmates at a state correctional facility. *American Journal of Public Health*, 95, 1793–1799.

Kushel, M., Hahn, J., Evans, J., Bangsberg, D., & Moss, A. (2005). Revolving doors: Imprisonment among the homeless and marginally housed population. *American Journal of Public Health*, 95, 1747–1752.

Lancaster, R. (1992). *Life is hard: Machismo, danger, and the intimacy of power in Nicaragua.* Berkeley: University of California Press.

Lanting, L. C., Joung, I. M., Mackenbach, J. P., Lamberts, S. W., & Bootsma, A. H. (2005). Ethnic differences in mortality, end-stage complications, and quality of care among diabetic patients: A review. *Diabetes Care*, 28, 2280–2288.

Laumann, E. O., Ellingson, S., Mahay, J., Paik, A., & Youm, Y. (2004). *The sexual organization of the city.* Chicago: University of Chicago Press.

Lavery, L. A., van Houtum, W. H., Armstrong, D. G., Harkless, L. B., Ashry, H. R., & Walker, S. C. (1997). Mortality following lower extremity amputation in minorities with diabetes mellitus. *Diabetes Research & Clinical Practice*, 37, 41–47.

Liguori, L., Gonzalez, M., & Aggleton, P. (1996). Bisexuality and HIV/AIDS in Mexico. In P. Aggleton (Ed.), *Bisexualities and AIDS: International perspectives* (76–98). Bristol, PA: Taylor and Francis.

MacNeil, J., Lobato, M., & Moore, M. (2005). An unanswered health disparity: Tuberculosis among correctional inmates, 1993 through 2003. *American Journal of Public Health*, 95, 1800–1805.

Magaña, R., Rocha, O., & Amsel, J. (1996). Sexual history and behavior of Mexican migrant workers in Orange County, California. In S. Mishra, R. Conner, & R. Magaña (Eds.), *AIDS crossing borders: The spread of HIV among migrant Latinos* (77–94). Boulder, CO: Westview Press.

Maguen, S. (1998). Bisexuality. In R. Smith (Ed.), *Encyclopedia of AIDS: A social, political, cultural, and scientific record of the HIV epidemic.* Chicago: Fitzroy Dearborn.

Mishra, S., Conner, R., & Magaña, R. (1996). Migrant workers in the United States: A profile from the fields. In S. Mishra, R. Conner, & R. Magaña (Eds.), *AIDS crossing borders: The spread of HIV among migrant Latinos* (3–25). Boulder, CO: Westview Press.

Monina-Klevens, R., Diaz, T., Lehan, P., Mays, M., & Frey, R. (1999). Trends in AIDS among Hispanics in the United States, 1991–1996. *American Journal of Public Health*, 89, 1104–1106.

de Moya, E. A., & Garcia, A. (1996). AIDS and the enigma of bisexuality in the Dominican Republic. In P. Aggleton (Ed.), *Bisexualities and AIDS: International perspectives* (121–135). Bristol, PA: Taylor and Francis.

Muñoz-Laboy, M., & Dodge, B. (2005). Bi-sexual practices: Patterns, meanings, and implications for HIV/STI prevention among bisexually-active Latino men and their partners. *Journal of Bisexuality*, 5, 81–100.

National Institutes of Health. (2001). Structural interventions to prevent HIV/STD infection; RFA: RFA-MH-02–006. Retrieved from http://grants.nih.gov/grants/guide/rfa-files/RFA-MH-02–006.html

Parker, R. (1985). Masculinity, femininity and homosexuality: On the anthropological interpretation of sexual meanings in Brazil. *Journal of Homosexuality*, 11, 155–163.

Parker, R. (1991). *Bodies, pleasures and passions: Sexual culture in contemporary Brazil*. Boston: Beacon Press.

Parker, R., & Aggleton, P. (2003). HIV and AIDS-related stigma and discrimination: A conceptual framework and implications for action. *Social Science & Medicine*, 57, 3–24.

Parker, R., Easton, D., & Klein, C. (2000). Structural barriers and facilitators in HIV prevention: A review of international research. *AIDS*, 14, S22–S32.

Perez, M., & Fennelley, K. (1996). Risk factors of HIV and AIDS among Latino farmworkers in Pennsylvania. In S. Mishra, R. Conner, & R. Magaña (Eds.), *AIDS crossing borders: The spread of HIV among migrant Latinos* (137–156). Boulder, CO: Westview Press.

Ramirez, J. R., Crano, W. D., Quist, R., Burgoon, M., Alvaro, E. M., & Grandpre, J. (2004). Acculturation, familism, parental monitoring, and knowledge as predictors of marijuana and inhalant use in adolescents. *Psychology of Addictive Behaviors*, 18, 3–11.

Rodríguez-Rust, P. (2000). Bisexuality in HIV research. In P. Rodríguez-Rust (Ed.), *Bisexuality in the United States: A social science reader* (355–400). New York: Columbia University Press.

Romero-Daza, N., Weeks, M., & Singer, M. (2003). "Nobody gives a damn if I live or die": Violence, drugs, and street-level prostitution in Inner-City Hartford, Connecticut. *Medical Anthropology*, 22, 233–259.

Ross, M., Harzke, A., Scott, D., & McCann, K. (2006). Outcomes of Project Wall Talk: An HIV/AIDS peer education program implemented within the Texas state prison system. *AIDS Education & Prevention*, 18, 504–517.

Schedlin, M., & Shulman, L. (2004). Qualitative needs assessment of HIV services among Dominican, Mexican and Central American immigrant populations living in the New York City Area. *AIDS Care*, 16, 434–445.

Schifter, J. (2000). *Public sex in a Latin society*. New York-London-Oxford: The Haworth Hispanic/Latino Press.

Schultz, N., & Moore, D. (1986). The loneliness experience of college students: Sex differences. *Personality and Social Psychology Bulletin*, 12, 111–119.

Simon, W., & Gagnon, J. (1984). Sexual scripts. *Society*, 22, 53–60.

Simon, W., & Gagnon, J. (1999). Sexual scripts. In R. Parker & P. Aggleton (Eds.), *Culture, society and sexuality: A reader* (29–38). London: UCL Press.

Singer, M. (1998). *The political economy of AIDS*. Amityville, NY: Baywood Publishing.

Singer M., & Clair, S. (2003). Syndemics and public health: Reconceptualizing disease in bio-social context. *Medical Anthropology Quarterly*, 17, 423–441.

Smith, C. A., & Barnett, E. (2005). Diabetes-related mortality among Mexican Americans, Puerto Ricans, and Cuban Americans in the United States. *Pan American Journal of Public Health*, 18, 381–387.

Smith, R. (2006). *Mexican New York: Transnational lives of new immigrants*. Berkeley: University of California Press.

Tewari, A., Horninger, W., Pelzer, A. E., Demers, R., Crawford, E. D., Gamito, E. D., . . . Menon, M. (2005). Factors contributing to the racial differences in prostate cancer mortality. *BJU International*, 96, 1247–1252.

Torres, H., & Gore-Felton, C. (2007). Compulsivity, substance use, and loneliness: The loneliness and sexual risk model (LSRM). *Sexual Addiction & Compulsivity*, 14, 63–75.

Weeks, J. (1986). *Sexuality*. London: Routledge.

Williams, D. R. (2001). Race and health: Trends and policy implications. In J. A. Auerbach & B. K. Krimgold (Eds.), *Income, socioeconomic status and health: Exploring the relationships*. Washington, D.C.: National Policy Association.

Wong, M. D., Tagawa, T., Hsieh, H. J., Shapiro, M. F., Boscardin, W. J., & Ettner, S. L. (2005). Differences in cause-specific mortality between Latino and white adults. *Medical Care*, 43, 1058–1062.

5

SEARCHING FOR IDEAL MASCULINITY

Negotiating Day Labor Work and Life at the Margins

Abel Valenzuela, Jr.
Maria C. Olivares Pasillas

Introduction

Don Ramon needed work badly. He was late on his rent and had failed to send money home for the past two months to assist his wife with feeding and caring for their three children. After several weeks of almost securing work at a well-known day laborer street corner in West Los Angeles, Don Ramon hit the day labor lottery of sorts. He was able to convince a prospective employer that his age (older than most of the day laborers at the hiring site) and size (short, medium build) would not disadvantage him at a job remodeling an older home. His job was to demolish a section of the garage and to load the discarded material in a pick-up truck. Towards the end of a long workday with little rest, Don Ramon stepped on a rusted nail, easily piercing his worn shoes and puncturing a tendon. After the injury, the employer who hired him told him to wait while he went to the nearby dump to unload his truck; he promised to return and take him to see a doctor. The employer did not return, and Don Ramon's injury eventually disabled him for several months as it mushroomed into a serious infection. Perhaps even crueler than this vanishing act was the fact that the employer never paid Ramon for his labor that day. For the near term, Ramon's family would have to do without his financial support.

Another worker, Artemio, conveys a similar story of day labor misery. After making the clandestine trek north (via foot, freight rail, car, and bus) from Honduras through Guatemala and then Mexico, Artemio arrived in Long Island, New York, looking for temporary work in Farmingville—a site notorious for its anti-immigrant and anti-day labor actions, including vigilante patrols, protests, and well-known beatings of day laborers by youths from the area (Buckley, 2008;

Fernandez, 2010). Securing work in Farmingville is desirable because the area is known to pay upwards of $100 per day—an excellent wage for day laborers who might normally earn $60 to $80 per day. Despite villainization, overt racism, and threat or real harm of violence (Valenzuela, 2006b), day laborers continue to search for work in sizable numbers in Farmingville. Artemio favors this site because he generally finds work more or less regularly that pays well, which, most importantly, allows him to remit resources home to care for his younger siblings and parents. But after several months of inconsistent work, Artemio is now subdued when speaking of his home in Tegucigalpa. He has grown tired of the constant epithets hurled his way by local protestors, the inconsistent work that has forced him into homelessness, the difficulty of competing with other desperate job seekers, and the constant awareness and fear of border vigilantes, local thugs, or Immigration and Customs Enforcement (ICE) officials.

The above two vignettes provide a glimpse into the very difficult life and work that day laborers confront at hundreds of similar hiring sites across the United States. Day laborers, mostly men, are primarily undocumented immigrants from Mexico and Central America who search for temporary employment in open-air markets—public spaces such as street corners, curbs, empty lots, home improvement store sites, or other high traffic spaces that might provide opportunities for employers to connect with workers. For day laborers, the job search, which may look basic and straightforward, is sporadic and nuanced, taking place in public settings but involving a complex array of negotiations and subtleties lost to a typical observer. Their search, already thorny by several measures, is made even more difficult with the bust in the housing market in recent years. The ensuing financial meltdown has made it difficult to refinance or secure a mortgage or equity line of credit—the lifeblood for contractors who rely on day laborers to keep their costs down. If a laborer is able to secure employment, it is usually fleeting, lasting a shift at best or, more often, just a few hours. The work is also grueling, dangerous, and with poor pay. Work, however, is the primary goal and day laborers will search daily and, if rewarded with a job, will accept almost any line of employment to secure wages.

Our chapter looks at the role that masculinity plays in day labor work. We are interested in exploring why thousands of men, despite their vulnerable immigration status and a labor market known to be one of the most difficult and abusive, would continue to search for and work day labor on a regular basis. Despite the current economic recession, the day labor market continues to grow, in part because of increases in unemployment and continued demand in some construction trades, but also because of other related occupations such as moving, landscaping, and painting. In this chapter, we first provide a portrait of day labor work, paying particular attention to key demographics and the difficulties suffered by this workforce in the form of poor pay, hazardous work, and abusive conditions (see Valenzuela et al., 2006).[1] We then review the literature on masculinity with a focus on Latinos and work. We concentrate our findings on three key issues:

(1) the significance of "responsible machismo," which we argue is performed as a type of day laborer masculinity; (2) interruptions—usually in the form of violence and injury—to the fulfillment of said masculinity; and (3) the role of competition in reinstating day labor masculinity.[2] These findings provide us with a window for understanding day labor fragility and related mental health vulnerabilities.

Working Day Labor: Poorly Paid, Hazardous, and Abusive

Day labor work is difficult and a few key demographic factors contribute to increased probability for differential outcomes regarding pay, abuse, and safety. For example, the mean age of day laborers is 34, relatively young but consistent with broader demographic trends that Latinos share, such as their general youthfulness. Almost all day laborers are male (98 percent), a demographic trait that enhances predicted increases in workplace violence when coupled with age (Valenzuela, 2006b). Most day laborers have low levels of education, with almost two thirds (59 percent) having fewer than eight years (Valenzuela et al., 2006). This translates into poor English proficiency in writing, reading, and speaking, leading up to a breakdown in communication with employers, often over issues of safety and wages. As a result, occupational dangers can easily turn into injuries, safety instructions become untranslatable, and mistrust ensues. Unfortunately for many day laborers, negotiating a wage, voicing a complaint, or articulating an abuse or labor violation in an unfamiliar language leaves them decisively disadvantaged.

A couple more examples further our point. Most day laborers (59 percent) are either married, living with a partner, separated, divorced, or widowed, while an even larger majority (64 percent) have children (Valenzuela et al., 2006). Due to poor pay and the high rate of inconsistency in day labor work, many children and spouses/mates are left wanting, not to mention the laborers themselves—many of whom reported going without meals and enduring homelessness and, as a result, social isolation.

One fifth of day laborers are recent arrivals in the United States, meaning they have been in the country for less than one year. Over one third (42 percent) have been in the U.S. between one and five years (Valenzuela et al., 2006). As a result, most day laborers are still adapting to U.S. mores and cultural nuances, in addition to learning about their civil, human, legal, and labor rights. With 75 percent lacking legal documentation, day laborers occupy a unique position that exposes them to abuse at the hands of unscrupulous employers who take advantage and exploit these types of workers to keep labor costs down.

No matter how you analyze the data, day labor pays poorly; despite a median hourly wage of $10 per hour, this market provides a difficult economic existence. For example, the monthly and yearly earnings of most day laborers place them among the working poor (Valenzuela et al., 2006). The instability of work combined with occasionally low hourly wages results in low monthly earnings for most day laborers, even during peak periods when work is relatively plentiful. In addition, workdays lost to job-related injuries and illnesses, and the under-payment of wages by some employers, contribute to the problem of low monthly earnings of day laborers. Valenzuela and his colleagues (2006) show that annual earnings for day labor rarely exceed $15,000 a year, a devastating statistic that puts most workers in this market at or below the federal poverty threshold.

Day labor is a dangerous and precarious occupation in which workers experience a high incidence of workplace injury. One in five day laborers has suffered an injury while on the job (Valenzuela et al., 2006). Lost work time due to injury is common among the day labor workforce and carries deeply felt consequences for their financial sustainability responsibilities. Two thirds of day laborers have missed work following an injury (Valenzuela et al., 2006). In many cases, work-related injuries have been severe, resulting in extended periods of time out of work or longlasting physical limitations. The National Day Labor Survey (Valenzuela et al., 2006) queried day laborers about their injuries during the previous year (2003), and 39 percent of injured day laborers reported missing one week or less of work due to injury, another 39 percent missed one to four weeks of work, and 22 percent missed more than one month of work. Illustrating their dire need for employment and their struggle to persevere, many day laborers continue to work despite having suffered an injury, with an alarming 68 percent working while in pain in the year prior to the survey.

Several factors contribute to the exceedingly high rates of on-the-job injury among the day labor workforce. These include exposure to hazardous substances (chemicals, dust, toxic emissions, etc.), use of faulty equipment (including shoddy scaffold construction and tools that are in poor condition), lack of protec-tive gear and safety equipment, and minimal safety training (Buchanan, 2004; Mehta & Theodore, 2006; Walter et al., 2002). To a certain extent, day laborers' concentration in the construction industry accounts for potentially dangerous exposures, as the construction industry itself carries high rates of work-related injury. Yet this fact alone cannot fully explain the levels of on-the-job injury experienced by day laborers. The inescapable conclusions are that day laborers are hired to undertake some of the most dangerous jobs at a worksite and there is little, if any, meaningful enforcement of health and safety laws. Day laborers endure unsafe working conditions, mainly because they fear that if they speak up, complain, or otherwise challenge these conditions, they will either be fired or not be paid for their work (Mehta & Theodore, 2006). Left with the prospect of losing a day's pay, day laborers find themselves with more than just empty pockets—they face the economic implications that affect their masculine roles within their connected and estranged families.

Employer violations of day laborers' rights and basic labor standards are an all-too-common occurrence in the day labor market. Wage theft ranks as the most typical abuse experienced by day laborers, followed by employer denial of food, water, and breaks; being verbally insulted or threatened; and being abandoned at a remote worksite with no access to public transportation. In another study, Valenzuela (2006b) documents the physical violence that day laborers endure by their employers and fellow co-workers who reported that violence is common among themselves, sometimes emerging during the keen competition to get work. Employers and passers-by also take their frustrations out on them, belittling their work performance or paying less than the contracted price, thereby inciting a violent response.

The above statistics on wage theft and other violations of basic labor standards indicate that the day labor market is rife with employer abuse, both psychological and physical. These indecencies further undermine the already low earnings of day laborers, and they add to the instability and insecurity of day labor work, feelings of discrimination, and anxiety associated with low socioeconomic status in a country that does little to value their worth. This belief is reinforced by the general climate of hostility that exists towards day laborers in widespread parts of the country and the current vitriol and anti-immigrant fever gripping the United States.

Why do these men endure the debilitating stress of perpetual economic struggle, perform hazardous labor, and put themselves at high risk for prevalent and pervasive employer abuse? Day laborers' self-sacrificing approaches toward work far exceed simplistic explanation. Their motivations for traversing arduous roads for the prospect of American opportunity cannot be essentialized as purely economic. What follows is a review of scholarship on masculinity as it relates to Latinos and work. We examine the existing literature on masculinity in order to better understand the symbolic meanings of traditional gender performance for this group of men, ways in which they exercise masculinity in this line of work, and how their inability to reach cultural prescriptions of masculinity may impact their mental and emotional well-being.

Masculinity Issues

Men are made, not born—so argued Gilmore (1990), positing masculinity as a ubiquitous, not universal, gender construct. Men's desire to exhort masculinity can be seen throughout varying societies, all of which possess their own culturally relative standards for masculinity (Gilmore, 1990). Several scholars have made strides past looking at "manliness" as one monolithic concept, asserting its homogeneous nature (Connell, 1995, 2000; Gilmore, 1990; Gutmann, 1996; Kimmel, 1987, 2006; Kimmel & Messner, 1992; Segal, 1990).

The Latino Masculinity Continuum

Through increasing scholarship aimed at disentangling the myth of monolithic masculinity, scholars have turned a critical eye toward the stereotypical Latino macho identity, characterized as constantly inebriated, aggressive, dominant, and brazen (Abalos, 2002; Chant and Craske, 2003; Gonzalez, 1996; Gutmann, 2001; Irwin, 2003; Lancaster, 1992; Melhuus and Stølen, 1996; Mirandé, 1997; Quintero & Estrada, 1998; Viveros-Vigoya, 2001). Machismo, the hegemonic form of Latino masculinity, is less concerned with establishing power relations between men and women (oppression and subordination of women are assumed within this social construct), and is instead fixated on a need to establish power relations among men (Courtenay, 2000; Lancaster, 1992) to prove utmost strength and dominance of one over the other. Similar to Donaldson (1993) and Carrigan and associates (1985), Lancaster (1992) believed that this cultural stereotype thrives on a social impulse to perpetuate competition among Latino men and eventually intra-personal competition to achieve "real" masculinity.

In response to one-dimensional typecasting of Latino men as unyielding machos, scholars have dissected the notion of Latino masculinity, transcending ambiguous and clichéd definitions and exploring more realistic behavior systems (De La Cancela, 1986, 1991; Mayo, 1994; Mirandé, 1988, 1997; Ruiz, 1981; Torres, 1998). This alternative view does not completely ignore negative characteristics inherent in the stereotypes (as instances of these should be expected in all humanity), but it explores the nuances, allowing for an understanding of Latino men as hard-working; dedicated to honoring, respecting, and protecting their families; autonomous; strong willed; responsible; and self-sacrificing, among other contextually and culturally realistic traits (Abad et al., 1974; De La Cancela, 1991; Falicov, 1998; Mirandé, 1997; Torres, 1998; Torres et al., 2002; Walter et al., 2002, 2004). The burgeoning critical exami-nation of Latino masculinities refutes a polarized perspective and instead supports a dynamic view of Latino gender roles, giving credence to the multifaceted nature of men's behavioral systems and positioning them on a positive-to-negative continuum (Gilmore, 1990; Mirandé, 1988, 1997; Torres et al., 2002).

Masculinity, Day Labor, and Mental Health

Despite the expanding scholarship on the multidimensionality of Latino masculinities, the ideals and standards of appropriate male behavior (hegemonic Latino masculinity) continue to pervade society and culture through communication media like television and radio, as well as via traditional cultural norms. Studies have found that an unwavering endorsement of this gendered male identity can pose a significant threat to the psychological health of Latino men who have come to perceive hegemonic Latino masculinity as culturally valuable and emblematic of bona fide manhood (Pleck, 1981; Walter et al., 2002, 2004). Researchers have found that pressures to uphold social conventions of gender are greater for men than they are for women (Golombok & Fivush, 1994; Martin 1995; Williams & Best, 1990), and the subsequent pursuit to embody the masculine mystique can prove detrimental to their physical and psychological health

(Clatterbaugh, 1997; Pleck, 1981; Walter et al., 2002, 2004). According to Pleck (1981), inconsistencies between men's idealization of hegemonic masculinity and their own authentic personal traits can result in damaging psychological dissonance, known as gender role stress. Dissonance in men's negotiation between *ideal* masculinity and actual masculinity can foster feelings of inadequacy and failure, particularly among Latino males, whose patriarchal roles as providers are a highly valued part of cultural tradition (Morgan, 1992; Walter et al., 2002, 2004).

By embodying dominance and aggressiveness toward fellow laborers when vying for employment and exhibiting docility and complacency toward employers when performing a job, day laborers are increasingly vulnerable to contradictory self-perceptions. In their 2002 study, Walter and associates explored how patriarchal responsibilities affect undocumented day laborers' experience of physical injury. The study found that physical injury negatively affected the laborers' already divergent sense of self by inhibiting the ability to work, which was a primary reason for immigrating to the United States. The inability to meet "internalized gender roles that require them to perform as patriarch and provider" (Walter et al., 2002, p. 225) can furthermore contribute to feelings of inadequacy and failure, dealing a harsh blow to day laborers' psychological well-being. Additionally, because volatile employment poses a significant threat to day laborers' ability to perform the patriarchal duty of supporting their family, this may usher in negative implications for their health. Stoical attitudes help mask the emotional and psychological suffering associated with meager sustainability and missing significant moments in their remote family's growth and development. Stoicism and tolerance help to stabilize psychological and emotional disparity superficially and to legitimate the hegemonic masculine traits of emotional callousness and the need to press on. Day laborers' stoic and tolerant attitudes have undoubtedly contributed much to their self-empowerment and their demonstrated emotional fortitude, but we must consider the serious emotional and psychological health detriments of living a life laden with diverse strife.

Several studies on the relationship between gender role conflict and the somatization of depression, anxiety, and low self-esteem testify to the emotional detriment experienced by Latino men (Good & Mintz, 1990; Lewis-Fernandez et al., 2002; O'Neil et al., 1995; Sharpe & Heppner, 1991; Stillson et al., 1991). Angel and Guarnaccia (1989) found that somatization—the process by which psychological and emotional stress become a physical psychosomatic illness—of psychological suffering was particularly prevalent among Latino cultures. While Angel and Guarnaccia's study is a good start to examining the relationship between somatization and culture, more research is needed to address the mental and psychological health implications of coping with inter- and intra-personal conflicts, social isolation, self-esteem, and, of course, ideals of Latino hegemonic masculinity. Below, we provide findings from a review of transcripts of 46 day laborers on how masculinity is played out in their work and lives.

Day Laborers' "Responsible Machismo"

With empirical evidence and narrative detail, we have conveyed that day labor is a dangerous, strenuous, and terribly paying job. The current economic downturn adds to the misery, transforming what is already a less than fruitful employment venture into an even worse one. Despite the impenetrability of this market as a viable and consistent source of income, a means by which family providers can attend to responsibilities to economically support their families (Morgan, 1992), thousands of immigrants, mostly Mexican and Central American, regularly search for and, when opportunity arise, take day labor jobs. Pitones' 2004 study found that day laborers "tended to associate to greater traditional values associated with their roles as men in the family" (p. 22), and generally agreed with statements that closely associated the responsibility of caring for and honoring a family with being masculine. In order to meet their family responsibility and cultural standards for acceptable masculinity, these men endure the dangerous trek to the United States in search of jobs that can help generate enough income to "push the family ahead."

Day laborers' willingness to meet these cultural standards is highly revered by family and friends in their sending countries due to the emotional, physical, and financial risks involved in migration, as well as the migrant's willingness to experience the ambiguous loss of family and community; while this loss is not permanent, though simultaneously not easily recuperated (Boss, 1991, 1999; Falicov, 2002), it is seemingly more permanent as the costs for clandestine migration have soared. In this way, patriarchal masculinity as embodied by day laborers takes the form of what Walter and colleagues (2004) have termed *responsible machismo*. Responsible machismo refers to the hyper-male identity (Gutmann, 1996; Limón, 1994; Lomnitz-Adler, 1992) embraced by men who are honorable, enduring, and courageous all for the sake of their families "and the dignity of their nation" (Walter et al., 2004, p. 1162). Responsible machismo conjures images of chivalry and men's self-sacrificing protection of women and children (and, increasingly, extended family members such as grandparents or grandchildren). It still assumes submissiveness, docility, and dependence of women on their men, yet it does not necessitate the aggression and insolence present in hegemonic masculinity.

The ability to complete physically taxing jobs and generate income serves as a form of validation and vindication for a group of people that experience constant villainization, discrimination, racism, employer abuses, distanced family relationships, and a compromised sense of masculinity (Theodore et al., 2006; Walter et al., 2002, 2004). Author-conducted interviews of day laborers from 1999 to 2001 provided telling stories of this validation. For example, Tomas, a married father of three children all still in Mexico, expressed that the successful completion of jobs increased his self-worth, giving him a sense of purpose despite dealing with society's constant treatment of day laborers as inferior beings. "I do a job well done and the days come and go and I pass by where I did the job. I feel proud at least in my way of thinking, that is what is good. That you feel satisfied that you are still useful." He later continued:

> People have a bad . . . well, they see the day laborer as an inferior person . . . there are a lot of day laborers that know a lot about the job, some that are even professionals . . . a lot of people think that day laborers are the lowest and no, they need to consider that just because we are day laborers, we do not always want to be there [at the corner]. We are there because we have not had the opportunities that other people have had of finding a better job.

The ability to earn a livable wage helps justify the multiple sacrifices of leaving family behind, living in a constant state of alienation and fear of deportation (Walter et al., 2002), and the inconsistent procurement of work. The daunting nature of these sacrifices is echoed by Arturo, a day laborer from Puebla, Mexico, "When I came to the United States, I left everything. I renounced the little bit of economy that I had so that I would be able to come here." Day laborers work hard, taking full advantage of jobs that come their way in order to recompense themselves and their families for mutual familial losses (Walter et al., 2002). Remittances serve to compensate for a lack in presence and to demonstrate continued dedication to family, allowing a real sense of contribution and fulfillment in being able to provide in any amount. It is through hard physical labor that many of these transplanted patriarchs seek to find a means of fulfilling their family duties even if accomplished remotely, inconsistently, and insufficiently.

Interruptions to the Fulfillment of Masculinity

The current state of economic recession in the country has fostered increased feelings of xenophobia, discrimination, and racism toward immigrants, resulting in governmental action such as the passage of state-level laws (e.g., Arizona's SB 1070) targeting Latinos under the proxy of "illegal immigration." As the availability of American jobs decreases, claims that immigrants are taking citizens' jobs and draining social services have spread like wildfire. As the most visible sign of a depressed economy, the urgent need for immigration reform, and the growing Latino presence in the United States (Purser, 2009), day laborer ubiquity mediated an increase in hate crimes, and seeing and feeling the wrath of a pervasive public panic. In November of 2008, Marcelo Lucero, an Ecuadorian immigrant who worked as a day laborer, was fatally stabbed by a group of Long Island youth who routinely assaulted Latino men for sport, calling it "beaner hopping" (Buckley, 2008; Fernandez, 2010). The killing of Mr. Lucero signified the fatal manifestation of hate; it was the third hate crime these youths had engaged in that evening. Before this final attack, the teenagers had shot at a Latino man in his driveway several times with a BB gun and had physically assaulted another Latino man on the street (Buckley, 2008).

In March 2010, the *New York Times* reported on the effort to find a jury for the case against these youths (Fernandez, 2010). A woman stated that her father's "huge opinion about illegal immigration" had become hers as well, while another man said that an illegal immigrant had broken into his house, negatively affecting his ability to be impartial. Some people expressed reasons for a positive bias toward immigrants and were additionally excused. By the third day of jury selection, 130 men and women had been questioned and only five had been selected. A large portion of the prospective jurors were excused because they held strong views on illegal immigration, and while many chose their words carefully, "so as not to condone the crimes for which Mr. Conroy stands accused," (Fernandez, 2010) the anti-immigrant sentiment was seemingly much stronger than the desire to bring justice to the murder of an innocent person targeted for looking Latino and being undocumented.

Unfortunately, the Lucero murder is not an isolated incidence of violence against Latinos, and increasingly against day laborers. In 2005, the National Day Laborer Organizing Network (NDLON) reported that simultaneous vigils would be held across the United States, from New York to California, in protest of what were then recent attacks against day laborers' physical safety and human rights. According to NDLON (2005), 2004 proved to be an especially treacherous year for the day laborer population nationwide:

> Day laborers across the country experienced a sharp rise in violent attacks, civil rights violations, and workplace rights abuses. In Jacksonville, FL, dozens of attacks against day laborers have resulted in at least two murders. In Redondo Beach, CA, over 60 workers were arrested merely for seeking work in public, in clear violation of human rights norms. After a Federal Court ordered the city to halt the arrests, an anti-immigrant group staged a protest and urged its members to, "Bring your bats, fellas. If we are lucky, we are going to need them."
>
> (NDLON, 2005)

More recently, San Francisco, like other large urban centers, has seen the breakout of a dangerous rash of assaults against day laborers (Smith, 2008) who have been beaten, shot, and even killed by local gang members. In April 2010, a street surveillance video from Jamaica, Queens, New York, recorded Hugo Alfredo Tale-Yax, a homeless day laborer, as he approached a quarrelling couple. Soon after coming to the woman's aid, Mr. Tale-Yax was stabbed by the man with whom she was arguing (Santos, 2010b). The video's notoriety is due not to its brutality, but to the unconcerned attitudes of passers-by as Mr. Tale-Yax lay on the ground for more than an hour, bleeding to death. In late June of the same year, the *Staten Island Advance* reported on the severe beating of a day laborer that left the victim with a broken eye socket and in critical condition. Apparently, this was but another incident in a rash of hate crimes against Mexicans in Staten Island, following a series of similar beatings in April (Annese, 2010). Additionally, without social security numbers, most day laborers are unable to secure bank accounts, and consequently receive their pay in cash. Assailants are aware of this and take advantage of it, dubbing day laborers "walking ATM machines" (Nossiter, 2009; Valdez et al., 2010; Valenzuela, 2006b). Fernando, a young day laborer from El Salvador, opened up about his numerous run-ins with local gang members and his subjection to frequent robberies that represented several months of work and savings:

> I would carry cash . . . when I wanted to send it to my wife I did not have time to wire the money and so I would carry it and I got bad luck . . . they robbed me several times and it wasn't little amounts . . . it was $700 and above.

The frequency and pervasiveness of attacks against day laborers affect more than just the victims directly. Latino immigrants, particularly day laborers, throughout the United States are fully aware of the negative perceptions associated with them, from which they experience feelings of social isolation and vulnerability. Jose, another day laborer from Los Angeles, elaborated on his experience of racial discrimination:

> They slam the door in your nose for the simple reason of being Latino . . . if you see them when they take somebody else, American, born here, or white . . . they give them their hand and they smile at them and talk to them and everything. But to us, they don't. They put us far away . . . they pass by us and if it is not to insult us, it is to give us problems about a plant not well planted. That is the only reason that they talk to us.

We believe that demoralizing experiences such as these foster a strong need in day laborers to counterbalance their perceived low social value with a strong sense of masculinity within their group of peers. Their conversations over this issue are tinged with resentment and anger; how can they not consider the multiple contradictions and ironies of what it means to be an immigrant—undervalued, overworked, praised, and similarly vilified for their hard work. Not lost on day laborers is the general disrespect and low-ranking position they occupy in the social hierarchy; to counterbalance this reality, they develop a strong sense of masculinity, which is played out daily not only in their search for work but also at the work sites and in non-work activities.

By feeling like strong, capable, skillful, and valuable workers relative to one another, day laborers help elevate their emotional sense of self. Additionally, earning enough money to survive and sending it to their families fulfill cultural prescriptions of masculinity as family providers, despite residing in perpetual social isolation, far from family.

Reaffirming Masculinity Through Competition

In a comparative study that analyzes the construction of masculinity, Gretchen Purser (2009) provided a closer look at masculinity among two groups of day laborers: one group solicited work on a street corner, the other sought work at a hiring hall. According to Purser, each group looked down on the other for searching for employment at their respective sites. Both found reasons for characterizing one another's methods of acquiring work as feminine and submissive. A worker at a center viewed street work solicitation as "begging" and a "desperate chase" (p. 131), while workers on the street "tend[ed] to evaluate those who search for work through the center as dependent, incompetent, deferential, and lazy, a set of attributes that collectively evoke the specter of the 'welfare queen'" (p. 128).

This form of competiveness is the manifestation of the hierarchical relationship that exists among multiple masculinities within a continuum, some of which are hegemonic while others are subordinate (Connell, 2000; Pitones, 2004). Purser (2009) argued that this back-and-forth condemnation among day laborers demonstrates that competition functions as a way of reclaiming and asserting their masculinity. She stated that their tendency to degrade one another has less to do with a need to construe the other as feminine and more to do with their need to uphold their own self-worth and dignity (p. 136). Competition in day labor is played out in multiple formats: over jobs, over space, over attention to oneself in attempting to secure work, over employers, and in the ability to survive on meager earnings. The regularity of competition similarly allows day laborers to recover and affirm their masculinity.

Previous studies have found that in societies where competition is central, individuals' self-perception and valuation are consequently informed by how they measure up to their peers and to social standards (Harter, 1993; Jordan, 2005). As central to day labor culture, competiveness proves influential in day laborers' self-esteem: "Groups that are 'outside' the dominant definitions of merit, who may have differing standards of worth, are thus disadvantaged by these privileged standards" (Jordan, 2005, p. 81). The makeup of day laborer self-esteem and self-concept is quite complex and contradictory; laborers are disadvantaged by social standards from the start for being primarily undocumented Latinos whose culture values their sacrifice and immigration as a true sign of family responsibility and masculinity (Walter et al., 2002) while their situational context in the United States devalues their presence and "illegal" status. The combination of both axioms is volatile and a stressor in the already difficult life and work circumstance of day laborers.

Discussion and Conclusion

Our chapter presents a roadmap for better understanding why day laborers continue, day after day, searching for work in a labor market that provides terrible pay, offers inconsistent employment, and is fraught with hazards and other abuses. Considering such hardship, a simple question emerges: why do so many men cross the Mexico–United States border to search for and work day labor? We argue that part of the answer lies in necessity—many poor people work terrible jobs to make ends meet. However, day labor is unique because it is poorly understood and, as we show, it is a job market with few opportunities, as well as being squalid and gloomy as an income-generating activity. We believe that day laborers in their search for employment, also search for an ideal masculinity, one well-known to immigrant workers from Latin America who honor family, venerate the ability to provide, and toil in the United States under harsh conditions so that they can remit resources and thereby fulfill their obligations to self and family.

Based on in-depth interviews and other sources, we argue that day laborers primarily undertake the difficulty of working day labor to fulfill their responsibilities to their families, many of whom remain in their country of origin. Day laborers do this because they are obligated and it fulfills their sense of worth as a worker, provider, and responsible family man in a household where space and long distance is part of the equation of transnational families (Abrego, 2009). As a result of a volatile and mean-spirited public discourse over undocumented immigration, a wave of vigilantism and new local and state ordinances, some specifically targeted at day laborers and undocumented immigrants in general, has swept the country (Archibold, 2010; Latino Justice PRLDEF, 2010; Miller, 2010; Murphy, 2010), provoking even more protests and violence directed toward day laborers. Thus, their search for employment and an affirmation of their masculine role are often interrupted. This interruption, we argue, creates an "us vs. them" dichotomy that further solidifies a strong need for day laborers to affirm their masculinity relative to one another. Consequently, day laborers often compete with each other (in multiple realms), which also provides a process for reaffirming their masculinity—our third major finding.

In a study conducted by Organista and Kubo (2005), migrant day laborers, when asked to indicate psychosocial problems encountered in the past six months, selected difficulties primarily having to do with underemployment, unemployment, and lack of money. Sadness and racism were the next set of most endorsed issues, followed by "sometimes" feeling socially isolated and lonely (p. 275). Because day laborers mostly come to this country for the specific purpose of working and earning resources to remit, economic stressors play a greater role in their mental and emotional well-being. Multiple respondents who we interviewed expressed feeling depressed, pressured, nervous, and worried due to economic stresses. In support of this point, longitudinal studies have shown a positive correlation between stressful life events and the manifestation of depressive symptoms (Aneshensel & Frerichs, 1982; Ensel & Lin, 1991; Turner & Noh, 1988).

For day laborers, these stressful events are numerous, and many are ever-present. Loss of employment and underemployment, endemic features of day labor and of the current economic recession, contribute to a rise in binge drinking, depression, and homelessness among this population (Theodore et al., 2006). Newspaper accounts have noted that "with their isolation and day-to-day existence, the laborers are perhaps the most invisible and hardest-to-reach victims of the recession" (Santos, 2010a). According to Dooley et al. (2000), the combined loss of earnings and social-psychological functions of work, resulting from loss of employment, leads to increased feelings of depression. Additionally, scholars have argued that the continuously unemployed suffer from more depressive symptoms than the employed because of the burden associated with a loss of income (Kessler et al., 1988). For unemployed day laborers, depression is compounded by the chronic anxiety of dealing with constant "competition, insecurity and public embarrassment of tenuous survival on the street" (Walter et al., 2004, p. 1162), including wage theft, violence, and police harassment (Valenzuela, 2006b; Valenzuela et al., 2006).

For day laborers who have risked their livelihoods, sacrificed their families, and worked under difficult circumstances, depression and chronic anxiety over competition, isolation, and other day labor realities are increasingly common. When income proves unattainable, the day laborer population becomes highly susceptible to feelings of failure, shame, and guilt for their inability to meet their masculine standards of providing for their families and, at worse, for themselves. When work dries up and subsistence becomes the norm, then no one benefits, not even the worker who barely survives on a day-to-day existence. An inability to adequately cope with these issues contributes to stressors and suffering, including gender role stress and somatization of illnesses, as discussed earlier. The inability to generate income creates an imbalance in tensions between anxiety over leaving family behind and sense of pride gained through acquiring, competing, and securing hard work (Walter et al., 2004).

Social isolation is positively associated with anxiety and depressive symptoms. Palacios' study (2010) on agricultural day laborers in California found that competition among the workers disrupts the potential for a sense of collectivity and, subsequently, the emotional strength that can be drawn from feelings of solidarity. This disruption inhibits inter-laborer harmony and in turn fosters a sense of mutual distrust (p. 464). Prolonged family separation, a lack of social and recreational interaction among laborers, and the cultivation of cynicism intensify feelings of depression, anguish, anxiety, and alcoholism (p. 469).

A day laborer's downward spiral toward depression, alcoholism, and potentially fatal outcomes demonstrate the very real and somber effects of intolerable stress. Feelings of pride and an inability to achieve the mystique of idealized masculinity can contribute to the progressive impairment of day laborers' psychological and emotional well-being. Precisely because day laborers persistently turn to street corners and hiring halls to earn a living, despite prevalence of low wages, worker abuses, social discrimination, and general hostility, it is important to analyze the ways in which attacks on their persona are internalized and to delve into the implications of constant struggle on the psyche and masculinity of day laborers.

Acknowledgments

We would like to thank Emily Erickson for assistance in compiling interview data for this chapter. Data collected on day labor was supported by grants from the Ford and Rockefeller Foundations.

Notes

1   Data for the portrait of day laborers conveyed in this section are published elsewhere (Valenzuela et al., 2006) and have been culled from the National Day Labor Survey (NDLS), a stratified random sample of 2,660 day laborers, conducted over the period of June–August 2004. The research team visited a total of 264 day labor hiring sites located in 36 metropolitan statistical areas across the United States. For a detailed overview of the survey's sampling framework and related methods, see Valenzuela et al., 2006.

2   The findings for this section and for all quotes in the chapter come from 46 in-depth interviews of day laborers and from case studies of day labor hiring sites in Los Angeles during the year 2000. Each interview was completed in Spanish and audio-recorded. Interviews lasted between four and eight hours and a modest ($25) incentive was provided at completion. We queried day laborers on various topics including their immigration to the United States, their work and family history, the abuses they experienced in their search for and work in day labor, how they made ends meet, their health, and their educational background. The interviews were conducted near the site, often inside a coffee shop, on a park bench, or in the interviewer's car. Recruitment was mostly snowball and non-random, though we took particular effort to interview a variety of day laborers—legal and unauthorized, young and old, and experienced and inexperienced. The participants were guaranteed anonymity and pseudonyms are used throughout this chapter.

References

Abad, V., Ramos, J., & Boyce, E. (1974). A model for delivery of mental health services to Spanish-speaking minorities. *American Journal of Orthopsychiatry*, 44, 584–595.

Abalos, D. T. (2002). *Latino male: A radical redefinition*. Boulder, CO: Lynne Rienner Publishers.

Abrego, L. (2009). Economic well-being in Salvadoran transnational families: How gender affects remittance practices. *Journal of Marriage and Family*, 71, 1070–1085.

Aneshensel, C. S., & Frerichs, R. R. (1982). Stress, support, and depression: A longitudinal causal model. *Journal of Community Psychology*, 10, 363–376.

Angel, R., & Guarnaccia, P. J. (1989). Mind, body, and culture: Somatization among Hispanics. *Social Science & Medicine* 28(12), 1229–1238.

Annese, J. M. (2010, June 25). Day laborer attacked in Port Richmond. *Staten Island Advance.* Retrieved from www.silive.com/northshore/index.ssf/2010/06/day_laborer_attacked_in_port_r.html

Archibold, R. C. (2010, April 23). Arizona enacts stringent law on immigration. *The New York Times.* Retrieved from www.nytimes.com/2010/04/24/us/politics/24immig.html

Boss, P. (1991). Ambiguous loss. In F. Walsh & M. McGoldrick (Eds.), *Living beyond loss: Death in the family* (237–246). New York: Norton.

Boss, P. (1999). *Ambiguous loss: Learning to live with unresolved grief.* Cambridge, MA: Harvard University Press.

Buchanan, S. (2004). Day labor and occupational health: Time to take a closer look. *New Solutions: A Journal of Environmental and Occupational Health Policy,* 14, 253–260.

Buckley, C. (2008, Nov 21). Teenagers' violent "sport" led to killing on Long Island, officials say. *The New York Times.*

Carrigan, T., Connell, B., & Lee, J. (1985). Toward a new sociology of masculinity. *Theory and Society,* 14(5), 551–604.

Chant, S., & Craske, N. (2003). *Gender in Latin America.* New Brunswick, NJ: Rutgers University Press.

Clatterbaugh, K. (1997). *Contemporary perspectives on masculinity: Men, women and politics in modern society* (2nd ed). Boulder, CO: Westview Press.

Connell, R. W. (1995). *Masculinities.* Berkeley: University of California Press.

Connell, R. W. (2000). *The Men and the boys.* Berkeley: University of California Press.

Courtenay, W. H. (2000). Constructions of masculinity and their influence on men's well-being: A theory of gender and health. *Social Science and Medicine,* 5, 1385–1401.

De La Cancela, V. (1986). A critical analysis of Puerto Rican machismo: Implications for clinical practice. *Psychotherapy: Theory, Research, Practice, Training,* 23, 291–296.

De La Cancela, V. (1991). Working affirmatively with Puerto Rican men: Professional and personal reflections. *Journal of Feminist Family Therapy,* 2(3 & 4), 195–211.

Donaldson, M. (1993). What is hegemonic masculinity? *Theory and Society,* 22, 643–657.

Dooley, D., Prause, J., & Ham-Rowbottom, K. A. (2000). Underemployment and depression: Longitudinal relationships. *Journal of Health and Social Behavior,* 41(4), 421–436.

Ensel, W. M., & Lin, N. (1991). The life stress paradigm and psychological distress. *Journal of Health and Social Behavior,* 32, 321–341.

Falicov, C. J. (1998). *Latino families in therapy: A guide to multicultural practice.* New York: Guilford Press.

Falicov, C. J. (2002). Ambiguous loss: Risk and resilience in Latino immigrant families. In M. M. Suárez-Orozco, C. Suárez-Orozco, & D. Qin-Hilliard (Eds.), *The new immigration: An interdisciplinary reader* (197–206). New York: Brunner-Routledge.

Fernandez, M. (2010, March 8). In jury selection for hate crime, a struggle to find tolerance. *The New York Times.* Retrieved from www.nytimes.com/2010/03/09/nyregion/09patchogue.html

Gilmore, D. (1990). *Manhood in the making: Cultural concepts of masculinity.* New Haven, CT: Yale University Press.

Golombok, S., & Fivush, R. (1994). *Gender development.* Cambridge, MA: Cambridge University Press.

Gonzalez, R. (1996). *Muy macho: Latino men confront their manhood.* New York: Anchor Books.

Good, G. E., & Mintz, L. B. (1990). Depression and gender role conflict and depression in college men: Evidence for compounded risk. *Journal of Counseling and Development*, 69, 17–21.

Gutmann, M. C. (1996). *The meanings of macho: Being a man in Mexico City*. Berkeley: University of California Press.

Gutmann, M. C. (2001). The vicissitudes of men and masculinities in Latin America. Introduction to a special issue on men and masculinities in Latin America. *Men and Masculinities*, 3(3), 237–260.

Harter, S. (1993). Causes and consequences of low self-esteem in children and adolescents. In R. Baumeister (Ed.), *Self-esteem: The puzzle of low self regard*. New York: Plenum.

Irwin, R. M. (2003). *Mexican masculinities*. Minneapolis: University of California Press.

Jordan, J. V. (2005). Relational resilience in girls. In S. Goldstein & R. B. Brooks (Eds.), *Handbook of resilience in children* (79–90). New York: Springer.

Kessler, R. C., Turner, J. B., & House, J. S. (1988). Effects of unemployment on health in a community survey: Main, modifying, and mediating effects. *Journal of Social Issues*, 44(4), 69–85.

Kimmel, M. S. (1987). Men's responses to feminism at the turn of the century. *Gender & Society*, 1, 261–283.

Kimmel, M. S. (2006). *Manhood in America: A cultural history* (2nd ed.). New York: Oxford University Press.

Kimmel, M. S., & Messner, M. A. (Eds.). (1992). *Men's lives*. New York: Macmillan.

Lancaster, R. (1992). *Life is hard: Machismo, danger and the intimacy of power in Nicaragua*. Berkeley: University of California Press.

LatinoJustice PRLDEF. (2010). NY day laborer organizations challenge anti-immigrant ordinance. Retrieved from http://latinojustice.org/briefing_room/press_releases/Orgs_challenge_oyster_bay_ordinance/

Lewis-Fernandez, R., Guarnaccia, P. J., Martinez, I. E., Salman, E., Schmidt, A., & Liebowitz, M. (2002). Comparative phenomenology of *Ataques de Nervios*, panic attacks, and panic disorder. *Culture, Medicine & Psychiatry*, 26(2), 199–223.

Limón, J. E. (1994). *Dancing with the devil: Society and cultural poetics in Mexican-American South Texas*. Madison: University of Wisconsin Press.

Lomnitz-Adler, C. (1992). *Exits from the labyrinth: Culture and ideology in the Mexican national space*. Berkeley: University of California Press.

Martin, C. L. (1995). Stereotypes about children with traditional and nontraditional gender roles. *Sex Roles* 33(11 & 12), 727–751.

Mayo, Y. (1994). The utilization of mental health services, acculturation, and machismo among Puerto Rican men. Garden City, NY: Adelphi University.

Mehta, C., & Theodore, N. (2006). Workplace safety in Atlanta's construction industry: Institutional failure in temporary staffing arrangements. WorkingUSA, 9, 59–77.

Melhuus, M., & Stølen, K. A. (1996). *Machos, mistresses, madonnas: Contesting the power of Latin American gender imagery*. London: Verso.

Miller, J. (2010, June 26). Utah among 18 states aiming to copy Arizona immigration law. *Deseret News*. Retrieved from www.deseretnews.com/article/700043391/Utah-among-18-states-aiming-to-copy-Arizona-immigration-law.html

Mirandé, A. (1988). *Qué gacho es ser macho*: It's a drag to be a macho man. *Aztlán: A Journal of Chicano Studies*, 17, 63–89.

Mirandé, A. (1997). *Hombres y machos: Masculinity and Latino culture*. Boulder, CO: Westview Press.

Morgan, D. H. J. (1992). *Discovering men*. London: Routledge.

Murphy, K. (2010, July 16). List sends chill through Utah's Latino community. *Los Angeles Times*. Retrieved from www.latimes.com/news/nationworld/nation/la-na-utah-immigration-20100716,0,6028318.story?track=rss

National Day Laborer Organizing Network (NDLON). (2005). Day laborers participate in nationwide vigil to denounce attacks, demand investigations, and urge reconciliation. Retrieved from www.ndlon.org/index.php?view=article&catid=59%3Apress-releases&id=296%3Aday-laborers-participate-in-nationwide-vigil-to-denounce-attacks-demand-investigations-and-urge-reconciliation-&option=com_content&Itemid=198

Nossiter, A. (2009, February 15). Day laborers are easy prey in New Orleans. *New York Times*.

O'Neil, J. M., Good, E. E., & Holmes, S. (1995). Fifteen years of theory and research on men's gender role conflict: New paradigms for empirical research. In R. F. Levant & W. S. Pollack (Eds.), *A new psychology of men* (164–206). New York: Basic Books.

Organista, K. C., & Kubo, A. (2005). Pilot survey of HIV risk and contextual problems and issues in Mexican/Latino migrant day laborers. *Journal of Immigrant Health*, 7(4), 269–281.

Palacios, S. P. I. (2010). Migración irregular y aislamiento social [Irregular immigration and social isolation]. *Revista Internacional de Sociología*, 68(2), 453–472.

Pitones, J. M. (2004, August). Perceptions of masculinity and machismo: An examination of Latino day laborers and Mexican American working class men. Paper presented at the annual meeting of the American Sociological Association, San Francisco.

Pleck, J. (1981). *The myth of masculinity*. Cambridge, MA: MIT Press.

Purser, G. (2009). The dignity of job-seeking men: Boundary work among immigrant day laborers. *Journal of Contemporary Ethnography*, 38(1), 117–139.

Quintero, G. A., & Estrada, A. L. (1998). Cultural models of masculinity and drug use: "Machismo," heroin, and street survival on the U.S.-Mexican border. *Contemporary Drug Problems*, 25, 147–168.

Ruiz, R. A. (1981). Cultural and historical perspective in counseling Hispanics. In D. W. Sue (Ed.), *Counseling the culturally different: Theory and practice* (186–216). New York: Wiley.

Santos, F. (2010a, January 2). In the shadows, day laborers left homeless as work vanishes. *The New York Times*. Retrieved from www.nytimes.com/2010/01/02/nyregion/02laborers.html?_r=1&partner=rss&emc=rss

Santos, F. (2010b, April 27). Here to aid his family, left to die on the street. *The New York Times*. Retrieved from www.nytimes.com/2010/04/28/nyregion/28laborer.html

Segal, L. (1990). *Slow motion: Changing masculinities, changing men*. New Brunswick, NJ: Rutgers University Press.

Sharpe, M. J., & Heppner, P. P. (1991). Gender role, gender-role conflict, and psychological well-being in men. *Journal of Counseling Psychology*, 38, 323–330.

Smith, M. (2008, January 23). Epidemic of violence against SF day laborers. *San Francisco Weekly*. Retrieved from www.sfweekly.com/2008-01-23/news/epidemic-of-violence-against-sf-day-laborers/

Stillson, R. W., O'Neil, J. M., & Owen, S. V. (1991). Predictors of adult male gender-role conflict: race, class, unemployment, age, instrumentality-expressiveness, and personal strain. *Journal of Counseling Psychology*, 38, 458–464.

Theodore, N., Valenzuela, A. J., & Meléndez, E. (2006). *La esquina* (the corner): Day laborers on the margins of New York's formal economy. *Working USA: The Journal of Labor and Society*, 9, 407–423.

Torres, J. B. (1998). Masculinity and gender roles among Puerto Rican men: A dilemma for Puerto Rican men's personal identity. *American Journal of Orthopsychiatry*, 68, 16–26.

Torres, J. B., Solberg, S. H., & Carlstrom, A. H. (2002). The myth of sameness among Latino men and their machismo. *American Journal of Orthopsychiatry*, 72(2), 163–181.

Turner, R. J., & Noh, S. (1988). Physical disability and depression: A longitudinal analysis. *Journal of Health and Social Behavior*, 29, 23–37.

Valdez, A., Cepeda, A., Negi, N., & Kaplan, C. (2010). Fumando la piedra: Emerging patterns of crack use among Latino immigration day laborers in New Orleans. *Journal of Immigrant and Minority Health*, 12(5), 737–42.

Valenzuela, A. J. (2006a). Economic development in Latino communities: Incorporating marginal and immigrant workers. In P. Ong & A. Loukaitou-Sideris (Eds.), *Jobs and economic development in minority communities: Realities, challenges, and innovation* (141–158). Philadelphia: Temple University Press.

Valenzuela, A. J. (2006b). New immigrants and day labor: The potential for violence. In Martinez and Valenzuela (Eds.). *Immigration and Crime: Ethnicity, Race, and Violence* (189–211). New York: New York University Press.

Valenzuela, A. J., Theodore, N., Meléndez, E., & Gonzalez, A. L. (2006). On the corner: Day labor in the United States (technical report). Center for the Study of Urban Poverty, UCLA.

Viveros-Vigoya, M. (2001). Contemporary Latin American perspectives on masculinity. *Men and Masculinities*, 3(3), 237–260.

Walter, N., Bourgois, P., Loinaz, H. M., & Schillinger, D. (2002). Social context of work injury among undocumented day laborers in San Francisco. *Journal of General Internal Medicine*, 17, 221–229.

Walter, N., Bourgois, P., Loinaz, H. M., & Schillinger, D. (2004). Masculinity and undocumented labor migration: Injured Latino day laborers in San Francisco. *Social Science & Medicine*, 59, 1159–1168.

Williams, J. E., & Best, D. L. (1990). *Measuring sex stereotypes: A multination study*. Thousand Oaks, CA: Sage Publications.

PART 2

The Construction of Masculinity

6

"WHERE THE BOYS ARE"

Macro and Micro Considerations for the Study of Young Latino Men's Educational Achievement

Aída Hurtado
Craig W. Haney
José G. Hurtado

In 2008 the American Association of University Women (AAUW) published its long-awaited report, "Where the girls are: The facts about gender equity in education" (Corbett et al., 2008). The report addressed the results of studies done in conjunction with a research agenda that had been established in the organization's 1992 landmark study, "The AAUW Report: How schools shortchange girls." The earlier report had sparked a national debate on gender equity in education, and the more recent publication presented updated, empirical analyses on a range of inter-related topics, including "school climate and sexual harassment, girls in science and technology, race and gender on campus" (p. xi). Although the recent report identified a number of obstacles that girls still face in the educational system, it also documented the ways that many of the research-based policy recommendations had been implemented over the years and the educational achievement of girls and women facilitated as a result.

In the same report, however, a new and important educational "crisis" was identified. The report noted that the successful implementation of many of the policy recommendations that the AAUW had helped to generate over the past decade and a half had led to an unexpected turn of events—one in which certain boys, not girls, could be "cast as the disadvantaged gender" (p. xi). Although it was clear that the overall educational achievement of girls *and* boys had improved dramatically as compared to nearly a generation ago, these overall improvements masked large disparities that existed on the basis of "race/ethnicity and family income level" (p. 4). Thus, the current crisis is "not specific to boys; rather, it is a crisis for African American, Hispanic and low-income children"

(Corbett et al., 2008, p. 4). Furthermore, the authors concluded that the inequalities that they had identified were both pressing and "longstanding."

With the AAUW analysis as a backdrop, we examine some dimensions of the educational inequality crisis, focusing on one subset of students who we believe are very seriously affected—young Latino men. Of course, the plight of young Latino men in the educational system has been examined by others (e.g., Sáenz & Ponjuan, 2009). Despite the clear value of these previous discussions, our focus is on some of the issues that remain largely unanalyzed, including why—despite the important commonalities that exist between young Latino men and women (or boys and girls)—their schooling experiences are nonetheless so very different. For example, we note that both groups are likely to attend poorly funded schools, to represent the first generation in the family to enter higher education, to be raised in poverty, to share immigrant status, and so on. In many ways, these common structural positions would seem to trump the effects of gender differences; but they do not. As we suggest here, each group both experiences and manifests the effects of the structural disadvantages to which they have been exposed in different ways that help to explain their differences in educational achievement. We argue that certain important differences in their life experiences and socialization histories help to account for their different levels of overall educational achievement.

From the theoretical perspective of intersectionality, there are certain dimensions or "axes" of difference in society that have special political, social, and economic implications. These axes traditionally include the social categorizations of race, class, sexuality, gender, and ethnicity (Collins, 2000; Hurtado, 1996). These particular social identities are part of the process of social categorization that is used by core societal institutions to allocate power and privilege. As such, these categorizations, and the social identities they produce, have enormous consequences for the members of the groups to whom they are applied. Therefore, they are critically important to take into account in interpreting research results where within-group differences might otherwise be masked or ignored.

Intersectionality allows us to understand why, although men in general may benefit in a number of ways from their masculinity and its accompanying male privilege, there are other dimensions of difference that men of Color encounter that complicate this generalization. Indeed, even within the larger category of men of Color, or Latino men in particular, there are diverse social categorizations and resulting social identities and life experiences that relate to differences along dimensions as phenotype, class, and sexuality (Hurtado & Sinha, 2008). For example, working class Latinos are more likely to experience harassment by the police and to have male friends and relatives who are in the criminal justice system (ibid).

In any event, in this chapter we use intersectionality to focus on the ways in which the social categorizations, social identities, and life experiences of young Latino men differ from those of young Latinas and help to explain the differences in educational outcomes between them. We suggest that the level of educational performance of Latinos can only be understood as a function of the multiplicity of powerful macro and micro forces that impinge on them over their life course.

Macro Forces at Work on Micro Experiences

To be sure, existing ethnic and racial group gender differences in educational achievement must be understood in the context of severe and persistent structural inequalities. Among Latinos, differences in educational achievement between girls and boys—including higher college graduation rates of girls—clearly do exist throughout the educational pipeline, as they do for African Americans, at an even more disproportionate level (Sáenz & Ponjuan, 2009). Some of these differences may be explained by recent historical developments and the different life experiences those events have produced for young Latino men and women. Most importantly, perhaps, the feminist revolution that occurred over the past several decades sought and achieved greater educational equity for girls in general. Even though many of the gender equity programs were designed primarily for White women, they brought about positive change for Latinas as well (Corbett et al., 2008). Primarily because White men did not seem to need a social and legal movement to enhance their already structurally privileged position, no comparable movement arose over the same time period from which Latino men could indirectly benefit. But there are other powerful forces at work as well.

We would argue that no meaningful analysis of educational achievement among Latino men can ignore the impact and influence of the criminal justice system. Unfortunately, the educational pipeline for young Latinos is closely interconnected with the prison pipeline; this interconnection is essential to understanding the educational trajectory of young Latino men. For one, the construction of educational institutions and funding for educational programs has been curtailed while correctional budgets have ballooned. States such as California appear to have consciously chosen to invest in prisons at the expense of schools, and to privilege policies on incarceration over education for many students of Color. Young Latino men are especially vulnerable to this ever-expanding reach of the criminal justice system. Among other things, young Latino men are more likely than their White counterparts to be placed under suspicion and surveillance in the public arena, and they report harassment by the police, even on college campuses where they are academically successful (Figueroa & Garcia, 2006). Moreover, because the behavior of young Latino men is typically viewed through a harsher criminal justice lens, the climate of suspicion and harassment to which they are subjected can have especially severe consequences. Thus, we know that behaviors that are ordinarily not criminalized among White middle-class youth result in arrest and incarceration for young Latinos (Fine et al., 2003). In addition, if and when they are labeled as "troublesome," young Latino men typically lack the family resources and "connections" to buffer them from potentially damaging justice system outcomes.

In fact, the overrepresentation of men of Color in penal institutions is so widespread that it has given rise to an acronym among corrections professionals — *disproportionate minority confinement (DMC)*—denoting the degree to which Latinos and African American youth greatly outnumber their White counterparts in juvenile justice facilities (Leiber, 2002). Criminal justice interventions that remove children from their families, schools, and neighborhoods are disruptive and potentially damaging to adolescent development; they may permanently impede a child's ability to acquire the educational and other life skills that he will need to succeed as an adult. Despite the criminogenic or crime-producing effects of incarceration—especially for young people—few if any efforts are made to ease the transition back to school or otherwise ensure their successful reintegration into free society.

The disruptive effect of justice system intervention on social and educational development, the poor quality of education typically received in juvenile justice institutions, and the lack of effective services to assist with reintegration all combine to dramatically increase the chances that formerly incarcerated juveniles will fail in school and beyond. The operation of these macro forces—the differential pull of the criminal justice system that results in disproportionate minority confinement and all of its potentially harmful effects—has micro consequences for the day-to-day lives of young Latino men that also need to be explained and understood. Indeed, as we have suggested, the only meaningful way to account for the life trajectories of young Latino men is to consider the interacting and compounding effects of the macro and micro forces that are at work (Hurtado & Sinha, 2005; 2006; 2008; 2012a; 2012b).

The Social Psychological Aspects of "Prisonization"

Juvenile and adult incarceration is a potentially life-altering experience that can have socially stigmatizing and structurally marginalizing consequences, undermining a person's chance for educational and occupational success. But the experience also has psychological consequences that can exacerbate these negative effects. Disproportionate minority confinement means that young Latino men are at greater risk of suffering these negative effects at structural, social, and psychological levels. As Haney (2003) has suggested, although much of the research on the negative consequences of incarceration has focused on "the most extreme or clinically diagnosable effects of imprisonment," there are "broader and subtler psychological changes that occur in the routine course of adapting to prison life" (p. 38). Specifically, the process of institutionalization—called "prisonization" when it occurs in correctional settings—is the shorthand expression for "a unique set of psychological adaptations that typically occur—in varying degrees—in response to the extraordinary demands of prison. In general terms, the process of prisonization involves the incorporation of the norms of prison life into one's habits of thinking, feeling, and acting" (Haney, 2003, p. 38,).

It is important to emphasize that the changes that prisonization brings about are natural and normal adaptations that occur in response to the unnatural and abnormal conditions of prison life. They become dysfunctional when they are taken to extremes, or when they become chronic and so deeply internalized that they persist even though surrounding conditions have changed (such as upon release from prison). These adaptations are not pathological in any traditional sense (that is, they do not derive from some defective trait in the persons who manifest them), but they can become severely problematic, even destructive.

The normal reactions to the abnormal treatment that prisonization brings about are experienced by the great majority of people who are incarcerated, albeit in varying degrees that relate to their personal resiliency, family and social support, and the nature and length of their prison confinement. However, most people—no matter their pre-existing level of mental health—are hard pressed to avoid at least some of the symptoms of prisonization if they are subjected to the typically dehumanizing practices and deprived conditions that prevail in our juvenile detention centers, jails, and prisons.

Haney (2003, 2006) has summarized the psychological consequences of the prisonization process. They include several distinct kinds of changes, all brought about by the need to accommodate to the harsh realities of prison life. Specifically:

1. Dependence on institutional structures and contingencies. Total institutions such as juvenile facilities and adult prisons force inmates to adapt to rigid institutional structures and regimens and to conform their conduct to whatever procedures and mandates are routinely enforced. They require inmates to obey an elaborate and encompassing set of rules and regulations that govern even the most mundane and minute aspects of their behavior. Because inmates are typically under very careful and nearly constant surveillance, violations are often identified quickly and, depending on the nature of the transgression, may be punished severely. Over time, inmates become dependent on the structure of the institution to regulate their behavior and correspondingly less capable of exercising autonomy or developing internal controls of their own. All other things being equal, the younger inmates are when they are first exposed to the prisonization process and the longer they experience it, the more chronic their dependency becomes and the more difficult it is to relinquish it upon release.

2. Hypervigilance, inter-personal distrust, and suspicion. Juvenile and adult correctional institutions can be frightening, dangerous places. In fact, for many inmates, they represent a form of "retraumatization"—immersion in an authoritarian, abusive, and largely uncaring setting that is psychologically reminiscent of experiences that they had earlier in their lives. Whether these dynamics are familiar or not, inmates frequently engage in a variety of psychological and physical defenses to avoid victimization. Juvenile and adult inmates quickly learn to carefully monitor their surroundings for signs of danger; hypervigilance becomes immediate and instinctive. Inmates learn to be wary of inter-personal closeness and to substitute suspicion for trust. Empathy, cooperation, love, and friendship are rare commodities in total institutions because they are perceived as jeopardizing survival. Obviously, this kind of hypervigilance and distrust can impede the formation of authentic relationships and intimate bonds once inmates re-enter the larger society.

3. *Emotional overcontrol, alienation, and psychological distancing.* Because outward signs of vulnerability or weakness in juvenile and adult prisons invite exploitation, inmates learn to suppress them. Many prisoners struggle to control their own internal reactions and to express only carefully measured emotional responses to facilitate the shaping of an outward image of tough invulnerability. Yet, "prisoners who labor at both an emotional and behavioral level to develop a 'prison mask' that is unrevealing and impenetrable risk alienation from themselves and others" (Haney, 2003, p. 42). The emotional flatness that often results can become chronic and debilitating in social interactions and intimate relationships in the world outside the institution, even though it may be a highly "functional" behavior inside.

4. *Social withdrawal and isolation.* Many inmates survive incarceration by creating their own psychological safe havens and withdrawing from the environment around them. Some accomplish this through social invisibility, by becoming as inconspicuous and unobtrusively disconnected as possible from the people and events around them. This self-imposed social withdrawal can lead to an isolated post-prison life of quiet desperation and, psychologically, to chronic apathy, hopelessness, and clinical depression.

5. *Incorporation of exploitive norms of prison culture.* Life inside juvenile and adult prisons is governed by an unwritten prisoner culture or code. Prisoners have their own set of elaborate rules and norms. Like the formal rules of the institution, prisoners must obey them or risk severe sanctions. Inmates learn to revere toughness, to safeguard their reputations, and to demand "respect" at all costs. Even seemingly insignificant insults, affronts, or signs of disrespect are responded to quickly and instinctively, sometimes with decisive (even deadly) force. In some contexts, the failure to exploit weakness is itself a sign of weakness and seen as an invitation for exploitation. Persons who internalize too many of these values and perspective are likely to encounter serious difficulties when they are released. The tough convict veneer can prevent them from seeking appropriate help for a range of problems with which they may re-enter society, and a learned tendency to strike out at others in response to minimal provocation—the sort of reaction that is not only tolerated but expected in prison—is highly dysfunctional in these other settings and may even ensure re-institutionalization.

6. *Diminished sense of self-worth and personal value.* Inmates frequently live under dehumanized and deprived conditions, and feel infantilized and degraded by the treatment they receive at the hands of their captors. Their sense of self-worth or value often diminishes as a result. They may internalize the symbolic meaning of their externally imposed treatment, coming to think of themselves as

"deserving" of the degradation and stigma to which they have been subjected. They may carry this internalized self-image with them when they are released.

Many aspects of the prisonization process represent the antithesis of developing what psychologists have called "self-efficacy." As defined by Bandura (1995), self-efficacy is "the belief in one's capabilities to organize and execute the courses of action required to manage prospective situations" (p. 2). Persons who are high in self-efficacy believe in their ability to succeed in many different situations, and, perhaps not surprisingly, this belief is significantly related to success and achievement in a range of settings. Prisonization undermines self-efficacy by teaching inmates to relinquish control to more powerful (and seemingly arbitrary) forces, to do so unquestioningly, and with respect to nearly every decision one might make on a daily basis (when, where, and how to eat, sleep, shower, and so on). In fact, in extreme cases, prisonization may not only suppress self-efficacy but even push inmates close to a state of "learned helplessness" (Seligman, 1975), where they are unable to engage in affirmative decision-making and initiating action on their own, and avoid situations where these assertions are called for because they experience them as painful and anxiety provoking.

The increasing exposure of young Latino men to the process of prisonization and the undermining of self-efficacy that it can bring about may help to explain the emergence of an alternative meta-ethos in many Latino communities. Institutional experiences that deplete self-efficacy and instill learned helplessness can lead inmates to narrow their social worlds when they are released, in an attempt to avoid anxiety-arousing situations where they are expected to perform. Previously incarcerated persons are often reluctant or unwilling to venture outside comfortable and familiar surroundings, and this means that they are unlikely to participate in educational settings that encourage and reward exploration, freedom, and intellectual risk-taking. They may become dependent on others to navigate these unfamiliar worlds on their behalf. For example, Valenzuela (1999) reported that young Chicanas in high school were more likely to deal with teachers and the principals to advocate on behalf of their "guys." They had sufficient self-efficacy not only to do their own schoolwork but their boyfriend's as well. In addition, they would "supervise" the comings and goings of their guys and negotiate their status with school authorities. In contrast, the young Chicano men were erratic in their school attendance and could not focus enough to accomplish the minimum requirements to survive in high school. Instead, many young Chicanos hid behind the hypermasculine pose of detachment, silence, and withdrawal that is functional in prison but that obviates any real engagement or investment in their schoolwork. The women in their lives negotiated these young men's survival while they remained more or less aloof.

Prisonization may lead to passivity in some settings, but it can lead to the mobilization of different kinds of problematic responses in others. As we noted above, the obsession with danger, insult, and affront, and the corresponding projection of an outward demeanor of invulnerability in prison, can lead to an exaggerated performance of some of masculinity's most negative traits—quick and forceful reactions to challenges of any kind, a hypersensitivity to even insignificant affronts, and an extreme investment in the appearance of control and "cool" detachment. However useful these survival strategies are in confinement, they are dysfunctional and counterproductive in the larger society, especially in settings where cooperation, trust, and affability are at a premium. Moreover, minor forms of aggression that may be tolerated by authorities in prison as expected forms of "mutual combat," or go unreported entirely because of the prohibition against snitching, precipitate entirely different and much more consequential responses from law enforcement officials in the free world. Ex-inmates who attempt to forcefully resolve disputes or protect their "reputations" by resorting to violence—habits they learned in prison—quickly find themselves re-institutionalized.

Notwithstanding the posturing about reputation and the air of invulnerability ex-convicts may project, they face a number of daunting social and structural obstacles that can exacerbate their pre-existing feelings of personal insecurity, doubts about self-worth, and hopes for any future success. Young men of Color suffer especially high unemployment rates that the stigma of incarceration and lack of effective educational and job training in prison only worsen. These bleak economic prospects can create a sense of helplessness and further undermine self-efficacy. In these ways, the process of prisonization may simultaneously exaggerate some of the worst outward aspects of male privilege for young men of Color, undermine their ability to effectively compete or achieve in the world outside prison, and make it difficult if not impossible for them to articulate (let alone seek help to overcome) their social and structural vulnerabilities.

Development of a "Carceral Consciousness"

Because mass imprisonment has swelled the prison system in the United States, each year literally hundreds of thousands of persons are released and returned to the communities where they once lived. As Haney (2003) pointed out:

> In the first decade of the 21st century, more people have been subjected to the pains of imprisonment for longer periods and under conditions that threaten greater psychological distress and potential long-term dysfunction. They will be returned to communities already disadvantaged by a badly frayed "safety net," and they will sorely need social services and supportive resources that their neighborhoods unfortunately will be often unable to provide.
>
> (p. 37)

Given the high rates of incarceration, it is now common for extended working-class Latino families to have at least one member confined in a juvenile or adult jail or prison. Many of these inmates will return home burdened with both the social stigma and psychological after-effects of their institutional experiences. Family members are often unaware of the challenges that their loved ones will face in trying to reintegrate into society and turn their life trajectories around. Often the personal and economic resources of the families are already stretched thin, as are those of the low-income communities in which they live. Many times, the family and the community are ill-equipped to assist in these transitions.

Although there is a stark gender difference among Latinas' direct exposure to the inner workings of the criminal justice system, it is important to recognize that they nonetheless grapple with its consequences. In effect, the state has decided that women are not as dangerous as men: they earn less, they are victimized more, and they do most of the emotional and social reproductive labor necessary for society to survive (women head most single households with children). Yet Latina women absorb many of the consequences of the increased incarceration and state surveillance of Latino men. Latino men returning to their communities after stints in juvenile detention halls, jails, and prisons rarely receive social or other governmental services designed to undo or ameliorate the effects of prisonization. Instead, their families—primarily the women in their families—are called upon to fill this void.

In these ways, Latino family members—even those who have not themselves been incarcerated—feel the pains of imprisonment and struggle to overcome its aftermaths. They also must remain hypervigilant against the ever-present threat of violence—violence administered at the hands of the state, seemingly without rhyme or reason, despite their best efforts at keeping it at bay, and the violence that plagues their surrounding communities. Indeed, some of the same dynamics that characterize prison life are lived not only inside the walls of total institutions but also in many poor and disenfranchised Latino communities.

There is another way in which the dynamics of prison life may spread into the communities where many young men of Color now grow up. Haney (2008) has argued that the massive increases in the "prison industrial complex" and the corresponding growth of correctional influence in social and political arenas have insinuated a criminal justice mindset—a kind of "carceral consciousness" —into the way many people think about themselves and others. The carceral consciousness has drawn increasing numbers of people into vicarious and direct participation in the crime and punishment process, such that punitive, prison-like norms, practices, and points of view have become increasingly merged with the everyday life of the larger society.

Referring primarily to African American communities but in terms that apply to Latinos as well, Dorothy Roberts (2004) has written about the increasing "normalization of prison in community life," and the way that mass incarceration has affected social norms so that prison has become "part of the socialization process" for many children (p. 1288). Haney (2008) has argued further that this consciousness has affected citizens more generally so that they are expected to, and increasingly do, "operate to some degree as extensions of the state," such that "their obligations have moved from caring to carceral—to increasingly scrutinizing, categorizing, and judging each other's behavior along largely legalistic or, more accurately, 'correctional' dimensions" (p. 135). The application of this carceral mentality is triggered by the perception of "difference"—something that is largely determined by race, class, ethnicity, sexuality, and gender. The emergence of this carceral consciousness is thus particularly problematic for persons of Color, whom White society continues to reflexively perceive and judge as problematic and potentially threatening "others."

Young men of Color are not only more likely to be categorized as deviant others through the lens of this carceral consciousness but also to be seen by the larger society as deserving of criminal justice-like sanctions. They are also more likely to be policed by the state, which is poised to intervene at the slightest indication of criminal behavior, sometimes turning the presumption of innocence on its head so that criminality is often assumed and innocence must be demonstrated or proven, increasingly including "prisonized" inner-city public schools where "zero tolerance" policies criminalize their behavior and newly installed security hardware and procedures subject them "to scrutiny by armed police, dogs, or metal detectors" (Hirschfield, 2008, p. 80). In these ways, the emerging carceral mentality produces a seamless continuation of the norms and dynamics of prison life into communities of Color themselves.

The Self as Mirror for Social Conditions: Micro Forces at Work

Individuals make sense of who they are in relation to those around them and from the social context in which they live (Cooley, 1902). If the state and its representatives (teachers, principals, counselors, and police) treat Latino boys and young men as if they are criminals, what is to prevent them from internalizing the implication of this message? If they have a family member in prison—as many do—what genealogical or even biological inference are they likely to draw? How many begin to fear, or assume, that they have inherited a "criminal gene," one that foretells their destiny? Does the fact that so many members of their community are incarcerated suggest to young Latino men that their entire ethnic group is biologically predisposed to crime? Will the sibling of an incarcerated young Latino assume that it is his freely chosen good choices—and his brother's bad ones—that account for their different outcomes in life, and is this assumption likely to create tension or distance between them? Should he police himself by repeating the messages of the carceral mentality: "do the right thing, obey the rules, do not stray, be hypervigilant, stay at home, do not venture out into the public sphere after certain hours, avoid 'bad people,' become like the guards and impose the rules on others."

The supposed reward for the internalization of the carceral mentality is that the individual will increase his chances of avoiding incarceration. According to the dominant narrative, those who violate these rules are the ones who should rightfully be labeled as deviants. The dynamics of the carceral mentality tear many Latino families apart, and oddly enough, mostly along gender lines—it is the girls (and young women) as a group who comply and the boys (and young men) who succumb. It is a perfect social system that has become normative, blaming poor, disenfranchised Latino men for their own conditions while simultaneously blaming the women in the same communities for being too "perfect," too "feminist," too "disciplined," to the ultimate disadvantage of the men. Under these persistent "dispositional attributions" (Haney & Zimbardo, 2009), the system remains innocent of any structural machinations at the same time that it achieves perfect control over its most vulnerable citizens.

Fortunately, in addition to the growing body of work that analyzes many of the macro forces that pull young men of Color generally, and young Latinos specifically, into the criminal justice system, there is new research examining the micro forces that operate to undermine young Latinos in educational settings. For example, in the "Latino Masculinities Study" (on which we rely heavily in the pages that follow), Hurtado and Sinha (2005) interviewed a non-representative sample of over 100 respondents from five southwestern states—California, Colorado, New Mexico, Texas, and Arizona—as well as in Illinois, Massachusetts, Michigan, New York, and Washington, DC—about a variety of topics, paralleling the design of an earlier study conducted with a similar sample of young Chicanas (Hurtado, 2003). Hurtado and Sinha (2005) identified several micro forces that negatively affected young Latino men, in addition to the more macro, public vulnerabilities described above. In particular, they learned that Latino families often pushed sons into premature independence, many times with little guidance or family supervision. An early independence from curfews and strictly enforced rules is often conceptualized as male privilege, but many respondents in the study expressed confusion and loneliness from the unguided freedom their families granted them. Unlike the women in their families, especially the respondents' sisters, who were subjected to restrictions, the young men were allowed many freedoms that they may have been ill-prepared to handle. Furthermore, young Latino men often belonged to peer cultures that pushed them in directions, especially sexual experiences, that they were not ready for or emotionally mature enough to manage (Hurtado & Sinha, 2005).

Latino families are deeply aware of their sons' public harassment by the agents of the state and of their potential vulnerability to violence and death. The terror of losing their sons may lead to overindulgence in the intimacy of family relationships; a "boys will be boys" mentality may prevail, in which they are allowed to dominate the household with no requirements or rules as possible compensation for the extreme surveillance they suffer in public spaces (Hurtado, 2003). From the perspective of poor Latino families, if they cannot protect their boys from violence and death, at least they can comfort them and even pamper them within the home—a dynamic especially salient in female-headed households.

The Police and Microaggressions

There is a variation of the carceral mentality that is enforced at the micro level of day-to-day social interactions and this has been termed "microaggressions." According to Pierce (1995), microaggressions are defined as

> subtle, innocuous, preconscious, or unconscious degradations, and putdowns, often kinetic but capable of being verbal and/or kinetic. In and of itself a micro-aggression may seem harmless, but the cumulative burden of a lifetime of microaggressions can theoretically contribute to diminished mortality, augmented morbidity, and flattened confidence. . . . [They are] probably the most grievous of offensive mechanisms spewed at victims of racism and sexism.
>
> (Pierce, 1995, as cited in Yosso et al., 2009)

The impact of microaggressions is intensified among the very large numbers of Latino men who have had direct experience with the criminal justice system. Microaggressions by representatives of the criminal justice system are one of the most common and efficient methods of spreading the carceral mentality among young Latino men; they fuse many of the adaptations required to survive prison life with the adaptations that must be made to live in vulnerable, poor communities of Color.

In the Latino Masculinities Study, all of the 105 respondents were educationally high achievers. Given the high dropout rates that characterized the communities from which they came—in some predominantly Latino high schools, the graduation rates for young Latino men are below 50 percent—the respondents' status as college students or graduates was an especially noteworthy achievement. They represent the young Latino educational elite. However, even among this select group of men, two-thirds (66 percent; n = 69) reported being harassed by the police. Obviously their educational achievement did not protect them from the enforcement of the carceral norms at the hands of the police.

Although many White citizens regard police harassment as rare, and witness only its most extreme examples (such as the brutal beating of Rodney King), it is less overt, and less visible, yet far more frequent in communities of Color, taking the form of police microaggressions, if you will. And so it was for the respondents in the study, who had learned to expect that harassment by the authorities might occur but not to talk about it when it did. The effects are undoubtedly cumulative but admittedly not easily measured. For example, one of the respondents, Nicholas, a 23-year-old from Texas who had attended college and was working at a natural history museum in San Antonio at the time of the interview, described his relationship with the police as follows:

I have been harassed more times than I can remember. As an adolescent I was an easy target (being both brown and young). . . . One tender recollection would be in San Antonio, after a 12 AM curfew, when I was pulled over with a group of friends. Two police cars [stopped us] later we were all standing (hands against the cars) and being thoroughly searched. My friendly officer thought he would amuse himself by tickling my nuts as he dug his hands into my pockets. He then gathered with the other cops as we waited (hands against the cars) forever for them to laugh about the whole thing. I don't know if anybody else was violated as such. I never asked.

Young men like Nicholas have few if any opportunities to even reflect on or discuss these transgressions. Although Nicholas obviously did not forget the incident, and could recount it in detail, he had no way of knowing whether it had a traumatic effect on him or how it might have influenced his reactions and emotions in subsequent, similar situations. There was (and is) no forum for victims of these microaggressions to explore the significance of these personal experiences. Indeed, there is no emotional discourse with which to label them, and no intellectual or therapeutic framework to assess and work through their consequences. Unlike the feminist movement that gave women a framework and discourse through which to understand and process the microaggressions to which they were subjected—sexual harassment, date rape, and sexism—there is no parallel set of concepts available to men of Color to legitimize and sensitize them to their vulnerabilities; whatever their injuries, they are largely suffered in silence and remain invisible.

Moreover, respondents in the study reported that there appeared to be very little they could do to protect themselves from microaggressions that were committed by the police. For example, Peter, a 20-year-old junior majoring in English at a college in Boston recalled being stopped by a policeman while driving with a group of friends from several prominent schools, including Tufts, Harvard, and Northeastern: "we were stopped and harassed. My boy had a broken tail light but the officer kept asking us where we were going, where were we coming from, what were we going to do, do we have anything in the car? I felt violated, I couldn't even speak." He thought that because he and his friends were college students from distinguished universities, the police would take a different approach. Similarly, Joseph, a 20-year-old junior from another distinguished Boston college, was stopped and asked to step out of his car in upstate New York. After he showed the state trooper his MIT student identification, the officer "refused to believe [he] went to school there and continued to badger [him] with stupid questions." Many young men like Peter and Joseph have acknowledged that, even though they have overcome the daunting educational and structural barriers placed in their way, arriving at the pinnacles of higher education, they are still vulnerable and helpless at the hands of a suspicious and distrustful criminal justice system, one that reflexively questions their credibility and calls their value and legitimacy into question.

Young Latino men also know that they are subject to having their appearance and behavior interpreted through the prevailing dominant narrative, poised to see them as potential gang members on the verge of committing gang-related crimes. As Eduardo, a 20-year-old junior at a California university, related:

> I have been pulled over numerous times because of my skin color and because I was bald. I have also been stopped, questioned, and searched while waiting for a bus. If you are brown, bald, and have a large jacket with baggy jeans you are labeled a gang member. I was suspected of this and searched for drugs.

Clothing, hairstyle, and skin color register as social signifiers of the gang meta-identity. Any overt display of these characteristics places young Latino men at risk of state harassment. However, even when these signifiers are muted, harassment still takes place. For example, Jesse, a 31-year-old college graduate who was working in an educational center at a California university at the time of the study, stated that when he was in high school,

> a group of friends and I were followed, pulled over and made to exit my friends' vehicle at gunpoint because we fit the profile of "gang members." We had just left campus to go and eat lunch and we were wearing our black football jerseys or lettermen jackets.

Again, what would otherwise be taken as official markers of belonging and success—lettermen jackets, an MIT identification card—earned no credibility from law enforcement. The brown skin of these young men served as a more powerful marker that attracted police attention and harassment.

The young men were often surprised at the emotion they felt as they relived the incidents they described in these interviews. Even though the specific incidents they recounted represented many similar ones that they had suffered, most also acknowledged that they had never told anyone about them before. There was a quality of subtle prisonization to these particular microaggressions; despite their status in the larger world, these young men were being taught (or re-taught) the dynamics of domination—the need to manifest unquestioning compliance, to guard against the ever-present possibility of unpredictable danger and victimization, and to suffer degradation and humiliation without complaint. Just as in prison, the social category to which these students belonged—in this case, young men of Color—represented their personhood and precipitated their mistreatment. Here, too, the social process by which these transgressions unfolded went unnamed, unacknowledged, and suffered without redress and with uncertain long-term consequences.

Indeed, these macro and micro social processes converge to create multiple vulnerabilities in young Latinos who often have very few material or emotional resources to navigate a smooth transition from adolescence to young adulthood. The natural *sturm und drang* that ordinarily characterizes this life stage is further complicated, amplified, and exacerbated for young Latinos because this is also the age when they are likely to be arrested and enter the destabilizing and potentially disabling criminal justice system. Between the ages of 13 and 22 years, when wise supervision and supportive guidance are most important—exactly the period when these boys-becoming-men are pulled by macro forces into the public arena and pushed by their families toward greater independence—the criminal justice system most often takes over. We know that those who can stay just beyond its grasp until they reach the age of 25 are likely to remain out of prison for the rest of their lives. But this is becoming an increasingly difficult feat to manage.

The combination of prisonization during incarceration, the carceral forces that operate in the larger society, and the targeted microaggressions to which Latino youth are subjected produce a kind of perfect storm of destructive influences that spread through neighborhoods and communities. There are few safe spaces where young men of Color can explore becoming full human beings possessing all of the vulnerabilities, hope, love, trust, and openness that the journey entails.

Implications for Education and Social Policy

Because the forces that adversely affect Latinos' educational achievement operate at both the macro and micro levels, the interventions designed to improve their educational success should target both levels as well. At the macro level, it is essential that social policies address the quality of education that young Latinos receive in their predominantly working-class neighborhoods. Geoffrey Canada's work exemplifies this macro approach (Tough, 2008). Canada grew up in the South Bronx and received his BA from Bowdoin College and Master's from the Harvard School of Education. Since 1990, he has been president of the Harlem Children's Zone, an organization that serves over 17,000 children in a nearly 100-block radius in Central Harlem. His model of intervention is implemented at key organizations within the neighborhoods on behalf of families and children living there. Canada's approach is to offer not only enhanced educational services but also a range of social service and community-building programs to children and families. The goal is to provide a healthy and safe environment for students and their families so that the enriched educational experiences they have in the classroom are not compromised or threatened by larger forces over which the children and teacher have no control.

Another important macro-level intervention reduces the harmful impact of the criminal justice system on young Latinos by minimizing their contact with it and ameliorating its negative consequences for those who are drawn in. In addition, inner-city schools that now resemble prisons—and there are more of these than ever in the nation's history (Schnyder, 2010)—must be restructured and restored to their original educational purpose and design. The criminalization of school discipline in which truancy is the first step in a fast-moving process that results in juvenile justice institutionalization must be reversed (Losen & Skiba, 2010).

Protection and Recovery—Minimizing and Exorcising the Pain

We have emphasized the various ways in which macro and micro social forces intersect and interact on a day-to-day basis to profoundly affect the life courses of the young men of Color who are exposed to them. Over time, these forces accumulate to influence whether and how young men of Color succeed in the classroom and beyond, reflecting the consequences of what, in another context, Haney (2004) has termed "biographical racism." Programs that effectively respond to this accumulation of forces are regrettably few in number. We believe that if and when they are devised, they must operate to both protect young students of Color as much as possible from the forces we have described and provide them with opportunities and services that facilitate their recovering from the traumas that they have experienced.

Social interventions that would protect young persons of Color from these pernicious forces are, of course, fundamentally different from therapeutic interventions that would facilitate their healing. As demonstrated in Canada's work in Harlem (Tough, 2008), restructuring the social environment and providing social guidance through programs designed to affect larger groups of people need not include individual-level counseling or treatment. However, there should also be room to develop micro interventions designed to enhance individual lives that are essentially social—rather than purely therapeutic—in nature. Here we propose to combine Canada's notion of geographical zones of interventions with Fine and her colleagues' notion of "safe spaces," which are intended as "pockets of possibility" (Fine & Weis, 1998, p. 275). For youth, structures such as neighborhood organizations can serve as urban sanctuaries (McLaughlin et al., 1994), offering temporary relief from gangs, drugs, violence, and poverty. Youth who enter these safe spaces receive both the encouragement and the structure necessary to confront the challenges many of them encounter daily in the poor urban communities where they live. Designed by and for community members, safe spaces offer opportunities for recuperation and resistance, places where groups can begin to imagine and organize for "what could be" (Fine & Weis, 1998, p. 243). In addition, safe spaces offer young people a place to "preserve their cultural connectedness, resist prevailing racism and sexism, and collectively transform the obstacles to their growth" (Pastor et al., 1996).

In fact, we would urge expanding the geographical reach of the safe space to a larger "safety zone." Young Latino men's personal lives are connected to the public realm in such a way that the concept of zones of safety more accurately captures the link between the personal display of masculinity and a constant vigilance of how the display is evaluated by the public. The masculine codes of conduct are a major hurdle to be addressed in scaffolding interventions to engage young Latino men (and men in general) in educational activities. Because the display of masculinity has a very important and crucial public component, larger zones of safety are needed to allow youths to display and expose vulnerabilities in the public sphere, without fear of ridicule, retribution, or harm.

Furthermore, because so many men of Color are under active surveillance by the state, especially by law enforcement and the criminal justice system, we believe this issue needs to be confronted directly. Such an intervention would include bringing microaggressions at the hands of the police into public and community view, both as a topic of in-depth scholarly analysis and political debate. We need to develop a much better understanding of what targeted surveillance and associated microaggressions, as well as prisonization, do to the psyches of Latino youth. Young men of Color need to learn avenues for redress—where and how to seek help for the potential symptoms that accompany prisonization, how to resist the microaggressions to which they are subjected in the community, and what kind of redress is available to them if and when they are victimized by law enforcement.

Note, for example, the progress that has been made on a set of roughly parallel issues for women, made possible in large part by the women's movement itself. Nowadays, in most of the country, if young women are sexually harassed in school or the workplace, there are designated officials who can help them report the incident and a forum in which to pursue their grievance. Organizations may be held legally (and sometimes financially) accountable for failing to prevent the incident. Perpetrators can be, and often are, sanctioned, and the victims of sexual harassment have avenues of redress, including seeking damages and obtaining counseling in the aftermath of their victimization. Moreover, pro-active steps are typically taken now—posters displayed in visible settings, pamphlets widely distributed, training sessions provided, and so on—to ensure that women know their rights in these circumstances and have adequate knowledge and assistance with which to pursue them. These public notices have heightened awareness and also serve as a deterrent to perpetrators.

In the Meantime: Counseling Safe Zones for Young Men

Canada's innovative and impressive approach in Harlem notwithstanding, the creation of these alternative social and education protective structures remains aspirational in most communities. In the meantime, traditional direct service and even therapeutic programs can be made more responsive to the needs of young people of Color. The realities of biographical racism in many communities ensure that countless young persons enter adolescence scarred by early traumatic lives and uncaring institutional responses. Far too many of them are in need of direct help, and have only existing social service agencies to which to turn. Child Protective Services (as they are called in California) or other similar agencies in other communities are (and will be in the foreseeable future) called upon to address the needs of many young persons of Color, many of whom suffer from unaddressed problems and issues, sometimes ones that were neglected, ignored, or overlooked by their families of origin, and frequently having been unsuccessfully placed in foster homes or even juvenile justice system institutions.

Social workers on the "front lines" of these cases continue to directly engage clients whose pressing practical problems need to be solved in order to prepare them for their eventual "freedom" and adult life. They must overcome their clients' suspicion and alienation by breaking down barriers by devising kind and creative ways to connect with them, providing assistance and guidance as well as consistent, caring attention. The best ones encourage their clients to acknowledge their vulnerabilities and fears, and facilitate the development of an outlook that is both empowered and realistic as they near their eventual "emancipation." The counseling process in these settings is fraught with uncertainty, and positive outcomes are by no means assured. Ideally, social workers in these settings are able to build on their clients' pre-existing, positive interests and encourage them to both perceive and to model "manhood" in a way that does not require the projection of an exaggerated image of competence or expertise. Young men who project a know-it-all demeanor are left alone with their own incompetencies and unaddressed vulnerabilities. As we noted earlier, there has been no social movement and few if any programs or resources to address this problem.

We know that the most effective learning takes place when people are taught manageable lessons, undertake small units of behavior or skills, receive immediate feedback, and then move on to the next, more challenging skill. Again, because most young men are reluctant to ask questions, they are often perceived as not needing help or guidance. By avoiding situations where they might be given ego-bruising feedback, they rarely get it. These socialized tendencies are part of the complex picture that must be acknowledged and addressed if this individual-level intervention is to succeed.

Young men of Color perceive themselves to be under "assault" in the larger society, and even more so in institutional settings. They are rarely socialized to listen to each other carefully or to talk openly and in-depth to one another about things that are important to them. Sensitive, authentic communication is often stereotyped as "women's work," something to be avoided by men. In the Latino Masculinities Study, many of the respondents reported hardly ever talking to their fathers. Instead, they reported talking directly to their mothers (or sisters) who, in turn, would give the father a brief summary of the conversation. Moreover, very few of the young Latino men reported having conversations with their brothers or even with male friends. Here, too, if they engaged in genuine, heartfelt communication of any kind, it occurred with the women in their lives—girlfriends, mothers, sisters, and even aunts. Counseling and therapy in this context often means assisting young male clients of Color in overcoming the difficult psychological challenge of relating in open and positive ways to other men.

Conclusion

Of course, these efforts are far from perfect and much remains to be done to improve them. However, no comparable avenues of redress exist for young men of Color who are likely to be subjected to a range of hostile and humiliating treatment at the hands of the criminal justice system in and outside its formal institutions. No similar pro-active steps have been taken in the places where this particular kind of victimization is likely to occur: none that even publicly name the problem, let alone provide a forum where it can be candidly discussed, avenues of redress through which it can be confronted or resisted, resources available so that the consequences for the young men are addressed, or meaningful legal or community-based steps taken to ensure that it is not repeated.

At the same time, we recognize that individual-level interventions like this one do little to address the macro- and micro-level problems—the structural inequalities that plague the lives of young men of Color, the disproportionate minority confinement to which they are exposed, and the greater number of microaggressions to which they are subjected at the hands of the police. It is critically important to conduct research to identify the key levers for structural change and institutional reform, and then to develop more powerful and effective interventions that reduce the pernicious effects of such transgressions on the lives of young men of Color. There is still much to be done.

References

Bandura, A. (1995). *Self-efficacy in changing societies*. New York: Cambridge University Press.

Collins, P. H. (2000). *Black feminist thought* (2nd ed.). New York: Routledge.

Cooley, C. H. (1902). *Human nature and the social order*. New York: C. Scribner's Sons.

Corbett, C., Hill, C., & St. Rose, A. (2008, May). *Where the girls are: The facts about gender equity in education*. American Association of University Women. Retrieved from www.aauw.org/learn/research/upload/whereGirlsAre.pdf.

Figueroa, J. L., & Garcia, E. (2006). Tracing institutional racism in higher education: Academic practices of Latino male undergraduates. In M. Constantine and D. W. Sue (Eds.), *Addressing racism: Facilitating cultural competence in mental health and educational settings* (195–212). Hoboken, NJ: John Wiley & Sons.

Fine, M., & Weis, L. (1998). *The unknown city*. Boston: Beacon Press.

Fine, M., Freudenberg, N., Payne, Y., Perkins, T., Smith, K., & Wanzer, K. (2003). "Anything can happen with police around": Urban youth evaluate strategies of surveillance in public places. *Journal of Social Issues*, 59(1), 141–158.

Haney, C. W. (2003). The psychological impact of incarceration: Implications for post-prison adjustment. In J. Travis & M. Waul (Eds.), *Prisoners once removed. The impact of incarceration and reentry on children, families, and communities* (33–66). Washington, DC: The Urban Institute.

Haney, C. W. (2004). Condemning the other in death penalty trials: Biographical racism, structural mitigation, and the empathic divide. *DePaul Law Review*, 53, 1557–1590.

Haney, C. W. (2006). *Reforming punishment: Psychological limits to the pains of imprisonment.* Washington, DC: APA Books.

Haney, C. W. (2008). Counting casualties in the war on prisoners. *University of San Francisco Law Review*, 43, 87–138.

Haney, C. W., & Zimbardo, P. G. (2009). Persistent dispositionalism in interactionist clothing: Fundamental attribution error in explaining prison abuse. *Personality and Social Psychology Bulletin*, 35(6), 807–814.

Hirschfield, P. (2008). Preparing for prison? The criminalization of school discipline the in the USA. *Theoretical Criminology*, 12, 79–101.

Hurtado, A. (1996). *The color of privilege: Three blasphemies on race and feminism.* Ann Arbor: University of Michigan Press.

Hurtado, A. (2003). *Voicing Chicana feminisms: Young Chicanas speak out on sexuality and feminism.* New York: New York University Press.

Hurtado, A., & Sinha, M. (2005). Restriction and freedom in the construction of sexuality: Young Chicanas and Chicanos speak out. *Feminism and Psychology*, 15(1), 33–38.

Hurtado, A., & Sinha, M. (2006). Differences and similarities: Latina and Latino doctoral students navigating the gender divide. In J. Castellanos, A. M. Gloria, & M. Kamimura (Eds.), *The Latina/o pathway to the Ph.D.: Abriendo Caminos* (149–168). Sterling, VA: Stylus.

Hurtado, A., & Sinha, M. (2008). More than men: Latino feminist masculinities and intersectionality. *Sex Roles* (special issue on "Gender: An Intersectionality Perspective"), 59 (5–6), 337–349.

Hurtado, A., & Sinha, M. (2012a). Beyond machismo: An intersectional analysis of young Latino's definitions of manhoods. Manuscript in preparation.

Hurtado, A., & Sinha, M. (2012b). Getting educated while brown: Young, educated Latinos' experiences with the criminal justice system. Manuscript in preparation.

Leiber, M. (2002). Disproportionate minority confinement of youth: An analysis of state and federal effort to address the issue. *Crime & Delinquency*, 48, 3–45.

Losen, D. J., & Skiba, R. J. (2010). *Suspended education: Urban middle schools in crisis.* Montgomery, AL: Southern Poverty Law Center.

McLaughlin, M., Irby, M., & Langman, J. (1994). *Urban sanctuaries: Neighborhood organizations in the lives and futures of inner-city youth.* San Francisco: Jossey-Bass.

Pastor, J., McCormick, J., Fine, M., & Andolson, R. (1996). Makin homes: An urban girl thing. In B. J. R. Leadbeater & N. Way (Eds.), *Urban girls: Resisting stereotypes, creating identities* (15–34). New York: New York University Press.

Roberts, D. (2004). The social and moral cost of mass incarceration in African American communities. *Stanford Law Review*, 56, 1271–1305.

Saenz, V. B., & Ponjuan, L. (2009). The vanishing Latino male in higher education. *Journal of Higher Education*, 8, 54–89. Doi:10.1177/1538192708326995

Schnyder, D. (2010). Enclosures abound: Black cultural autonomy, prison regime, and public education. *Race, Ethnicity, and Education*, 13(3), 349–365.

Seligman, M. E. P. (1975). *Helplessness: On depression, development, and death.* San Francisco: W. H. Freeman.

Tough, P. (2008). *Whatever it takes: Geoffrey Canada's quest to change Harlem and America.* New York: Houghton Mifflin.

Valenzuela, A. (1999). "Checking up on my guy": High school Chicanas, social capital, and the culture of romance. *Frontiers: A Journal of Women Studies,* 20(1), special issue on Educated Latinas Leading America.

Yosso, T., Smith, W. A., Ceja, M., & Solorzano, D. G. (2009). Critical race theory, racial microaggressions, and campus racial climate for Latina/o undergraduates. *Harvard Educational Review,* 79(4), 659–690.

7

TAKING COUNT OF GENDER AND LEGAL STATUS WITHIN LATINO MEDIA POLICY

Dolores Inés Casillas

> In a transnational world typified by the global circulation of images and sounds, goods and peoples, media spectatorship impacts complexly on national identity, communal belonging and political affiliations.
>
> (Shohat, 1997, p. 209)

> What viewers have learned is that too often Latinos are portrayed as problem people living on the fringes of U.S. society.
>
> (Frederico et al., 2005, p. 5)

Recent shifts in both telecommunications and Latino population numbers have placed an increased significance on Latino-oriented media policy (Subervi-Vélez, 1999, 2008). A number of reputable think tanks, non-profit groups, and professional organizations conduct timely research on Latino representation in English-language television programming (see National Association for Hispanic Journalists [NAHJ], Tomás Rivera Policy Institute, Center for Media and Public Affairs, and Children NOW); gauge the media use and practices of Latinos (in particular, Project of Excellence in Journalism and PEW Research Center); and ultimately attempt to counsel and apply pressure on media industries to diversify their programming as well as their production and employment opportunities (especially the National Association for Hispanic Journalists, Latino Entertainment Media Institute, National Latino Media Council, National Council for La Raza, and the National Chicano News Media Association).[1] For instance, the National Hispanic Media Coalition since 1986 has filed more than 100 petitions before the Federal Communications Commission (FCC) in a bureaucratic gesture to bring television and radio stations into compliance with Equal Employment Opportunity laws (Noriega, 2002). They also ignited national media action by spearheading a one-week Latino "brownout" or boycott of network television in 1999 in response to the grim numbers of Latinos represented on television (Wilkinson, 2003). Despite the then news media coverage of the "majority-minority" predictions for the 2000 U.S. Census, Latinos accounted for fewer than 2 percent of individuals on television, yet made up 11 percent of the U.S. population (Kolker, 1999).

That same year the National Association for the Advancement of Colored People (NAACP), equally displeased, threatened legal action against the major networks for the lack of minorities featured within primetime lineups. Jennifer Fuller (2010) argued that the NAACP campaign accentuated what communities of Color had noted for years—that highly ranked sitcoms, such as NBC's Seinfeld (1990–1998) and Friends (1994–2004), "had casts that were not only exclusively White, but seemed to live in urban spaces bereft of people of color" (p. 285).

The media as a social institution broadcast messages about race, gender, and class, often instructing audiences about these concepts. According to Otto Santa Ana (2002), the news media in particular are "undeniably powerful" and armed with a "unique access to the public ear, and nearly full control over the form of the message they disseminate" (p. 50). A survey study conducted by Dana Mastro, Elizabeth Behm-Morawitz, and Michelle Ortiz (2007) with 362 undergraduate participants found that "the relationship between the perceptions of television portrayals of Latinos and real-world evaluations of Latinos is stronger for heavier [television] viewers" (p. 357). Given this influence, television serves as a site of symbolic and political contestation (Gray, 1995). If, as Ella Shohat has claimed, media spectatorship bears influence on political and communal notions of belonging, then the framing and coverage of Latinos on network news—noted above as "problem people" in the *Network Brownout Report*—influence how Latinos are imagined as a part of the broader U.S. citizenry.

To be sure, these professional policy organizations, comprised of researchers, industry professionals and the occasional Hollywood actor, generate briefs, studies, and/or reports that are immeasurably useful to scholars of race, media, and communications. In many ways, the emerging field of Latina/o Media Studies—wherein academics survey the same media landscape with a critical, discursive eye—relies on these organizations' statistical profiles that confirm the absence and disproportionate representation of Latinos in English-language television. Participants active in Latino media policy and those engaged in academic inquiry on Latinos in and of the media regard media policy and the goal of achieving fair and equitable access as a key facet of civil rights. As Isabela Molina-Guzmán (2006) succinctly stated, "the right to communicate is one of the basic tenets necessary for political recognition within the public sphere" (p. 283).

This chapter calls for a more complex tabulation of the representations of Latinos within English-language television through an analysis of Latino media briefs known as the *Network Brownout Report* and prepared by NAHJ from 1996–2006. I argue that the *Network Brownout Report* effectively articulated the woeful absence of Latinos in the media but would clearly have benefitted by including the role of gender and legal status in its findings. The *Network Brownout Report* exemplifies the challenges involved in researching Latinos as a racial construct in isolation of gender and legal status, and beyond the related factors of phenotype, sexuality, and language. Despite the *Network Brownout Report*'s annual summations stating that Latinos are more often than not represented through news stories that deal with either immigration or crime, a substantive discussion of the perceived legal status of Latinos as well as the gender representation of Latinos remains elusive. It is not sufficient to "count" Latinos through racially codified terms; it is also critical to understand how gender and perceived legal status position Latinos as well as Latino issues. An analysis of these findings through the perspective of gender and legal status complicates the ways in which race matters in media representations of Latinos.

In this chapter, I employ Lucila Vargas's (2000) feminist concept of "newsroom processes of genderization" to argue that several of the *Network Brownout Report*'s key findings on immigration and crime reveal instances of racialized *and* gendered news coverage. Vargas (2000) argues that newsroom practices and news texts "gender social groups by imprinting markings of sex" (p. 262) through linguistic and visual practices. According to Vargas, social and ethnic groups, under advanced capitalism, are depicted as racialized and gendered subjects as a means of undermining their journalistic authority. For instance, Vargas monitored whether Latino news pieces were covered under female-identified domains, such as food or education, versus male-identified domains, politics or business. Vargas contended that these gendered techniques work to isolate and/or delegitimize Latinos' participation from the larger male body politic. In this essay, I examine press releases by NAHJ coupled with their annual *Network Brownout Reports* that disclose patterns of English-language news references to Latinos as racialized and gendered "brown masses." Ultimately, I argue for the use of a more nuanced lens that takes into account both gender and legal status and how these additional variables alter our understanding of racial representations of Latinos.

Network Brownout Report

In response to the disparate presence of Latinos and Latino news stories within the English-language media, NAHJ launched the *Network Brownout Report*, an aggressive and impressive watchdog effort monitoring and documenting Latino media representation. Between 1996 and 2006, NAHJ compiled quantitative and increasingly qualitative data on news shows from several major network sources, including *ABC World News Tonight*, *CBS Evening News*, *NBC Nightly News*, and later *CNN News Night*. These findings are readily available to the public via the Internet. They focus on the structure and content of news stories, including number of stories; story topics; story length; and use of Latino reporters and anchors over a one-year period, as well as content analyses conducted on random two-week samples of news from each network.

The online availability of the *Network Brownout Report* gestures towards its media-savvy, or at the very least, its Internet-connected targeted audience. But a well-documented "digital divide" indicates that Latinos and lower-income communities of Color generally do not have Internet access. Admittedly, findings from the *Report* can be read through journalists' and newspapers' reports of the statistics. In addition, despite NAHJ's focus on Latino representation, the organization targeted media executives (vis-à-vis journalists), revealing their faith in generating sustained change from within the media. In a similar vein, Chon Noriega (2000) documented how Chicana/o media activism during the 1960s to 1980s made industry opportunities possible for more Latinos in film and television; yet these gains did not necessarily translate into healthier representations of Latinos in either film or television.

NAHJ's emphasis on increasing the number of Latinos in newsrooms reflects the organization's belief that like-minded journalists tend to "make sense of the news in ways that reflect their own identity politics" (Zelizer, 2004, p. 102). Every year NAHJ requests that the major networks share data on the racial and ethnic makeup of their newsrooms and every year the networks refuse, offering no rationale for doing so (Méndez-Méndez & Alverio, 2003; Montalvo & Torres, 2006; Subervi et al., 2005). NAHJ strategically used the *Network Brownout Reports* to reason that diversity in newsrooms correlates with when and how viewers see particular newsroom coverage of Latinos. It is unclear whether this political strategy has influenced or impacted the profession. By NAHJ's own admission, the numbers of Latina/o journalists in general-market news outlets remains fewer than 5 percent (Montalvo & Torres, 2006).

The presentation of the *Network Brownout Report*'s statistical data, assembled within a tidy twenty-or-so page document, made it easy for journalists to digest and quote in various news pieces (see, for example, Associated Press, 2004; Elber, 2003). It also provided ample fodder for blogs and websites. The inaugural issue, for instance, found that salsa and mariachi music were used on several occasions as background soundtrack, regardless of the tone of the news story (Carveth & Alverio, 1996). For many, these findings serve as an argument to abandon network viewing altogether for the more inclusive programming available on cable television. But Jennifer Fuller (2010) recently cautioned against the promise of cable diversity, noting that cable television revenue relies on member subscription and less on advertising revenue. Online *TV Eye* writer Belinda Acosta (1999) urged her readers to pay attention to the fact that "cable television is where the most diverse programming can be found, though, alas, it's not free" (para. 3).

The *Network Brownout Report*'s vast public reach demanded that media industries take note of the not-so-subtle lack of diversity on network news.

Several Latino Studies scholars have identified discursive constructions of Latinos in the media through more qualitatively driven sets of data within various genres of film (Fregoso, 1993; Noriega, 1992; Ramírez-Berg, 2002; Rodríguez, 1997, 2004), print (Cepeda, 2010; Chavez, 2001, 2008; Inda, 2006; Molina-Guzmán, 2010; Santa Ana, 2002), and television (Dávila 2001; Rodríguez, 1999). According to these qualitative studies, Latinos are regularly cast as dark-skinned immigrants, light-skinned ethnics, deceitful villains, loyal consumers, and/or threats to national security. Few have focused on Latino-specific network news coverage (Dixon & Linz, 2000; Santa Ana et al., 2007) and even fewer incorporate longitudinal *and* quantitative approaches. The paucity of such studies speaks to the unique positioning of the *Network Brownout Report* as a quantitative, policy-oriented, packaged report for mass consumption.

Counting Race, Discounting Gender

Popular culture's relentless circulation of the socially constructed "macho" to portray Latino masculinities has produced disparaging portrayals of Latino men (Gutmann, 1996; Ramírez-Berg, 2002; Rodríguez, 1997). Despite the mid-to-late 1990s academic fetish regarding masculinity studies—dubbed an era of "academic Viagra" (Traister, 2000)—race and immigration were not central tenets of the discourse. Questions of gender, however, transformed academic approaches to immigration studies. Legal status also became a salient and critical category of difference in examining the social construction of masculinity. Sociological and anthropological studies, particularly those with a feminist focus, documented how experiences of migration reconfigured gender roles in newfound residences (Espiritu, 1999; Hondagneu-Sotelo & Messner, 2001; Rodriguez & Mahler, 1999; Schaeffer-Grabiel, 2006). This wave of research emphasized how gender plays a crucial role in the social status, performances, and expectations of livelihoods among immigrant men and suggested that immigrant men wrestle with gender anxieties often manifested through more masculinist displays (Goldring, 2003; Hondagneu-Sotelo, 1994a, 1994b).

However, the portrayals of Latinos as reported by the *Network Brownout Report* (and discussed later in this chapter) suggested a more de-masculinized and racial-ized framing of Latinos within newsprint and television. Vargas (2000) stressed the significance of this type of newsroom gendering, stating "under advanced capitalism the construction of a social group as female justifies its social, political, and economic subordination" (p. 267). Specifically, her concept of "newsroom processes of genderization" refers to "newsroom practices, especially those uses of language, by which markings of sex are imprinted on journalistic products" (p. 264). Vargas argued that the systematic framing of Latino current affairs as "feminine" reifies classed stereotypes and associations of Latinos as an "underclass of peons" (p. 261). Her longitudinal case study focusing on news coverage of Latinos within the North Carolina-based newspaper *Raleigh News & Observer* found that Latino stories were often covered as "soft" (female) interest pieces rather than as "hard" (male), and hence more politically significant, news. She found that the majority of news pieces written by female reporters fell under the topic categories of Local Community and Nation. Notably, topics under the Nation included traditional female domains such as family, health, and education (p. 273) while male reporters covered the male-identified domains of Sports and Business (p. 274). An overwhelming 60 percent of Latino news stories within Vargas's study were covered by female reporters, which gestures towards a "softer," less politically serious sentiment tied to Latino news stories. Vargas's approach and detailed case study provide a compelling lens through which to analyze how news coverage connotes gendered, raced, and classed underpinnings.

Although visuals and linguistic references to Latinos do not, in my estimation, effectively "feminize" Latinos in accordance to Vargas's concept, at the very least, Latinos are de-masculinized by these portrayals. The distinction is significant in that Latino men framed as de-masculine continue to be regarded as men, albeit with weak and un-gallant-like features. To feminize the portrayals infers an undressing of masculinity altogether, in favor of more socially constructed female traits, such as domesticity and/or defined through physiological structures. Certainly, the construction of one's masculinity has a history of functioning as a means of policing discourses of race in the United States. David Eng (2001), for instance, in *Racial Castration* argued similar limitations assigned to Asian American masculinities. Together with historical experiences Latinos have had with proletarianism and colonialization, the televised news representation of Latino masculinities as emasculated and exclusively immigrant works to further disenfranchise Latino men. Whereas being a macho connotes an excessive display of patriarchy widely associated with men of Color, being de-masculinized strips men of any degree of masculine authority; both extremes signify an utter lack of social and/or political power. As the work of R. W. Connell (1995) has reminded us, masculinities are dependent on a social hierarchy and in relationship to other men's status of power. In essence, not all men have to be seen as feminine in order to have their masculinity compromised.

"Alien" Versus "Undocumented"

Questions of media policy or media activism in relation to raced and gendered representations of Latinos within the media are infrequently raised. Yet public appeals made by NAHJ unveil how race and gender are latently embedded within certain journalistic styles and word choice. An analysis of both the *Network Brownout Report* and NAHJ's press releases stressing that specific terminology be used to report race and immigration highlights how gender adds another layer to the discussion of the representation of Latinos and Latino issues.

The topic of immigration—often described as a dominant theme within media reports of Latinos on television (Méndez-Méndez & Alverio, 2003; Montalvo & Torres, 2006; Subervi et al., 2005)—is rarely identified as a gendered or racial construct. For instance, in the midst of health reform debates, NAHJ (2009, Sept.) urged journalists to "stop using the dehumanizing term 'illegals' as a noun to refer to undocumented immigrants" (para. 1). According to Santa Ana and colleagues (2007), the term *illegal* invokes criminality and inherently places blame on individuals while *undocumented* implies an error. NAHJ (2009, Sept.) recommended *undocumented immigrant* or *undocumented worker* to refer to the nearly 12 million undocumented people living in the United States and called for the abandonment of the shorthand *illegal* and *illegal alien* as these word choices "dehumanizes the subjects [during times of] important public policy debate" (para. 4). Arguably, NAHJ's preference for *undocumented worker* does not fare much better because it reinscribes immigrants as units of labor, not as individuals with families or social lives. The word choice of *illegal* or *illegal alien* lends individuals less journalistic authority as, according to NAHJ Executive Director Iván Román, the use of "these terms not only distorts the debate, but it takes away their identities as individuals and human beings. When journalists do that, it's that much easier to treat them unfairly and not give them an equal voice in the controversy" (NAHJ, 2009, Sept., para. 4). Perhaps most troubling is that NAHJ (2009, Sept.) also called on editors and journalists to "refrain from reporting a person's legal status unless it is relevant to the story in question" (para. 8). Although NAHJ was concerned with the reporting of immigrants, Román's statement that *illegal* marks persons without identities, and are thus vulnerable to partial coverage, infers gendered journalistic binaries of authority/subjection and male/female while the consistent use of reporting a person's status regardless of storyline connotes racialized connotations of unmarked/marked and non-White/White. Both gendered and racialized markings work together to question and/or undermine the story's perceived objectivity.

Even when gender as a reporting topic is blatantly dressed as a woman, the inclusion or mention of race and/or immigration undermines the female subject's authority and the significance of the news event. For instance, during the confirmation hearings of Supreme Court nominee Judge Sonia Sotomayor, NAHJ (2009, May) issued a press release urging news organizations "to avoid any confusion over Judge Sotomayor's ethnic background. Her Puerto Rican parents are not immigrants, as some journalists have reported, since island-born residents are U.S. citizens, conferred by an act of Congress in 1917" (para. 1). Here NAHJ (2009, May) not only served as media watchdog for linguistic accuracy but also as "history teacher" to journalist colleagues, emphasizing that "people who move to the U.S. mainland from Puerto Rico are no more immigrants than those who move from Nebraska to New York" (para. 1). Despite the historic distinction of the appointment of Sotomayor as the first Latina to sit on the highest court, the linguistic marking of "immigrant" also signified racial underpinnings.

Vargas (2000) argued that even when women in politics are covered in the media, the emphasis on their "family" and/or "cultural heritage" gestures to more feminine discussions, despite their prominence within the male body politic (pp. 273, 276). For better or worse, the repetitive emphasis on Sotomayor effectively made her an "identifiable Latino" with some degree of political authority within the news, only to be later vilified for her infamous comment about "wise Latina" women (Savage, 2009).[2] Both gender and race complicate her authority and highlight how illegality is often racialized.

Immigration/Crime as "Newsworthy"

From 2000 to 2006, the major networks devoted less than 1 percent of their news coverage to Latinos. The latest *Network Brownout Report* found that when Latinos were reported in the network news, the most newsworthy components consisted of crime, immigration and, to a lesser extent, sports and celebrity personalities (Montalvo & Torres, 2006). Between 1995 and 2004, the *Network Brownout Report* found that immigration, specifically *undocumented* immigration *and* crime, had occupied much of the news coverage on Latinos (Subervi et al., 2005), reporting specifically that "out of 1,201 stories, these two topics accounted for 36 percent of coverage" (p. 5). In 2002 alone, 39 percent of all stories that aired about Latinos were about crime (Méndez-Méndez & Alverio, 2003, p. 4). In addition to these convincing tabulations, the *Network Brownout Report* has modified its methodology to account for more nuanced categories of representations, as discussed below.

Brown Masses, Latino Brown-Ins, and Unidentifiable Latinos

While the *Network Brownout Report* began as a quantitative analysis of Latinos on network television, over the years it underwent key methodological modifications that in turn produced new and insightful pieces of information. In 2000, a Critical Viewing component of a random two-week sample of news content accompanied the usual analysis of one year of news coverage. In 2002, the *Network Brownout Report* included a bi-coastal (Los Angeles and New York) focus group sample in which participants were asked to comment on specific news clips. As demonstrated in the previous discussion, although many of these findings—both quantitative and qualitative—were primarily presented through a racial perspective, they also simultaneously worked to gender Latinos and Latino-specific issues.

One of the most compelling findings tracked in several issues of the *Network Brownout Report* was the visual depiction of Latinos as either individuals or in groups, and the perceived significance of this framing within news coverage. Just as NAHJ stressed how word choice lends credence to news topics and people, the *Network Brownout Report* found visual evidence of news coverage grouping Latinos without regard to their identities. In 2000, for instance, the *Network*

Brownout Report noted the frequent visual use of unidentified Latino groups or "brown masses" (to use their term) as background scenery for Latino stories (Méndez-Méndez & Alverio, 2000). Focus groups conducted in New York in 2002 confirmed this perception of brown masses, with participants remarking on the images of "hordes" and "herds" of brown people seen on network television (Méndez-Méndez & Alverio, 2003, p. 14). Such infamous shots usually featured a Latino neighborhood or barrio (p. 13). Despite the fact that Latinos have increasingly chosen to settle in more rural areas and now represent the largest minority population in rural and suburban landscapes (Mahler, 1992), the classed and racialized perceptions of the urban barrio continue to follow Latinos.

These visual couplings of unidentified groups of brown people with geographical and classed signifiers of barrios contribute to a "discursive economy of Otherness," in which the experiences of the marginalized are effaced and trivialized in newsprint (Allan, 1998, p. 132). Furthermore, the *Network Brownout Report* found that "stories placed special emphasis on linking criminal activity with Latinos by interviewing heavily accented acquaintances of the subject matter to visually establishing a shot of a heavily populated Latino neighborhood" (Méndez-Méndez & Alverio, 2003, p. 12). The continuous linking of "accent" with barrio signifiers strengthens the perception of immigrants as residents of crime-inflicted dwellings.

In 2005, the *Brownout Network Report* began to classify this section of its report as Identifiable Latinos versus Unidentifiable Latinos, which tracked when unspecified Latino voices or identified individuals were used for a news segment (Subervi et al., 2005, p. 11). Specifically, the category of unidentifiable Latinos designates when Latinos are shown in large groups, such as undocumented immigrants crossing the border, groups on a crowded street, and day laborers standing in a parking lot; in these instances, the screened Latinos are neither named nor spoken to on camera. Using this criteria, the 2005 *Report* found that 47 out of 115 (or 41 percent) of Latino-oriented stories featured "unidentified Latinos" and of those "31 (or 66 percent) featured shots of immigrants" (Subervi et al., 2005, p. 11). Altogether, nearly 27 percent of news coverage from the major network news shows screened unidentified Latinos or masses and groups of (perceived brown) immigrants, and a significant majority (66 percent) of Latino-oriented stories displayed visual shots of immigrants.

As documented over the years by NAHJ, these recurring visual sceneries of mass immigrants often accompanied the frequently discussed topic of immigration on news programs. These groupings of immigrants reify already negative connotations of immigrants as contributors to overpopulation due to extraordinary migration and fertility rates (Chavez, 2008; Santa Ana, 2002). These images also tap into existing notions of delinquency associated with groups of Black and Brown youth and day laborers, both of whom are seen as "loitering" outside public venues and street corners. To be sure, these trite images—despite the fact that the *Network Brownout Report* fails to explicitly recognize them as such—are innately gendered as male and criminalized because both crossing the border and loitering are considered illegal activities. These Latino "brown-ins" are seen as pre-criminalized behavior wherein appearance (phenotype, accented) and perceived legal status subject Latinos to legislative policing (Covington, 1995). Just as word choice inappropriately groups all Latino-origin populations as immigrant, these brown-in visuals overwhelmingly group Latinos as male and even legally undocumented or, at best, cast doubt on their legal status. Without being interviewed or explicitly mentioned, these visual images of brown masses simultaneously connote a sense of docility among immigrant men and the potential threat of rebelliousness among male youth—Latino masculinities that rely on stereotypes regarding race and perceived immigrant status.

Identifiable Latinos and Latino Experts

Given the lack of a Latino voice on network news, a critical viewing of when Latinos are deliberately on camera versus simply window dressing has become increasingly significant. According to the *Network Brownout Report*, those individuals regarded as identifiable Latinos—that is, who are spoken to and heard on camera—are presumably given more journalistic authority. In 1999, Latinos were quoted as experts a total of 15 times, including twice on non-Latino topics; just three years earlier the 1996 *Network Brownout Report* found that not a single Latino was quoted as an expert. Instead, "white federal and state government officials were interviewed" on Latino topics (Carveth & Alverio, 1996 p. 1), not Latino experts or Latinos. The chronic reporting of Latinos with implicit screen group shots gestures to infantilized and paternalistic attitudes toward Latinos. Clearly, this view both exacerbates and masks existing differences in racial and legal privileges between Latino communities and news networks.

Vargas (2000), however, observed that when Latinos are cited as a news source, they are often quoted as "ordinary people talking about their personal experience," (p. 272) not as experts. The orientation toward the personal, the subjective, and hence the feminine, according to Vargas (2000), uses the narratives of Latinos to solidify public and private spheres rather than serve as "authoritative sources of information" (p. 272). Often framed as human interest features, these pieces rely on emotional narratives, rather than sources of information, to guide a story.

Indeed, the *Network Brownout Report*'s immigration-related findings determined that most news pieces were either crime-related or human interest stories that reported immigration as a pursuit of the American Dream. As Ali Behdad (2005) noted in *A Forgetful Nation*, the American Dream is a spoon-fed narrative for immigrants that masks the strong current of nativism upon which the United States was founded (and continues to thrive) and the very real economic benefits that immigrants have provided the nation. To acknowledge this narrative, however, would counter the "give me your tired, your hungry" ideology, from which Americans take a perception of being selflessly democratic. The use of the

American Dream theme as a means of structuring Latino-oriented stories was found in reports, for instance, of Latino soldiers, Latino athletes, and Latino politics (Subervi et al., 2005, p. 3) while male-identified Latino topics of interest (e.g., war and sports) were reported through a more feminine journalistic frame (again, human interest).

The *Network Brownout Report* does not differentiate whether news pieces on immigration focused more on male migrants, children of undocumented parents, or female immigrants. In contrast, an increased focus on issues regarding gender or family would encourage future inquiries examining how family-oriented segments of immigration versus male-centric segments of immigration differ in tone and perhaps provide a more humanized, less criminalized tenor to immigration.

Conclusion

These findings of Latino representation as a racial category, one of the many legacies of the *Network Brownout Report*, are extremely useful. While communications studies "count" race as a primary factor in representations, they often *discount* the role of gender and altogether ignore legal status as a viable factor. When represented within crime-related television segments, Latinos were often the perpetuators, not the victims. While one may assume, given the gendered nature of crime-related coverage, that most of these projected perpetrators were male, NAHJ does not differentiate between representations of Latino males and Latina females. Doing so would help with investigations that monitor whether Latinos are reported within more masculine or feminine framings and gesture toward the larger implications of network news coverage.

Even more critical than counting Latinos through racially codified categories would be the study and determination of how gender and perceived legal status position Latinos as well as Latino issues. For instance, reporting on Latino-specific issues while speculating on legal status undermines the journalistic authority given to subject matters. By considering the gender and legal status perspective, media policy discussions would produce a different set of demands for Latino representation. It is not sufficient to insist on equitable or proportionate coverage of Latino communities; we must also ensure that reports move beyond gendered depictions of Latino men as overwhelmingly immigrant, criminally suspect, and de-masculine in nature. Such representations help create an environment for hate speech and an assumption that Latinos, as non-Americans or as foreigners, are a source of society's ills and not a valued part of our larger citizenry.

Acknowledgments

I thank Aída Hurtado, Pedro Noguera, and Edward Fergus for their invitation to this important forum on the status of U.S. Latino males; María Elena Cepeda,

Nicholas Syrett, and Gabriela Soto Laveaga for their insights on key points; Felicity Schaeffer-Grabiel for coming to the paper's rescue; and Sara Veronica Hinojos for her excellent research assistance.

Notes

1   Many of these organizations do not self-identify their work as advocacy or Latino-specific although their research reports serve as cornerstone arguments for more racially inclusive media programming.
2   Specifically, the remark in question was, "I would hope that a wise Latina woman with the richness of her experiences would more often than not reach a better conclusion than a white male who hasn't lived that life."

References

Acosta, B. (1999, August 9). TV eye. *Weekly wire*. Retrieved from http://weeklywire.com/ww/08–09–99/austin_screens_tveye.html

Allan, S. (1998). (En)gendering the truth: Politics of news discourse. In C. Carter, G. Branston, & S. Allan (Eds). *News, gender, and power*. New York: Routledge Press.

Associated Press. (2004, December 14). News coverage of Latinos is 'dismal'. *Los Angeles Times*. Retrieved from http://articles.latimes.com/2004/dec/14/entertainment/et-latino14

Behdad, A. (2005). *A forgetful nation: On immigration and cultural identity in the United States*. Durham, NC: Duke University Press.

Carveth, R., & Alverio, D. (1996). The portrayal of Latinos in network television news, 1995. *Network brownout report 1996*. Washington, DC: National Association of Hispanic Journalists.

Cepeda, M. E. (2010). *Musical ImagiNation: U.S.-Colombian identity and the Latin music boom*. New York: New York University Press.

Chavez, L. R. (2001). *Covering immigration: Popular images and the politics of the nation*. Berkeley: University of California Press.

Chavez, L. R. (2008). *Latino threat: Constructing immigrants, citizens, and the nation*. Palo Alto: Stanford University Press.

Connell, R. W. (1995). *Masculinities*. Berkeley: University of California Press.

Covington, J. (1995). Racial classification in criminology: The reproduction of racialized crime. *Sociological Forum*, 10(4), 547–568.

Dávila, A. (2001). *Latinos inc.: The marketing and making of a people*. Berkeley: University of California Press.

Dixon, T. L., & Linz, D. L. (2000). Overrepresentation and under representation of African Americans and Latinos as lawbreakers on television news. *Journal of Communication*, 50(2), 131–154.

Elber, L. (2003, December 12). Latinos rare on the air. *Los Angeles Times*. Retrieved from http://articles.latimes.com/2003/dec/12/entertainment/et-elber12

Eng, D. (2001). *Racial castration: Managing masculinity in Asian America*. Durham, NC: Duke University Press.

Espiritu, Y. L. (1999). Gender and labor in Asian immigrant families. *American Behavioral Scientist*, 42(4), 628–647.

Fregoso, R. L. (1993). *The bronze screen: Chicana and Chicano film culture*. Minneapolis: University of Minnesota Press.

Fuller, J. (2010). Branding blackness on US cable television. *Media, Culture, Society*, 32, 285–305.

Goldring, L. (2003). Gender, status, and the state of transnational spaces: The gendering of political participation and Mexican hometown associations. In P. Hondagneu-Sotelo (Ed.), *Gender and U.S. immigration, contemporary trends*. Berkeley: University of California Press.

Gray, H. (1995). *Watching race: Television and the sign of Blackness*. Minneapolis: University of Minnesota Press.

Gutmann, M. C. (1996). *The meanings of macho: Being a man in Mexico City*. Berkeley: University of California Press.

Hondagneu-Sotelo, P. (1994a). *Gendered transitions: Mexican experiences of immigration*. Berkeley: University of California Press.

Hondagneu-Sotelo, P. (1994b). Overcoming patriarchal constraints: The reconstruction of gender relations among Mexican immigrants women and men. *Gender & Society*, 6(3), 393–415.

Hondagneu-Sotelo, P., & Messner, M. (2001). Gender displays and men's power: The "new man" and the Mexican immigrant man. In H. Bord & M. Kauffman (Eds.), *Theorizing masculinities* (200–218). Thousand Oaks, CA: Sage Publications.

Inda, J. X. (2006). *Targeting immigrants: Government, technology, and ethics*. Malden, MA: Blackwell Publishing.

Kolker, C. (1999, 28 July). Latino groups urge boycott of network TV. *Los Angeles Times*. Retrieved from http://articles.latimes.com/1999/jul/28/news/mn-60272

Mahler, S. J. (1992). First stop: Suburbia. *NACLA Report on the Americas*, 26(1), 1–5.

Mastro, D., Behm-Morawitz, E., & Ortiz, M. (2007). The cultivation of social perceptions of Latinos: A mental models approach. *Media Psychology*, 9, 347–365.

Méndez-Méndez, S., & Alverio, D. (2000). The portrayal of Latinos in network television news, 1999. *Network brownout report 2000*. Washington, DC: National Association of Hispanic Journalists.

Méndez- Méndez, S., & Alverio, D. (2003). The portrayal of Latinos in network television news, 2002. *Network brownout report 2003*. Washington, DC: National Association of Hispanic Journalists.

Molina-Guzmán, I. (2006). Competing discourses of community: Ideological tensions between local general-market and Latino news media. *Journalism*, 7(3), 281–298.

Molina-Guzmán, I. (2010). *Dangerous curves: Latina bodies in the media*. New York: New York University Press.

Montalvo, D., & Torres, J. (2006). The portrayal of Latinos and Latino issues on network television news, 2005. *Network brownout report 2006*. Washington, DC: National Association of Hispanic Journalists.

NAHJ. (2009, May 26). Avoid confusion on Sotomayor. National Association of Hispanic Journalists. Retrieved from www.nahj.org/2009/05/nahj-avoid-confusion-on-sotomayor/

NAHJ. (2009, September 15). NAHJ urges news media to stop using the term "illegals." National Association of Hispanic Journalists. Retrieved from www.nahj.org/2009/09/nahj-urges-news-media-to-stop-using-the-term-illegals-when-covering-immigration/

Noriega, C. A. (Ed.). (1992). *Chicanos and film: Representation and resistance.* Minneapolis: University of Minnesota Press.

Noriega, C. A. (2000). *Shot in America: Television, the state, and the rise of Chicano cinema.* Minneapolis: University of Minnesota Press.

Noriega, C. A. (2002). Making a difference. *Politics and Culture,* 1. Retrieved from http://aspen.conncoll.edu/politicsandculture/page.cfm?key=145

Ramírez Berg, C. (2002). *Latino images in film: Stereotypes, subversion, and resistance.* Austin: University of Texas Press.

Rodriguez, A. (1999). *Making Latino news: Race, language, class.* Thousand Oaks, CA: Sage Publications.

Rodriguez, A. P., & Mahler, S. J. (1999). Engendering transnational migration: The case of Salvadorans. *American Behavioral Scientist,* 42(4), 690–719.

Rodríguez, C. E. (Ed.). (1997). *Latin looks: Images of Latinas and Latinos in the U.S. media.* Boulder, CO: Westview Press.

Rodríguez, C. E. (2004). *Heroes, lovers and others: The story of Latinos in Hollywood.* Oxford: Oxford University Press.

Santa Ana, O. (2002). *Brown tide rising: Metaphors of Latinos in contemporary American public discourse.* Austin: University of Texas Press.

Santa Ana, O., Treviño, S. L., Bailey, M. J., Bodossian, K., & De Necochea, A. (2007). A May to remember: Adversarial images of immigrants in U.S. newspapers during the 2006 policy debate. *Du Bois Review: Social Science Research on Race,* 4, 207–232.

Savage, C. (2009, May 14). A judge's view of judging is on the record. *New York Times,* p. A21. Retrieved from www.nytimes.com/2009/05/15/us/15judge.html?_r=1

Schaeffer-Grabiel, F. (2006). Planet-Love.com: Cyberbabies in the Americas and the transnational routes of U.S. masculinity. *SIGNS: Journal of Women in Culture and Society,* 31, 331–356.

Shohat, E. (1997). Post-third-worldist culture: Gender, nation and cinema. In M. J. Alexander & C. T. Mohanty (Eds.), *Feminist genealogies, colonial legacies, democratic futures* (183–209). New York: Routledge.

Subervi-Vélez, F. A. (1999). The mass media and Latinos: Policy and research agendas for the next century. *Aztlán,* 24(2), 131–147.

Subervi-Vélez, F. A. (Ed.). (2008). *The mass media and Latino politics: Studies of U.S. media content, campaign strategies and survey research: 1984–2004.* New York: Routledge.

Subervi, F. A., Torres, J., & Montalvo, D. (2005). The portrayal of Latinos & Latino issues on network television news, 2004 with a retrospect to 1995. *Network brownout report 2005.* Washington, DC: National Association of Hispanic Journalists.

Traister, B. (2000). Academic Viagra: The rise of American masculinity studies. *American Quarterly,* 52(2), 274–304.

Vargas, L. (2000). Genderizing Latino news: An analysis of a local newspaper's coverage of Latino current affairs. *Critical Studies in Media Communication,* 17(3), 261–293.

Wilkinson, K. T. (2003). Blackout, brownout, or both?: The dynamics of ethnic-oriented media advocacy. In D. I. Rios & A. N. Mohamed (Eds.), *Brown and Black communication: Latino and African American conflict and convergence in mass media* (217–232). Westport, CT: Praeger Publishers.

Zelizer, B. (2004). When facts, truth and reality are God-terms: On journalism's uneasy place in cultural studies. *Communication and Critical/Cultural Studies,* 1(1), 100–119.

8

ANCHORING THE MEASUREMENT OF MACHISMO AND LATINO MALE IDENTITY IN CONTEMPORARY DEFINITION AND THEORY

María Félix-Ortiz
Ian Ankney
Megan Brodie
Harold Rodinsky

A basic problem in measuring machismo has been in defining machismo. Some scholars conceptualize machismo as Latino male identity; however, others suggest it defines individuals from a variety of ethnoracial identities, genders, sexualities, socioeconomic classes, and sexual preferences. There has been a failure to distinguish *machismo* from similar constructs, or to contextualize it within a larger theory. Measures have usually served to reinforce insufficiently elaborated theory rather than reflect the various evolving conceptualizations of masculinities. Inadequate definitions of machismo lead to inadequate measurement and these inadequate measures then "confirm" the original weak theory or definition of machismo. We review definitions of machismo, comment briefly on psychometric issues related to its measure (e.g., discriminant validity), and anchor these within a larger context of gender studies and psychological theory.

Defining Machismo

Over fifty years ago, Rogelio Díaz-Guerrero (1955) initially defined *machismo* in psychoanalytic terms as a defense mechanism against feelings of powerlessness, inferiority, or low self-esteem resulting from a poorly resolved Oedipal conflict. In Mexican psychology especially, machismo has been described as a hyper-polarized masculine gender role, rooted in veneration of the mother and reflecting a fundamental ambivalence towards women (Díaz-Guerrero, 1955; Penalosa,

1968). Although some investigators have described machismo as the denial of feminine feelings and a reaction formation against them, they grounded the psychodynamic conflict in the legacy of Spanish *conquistadores* and the Mexican revolution. The modern macho compensates for the trauma of the Spanish conquest of the Mexican Indians or "still-unhealed rape" of the Spanish conquistadors (Stavans, 1996) by assuming "the hypermasculine Hispanic role" and asserting dominance over women (Goldwert, 1985). Order was maintained through power/force, and power was manifested through physical strength. Consistent with psychoanalytic and psychodynamic theory, aggression is conceptualized as a basic drive.

Across psychodynamic theories, machismo develops through early conflicted interactions (between child and family, or in the history of their culture), leading to a need to establish a powerful position within a hierarchy. Although psychology's contemporary emphasis is on behavior being determined by the environment, cognition, and biology in addition to psychodynamic factors, machismo continues to be described primarily in psychodynamic terms. Conceptualized this way, machismo is a deficit-oriented construct (e.g., "hypermasculine"), a personality trait fraught with tension and anxiety. This deficit orientation is typical of the older medical tradition of looking for and diagnosing illness or "what's wrong" with an individual rather than also considering strengths (Levine et al., 2005). Community psychology (e.g., Levine et al., 2005) and positive psychology (Seligman & Csikszentmihalyi, 2000) mostly reject Freudian theory and emphasize personal and community resilience and environmental, cognitive, and biological determinants of behavior and emotion.

In contrast to psychodynamic theories, social modeling theories suggest that machismo is an exaggerated, hypermasculine gender "script" transmitted from parent to child through socialization (Mosher & Tomkins, 1988). Boys are taught to show no distress, to feel shame about feelings of fear or distress, to be proud of aggressive or daring action, and to exert inter-personal control through aggressive dominance. As a rite of passage, adolescent boys undergo trials of manliness that are judged by their peers and older male family members. Again, this theory defines machismo as abnormal (e.g., hypermasculine). However, this script theory foreshadowed contemporary gender theory in that it implies the "performative" nature of gender (Butler, 2006). Rather than being an essential part of the unconscious, machismo is something taught and transmitted across generations. Some have detailed how these aspects of male identity characterize a larger, American way of socializing boys (Pollack, 1998). This conceptualization allows for the disconnection of machismo from biological sex, allowing women and gay men to be as "macho" as any Latino man. Therefore, machismo is probably not a personality trait, but rather something that can change over time or with experience. Nevertheless, this definition of machismo still represents a psychological/psychiatric approach to conceptualizing machismo since it retains an emphasis on machismo as a deficit.

Culturalist theories of machismo integrate the social and political with psychological aspects of Latino masculinity to legitimize machismo as part of Latino culture and history. For example, Victor De La Cancela's (1986) description of machismo includes stoicism, and attempts to avoid shame and gain respect and dignity for oneself and one's family. While psychodynamic scholars suggest intimacy is achieved only through aggression, culturalists suggest that machismo requires openness in some relationships (spousal, familial) and guardedness in others (with other men, strangers). As with some psychodynamic theories (e.g., Goldwert, 1985; Stavans, 1996), machismo is rooted in specific historical contexts and reflects Latino sex role ideals institutionalized through the division of labor between the home and outside world. However, contemporary social pressures are also considered. For example, machos are providers because patriarchal capitalism denies women this opportunity. Furthermore, women are highly valued for their capacity to bear children who will help maintain the family (De La Cancela, 1986).

Culturalists' definitions of machismo also have some limitations. Culturalists viewed machismo as a cultural manifestation to be respected and believed that "machismo needs to be defended as a conscious affirmation of the Latino in the face of discrimination and prejudices" (De La Cancela, 1986, p. 292). The latter is a more positive definition of machismo, though still problematic. Rather than being the result of intrapsychic conflict, machismo is a reaction against pressures in the larger social context. These culturalist definitions of machismo are more contextually grounded compared to earlier psychodynamic definitions, but still do not account for some contexts like socioeconomic class. For example, both men and women who are professionals defy traditional sex role ideals, and this may evoke either more or less machismo in their partners. For some men/partners, this situation may inspire a more egalitarian relationship based less on rigid gender role prescriptions. For others, however, a woman's rejection of traditional roles may provoke increased pressure, resentment, and even violence in a partner who is not ready to abandon the negative aspects of machismo. Also, culturalists have not considered the full extent to which race *and* class influence machismo. In some South American and Caribbean nations where African ethnic groups settled (as part of a slave trade), some investigators identified societal beliefs particular to Black men as well as some particular to "rich men": Black (or any non-White) men are dangerous and animalistic (Gutmann & Viveros Vigoya, 2005; Halberstam, 2002), while rich men are feminized because "rich men are seen as more interested in themselves and more subject to restrictions imposed by their wives" (Gutmann & Viveros Vigoya, 2005, p. 122).

Measurement Issues

The various definitions of machismo are reflected in a number of different machismo measures. Table 8.1 shows results from an earlier review of machismo

TABLE 8.1 Strengths and Limitations of Earlier Machismo Measures (as reviewed in Félix-Ortiz et al., 2001)

Scale	Strengths	Limitations
Cuellar, Arnold, & González (1995), Multiphasic assessment of cultural constructs	• Represents cognitive referents of acculturation • Correlated with acculturation	• Items derived from the literature, not developed from focus groups or other qualitative research • Negative definition of machismo
Díaz-Guerrero (1994), *Premisas histórico-socioculturales* (socio-cultural premises)	• Items derived from qualitative research • Tested over time using various Mexican samples	• Included psychometrically limited items that were heavily endorsed • Negative definition of machismo
Lara-Cantú (1989), Masculine-feminine personality traits scale	• Extends Bem's work • Includes a factor for both negative and positive masculinity	• Items derived from the literature • Machismo defined as a state rather than as a state that changes over time or with education
Mirandé (1997), Sex role inventory	• Items derived from popular literature reflecting Latino values (e.g., dichos)	• Psychometric limitations (e.g., factor extraction not empirically driven)
Mosher & Sirkin (1984), Hypermasculinity inventory	• Items derived from focus groups • Supported by other studies	• Focus group discussion guided by leading questions? • Extremely negative definition of machismo (e.g., "calloused sex")
Nagelschmidt (1981), Machismo/modernism measures	• Conceptualized "modernism" as distinct from machismo • Items derived from interviews	• Sample was female, not male • Minimal evidence of reliability and validity
Neff, Prihoda, & Hoppe (1991), Machismo measure	• Some items derived from interviews + careful sampling • Machismo varied across Mexican and other ethnic group samples	• Rejection of more complex factor structure (e.g., family responsibility, honor) • Limited convergent criterion validity
Strong, McQuillen, & Hughey (1994), Macho belief inventory	• Use of expert panel to derive items • Attempt to represent "ethical machismo"	• Factor structure issues • Lengthy • Negative definition of machismo
Villemez & Touhey (1977), The macho scale	• Discriminant validity • Supported by other studies	• Based on college student samples • No other demographics reported for the norm samples

measures (Félix-Ortiz et al., 2001). A review of the literature since 2000 revealed one new measure of machismo (Arciniega et al., 2008) and one measure that was reanalyzed to include positive characteristics that had been dropped in the original analysis (Neff, 2001). In addition to basing the measure on a negative/pathological definition of machismo, other common problems included psychometric limitations like limited reliability or validity and reliance on very old literature for deriving items rather than conducting new qualitative research to examine how the conceptualization of machismo may have evolved. Some of these problems also reflect biases brought to the study of machismo.

Reliable and valid measurement begins with identifying and including appropriate items that describe all content areas of the psychological construct (i.e., content validity). Few investigators used an emic approach to understanding machismo, one that entailed distilling factors from responses obtained through varied methods of qualitative research (e.g., Sternberg, 2000). Generally, items were borrowed from older scales or items from scales were combined; sometimes items were added based on interviews (e.g., Neff et al., 1991). With rare exceptions (e.g., Díaz-Guerrero, 1994), studies were not replicated on other Latino male samples to examine content validity, or were not tested with women, other ethnic groups, or gay men to look for discriminant validity. These samples should show weak scores on any machismo measure to confirm that machismo is a construct unique to Latino men, and provide evidence of discriminant validity.

Attention to research design can overcome problems in content validity when defining machismo. Investigations of machismo have not regularly examined how the definition of machismo may vary across time (across generational cohorts, or how it changes across time in a single cohort), socioeconomic class, gender, race, or cultures. Only one investigator used the same scale across several generational cohorts: in comparing data collected in 1994 to data collected in 1959, Díaz-Guerrero (2000) found that the authoritarianism component of machismo had declined most. Recently, an ambitious study conducted in Nicaragua with a diverse group of 90 men from both urban and rural Nicaraguan communities examined machismo through plenary sessions, questionnaires, and focus groups (Sternberg, 2000). Furthermore, Sternberg noted how norms defining masculinity were defined and maintained by societal institutions like faith-based communities, the government, the media, the medical community, and the family. In these studies, machismo is defined more fully, with both positive and negative aspects, and is less likely to be defined in a tautological manner. When the Latino community is involved in defining the construct of machismo, there is also less likely to be reification of a construct due to an investigator's biases (Moritsugu et al., 2010).

Social identity theory (SIT) (Tajfel, 1982) may explain why definitions of machismo have been so monolithically negative. SIT suggests that a person forms an in-group bias *in favor of the group with which we identify*, and an out-group homogeneity bias where we recognize fewer within-group differences in the out-group (Tajfel, 1982). SIT suggests that social scientists, who have had "the power to define" (e.g., Stobbe, 2005), may have overlooked the influence of their own in-group and out-group biases on their theory development. Because many social scientists studying machismo have hailed from privileged groups (indeed all enjoy the privilege of membership in the elite intellectual class), there has been little challenge to their perspectives until recently. Careful research design that includes focus groups and other qualitative methods bolstered by the community's involvement in data interpretation can address some of these biases.

Another issue important to understanding machismo is whether or not the attitude or behavior is relatively permanent (i.e., a trait) or relatively open to change (i.e., a state), and how this hypothesized characteristic is reflected in the psychometrics of the measure. Such questions have implications for clinical, educational, or social interventions designed to change behavior. Tests of reliability usually reflect whether or not the construct being measured is defined as a stable trait or a highly volatile state of mind (Anastasi & Urbina, 1997). Usually, machismo is defined as an enduring personality trait, but measured like a state of mind, as indicated by the psychometric tests of reliability used to evaluate the accuracy of the machismo measure. In evaluating the reliability of a measure of machismo, one can use the Spearman-Brown coefficient to examine whether or not test results obtained at two different times correlate with each other. Strong correlation would suggest that (1) the measure is accurate, and (2) that machismo is a relatively immutable trait. Instead, Cronbach alpha, a measure of item intercorrelation, has been often used for testing machismo measure reliability, implying that machismo is expected to vary over time. Use of the Cronbach alpha is inconsistent with the expectation that machismo is a relatively immutable personality trait. If machismo varies over time (e.g., Díaz-Guerrero, 2000), one could also investigate this through longitudinal research. However, no prospective studies follow boys over time to determine how biological development (e.g., aggressiveness linked to testosterone levels) may influence machismo. The issue of construct stability is important because machismo is often defined negatively: Is machismo an attitude that is open to change?

Probably the most important issue of machismo measurement is construct validity, the idea that the measure one develops is indeed a measure of the hypothesized phenomenon or "construct" (Messick, 1995). Factor analysis is a common statistical method used to establish construct validity; it allows for an investigator to identify a set of interview questions or scale items that are highly correlated with each other and define a "factor" or construct. In conducting a factor analysis, however, choices about the method of estimation, factor extraction, and factor rotation imply specific hypotheses. Nonetheless, choices in factor analysis are rarely explicitly discussed in machismo measurement, and are not usually tied to hypotheses about machismo theory. For example, principal component analyses is often favored over maximum likelihood estimation (MLE) despite the problem of inflated estimates of explained variance. MLE better distinguishes between shared and unique variance, yielding more accurate estimates, even when data are not distributed in the usual bell curve shape (Costello & Osbourne, 2005). Also, a failure to consider the scree test may lead to an under- or over-estimation of the number of essential components of machismo (ibid). Orthogonal rotation is often selected over oblique rotation because it yields easily interpretable factor loadings. However, comparing an oblique rotation to an orthogonal rotation is an extra step in factor analysis that can show whether or not the construct is more complex than hypothesized. This is particularly important in examining a complex construct like machismo that may have various second-order factors that define positive and negative macho profiles (Torres et al., 2002). These choices are rarely if ever discussed in the machismo literature.

Another way of establishing the construct validity of machismo is to submit the measure to tests of discriminant and convergent validity (or criterion validity). Unfortunately, these are usually missing from machismo measurement. Convergent validity could be determined by correlating machismo with other measures that capture elements of machismo. Essentially, discriminant validity establishes how a measure is sufficiently specific to describe the target construct *and* differentiate it from something else. Discriminant validity could be established by showing how the machismo measure is *not* correlated with a measure of feminism. However, some investigators have suggested that elements of machismo are also evident in Latina psychology (Arciniega et al., 2008; Nagelschmidt, 1981), in which case one might expect to find weak, or even moderate machismo scores in some Latinas.

Another important type of measure validity is predictive validity, the measure's ability to predict a future behavior or condition. Some theorists have suggested that machismo has been defined so variously across ethnic groups and historical time that it may be inappropriate to use it to predict behavior (e.g., Sternberg, 2000). Instead, it may be more fruitful to examine how specific behaviors or attitudes that have defined machismo predict behavior or attitudes. Hector Betancourt and Steven Lopez (1993) have suggested that measures of cultural phenomenon often suffer from a lack of specificity in definition and that this renders them useless in predicting behavior.

Another problem in measuring machismo is the negative influence of social desirability. Social desirability is a respondent's tendency to reply in a way that will be viewed favorably by others. When negative aspects of machismo are assessed, such as aggression that might be associated with domestic abuse, how can a researcher confirm that respondents' responses are not influenced by social desirability? Even though such behavior may be socially and culturally acceptable, it is unlikely that a man who engages in aggressive behavior (e.g., beats his wife or children) will be honest and admit such behavior, particularly when reporting it to someone perceived as an "outsider" or on paper when such behavior might be a punishable criminal offense. Researchers might create questionnaires that gauge specific beliefs or attitudes as opposed to specific actions. A question such as "Do you beat your wife when she displeases you?" would be susceptible to a great deal of social desirability bias. However, a question such as "Does your wife know that there are consequences to disagreeing with you?" may also flag the respondent as someone who is potentially abusive without requiring the person to implicate himself by admitting some undesirable or even illegal behavior. In their study of versions of the Marlowe-Crowne Social Desirability scale, Loo and Thorpe (2000) found that "the 18 keyed-true items could reflect a tendency to attribute socially approved, but improbable statements to oneself" (p. 629). An example of this approach for a study of machismo could be, "Your wife always agrees with your decisions." They also found that "the 15 keyed-false items could reflect the tendency to deny socially disapproved, but probably true, statements about oneself" (p. 629). An example of an item reflecting this approach is, "I have the right to force my wife to comply, using any means I desire." Because the questions target a way of thinking, they identify beliefs that can be the focus of therapy and other broader interventions.

Implications for Definition of Machismo

Power/Control

In spite of the differences across definitions and measurement of machismo, one common element emerges: there is an explicit emphasis on power or personal control. For example, the capacity to function as "breadwinner" seems to be especially important to Latino men (Sobralske, 2006; Sternberg, 2000; Stobbe, 2005). Some researchers have conceptualized this as a gender role endowed with power (e.g., Casas et al., 1994), others in terms of ego integrity or psychological power (e.g., Díaz-Guerrero, 1955; Sobralske, 2006), while still others as economic power (e.g., De La Cancela, 1986; Stobbe, 2005) or power to demand or evoke respect from the family (Torres et al., 2002). More specifically, attitudes that reflect the power of natural differences (e.g., "Men are natural leaders"), the power of denial, the power of the male standard, and pastoral power (e.g., the belief that women must be protected) might be elements of machismo that may account for cultural divisions of labor observed in Latin America (Stobbe, 2005). In considering African male identities, other researchers have noted a tension between violence as power and emotional control as power (Morrell & Swart, 2005), a dynamic that may underlie the negative and positive aspects of machismo. Espín (1994) hypothesized that when men of Color cannot exercise dominance or control in other domains of life, they exert it within their family, and domestic violence ensues. However, even when one includes responsibility as a component of machismo (i.e., pastoral power), this may inadvertently support a system of gender inequality (Morrell & Swart, 2005).

Aside from specific beliefs/attitudes, psychological constructs reflecting personal power such as locus of control (Rotter, 1992), self-efficacy (Bandura, 1992), and learned helplessness (Seligman, 1992) might be correlated with machismo to establish convergent and discriminant validity in machismo measurement. For example, fatalism has been identified with Latino culture (Sobralske, 2006). But is fatalism associated with machismo, and does it differ across genders? Personal control may be important across many definitions of machismo because personal control can be influenced by the individual's perceptions of their place in society, as well as by their own sense of how they can function within that position.

If machismo is a socioeconomic phenomenon with psychological roots in personal control, and possible biological bases, then the behavior might be descriptive across various ethnic male groups (e.g., Neff et al., 1991). Yet the Spanish term *machismo* continues to be used to describe the construct rather than another term that suggests a more universal construct. Some investigators have suggested that machismo has its historical roots in the Spanish class system, which exalted descendents of those who fought in the Crusades and rewarded horsemanship, chivalry, and swordsmanship (Lockhart & Schwartz, 1983; Torres et al., 2002), while others suggest that machismo is a relatively new American anthropological construction (Gerardo, 2000; Gutmann & Viveros Vigoya, 2005). The use of the Spanish *machismo* may suggest that the trait is specific to Latinos and indicative of homogeneous Latino male identity. Arguments made in gender studies have claimed that language use can constrict gender identities to "male" and "female" (Butler, 2006). Furthermore, "the fixity conferred by names also traps people into many different identities, racial as well as gendered" (Halberstam, 2002, p. 359). Likewise, the use of the term *machismo* artificially restricts Latino male identity. But Latino male identities vary (Stobbe, 2005; Torres et al., 2002), and the negative (and positive) elements of machismo can be found across ethnic groups (Neff, 2001).

Changing Cultures and Machismo

The definition of machismo is also influenced by cultural changes in sports, the military, and definitions of ability and disability. Displays of machismo in Latin American sports have been linked to context and do not exclude expressions of tenderness. In one study of Mexican baseball players, expressions of emotion were more commonly seen among the Latinos than among their North American counterparts (Klein, 2007). This led to behavior that would not be considered macho from men who are typically thought of as very, very macho. For example, a player who was prone to violent outbursts if a play did not go his way, was observed to dramatically shift into a kind, caring exchange with a mother and her young daughter (Klein, 2007). Klein's study illustrates how machismo can be dependent upon the situation, and something that can be controlled by the individual. This study suggests that men who display machismo may also be fully capable of keeping it in check or displaying very different characteristics.

This capability was confirmed in another study of masculine identity conducted among college men. Harris (2008) found that college men identified many positive aspects of masculinity as "truly" defining the term (e.g., character, respect, integrity), yet also reported having conversations with their male peers that featured demeaning references to women, boasts about sexual "hooking up," and other "hypermasculine performance" that would not be displayed with women peers. Different aspects of a male identity can be evoked by demand characteristics of the situation: environment and identity interact.

In recent years, greater numbers of women have entered the U.S. military and law enforcement. This trend has complicated and extended the usual gendered expression of war beyond men as "aggressors" or "defenders," and women as "victims" and "survivors" to include ideas like "discipline," "civility," activities like "peace keeping," less use of excessive force, and improved relationships between the community and the policing/military force (Higate & Hopton, 2005; Morrell & Swart, 2005; National Center for Women and Policing, 2002). Some service women, however, allow for or use macho terms and beliefs to define themselves or protect themselves, or to show group affiliation (Harrell & Miller, 1997). Finally, certain physical conditions previously conceptualized as "weak" have been redefined as a new kind of strength or machismo. For instance, some athletes using prosthetics can perform better in competition than athletes relying on their natural limbs (e.g., Oscar Pistorius who raced on prosthetic legs referred to as "blades").

Gender Studies and Recent Psychological Theory

The emergence of gender and queer studies has provided a new lens through which one can view machismo. One important theme is that gender identity can no longer be restricted to only two genders (e.g., Butler, 2006; Fausto-Sterling, 2002; Halberstam, 2002). Themes common to gender studies also illuminate understandings of machismo: hegemonic masculinity being dependent on minority masculinities, gender as a basis for assigning privilege/power, gender being limited by the absence of commonly accepted names for alternative genders, and gender as a violently enforced tool of oppression (Butler, 2006; Halberstam, 2002).

Many researchers in gender studies have discussed how a hegemonic masculinity (e.g., Halberstam, 2002), and even feminism (Butler, 2006), depends on a power structure that recognizes men as powerful and women as submissive. As originally conceived, machismo was a male identity, and, as such, was often contrasted with marianismo, a supposedly common female identity in Latin American cultures. *Marianismo* is an attitude rooted in the archetype of the Virgin Mary, connoting a woman who is pure and who sacrifices herself to the duties of motherhood. However, even here we confront the problem of limiting Latino identities to just two constructions. Latina feminists have pointed to many Latina archetypes—*la Llorona, la Malinche, la Adelita,* and others—to define themselves or various aspects of themselves. Although *la Llorona* refers to the legend of the weeping woman (who wanders along riverbanks searching for the children she drowned to win the love of a man who ultimately rejected her) and *la Malinche* refers to an indigenous traitor to her people (Taylor, 2000), *la Adelita* is a completely positive and strong archetype, representing the women soldiers of the Mexican Revolution (Norris & Reiss, 2006).

Another challenge to gender identity as a simple dichotomy is that gender identities are not anchored to biological sex. Some recent research has suggested that machismo can be measured in women as well as men (LaFranchi, 2001; Nagelschmidt, 1981) and, conversely, that feminine traits are part of Latino male identity (Diaz-Guerrero, 1994; Gutmann, 1996; Lara, 1999; Mirandé, 1997). Even in the gay community, some men are very macho and violate common gay stereotypes. Some investigators have suggested that a partner's machismo is considered by gay men in deciding what sexual behavior they will select (Carballo-Diéguez et al., 2004). Others have suggested that the idea of dichotomy in biological sex is as troublesome as dichotomy of gender (Butler, 2006; Fausto-Sterling, 2002).

Various Latino male identities are being recognized and labeled in new ways (e.g., *caballerismo*), and this might identify experiences that form and transform identity. As noted by some investigators, men seek transformation but will use local cultural systems and language to change within "existing parameters rather than aspiring to externally prescribed norms" (Sampath, as cited in Morrell & Swart, 2005). This is evidenced in modern evangelical programs that aim to mentor and serve men, such as the Promise Keepers ("men transformed worldwide"; www.promisekeepers.org) and men's ACTS (Adoration, Community, Theology, and Service) retreats in the Roman Catholic Church. However, such transformation might require a context that includes relationships to women, similar to how postmodern theorists have discovered that women in developing countries cannot benefit from assistance in an enduring way unless their male partners are included in the plan (Morrell & Swart, 2005).

Machismo can be viewed as a response to challenges and a form of adaptation to an ever-changing context. A critical component of SIT is that a person has multiple identities or "categories" of self and group membership, and that "category salience" varies with the context (Tajfel, 1982). Every bicultural person knows this phenomenon intuitively as they select which identity and behaviors they will present in a given situation. Similarly, elements of a macho identity may be selected or de-emphasized based on situational demands (e.g., Harris, 2008). Cultural identity theory and acculturation also inform the understanding of machismo. As a type of cultural identity, both feminism and machismo are products of ethnoracial socialization and may change as immigrants acculturate (Cuellar et al., 1995; Félix-Ortiz et al., 1994).

Ecological Theory

According to ecological theory (e.g., Bronfenbrenner, 1979), two proximal environments/contexts might be most important in determining the Latino man's behavior: the male peer network and his relationship with his partner. The male peer network is a social network whose rules for establishing status are culturally determined. This peer network responds to pressures and demands of the larger economic and political environment. The Latino man's partner would create the other important environment in determining the man's behavior: the most proximal and influential environment of "the couple." These environmental influences would not, however, completely overshadow the importance of other environments such as the immediate neighborhood community or the local ethnic enclave, various peer communities, the larger local government, and the most distal national or global environment.

One example of how proximal influences interact with more distal influences to shape a Latino man's identity is how a couple's relationship undergoes changes with the fortunes of the economy within which it functions. Work or the ability to support a family may be important to machismo. The division of labor has been gendered for millennia, beginning with hunter-gatherer societies when women may not have participated in the hunt due to pregnancy or child rearing. The industrial revolution also affirmed a gendered division of labor, luring the husband away from the homestead farm and leaving the wife to raise children and oversee the homestead (Gutmann & Viveros Vigoya, 2005). When economic opportunities at home disappear or dwindle to unattractive options (like joining or being absorbed into drug gangs), some Latino men will try to find work elsewhere. Immigration earns Latino men money and power, but the dislocation can damage ties to community and family in their native country and force a renegotiation of identity. This can be particularly problematic for the Latino male if he defines himself through his connection to family and status in his local community. These feelings may explain why some immigrant men establish a *casa chica*, a lover and children, in the host country, while maintaining their legitimate wife and children in their home country (Wertheimer, 2006). On the other hand, a Latino man may not be able to find work in some economic environments. Even more disruptive to a Latino man's power and gender identities may be when his wife is able to find work but he cannot (Hondagneu-Sotelo, 1994). In such cases, fatherhood might become an important outlet for enacting authority and power when there are few opportunities for doing so in the larger society. Some researchers have conceptualized the domestic abuse of women and children as the expression of a minority man's frustration with reduced economic opportunity (e.g., Espín, 1994). In any case, economic and class pressures might account for the "violent enforcement" and policing of gender norms (Butler, 2006; Halberstam, 2002, p. 369).

It is interesting to note that this environmental perspective may not be so radically different from older psychodynamic perspectives. In the older psychodynamic models, healthy outcomes resulted from the person's ability to resolve a conflict and adapt; "fixation," an inability to move beyond old conflicts, resulted in maladaptive behavior. Even in the oldest Spanish definitions of machismo, horsemanship, swordsmanship, and chivalry were about rising to and surmounting a challenge, about asserting power, coping, adapting. The need to effectively confront challenges continues to be a central part of the contemporary Latino man's life—and challenges abound: racism that persists in the sheep's clothing of "immigration issues"; shifting economic power within the couple, related to restricted job opportunities; unfriendly educational environments; and many others. Some recent investigations have examined how role stress or the tension between the real and ideal can influence men's health (Sternberg, 2000; Torres et al., 2002). The capacity to adapt may be an important, unrecognized element of machismo and essential to the health and well-being of Latino men.

Concluding Remarks

Measures of machismo have a long history of theoretical and psychometric shortcomings that seem to reflect an uncertainty about how to define machismo, as well as some lack of scientific rigor in measurement development. Studies of machismo have suffered from investigators' investment in theories that are inadequate for explaining modern realities and from investigators' failures to adopt an interdisciplinary perspective on a subject that spans anthropology, psychology, sociology, economics, and biology. While there is a constellation of hypermasculine behaviors that seem to appear together reliably (when they appear), it is not clear that these behaviors define a typical Latino man; they do seem to appear in some women, gay men, and men of other ethnicities too. Furthermore, this constellation of behaviors is one that can be summoned to "impress the guys" and suppressed to not "offend the ladies" (e.g., Harris, 2008). As such, it seems a misnomer to continue referring to a monolithic Latino male identity that might be labeled *machismo*.

Latin American history is a history that includes 300 years of slave trade and extensive colonialization, experiences that have left a psychic wound in many Latino communities and economic difficulties in settling into independence (Morrell & Swart, 2005). As with measures of other cultural phenomena (e.g., acculturation), machismo measures have not captured the transaction between the socioeconomic environment and the individual, the transaction between the individual and other men, or the transaction between the woman and the man. As power and control appear to be a definitive element of this constellation of masculine behaviors, maybe Latino male identity can be best described as reflecting a Latino man's attempts to adapt effectively to constantly evolving social and cultural contexts, while retaining positive personhood and productivity vis-à-vis a partner (male or female) and family. In some contexts, negative aspects will predominate, while in other situations or environments more positive aspects will be evoked. This type of transaction between person and environment is not easily captured in cross-sectional research of identity.

Future research might look at Latino male identity in a way that follows men of diverse socioeconomic classes and races within one Latino nationality across time, particularly from adolescence to middle or even older adulthood, and detail how endorsement of values and behaviors may persist or change over time. Such a study would have to document significant experiences that might influence male identity development like fatherhood, changing roles in the man's romantic/intimate relationships, job loss, retirement, "coming out" to family and friends, and disability. It would be important to include a "control" group of Latina women, similarly diverse, against whom to compare the development and evolution of Latino machismo or other male identities and establish Latino male identities as distinct from other Latino/a genders. Finally, it might be important to empirically establish this male identity as particular or unique to Latinos.

With the growing exchange of cultural elements between the U.S. and Latin American countries, the distinction between "uniquely Latino" and "uniquely American" may be increasingly difficult to identify reliably. We might be surprised to discover more similarities across Latino and American men (and, perhaps, across men and women) than we've been willing to see. "Machismo" may be a term that, like "race," is a reality only in the mind of the believer.

Such discovery might suggest that health disparities may reflect problems in the system of care (i.e., prejudice and discrimination) rather than true differences across human beings. This complexity in the study of machismo might remind policy makers of the imprecision inherent in social science, and warn against extrapolating findings far beyond what is appropriate, sometimes to support xenophobic ideology. It might be important to abandon illusions of a homogeneous Latino masculinity called "machismo" and strive to better delineate the diversity of Latino gender identities as they exist now and as they continue to evolve.

References

Anastasi, A., & Urbina, S. (1997). *Psychological testing* (7th ed.). Upper Saddle River, NJ: Prentice-Hall.

Arciniega, G. M., Anderson, T. C., Tovar-Blank, Z. G., & Tracey, T. J. G. (2008). Toward a fuller conception of machismo: Development of a traditional machismo and caballerismo scale. *Journal of Counseling Psychology*, 55(1), 19–33.

Bandura, A. (1992). On rectifying the comparative anatomy of perceived control: Comments on "Cognates of personal control." *Applied & Preventive Psychology*, 1, 121–126.

Betancourt, H., & Lopez, S. (1993). The study of culture, ethnicity, and race in American psychology. *American Psychologist*, 48, 629–637.

Bronfenbrenner, U. (1979). *The ecology of human development: Experiments by nature and design.* Cambridge, MA: Harvard University Press.

Butler, J. (2006). *Gender trouble: Feminism and the subversion of identity.* New York: Routledge.

Carballo-Diéguez, A., Dolezal, C., Nieves, L., Díaz, F., Decena, C., & Balan, I. (2004). Looking for a tall, dark, macho man . . . Sexual-role behaviour variations in Latino gay and bisexual men. *Culture, Health & Sexuality*, 6, 159–171.

Casas, J. M., Wagenheim, B. R., Banchero, R., & Mendoza-Romero, J. (1994). Hispanic masculinity: Myth or psychological schema meriting clinical consideration. *Hispanic Journal of Behavioral Sciences*, 16, 315–331.

Costello, A. B., & Osborne, J. W. (2005). Best practices in exploratory factor analysis: Four recommendations for getting the most from your analysis. *Practical Assessment Research & Evaluation*, 10, 1–9.

Cuellar, I., Arnold, B., & Gonzalez, G. (1995). Cognitive referents of acculturation: Assessment of cultural constructs in Mexican Americans. *Journal of Community Psychology*, 23, 339–356.

De La Cancela, V. (1986). A critical analysis of Puerto Rican machismo: implications for clinical practice. *Psychotherapy*, 23, 291–296.

Díaz-Guerrero, R. (1955). Neurosis and the Mexican family structure. *American Journal of Psychiatry*, 112, 411–417.

Díaz-Guerrero, R. (1994). *Psicología del Mexicano: Descubrimiento de la etnopsiclogía* (6th ed.). Mexico City: Editorial Trillas.

Díaz-Guerrero, R. (2000). La evolución de machismo. *Revista de Psicologia Contemporanea*, 7(2), 4–11.

Espín, O. (1994). Feminist approaches. In L. Comas-Díaz & B. Greene (Eds.), *Women of color: Integrating ethnic and gender identities in psychotherapy* (265–286). New York: Guilford Press.

Fausto-Sterling, A. (2002). "That sexe which prevaileth." In R. Adams & D. Savran (Eds.), *The masculinity studies reader* (375–385). Malden, MA: Blackwell Publishing.

Félix-Ortiz, M., Abreu, J. M., Briano, M., & Bowen, D. (2001). A critique of machismo measures in psychological research. In F. Columbus (Ed.), *Advances in psychological research, Vol. III* (63–90). Hauppauge, NY: Nova Science.

Félix-Ortiz, M., Newcomb, M. D., & Myers, H. (1994). A multidimensional measure of cultural identity for Latino and Latina adolescents. *Hispanic Journal of Behavioral Sciences*, 16 (2), 99–115.

Gerardo, G. M. (2000). Reactionary gender studies? The historiography of Mexican masculinity. *Ex Post Facto*, 9, 53–63. Retrieved from http://userwww.sfsu.edu/~epf/2000/gerardo.html

Goldwert, M. (1985). Mexican machismo: The flight from femininity. *Psychoanalytic Review*, 72, 161–169.

Gutmann, M. C. (1996). *The meaning of macho: Being a man in Mexico City.* Berkeley: University of California Press.

Gutmann, M. C., & Viveros Vigoya, M. (2005). Masculinities in Latin America. In M. S. Kimmel, J. Hearn, & R. W. Connell (Eds.), *Handbook of studies on men and masculinities* (113–128). Thousand Oaks, CA: Sage Publications.

Halberstam, J. (2002). An introduction to female masculinity. In R. Adams & D. Savran (Eds.), *The masculinity studies reader* (375–385). Malden, MA: Blackwell Publishing.

Harrell, M. C., & Miller, L. L. (1997). *New opportunities for military women: Effects upon readiness, cohesion, and morale (MR-896-OSD)*. Santa Monica, CA: Rand Corporation.

Harris, F. (2008). Deconstructing masculinity: A qualitative study of college men's masculine conceptualizations and gender performance. *NASPA Journal*, 45(4), 453–474.

Higate, P., & Hopton, J. (2005). War, militarism, and masculinities. In M. S. Kimmel, J. Hearn, & R. W. Connell (Eds.), *Handbook of studies on men and masculinities* (432–447). Thousand Oaks, CA: Sage Publications.

Hondagneu-Sotelo, P. (1994). *Gendered transitions: Mexican experiences of immigration.* Berkeley: University of California Press.

Klein, A. M. (2007). Tender machos: Masculine contrasts in the Mexican baseball league. *Sport in Society*, 10(6), 1014–1034.

LaFranchi, H. (2001, April 6). Candidate battles machismo—in women. *Christian Science Monitor*, 93, 1.

Lara, M. A. (1999). Estereotipos sexuales, trabajo extradoméstico y depresión en la mujer: Hacia una perspectiva de género en el estudio de la salud mental femenina [Sexual stereotypes, housework, and women's depression: Towards a gendered perspective in the study of women's mental health]. *Salud Mental*, 20, 121–127.

Lara-Cantú, M. A. (1989). A sex role inventory with scales for "machismo" and "self-sacrificing woman." *Journal of Cross-cultural Psychology*, 20, 386–398.

Levine, M., Perkins, D. D., & Perkins, D. V. (2005). *Principles of community psychology* (3rd ed.). New York: Oxford University Press.

Lockhart, J., and Schwartz, S. B. (1983). *Early Latin America: A history of colonial Spanish America and Brazil*. Cambridge, England: Cambridge University Press.

Loo, R., & Thorpe, K. (2000). Confirmatory factor analyses of the full and short versions of the Marlowe-Crowne social desirability scale. *The Journal of Social Psychology*, 140, 628–635.

Messick, S. (1995). Validity of psychological assessment: Validation of inferences from persons' responses and performances as scientific inquiry into score meaning. *American Psychologist*, 50, 741–749. doi: 10.1037/0003-066X.50.9.741

Mirandé, A. (1997). *Hombres y machos: Masculinity and Latino culture*. Boulder, CO: Westview Press.

Moritsugu, J., Wong, F. A., & Duffy, K. G. (2010). *Community psychology* (4th ed.). Boston: Allyn & Bacon.

Morrell, R., & Swart, S. (2005). Men in the third world: Postcolonial perspectives on masculinity. In M. Kimmel, J. Hearn, & R. W. Connell (Eds.), *Handbook of studies on men and masculinities* (90–113). Thousand Oaks, CA: Sage Publications.

Mosher, D. L., & Sirkin, M. (1984). Measuring a macho personality constellation. *Journal of Research in Personality*, 18, 150–163.

Mosher, D. L., & Tomkins, S. S. (1988). Scripting the macho man: Hypermasculine socialization and enculturation. *Journal of Sex Research*, 25, 60–84.

Nagelschmidt, A. M. (1981). Una medida de modernismo individual entre mujeres de Brazil [A measure of modernism among Brazilian women]. *Revista de la Asociación Latinoamericana de Psicología Social*, 1, 63–74.

National Center for Women and Policing. (2002). A content analysis of civil liability cases, sustained allegations & citizen complaints. Retrieved from www.womenandpolicing. org/PDF/2002_Excessive_Force.pdf

Neff, J. A. (2001). A confirmatory factor analysis of a measure of "machismo" among Anglo, African American, and Mexican American male drinkers. *Hispanic Journal of Behavioral Sciences*, 23, 171–188.

Neff, J. A., Prihoda, T. J., & Hoppe, S. K. (1991). "Machismo," self esteem, education and high maximum drinking among Anglo, Black and Mexican American male drinkers. *Journal of Studies on Alcohol, 52*, 458–463.

Norris, L., & Reiss, J. (2006). *La Adelita.* Retrieved from www.umich.edu/~ac213/student_projects06/joelan/adelita.html

Penalosa, F. (1968). Mexican family roles. *Journal of Marriage and the Family, 30*, 680–689.

Pollack, W. (1998). *Real boys: Rescuing our sons from the myths of boyhood.* New York: Henry Holt.

Rotter, J. B. (1992). Some comments on the "cognates of personal control." *Applied & Preventive Psychology, 1*, 127–129.

Seligman, M. E. P. (1992). Power and powerlessness: Comments on "cognates of personal control." *Applied & Preventive Psychology, 1*, 119–120.

Seligman, M. E. P., & Csikszentmihalyi, M. (2000). Positive psychology: An introduction. *American Psychologist, 55*(1), 5–14.

Sobralske, M. (2006). Machismo sustains health and illness beliefs of Mexican American men. *Journal of the American Academy of Nurse Practitioners, 18*, 348–350.

Stavans, I. (1996). The Latin phallus. In R. Gonzalez (Ed.), *Muy macho: Latino men confront their manhood* (143–164). New York: Anchor Books/Doubleday.

Sternberg, P. (2000). Challenging machismo: Promoting sexual and reproductive health with Nicaraguan men. *Gender and Development, 8*, 89–99.

Stobbe, L. (2005). Doing machismo: Legitimating speech acts as a selection discourse. *Gender, Work and Organization, 12*, 105–123.

Strong, W. F., McQuillen, J. S., & Hughey, J. D. (1994). En el laberinto de machismo: A comparative analysis of macho attitudes among Hispanic and Anglo college students. *The Howard Journal of Communications, 5*, 18–35.

Tajfel, H. (1982). *Social identity and intergroup relations.* Cambridge, United Kingdom: Cambridge University Press.

Taylor, J. (2000). Reinterpreting Malinche. *Ex Post Facto, 9*, 21–33. Retrieved from http://userwww.sfsu.edu/~epf/2000/jt.html

Torres, J. B., Solberg, V. S. H., & Carlstrom, A. H. (2002). The myth of sameness among Latino men and their machismo. *American Journal of Orthopsychiatry, 72*, 163–181.

Villemez, W. J., & Touhey, J. C. (1977). A measure of individual differences in sex stereotyping and sex discrimination: The macho scale. *Psychological Reports, 41*, 411–415.

Wertheimer, J. W. (2006). Popular culture, violence, and religion in Gloria's story. *Law and History Review, 24*(2), 375–422. Retrieved from www.historycooperative.org/journals/lhr/24.2/wertheimer1.html

9

TRANSFORMING BOYS, TRANSFORMING MASCULINITY, TRANSFORMING CULTURE

Masculinity Anew in Latino and Latina Children's Literature

Phillip Serrato

> Do we have ... dialogue about machismo going on in our community today? Or have we accepted old rules conditioned by forces beyond our control?
>
> (Rudolfo Anaya, 1996, pp. 62–63)

Since the early 1990s, artists working within a variety of disciplines have exhibited a growing interest in Latino masculinity. For example, theatre and performance practitioners such as Guillermo Reyes, Luis Alfaro, Maria Costa, Rick Najera, and John Leguizamo have crafted stage pieces that probe and problematize the nature and underpinnings of machismo. At the same time, literary offerings by Denise Chavez, Helena María Viramontes, Sandra Cisneros, Ana Castillo, and Carla Trujillo have proven to be valuable in numerous ways, not the least of which is their indictment of male violence against women. Not to be overlooked, films as diverse as *American Me* (1992), *Latin Boys Go to Hell* (1997), *Price of Glory* (2000), *Manito* (2002), and *La Mission* (2009) have also explored—with admittedly mixed results—some of the social, cultural, and personal issues that Latino males face. All told, a substantial body of creative work exists that examines and exposes the multifarious ways that boys and men experience, embody, and express masculinity.

Because children are at a point in their lives when they are forming their opinions and values and fashioning understandings of themselves, others, and the society around them, it is not surprising that Latino and Latina authors with progressive gender politics have begun to write books for younger audiences. After all, as noted by children's literature scholar Troy Potter (2007), "Literature is of significant cultural importance in reaffirming or challenging cultural ideologies, including those of gender and masculinity" (p. 28). To be sure, one implication of Potter's statement is that literature—especially literature for children—carries the potential to simply perpetuate the ideological status quo. Terry Eagleton (1990) suggested as much in *The Ideology of the Aesthetic*, in which he asserted, "From the infant school to the University faculty, literature is a vital instrument for the insertion of individuals into the perceptual and symbolic forms of the dominant ideological formation, able to accomplish this function with a 'naturalness,' spontaneity and experiential immediacy possible to no other ideological practice" (p. 56). With Eagleton's formulation in mind, it becomes possible to see books for children as potentially insidious instruments of integration propaganda. Yet if literature for children can suture readers into the dominant ideology, it alternatively follows that literature can be put into the service of progressive or even transgressive politics. Along these lines, Jack Zipes (2008), in his foreword to a recent anthology of radical children's literature, pointed out the flipside to Eagleton's approach, "The rise of strong political and social oppositional groups [at the end of the nineteenth century] led to the formation of socialist, communist, anarchist, feminist, and social rights organizations at the beginning of the twentieth century, and they produced diverse works for children that countered, contradicted, and opposed the mainstream products" (p. viii). Between the examples of Eagleton and Zipes exists a multiplicity of ideological stances available to children's authors. Encapsulating the specific capacity of children's literature to critically engage the subject of masculinity and prompt in younger readers a reassessment of prevailing gender expectations and definitions, Perry Nodelman (2002) stressed in his essay "Who the Boys Are: Thinking About Masculinity in Children's Fiction," "The more aware of [matters of gender and gender relations] we work to become, the more we can help children to become aware of them also—and, then, to make more conscious commitments for or against them" (p. 17).

   Within the field of contemporary Latino/a children's literature, authors are certainly working to actualize the type of potential described by Nodelman. Rudolfo Anaya, Luis Rodríguez, Pat Mora, Juan Felipe Herrera, Gloria Anzaldúa, Rigoberto González, and René Colato Laínez are just some of the authors who have written books for children that productively broach the subject of masculinity. In effect, they have made the genre of children's literature a vibrant site for efforts at cultural transformation. In their respective texts, these authors, all leery of rearticulating or otherwise sustaining traditional or stereotypical definitions of masculinity, offer younger readers opportunities not only to broaden their conceptualization of masculinity by deconstructing its definitions and parameters and providing a greater range of images of it; they also offer younger readers opportunities to acknowledge, understand, and question the various issues that Latino boys and men must negotiate. Perhaps above all else, this literature invites boy readers in particular to think about the examples of masculinity surrounding them, to reflect upon the pressures that they themselves have faced or will face as they grow up, and to figure out what kinds of men they want to become. Of course, although this literature carries tremendous potential, helping real children—especially real boys—to actually benefit from these texts remains a challenge. Fortunately, it seems that with some initiative, the potential of this literature to participate in the enlightenment of young people and contribute to social and cultural transformation can be realized.

Deconstructing the Macho Will to Power

To properly contextualize and appreciate the critical breakthroughs managed by recent artistic productions of all varieties, one must recognize the significant role that Latina feminism has played in enabling and inspiring this body of work. Over the years, as Latina feminists have drawn attention to gender roles and relations within Latino communities, they have progressively implicated Latino male privilege and behaviors in the oppression of Latina women. For example, in "Women: New voice of la raza" (1971), a key document in the emergence of Chicana feminism, Mirta Vidal directed a critical eye at machismo. Attempting to organize and articulate the premises of Chicana feminism at a crucially early moment in the movement's history, she asserted, "In part this awakening of Chicana consciousness has been prompted by the 'machismo' she encounters in the [Chicano] movement" (p. 5). With a subsequent reference to a contemporaneous article that delineated and indicted different "macho" behaviors, including a "lack of respect for Chicanas," Vidal foregrounded Chicano masculinity as an issue that must be addressed in order to fully understand and redress the condition of Chicana women. Later works ranging from Lea Ybarra's "Marital decision-making and the role of *machismo*" (1982) to Gloria Anzaldúa's *Borderlands/La frontera* (1987) have continued to cite masculinity as an integral factor in Latina lives. In many cases, the upshot of this work is that the state of Chicano/Latino masculinity, as it has predominately been defined and lived, requires revision.

Many recent picture books for children extend the work of Latina feminism by bringing to light and critiquing problematic masculine tendencies. Gloria Anzaldúa's *Friends from the other side* (1993), for example, portrays male bullying as an empty and cruel display of bravado. The story is set in south Texas and features the development of a friendship between Joaquín, an undocumented immigrant boy from Mexico, and Prietita, a young Chicana. In a key scene of intracultural racism, Joaquín finds himself threatened by a group of Chicano boys. Besides calling him "wetback" and "*mojadito*," one of the antagonists chides him, "Hey, man, why don't you go back where you belong? We don't want any more *mojados* here." At this instant, Prietita, whose ire is raised by the injustice of the boys' actions, boldly assumes the role of a clear-thinking New Mestiza—the critically enlightened figure that Anzaldúa valorizes in *Borderlands*. She intercedes in the scene, chastising the boys, "What's the matter with you guys? How brave you are, a bunch of *machos* against one small boy. You should be ashamed of yourselves!" As the bullying boys are thus humiliated, the text encourages readers to share not only in Prietita's outrage, but also in her insight into the bankrupt and reprehensible underpinnings of some forms of masculinity.

Similarly, Rudolfo Anaya's *Roadrunner's dance* (2000) is a tale about masculinity and bullying. In this story, the bully takes the form of a rattlesnake that terrorizes other animals whenever they travel through the road that he has claimed as part of his turf. Rattlesnake, set up not-so-subtly as an emblem of phallic masculinity via the suggestive set of rattles that he wields and ostentatiously flaunts, emerges as a figure through which one can rebuke the macho will to power that Anaya first took to task in his earlier essay, "'I'm the king': The macho image" (1996). Indeed, one need only consider Rattlesnake's boastful proclamation—"Look at me . . . . I rattle and hiss, and my bite is deadly. I am king of the road, and no one may use it without my permission"—to realize the picture book is an adaptation of the author's essay. Notably, as occurs in Anzaldúa's *Friends from the other side*, a female figure orchestrates the eventual disciplining of masculinity that takes place in *Roadrunner's dance*. After much supplication, a magical figure, Desert Woman, comes to the aid of Rattlesnake's numerous victims by cobbling together a new creature, Roadrunner, whom she instructs, "You will dance around Rattlesnake and peck at his tail. He must learn he is not the king of the road." When Roadrunner confronts Rattlesnake, he "[spins] around Rattlesnake until the serpent [becomes] dizzy" and acquiesces, "You win! You win!" Thus defeated, Rattlesnake disavows his former ways. With Roadrunner's proclamation that "there is no [longer any] king of the road," the reformation of Rattlesnake ultimately betokens a social transformation. Interestingly, one way to read the similarly integral roles of the female characters in *Friends from the other side* and *Roadrunner's dance* is as a symbolic reflection and acknowledgment of the Latina feminist's status as an individual who, with her astute perspective on patriarchal gender dynamics, can intervene in and interrupt the patriarchal status quo. In the texts of Anzaldúa and Anaya, and specifically through the distinctively proactive roles of Prietita and Desert Woman, we witness the insights and efforts of the Latina feminist leading to the positive transformation of masculinity.

Another savvy commentary is delivered by Pat Mora in *Doña Flor: A tall tale about a giant woman with a great big heart* (2005). With its storyline about an unseen puma that terrorizes a small village with its "terrible '*Rrrr-oarrr!*,'" this picture book is an exceptionally crafty exposé and indictment of the same masculine will to power that underwrites the bullying behavior found in the texts by Anzaldúa and Anaya. According to the narrative, the roar of the puma is enough to instill in the villagers a fear so tremendous that they refuse to leave their homes. In the process, the puma seizes for himself the ability to keep the villagers under his control. Notably, in this manner Mora suggests patriarchal gender relations. The puma resembles a domineering male whose empowerment depends on the coercion of others into marginalized social spaces. In particular, the fact that the villagers are compelled to stay in their own homes calls to mind the historical disempowerment of women via their relegation to domestic spaces. However, when Doña Flor, the story's eponymous giant woman, decides to investigate, she uncovers the reality of the situation. When the woman approaches the mesa from which the terrible sounds have been emanating, "All she saw was the back of a cute little puma." As she proceeds to "[watch] him very quietly," she basically studies him in an effort to understand the situation as clearly and completely as possible.

Soon enough, the sham of the puma's power is revealed: "Doña Flor began to tiptoe toward the puma when all of a sudden he roared into a long, hollow log. The sound became a huge '*Rrrr-oarrr!*' that echoed down into the valley." Interestingly reminiscent of Judith Halberstam's discussion (1998) of the "prosthetic" nature of masculinity in patriarchal social formations, Mora literally depicts masculine prominence as a technology, a process whereby males manufacture their own dominance over others. Ultimately, the puma's artificial amplification of his unexceptional roar into an intimidating assertion of social control serves as a rich metaphor for the different means (social, economic, cultural) by which patriarchal dominance has been instituted and maintained. Moreover, Mora suggests that the daunting veneer of masculinity masks a rather indistinctive reality:

> *Aha!* thought Flor. "Are you the little *chico* who's causing all the trouble?" she asked. The little puma tried to look very fierce. His eyes sizzled with angry sparks. He opened his mouth wide, and his teeth glinted. He roared his meanest roar. "*Rrrr-oarrr!*" he growled, but without the log, the growl wasn't really very fierce.

While some of the more theoretical aspects of the portrayal of the puma and his exposure by Doña Flor—who can be read as yet another incarnation of Latina feminism—may be lost on younger readers (including the allusion to the illusory nature of phallic masculinity vis-à-vis the hollow log), at the very least it can be said that Mora invites and enables a critique of masculinity and the will to power. In addition, her story promotes a skeptical reconsideration of the bases and nature of masculine primacy.

Stretching the Imagination

Alongside the indictment of problematic aspects of Chicano/Latino masculinity that one finds in texts such as *Friends from the other side*, *Roadrunner's dance*, and *Doña Flor*, Latino/a books for children have increasingly begun to present diverse versions of masculinity that explode rigid and narrow configurations of Latino masculinity. Such is clearly the objective of Mora in another of her picture books, *Pablo's tree* (1994). In this text, Mora presents two male characters who embody none of the negative attributes of stereotypical masculinity. As I have noted elsewhere in a fuller treatment of this book (Serrato, 2010), the story features a loving relationship between the eponymous 5-year-old child and his grandfather. Besides illustrating the possibility for males to be emotionally open, the portrayal of Pablo and Lito taking pleasure in music, stories, and the beauty of the tree that Lito has decorated for his grandson orients masculinity toward distinctly aesthetic interests and delights and away from stereotypically rougher and tougher physical activities. Especially important in Mora's strategic depiction of Pablo and Lito is the fact that the book targets readers similar in age to that of the title character. As such, it can be said that Mora's book attempts to intervene in young readers' conceptualization of masculinity before their socializing experiences delimit it. In this regard, we might situate *Pablo's tree* within the progressive effort that is presently afoot to model a broader range of modes of masculinity for boys who are at a presumably impressionable age. In his preface to *Ways of being male: Representing masculinities in children's literature and film* (2002), John Stephens pointed out the recent proliferation of such efforts:

> In recent literature and film addressing preadult audiences masculinity has emerged as an increasingly overt theme. Of particular note here is the propensity for such texts to engage in attempted social intervention by privileging variants of a "sensitive male" schema (or postfeminist masculinity) and pejorating the hegemonic masculinity associated with patriarchy and against which preferred masculinities are depicted.
>
> (Stephens, 2002, p. xi)

For boys in the midst of fashioning their gender identities, the representation of a panoply of modes of masculinity potentially frees them to experience and express themselves in ways that transcend the narrowness of dominant gender prescriptions. Moreover, it can prepare readers—both boys *and* girls—to accept a more expansive range of masculinities.

A compelling means by which children's understanding of masculinity can be broadened beyond dominant definitions is through the dramatization—and thus validation—of emotional vulnerability in boys. Recently, much attention has been devoted to the fact that the socialization of boys often demands their emotional foreclosure and invulnerability. Discussing the limits imposed on the emotional lives of boys, psychologist William Pollack (1998) asserted:

> Many of the boys I see today . . . [live] behind a mask of masculine bravado that hides the genuine self to conform to our society's expectations; they feel it necessary to cut themselves off from any feelings that society teaches them are unacceptable for men and boys—fear, uncertainty, feelings of loneliness and need.
>
> (Pollack, 1998, p. 5)

Consequently, Pollack has urged that boys need "to feel less ashamed of [their] own vulnerable feelings" (p. 8). By acknowledging the different emotional challenges that real boys face, contemporary children's literature can be seen as attempting to undo the emotional stranglehold to which dominant gender norms have subjected them.

Incidentally, autobiographical immigrant narratives such as Juan Felipe Herrera's picture book *The upside down boy* (2000) and Francisco Jiménez's *The circuit: Stories from the life of a migrant child* (1997) perform this kind of service quite powerfully. Both works stand out as texts that illustrate the distinctive susceptibility of immigrant boys to their fears and lack of confidence as the protagonists deal with new schools, few friends, and a feeling of dislocation. In *The upside down boy*, the author shares with readers his adjustment to a new school after years of life on the road with his *campesino* (migrant farmworker) parents. Estranged from everything and everyone around him on multiple levels, Juanito, the narrator, relates, "My feet float through the clouds/when all I want is to touch the earth./I am the upside down boy" (p. 14). Similarly, Panchito in Jiménez's text contends with feelings that range from loneliness at school (especially as he never stays at one school for long because his family is always on the move) to fear of being caught by the Border Patrol. To be sure, the emotional challenges that Juanito and Panchito endure are not particular to immigrant Latino boys. Various studies document the multifaceted struggles that both Latino boy and Latina girl immigrants face as they try to adjust to life in the United States (Dumka et al., 1997; Kao, 1999). Accordingly, in the children's literature marketplace there are several books for young readers that portray immigrant Latina narratives, including Irene Beltran Hernandez's *Across the great river* (1989), Anilú Bernardo's *Fitting in* (1996), and Luis Rodríguez's *América is her name* (1998). But what is unique— and valuable—about *The upside down boy* and *The circuit* is the books' ability to open up a space for emotional vulnerability in boys, who are often expected to be emotionally uncomplicated vis-à-vis emotional invulnerability.

It's Complicated but not Hopeless

Elsewhere the complication of the subjectivity of boys is developed exceptionally well by Herrera in his verse novel *Downtown boy* (2005). The novel is narrated from the first-person perspective of Juanito Palomares, a 10-year-old boy whose family is constantly moving due to his father's restlessness. Particularly noteworthy is Herrera's handling of the convoluted dynamics of Juanito's subjectivity and the complicated formation of his masculine identity. As the author portrays Juanito adjusting to life in different California cities, recurrently surrounded by unfamiliar people, readers see Juanito's maturation crisscrossed by numerous voices foisting their gender-based expectations on him. Through a motley cast of characters that includes cousin Chacho, cousin Tito, Chacho's friend Edda, and Coach Egan, not to mention Juanito's mother and father, readers find that the messages about masculinity that Juanito receives are not only inconsistent, but frequently conflict with each other. For example, in the opening pages of the book, we find Juanito exhorted by Chacho to take up boxing. With the insistence, "You're gonna love boxing!" (p. 5), Chacho ultimately challenges his younger cousin, "You wanna be a chump/or a champ?" (p. 7). All the while, Juanito is hesitant, not only because boxing is not in his nature, but because of his parents' rules. Feebly, he protests,

> Chacho . . . I, uh, don't think my mom
> likes me doing stuff like that and . . .
> Papi said, back in Ramona Mountain,
> that I shouldn't fight.
>
> (Herrera, 2005, p. 6)

Unwilling to let Juanito's parents have the final say (and sway), Chacho eventually commands the boy, "Get with it, *Primo!*/Get tough, *Primo!*" (p. 7). Shortly thereafter, while Juanito is still uncertain about how to adjudicate the competing viewpoints of Chacho and his parents, he encounters another imposition. Cousin Tito, who is older than Chacho, adds to the psychic fray within Juanito by challenging Juanito and Chacho, "I bet neither of you cats/can do the 'Morgue Run.' Are you squares/or are you cool Daddy-os?" (p. 35). The reference here is to an alleged rite of passage in which one sneaks into the ventilation system of the local morgue to shoot spitballs into opened cadavers. As the rest of the novel unfolds, we see Juanito increasingly confused and emotionally in turmoil from the mixed messages that threaten to overwhelm him.

Importantly, in dramatizing the formation of Juanito's selfhood, Herrera refuses to present the condition of being a boy as a confident, stable state of selfhood that boys naturally assume and enjoy. Instead, Juanito's maturation is presented as a tumultuous journey that is shot through with numerous competing influences and feelings. In the process, Herrera throws into relief the unstable nature of masculinity. As Chacho, Tito, and all the others advise Juanito on how to be a boy, readers witness the fundamentally indeterminate and inconsistent nature of gender definitions. In addition, readers are invited to consider the formation of gender identity as a messy process that carries very high stakes. To Herrera's credit, however, rather than portray Juanito as a helpless boy pulled in every direction by the various others around him, *Downtown boy* drives toward a suggestion of the boy's agency. The implication that progressively emerges is that at some point, Juanito, like any other boy, will decide for himself what kind of boy and, by extension, what kind of man, he wants to become.

A similar emphasis on the agency of boys is the primary message of *It doesn't have to be this way* by Luis Rodríguez (1999). This particularly bold picture book tells the story of Monchi, a boy who finds himself pressured to join a local street gang. Reflective of the author's commitment to counseling young people away from crime, drugs, and gangs, the story first depicts Monchi's inclination to accept the invitation. However, as the day of his initiation into the Encanto Locos Pee Wees approaches, he begins to realize just how dangerous *la vida loca* (or "crazy life" of a gangbanger) is. With a portrayal of the perils that are a fact of gang life, the book ultimately becomes a warning for young readers. The story's defining moment occurs near the end after Monchi's cousin, Dreamer, has been gunned down in a drive-by shooting. All along, Dreamer has been trying to convince Monchi not to join the gang, and in one last desperate effort she goes to the lot where her cousin and the Pee Wees are hanging out. When members of a rival gang pass by and start firing, Dreamer is shot. As Monchi, who is wracked by guilt, waits in the hospital to hear Dreamer's prognosis, his uncle Rogelio advises him, "It doesn't have to be this way, *m'ijo*. I know you want to be a man, but you have to decide what kind of a man you want to be." Without a doubt, this advice is intended as much for the implied boy reader as it is for Monchi. Evidently impressed by his uncle's words, Monchi, acting as a model for readers, exercises the agency that Tío Rogelio suggests. The next time he encounters Clever, the leader of the Pee Wees, Monchi declines the invitation and decides to follow a different life course.

Certainly, Rodríguez's effort to empower readers via a declaration of their agency is admirable. But the efficacy of his methodology is questionable at best, and it throws into relief the challenges that literature with progressive politics face in effecting social, cultural, and individual change. As regards masculinity and children's literature, Stephens and Nodelman both noted that any presumption that social change can be implemented simply by portraying masculinity differently in books would be naïve. Granted, Stephens has posited:

> children's literature can make a significant contribution to whether or not child readers understand the conflict between the possibilities of forging a new subjective agency and the propensity of a hegemonic social structure to represent itself as always already given and inevitable.
>
> (Stephens, 2002, p. xiii)

But he also acknowledged a dialectic between symbolic representation and intervention on one hand and lived reality on the other. Observing that "the dynamics of representation may be grappling with a complex network of possibilities," he noted that literary representation necessarily runs into "the historically situated embodied practices (repetitive, lived aspects of sexual identity) of adult males and boys themselves" (p. xii). Even more bluntly, Nodelman offered the sobering prospect that:

> the portrayals of boys defying cultural machismo so common in children's fiction may have little influence on boy readers when compared to the huge power of cultural conventions which reinforce traditional desirable masculinity. When it comes to what it means to be a man, boys are less

likely to listen to their mothers and librarians than to other boys and older male figures.

(Nodelman, 2002, p. 12)

The gap, as suggested by Stephens and Nodelman, between the efficacy of well-intentioned literature and the reality of the playground, the street, and other venues where the socialization of boys occurs becomes all too clear with the ending of *It doesn't have to be this way*. As I have discussed in a separate essay on Rodríguez's picture books (Serrato, 2009), the agency that Monchi exercises at the end of the book seems too idealistic. In reality, many boys living in gang-infested areas cannot simply walk away from an "invitation" to join a gang because in many cases these invitations are non-negotiable (Spergel, 1995). Thus, Rodríguez's particular suggestion for a boy's agency to choose his own path of selfhood is, in the real world, a rather fraught proposition. This begs the question, then, how can we actualize the socializing potential of Latino/a children's books that otherwise productively problematize, broaden, and complicate masculinity?

Policy Possibilities for Change

Given the legitimate reservations of Stephens and Nodelman about the capacity of children's literature to have any bearing on the ways that real boys think about and embody masculinity, the challenge that parents, teachers, and other concerned parties face is how to facilitate real boys' meaningful engagement with the literature that exists? Because school years constitute a major part of a boy's life —and in all likelihood school is the place where he does most of his reading— the classroom emerges as a site where critical thinking about masculinity can be groomed. In this respect, the work of Wayne Martino is both helpful and inspiring. A passionate advocate for the development of progressive pedagogies, especially with regard to gender, Martino has published a number of books and articles that highlight the potential for the classroom to facilitate the institution of progressive praxis. For instance, in his piece "Deconstructing masculinity in the English Classroom: A Site Reconstituting Gendered Subjectivity" he suggested,

> Through deconstructive praxis … an emancipatory politics can be elaborated in the English classroom, providing the basis for the reconstitution of gendered subjectivity and ways of knowing that are freed from a phallocentric symbolic order. It is in this sense that other less oppressive forms of masculinity can be promoted and validated, ones which are not tied to an oppressive symbolic order.
>
> (1995, p. 206)

Given the attributes of the books discussed above, it goes without saying that they could provide a powerful core for the sort of curriculum that Martino envisions.

Of course, Martino's proposal that the literature curriculum can be tailored to "[stimulate] discussion about the social construction of masculinity" and thus "deconstruct gender regimes" (p. 217) is contingent on certain factors. For starters, any curricular changes or innovations always run the risk of parental, community, and administrative objections. In particular, the issues of gender and sexuality never fail to be lightning rods for protestations. Consequently, one can wonder how willing and/or able a teacher may be to facilitate student engagement with, for example, Gloria Velásquez's *Tommy stands alone* (1995) or Rigoberto González's *The Mariposa Club* (2009), both of which depict gay Latino male characters contending with homophobia. Even works such as *It doesn't have to be this way*, with its references to gangs and its portrayal of a drive-by shooting, and *Downtown boy*, with a scene in which Juanito nearly falls into the clutches of a pedophile, could elicit objections. Although Rodríguez and Herrera handle the content of their texts tactfully and purposefully, the reality is that sometimes it only takes a textual detail and a complaint—or a teacher's fear of a complaint—to keep a book out of the curriculum. Add to such concerns the intensifying emphasis on standardized test performance over curricular innovation, as well as tightening school budgets, and the institution of a critically progressive literature curriculum seems more and more challenging.

Nonetheless, there are models in place for involving Latino youth in workshops about masculinity. Recently, the North Carolina Coalition Against Domestic Violence announced an initiative to "create statewide public school programs to teach boys about masculinity and gender roles" (Changing the Culture, 2010). The ambitious scope of the ten-year, federally funded endeavor is especially laudable given its professed commitment to actualize a "paradigm shift" in thinking about gender and gender relations across the state. At the very least, the pursuit of social and cultural transformation, especially among Latino boys, can take place or begin on a smaller scale.

In fact, such a project could be modeled after the Latino male discussion groups that began convening in cities across the country around the year 2000. As reported by Jennifer Mena in the *Los Angeles Times* (2000), the original idea behind the *círculos de hombres* (or "circles of men") was to "redefine 'macho man'" (p. E1) by giving Latino men the opportunity to confront and explore the issues that they face. One special objective was for these men to "unravel" their own "condition[ing] to be rough and even uncaring" and thereby "reconstruct manhood" (p. E3). Incidentally, Jerry Tello, one of the featured organizers of the discussion groups, recognized the importance of involving younger men in these *círculos*, too. He is quoted by Mena as saying, "I have seen a growth of young men who see a different way of seeing themselves. We want to engage young men with themselves, with each other, and with older men" (p. E3). Under the aegis of the National Compadres Network (n.d.), the *círculos* continue to be active in over fifty cities in the United States, and Tello himself presently serves as consultant for the curriculum he has developed titled *El Joven Noble* (or the

Noble Young Man). One can conceive that a discussion and support network (quite possibly involving the aforementioned literature) similar to the *círculos* could be developed for Latino boys.

In the final analysis, it seems that a critically informed literature for young readers about masculinity could serve as the starting point for the *conscientización* of boys and the reconceptualization of gender definitions. The critical thinking and reconsiderations that this literature enables can help broaden the socialization of boys beyond the narrowness of the images and expectations that have historically prevailed. Indeed, the texts explored in this chapter lend themselves to the initiation of rigorous and sincere discussions about gender definitions and relations. But because literature by itself cannot effect social change, ancillary programs that integrate and build upon the literature are necessary if its potential for cultural, social, and individual transformation is to be actualized and maximized. Once Latino boys are able to grow up with a less rigid, less problematic understanding of what it means to be male and realize that they have agency in deciding what kind of men they want to become, the sort of cultural transformation that Latina feminists began describing years ago becomes possible.

References

Anaya, R. (1996). "I'm the king": The macho image. In R. González (Ed.), *Muy macho: Latino men confront their manhood* (57–74). New York: Anchor.

Anaya, R. (2000). *Roadrunner's dance*. New York: Hyperion.

Anzaldúa, G. (1987). *Borderlands/La frontera*. San Francisco: Aunt Lute.

Anzaldúa, G. (1993). *Friends from the other side*. San Francisco: Children's Book Press.

Bernardo, A. (1996). *Fitting in*. Houston: Piñata Books.

Changing the Culture. (2010, June 6). *Winston-Salem Journal*. Retrieved from www2. journalnow.com/content/2010/jun/06/changing-the-culture/opinion/

Dumka, L. E., Roosa, M. W., & Jackson, K. M. (1997). Risk, conflict, mother's parenting, and children's adjustment in low-income, Mexican immigrant and Mexican American families. *Journal of Marriage and Family*, 59, 309–323.

Eagleton, T. (1990). *The ideology of the aesthetic*. Cambridge: Blackwell.

González, R. (2009). *The mariposa club*. New York: Alyson Books.

Halberstam, J. (1998). *Female masculinity*. Durham: Duke University Press.

Hernandez, I. B. (1989). *Across the great river*. Houston: Arte Público.

Herrera, J. F. (2000). *The upside down boy*. San Francisco: Children's Book Press.

Herrera, J. F. (2005). *Downtown boy*. New York: Scholastic.

Jiménez, F. (1997). *The circuit: Stories from the life of a migrant child*. New York: Houghton Mifflin.

Kao, G. (1999). Psychological well-being and educational advancement among immigrant youth. In D. J. Hernandez (Ed.), *Children of immigrants: Health, adjustment, and public assistance* (410–477). Washington, D.C.: National Academy Press.

Martino, W. (1995). Deconstructing masculinity in the English classroom: A site reconstituting gendered subjectivity. *Gender and Education*, 7, 205–220.

Mena, J. (2000, December 12). Creating the new macho man. *Los Angeles Times*, pp. E1, E3.

Mora, P. (1994). *Pablo's tree*. New York: Simon & Schuster.

Mora, P. (2005). *Doña Flor: A tall tale about a giant woman with a great big heart*. New York: Knopf.

National Compadres Network. (n.d.). About us. Retrieved from www.nationalcompadres network.com/?page_id=21

Nodelman, P. (2002). Who the boys are: Thinking about masculinity in children's fiction. *The New Advocate*, 15(1), 9–18.

Pollack, W. (1998). *Real boys: Rescuing our sons from the myths of boyhood*. New York: Random House.

Potter, T. (2007). (Re)constructing masculinity: Representations of men and women in Australian young adult literature. *Papers: Explorations into Children's Literature*, 17, 28–35.

Rodríguez, L. (1998). *América is her name*. Willimantic, CT: Curbstone Press.

Rodríguez, L. (1999). *It doesn't have to be this way*. San Francisco: Children's Book Press.

Serrato, P. (2009). Conflicting inclinations: Luis J. Rodríguez's picture books for children. In M. Pagni Stewart & Y. Atkinson (Eds.), *Ethnic literary traditions in American children's literature* (191–204). New York: Palgrave.

Serrato, P. (2010). Promise and peril: The gendered implications of Pat Mora's *Pablo's tree* and Ana Castillo's *My daughter, my son, the eagle, the dove*. *Children's literature*, 38, 133–152.

Spergel, I. (1995). *The youth gang problem: A community approach*. New York: Oxford University Press.

Stephens, J. (2002). Preface. In J. Stephens (Ed.), *Ways of being male: Representing masculinities in children's literature and film* (ix–xiv). New York: Routledge.

Velásquez, G. (1995). *Tommy stands alone*. Houston: Arte Público.

Vidal, M. (1971). Women: New voice of la raza. In *Chicanas speak out* (3–11). New York: Pathfinder Press.

Ybarra, L. (1982). Marital decision-making and the role of *machismo*. *De Colores*, 6, 32–47.

Zipes, J. (2008). Foreword: The twists and turns of radical children's literature. In J. Mickenberg & P. Nel (Eds.), *Tales for little rebels: A collection of radical children's literature* (vii–x). New York: New York University Press.

10

UNDOCUMENTED LATINO YOUTH

Strategies for Accessing Higher Education

Daysi Diaz-Strong
Christina Gómez
María E. Luna-Duarte
Erica R. Meiners

> It makes me angry a lot when some people have their citizenships and they don't appreciate what they have. I know some students that are from high school and have citizenship and they don't care. They use drugs, they don't care about school. They just care about their friends and having fun. They don't think about their future. And I would like to have that opportunity—the citizenship—so I can go to college, so I can have a better future for me and my family. . . . Well, I say they should give us a chance because we deserve it, and if they give us a chance, I think we will appreciate real good and work really hard towards our career.
>
> Josue, age 18

Josue, who arrived in the United States when he was 11 years old, is just one of the approximately 42 out of 210 undocumented graduates of a Chicago open enrollment high school (class of 2008). This number does not include the many students who already dropped out of school in tenth or eleventh grade to work, convinced that a high school diploma offered no real route to a future. Josue and the many other undocumented students we interviewed are all too aware of the pathways awaiting them in the United States—namely, physically demanding low-wage work and possibly deportation. As Pedro A. Noguera (2008) has stated, "many Latino youth will remain like so many immigrant youth of the past, hard-working and hopeful but caught in the circumstances that erode their dreams of a better future" (p. 82). For undocumented youth, this loss of optimism is particularly true.

In this chapter, we explore the relationship between criminalization and access to citizenship and education. Building from our activist fieldwork, including the collection of forty interviews with undocumented and formerly undocumented youths in the Chicago area, we examine the role of the prison industrial complex in conferring "civil death" on growing segments of the population, including undocumented Latino students, especially Latino males. We use the term *social* or *civil death* as defined in Ruth Gilmore's work on our expanding carceral state and the consequences of conviction and incarceration that extend beyond one's time in prison (Gilmore, 2002, 2007; Patterson, 1982). Civil death refers to the fact that many in the United States possess no basic civil rights. For example, in some states, those with criminal convictions are restricted from voting and employment and do not have access to educational resources and other social services.

The concept of civil death can also encompass how U.S. immigration policies and practices continue to be an integral component of our expanding prison industrial complex (Rodriguez, 2008). According to the Pew Hispanic Center, in 2007:

> Latinos accounted for 40% of all sentenced federal offenders—more than triple their share (13%) of the total U.S. adult population. By 2007, immigration offenses represented nearly one-quarter (24%) of all federal convictions, up from just 7% in 1991. Among those sentenced for immigration offenses in 2007, 80% were Hispanic.
>
> (Lopez & Light, 2009, p. i)

Immigration offenses include entering the United States unlawfully and living in the country without authorization or "papers," as well as smuggling, transporting, or harboring an undocumented person, filing false statements on applications, marriage fraud, and failing to report the arrival of undocumented individuals. In 2007, 75 percent of sentenced immigration offenders were convicted of unlawfully entering or living in the United States (Lopez & Light, 2009, p. 4).

While the youths we interviewed have not been incarcerated, they too are subjected to civil death; in daily life their experiences are similar to that of formerly (or currently) incarcerated men and women who lack civil rights. Some of the students interviewed struggled to determine what rights, if any, they could claim. When asked if he had any rights in the United States, Ricky, age 20, responded:

> I mean, besides most human rights I don't think I do. I mean, I have no say in anything really. I mean, I could protest but there's nothing really I can do. I can't vote or anything. If I'm arrested in some cities or counties I can be deported. Sometimes I feel like I don't have any rights. There's nothing I can ever really do. If they ever find that out, they can just deport

me. I don't feel I have any rights other than civil liberties, and I don't even know if I have those.

In reality, undocumented individuals do not have the right to vote and are denied access, either directly or indirectly, to most avenues of post-secondary education, social assistance benefits, and legal employment. Many fear public spaces, frightened of being apprehended by the police or Immigration and Customs Enforcement (ICE) agents. Yet, in our interviews with currently and formerly undocumented youths, their desires for access to higher education and citizenship situate them in opposition to criminal figures. In our nation of over two million (and counting) behind bars, their strategies for accessing citizenship work to augment this "prison nation" by animating old racialized stories of "those other people" who are unworthy, undesirable, and lazy.

Study Cohort and Process

Over a two-and-a-half-year period (2007–2010), we interviewed forty currently and formerly undocumented youths and collected their oral histories, centering on educational experiences and addressing other issues, including family, border crossings, relationships to U.S. identity, and future plans. This research evolved from our outrage with the escalating anti-immigrant and anti-Latino climate in recent years that many undocumented immigrants face in our country. The media coverage has further exacerbated this condition by routinely depicting Latino immigrants as "illegal aliens" while offering little historical context to the nation's immigration policies and trends. We also work at institutions where students have disclosed to us that they are undocumented and turn to us for guidance.

Respondents in this project self-identified to participate. We accessed formal and informal networks, and interviewed youths through snowball sampling. Our participants are self-identified Latino students (at least 18 years of age) already enrolled in high school or college and working to be academically successful. Clearly, this is a select sample and not representative of the total population of undocumented youth in the Chicago region or the nation. In total, we interviewed twenty-seven female and thirteen male students.

The youths we interviewed, especially the young men, have a complicated relationship with the vast and growing criminalized population in the United States. Despite their undocumented status, these students strategically elect to not identify as participants in the expanding criminalized class. We have found that students deploy strategies of social dis-identification to separate themselves from "criminals" or "bad and undeserving Latinos or Blacks" in order to survive in the United States and to navigate the narrow, and often impossible, path towards citizenship. Most of these students view themselves as "good" and "hard working," unlike their more acculturated and assimilated second- and third-generation Latino counterparts or Black youth (Noguera, 2008; Suarez-Orozco

& Suarez-Orozco, 2001). They often disassociate themselves from targeted groups (perceived as lazy, felons, undeserving) so as not to be mistaken for one of them and suffer any negative consequences. Because they are acutely aware of the media portrayal of their status, and because of the history of how citizenship has often been acquired by new non-White immigrants, disassociation from other marginalized groups makes strategic sense. Their approach helps them preserve their individual identities as hard working and "deserving of a chance" within an oppressive and acquisitive prison industrial complex that is quick to incarcerate and deport. Thus, ventriloquating the rhetoric of the "good immigrant" reflexively perpetuates the same racist structures that constrain many undocumented individuals in everyday life.

Our discussion of this topic is divided into two parts. The first offers a brief overview of the undocumented population within the growing U.S. prison industrial complex and introduces our research within this theoretical context. The second part analyzes a key finding from our interviews with undocumented Latino students—namely, how these youths frame access to citizenship within a nation-state where prisons, jails, and borders continue to be fortified. While this chapter looks critically at how the youths we interviewed narrate their complex location in the United States, we acknowledge that each of the students involved in this project struggles to survive and flourish in annihilating contexts. As scholars and activists deeply invested in social, economic, and racial justice movements, we offer this analysis in the spirit of building a movement for change and in the hope of better understanding the disenfranchisement of Latino males.

The Prison Industrial Complex

The *prison industrial complex* (PIC), a term used to refer to the privatization and profit in the expanding prison system, devastates communities of Color (Mauer & Chesney-Lind, 2003). The Pew Center on the States Public Safety Performance Project (2008) documented that at the start of 2008 American prisons or jails held 2,319,258 adults, accounting for one prisoner for every 99.1 men and women. This high incarceration rate is a direct result of a national punitive law-and-order agenda and public policies that target women, poor people, and/or people of color—the war on drugs, mandatory minimum sentencing—not from a rise in violent crime (Davis, 2000; Mauer, 1999). With the merger of the Immigration and Naturalization Services (INS) into the Department of Homeland Security (DHS) in 2001, and the corresponding shift from immigration as a service to an enforcement agency and the establishment of a network of 400-plus private and public detention centers nationwide, undocumented immigrants are an integral, and expanding, component of this criminalized class.

Between 1991 and 2007, the number of those sentenced in federal court more than doubled, largely due to an increase in sentenced Latinos. In fact, the number of Latinos sentenced quadrupled (270 percent) and accounted for 54 percent of the growth in the total number of those sentenced. In 2007, Latinos without U.S. citizenship represented 29 percent of all people convicted of federal offenses, and among all Latinos convicted of crimes, some 72 percent were not U.S. citizens (up from 61 percent in 1991). In comparison, only 8 percent of White people and 6 percent of Black people who were sentenced in federal courts in 2007 were not U.S. citizens (Lopez & Light, 2009).

Immigration has always played a central role in our nation's prison industrial complex. Criminalization and imprisonment have been used both as a form of labor control and, more broadly, as a means of disciplining marginalized populations. As Angela Davis (2000) wrote in *From the Convict Lease System to the Super-max Prison*, recently freed African-Americans were criminalized after the American Civil War through the Black Codes practiced in the Southern states. Once incarcerated in conditions worse than slavery, these men constituted a ready supply of laborers following the War. Ex-slaves were not the only targets of these Codes; numerous laws also addressed Indigenous Peoples, criminalizing their behavior and subsequently framing them as exploitable labor (Ogden, 2005).

The detention and incarceration of marginalized populations is profitable business. Labor within prisons is contracted out to for-profit companies (such as Victoria's Secret), often for as little as 25 cents a day (Evans, 2005). In U.S. prisons, minimum wage laws do not apply, and overtime and healthcare benefits are not an issue because companies simply do not offer them; large profits are there to be made. The exploitable labor of those incarcerated is parallel to the labor of the undocumented. For instance, in 2008, state officials in Colorado proposed that incarcerated workers could simply replace the potentially diminishing supply of migrant workers. Colorado employers and state politicians believed that the raids conducted by ICE would result in fewer migrant workers willing to do migrant labor in their state; they suggested replacing this labor force with the state's prison population. Those in prison would be paid "60 cents a day" for weeding, harvesting, and other manual labor, aiming to address the gap in labor, estimated at 150,000 undocumented workers in the state (Frosch, 2007).

More central than the possibility of exploiting the labor of the incarcerated is the construction of multi-billion dollar detention centers and prisons and the subsequent staffing and maintenance of these institutions, touted by supporters as an economic engine for depressed rural communities (Gilmore, 2007). With this landscape of "surplus" land, deindustrialization, and corresponding under- and unemployment, the criminalized and undocumented, from one vantage point, are commodities. Seduced by planners' promises of steady employment and economic revitalization, towns are betrayed by the mobility of employees at prisons and the inability of locals to qualify for the "new" employment (Gilmore, 2007). Rather than sound economic investment, the prison industrial complex is *anti-developmental* (Ferguson, 1994). While prisons and detention centers are the result of intricate economic planning, the consequences of this planning do not develop the region's capacity for long-term economic growth; rather, they offer maximum profit to certain stakeholders, including construction corporations, utilities, prison guard unions, and the producers and marketers of surveillance technologies.

If the 1980s were characterized by prison construction fueled by the war on drugs, the post 9/11 decade is about detention center expansion, scaffolded by the war on terror. In 2008, ICE removed 356,739 undocumented immigrants from the United States—a 23.5 percent increase from 2007. With a workforce of over 17,000 and a 2008 budget that topped $5 billion, ICE is the largest enforcement agency, deporting an average of 977 non-citizens on a daily basis:

> [ICE] is responsible for one of the largest, most transient and most diverse detainee populations in U.S. custody. On any given day, at more than 300 ICE-managed detention facilities and contract facilities nationwide, the agency is responsible for overseeing the well-being of thousands of detainees hailing from countries around the world. ICE detainees include men, women and juveniles of all ages, including families. . . . ICE detention bed space has grown from 18,500 beds in FY03 to approximately 32,000 beds in FY08.
>
> (U.S. Immigration and Customs Enforcement, 2008, p. 19)

Reporters with the *Washington Post* recently calculated that:

> with roughly 1.6 million immigrants in some stage of immigration proceedings, the government holds more detainees a night than Clarion Hotels have guests, operates nearly as many vehicles as Greyhound has buses and flies more people each day than do many small U.S. airlines.
>
> (Hsu & Moreno, 2007, p. 8)

With the proliferation of detention centers and borders (including internal border checkpoints), the advent of raids such as Operation Return to Sender that result in the deportation of non-citizens, and the militarization of border areas, border control is an integral part of the nation's expanding prison industrial complex. In public and private facilities across the nation and outside, this detention does not just confer civil death but physical death. As of August 2009, 104 immigrants have died at federal detention centers since 2003 (Farrell, 2009).

The consequences of detention and/or conviction directly shape individual (and community) participation in our democracy and in our public sphere. The Sentencing Project (2007) has indicated that "5.3 million Americans, or one in forty-one adults, have currently or permanently lost their voting rights as a result of a felony conviction" (p. 1). The Sentencing Project has documented a national landscape of inconsistent disenfranchisement restrictions and cumbersome voting-rights restoration processes. The undocumented individual faces similar prohibitions and current policies; Arizona's SB1070 act – which gives police broad power to detain individuals who look suspicious and to criminalize the failure to carry immigration documents – has been compared to apartheid in South Africa and the World War II internment of Japanese-Americans, and exacerbates the growing criminalization of the undocumented.

The Undocumented Youth

Although the issue of undocumented individuals residing in the United States is an on-going media story, little has been written about undocumented youth specifically. Most of these youths came to the United States with their parents or adult guardians, and in some cases arrived by themselves. Many of these children have grown up in the United States, attended grammar and high schools, and lived typical "American" lives. Approximately 65,000 undocumented students graduate from high school each year across the United States (UCLA Center for Labor Research and Education, 2007), and estimates suggest that 7,000–13,000 undocumented immigrants are enrolled in colleges across the country (Passel, 2005). Existing qualitative research has documented that immigration status directly shapes academic persistence and "strongly influences" students' decisions to leave school (Norrid-Lacy & Spencer, 1999). Lack of financial resources was another primary barrier identified in the research. Undocumented students do not qualify for federal aid and in most states cannot apply for state aid. Additionally, many schools require citizenship or permanent residency for scholarship monies, disqualifying undocumented students from most forms of financial assistance. Undocumented students lack the proper documentation to have a "normal life" in the United States; they do not have valid social security numbers, visas, resident alien cards, or other documents that would allow them to reside and work legally in this country.

Most of the undocumented persons in the country are Latinos, with Mexicans comprising 57 percent of the undocumented population and other Latin Americans making up 24 percent. Nationally, approximately 9 percent of the undocumented are from Asia, 6 percent from Europe and Canada, and 4 percent from Africa and other countries; 1.7 million undocumented immigrants are children under the age of 18 years. One in every six undocumented persons is a child. Additionally, 60 percent of undocumented immigrants between the ages of 18 to 39 are male; there are 146 men for every 100 women (Passel, 2005).

Available research suggests that approximately 20,000 undocumented high school students live in Chicago, and approximately 6.1 percent of all undocumented students are enrolled in a post-secondary institution (IBHE, 2002; Mehta & Ali, 2003). Because of the escalating cost of colleges and universities, many students, including those eligible for most financial aid, simply cannot afford higher education. Even when they are accepted to public or private four-year institutions, most undocumented students will attend the overflowing public community colleges in the states where they reside (as long as there is no law that prohibits their access to higher education, such as that found in South Carolina).

Imagined Access to Citizenship: Hard Work and Good People

Citizenship, and access to the benefits and rights associated with it, is commonly linked to labor and "hard work" (Ngai, 2004). "Good" citizens usually contribute to society through their labor. In addition, citizens are assumed to act responsibly, pay taxes, obey laws, and improve society overall; they are responsible people of good character (Westheimer & Kahane, 2004). It follows that "bad" citizens behave irresponsibly, break laws (and consequently are imprisoned), and harm society. This paradigm of the "good immigrant" versus the "bad immigrant" is persistent in U.S. history, especially during economic downturns. For example, during the 1920s the right to U.S. citizenship for Mexicans was questioned; anti-immigrationists tried to prove that Mexicans were a menace to society by exploiting the image of the racially inferior and diseased Mexican (Molina, 2006).

Not surprisingly, when asked whether they saw themselves as American citizens, the undocumented youths we interviewed frequently answered yes, and offered their "hard work" as evidence for citizenship. This response was a consistent theme across all our interviews; when youth were asked about their desire for citizenship, they often included in their discussion the fact that they and their family worked hard. These messages about hard work and success, about American-ness and access to citizenship, directly oppose the identity and the figure of the "criminal." The criminal was defined by respondents as a gangbanger, drug dealer, lazy non-productive non-worker, and terrorist, in contrast to the hard-working, good citizen and other loved ones who merit access to the rights associated with citizenship.

Some students blamed individuals who "mess up" and do not appreciate their citizenship as the reason they cannot gain access to citizenship. If it were not for those "bad apples," then everything would be good for them. Cristobal, age 23, explained why he believes not everyone should be granted citizenship:

> I think they would take it (citizenship). And I think if they pass such a thing (amnesty) there will be plenty of people who would take advantage of it, and it will make the ones who really do care about becoming Americans, it will make them look bad and it could hurt them in the future.

When pressed on who really cares about becoming American, Cristobal explained:

> I would say it's the younger people that are not getting in trouble. I mean it's undeniable to say—there are rotten apples in every barrel. . . . There are people who care and people who don't care. I just don't want the ones who care to be hurt by those who don't care.

Logically, these youths are quick to self-identify themselves and their families as good and are highly conscious of the consequences of not being perceived as good. In order for them to argue for the ability to stay in the United States or negotiate for a visa or amnesty, they articulate the need to place themselves on the side of the "worthy" citizen or immigrant. They are not allowed to mess up, or do "illegal things." Interestingly, they do not view their status of being undocumented as an illegal activity. Instead those "other people" who are not working hard (gangbangers, etc.) are the bad immigrants, and they (the students) are not like them. Even when students identify being in the United States without permission or driving without a license as a criminal activity, they are quick to qualify and differentiate themselves from the others.

> I've got to go to work, and I have to have somewhere to live, and I've got to go to school; I've got no choice. I hate committing a crime, but . . . so I'll just say I don't commit any crimes because I feel like it.
>
> (Cristobal, age 23)

This method of dis-identifying with a group (often other native-born Latinos or Blacks) allows undocumented students to articulate a space for themselves that might permit access to citizenship. In addition, showing that they are contributors, not takers, and succeeding without the help of the government (no handouts) becomes an important factor in this construction. Students correctly point out the important talking points that they would bring up if given the opportunity to share their story with policy makers:

> I would like to share my story in front of the Senate so that they can see that I'm not a bad person; that I'm trying to contribute to this country as much as I can.
>
> (Luis, age 24)

> If I could share my story with anyone I think it would be [with] Congress . . . and make them understand, I'm not here to ruin their economy or use their resources carelessly.
>
> (Ricky, age 20)

These youths see their access to citizenship through the pathway of hard work and the American dream; it is because they are good that they can identify as American and therefore belong in the United States.

Media Representations

The labels of good and bad are pre-existing tropes that are racialized, sexualized, and genderized: girls are good, neat, follow orders, and are not supposed to get pregnant or be involved in gangs. The pathways to "badness" for young Latino males are through gangbanging, drug dealing, and dropping out of school. The undocumented youths interviewed respond to, and reflect, the tropes of immigration represented in mainstream media. While the National Association of Hispanic Journalists has issued a press release requesting that aliens not be used as a noun, the request has seemingly had no impact (Montalvo & Torres, 2009). Mainstream media recycles the terms *illegal* and *alien* again and again, using headlines such as "Illegal aliens cost Florida hospitals $100 Million" (Amato, 2009) and "Illegal aliens with fake documents caught at border" (Vaugh, 2009). Such headlines, always referring to Latinos, inflame the nation's anxieties. Whether it is voter fraud, falsely attributing the current financial crisis to undocumented workers acquiring mortgages, or arousing anxiety about drug wars in Mexico, mainstream U.S. media play a significant role in shaping perceptions about Latino immigration and U.S. national security.

Politicians and the media will frequently resort to narratives of how America's limited resources are being diverted away from the deserving, hard-working taxpayer to the undeserving, selfish, benefit-seeking criminal (e.g., California's Prop 187 or Arizona's SB 1070). In this situation, hard-working Americans are the victims of those immigrants who come to the country to take advantage of America's generosity. The impact of scapegoats is another old story in the United States.

When asked about their perceptions of media coverage of Latinos and immigration, most of the youths we interviewed accurately pointed to the misrepresentation of Latinos in mainstream media. They understand how the media has constructed them in the public eye. The students were acutely aware of the framing of the debate over immigration: immigrants (in particular the undocumented) take jobs away from deserving Americans, use up scarce resources, and are viewed as criminals. As criminologist Ramiro Martinez, Jr. (2006) stated, "rising immigration into the United States coincided with increased fear of crime in many areas—a presumed connection dating back to at least the early 1900s" (p. 7). The students' analysis of media was finely tuned; they understood how different media outlets (Univision verses Fox News, for example) represented them. As Jorge, age 22, describes:

> Again, with the media it's a lot of propaganda—the pro immigrants trying to accomplish one thing and the anti-immigrants another thing. . . . I mean it depends on what station you watch but for the most part they say we're criminals, and we're here to take jobs, and we're raising taxes, and we're depleting services.

The students are very aware of the narrative that is played out in the media, portraying immigrants as "criminals" not worthy of access to citizenship. When asked about his opinion on the portrayal of Latinos in the media, Luis, age 24, responded:

It depends on the reporter, but on the general media I believe the word *immigrant* has become I guess connected with the word *illegal* and that creates a chain, because from immigrant you create that word *illegal*, or people believe it's illegal and from being illegal they connect it with criminal.

Yet, even though these students understand that the media represents them as criminals, they do not view themselves this way. However, their understanding of the complicated position they hold does not extend to other groups that are portrayed as criminal. In other words, criminals are other people who break the law.

Negotiating Access

While the youth in our sample understood that myths and inaccurate stories are carelessly portrayed in the media, they were often acutely aware that these are the narratives to ventriloquate in order to seem "fit" for citizenship. And, more astutely, the youth often named these representations as labels that shape the routes individuals pursue to gain legalization. Stories about good youth, worthy youth, working and ideologically appropriate youth, are the identities required to map onto mainstream avenues for legalization. Josue, age 18, is able to name the right path to market oneself to a legislator:

To a legislator it depends if it is in an election season or not, but you have to try to build your resume, build yourself up by being involved in the community, by being involved in school, getting good grades and so forth, and then you can present to the legislator. I've done the best I can. I'm in the top 5 percent of overall students in the university and when I graduate I will have a degree and I won't be another negative statistic for Latinos that hasn't graduated and is working on minimum wage and stuff like that. . . . How can you help me? What can I do? You just can't go to the legislator and say I need my legal status. It is a catch for both sides. If you've been a good student, it is easier for them to work for you if you're trying to be the best you can compared to you just wanting the legal status.

In response to questions about how to build a movement for comprehensive immigration reform, Ricky, age 22, identified how the labor and economic tensions, layered onto a racialized landscape, present a barrier to unity and movement building.

I think they [the media] use them as scapegoats. . . . I think they praise them when they're necessary but when something goes bad they're pretty much the first people that they blame it on. . . . They portray them as a good thing when they need cheap labor, but then when the economy is going bad all of a sudden we're like a burden on everyone.

Yet, despite their ability to recognize that labor and economic anxieties fuel the mainstream media's portrayal of their struggles and that this is the story to ventriloquate to get access to resources, this circulation of the criminal and deviant persists with consequences. We focus on the trope of the criminal, the bad person, because immigration is an intimate piece of our nation's expanding prison industrial complex. While criminalizing immigrants facilitates deportation, and some of the immigrants targeted for deportation have committed crimes in the United States (or in their home country), the undocumented students elect not to identify with this criminal figure.

Criminality in the United States has been, and continues to be, racialized. Disassociation with the figure of the criminal is also a racial distancing strategy. Yen Le Espiritu (1992) reported that before the 1960s, Asians in the United States sometimes distanced themselves from one another so as not to be mistaken or blamed for the presumed transgressions of that group. She has explained how external threats (such as violence or possible deportation) can intensify solidarity or distance them from stigmatized members. Rather than joining in combating racist forces, early Asian immigrant communities disassociated themselves from the group under attack for fear of being aligned with them. Like the Chinese who displayed buttons proclaiming "I'm Chinese" during World War II for fear of being considered Japanese and incarcerated (Espiritu, 1992, p. 23), so do our young Latino students differentiate themselves. They understand that as Latinos, especially Latino males, they are all being lumped into a category that views them as criminals. In order to negotiate a possible space for themselves, especially given their status as undocumented individuals, they disassociate themselves from the other groups that are stigmatized.

Conclusion

The undocumented youths we interviewed recognize that in order to have access to citizenship they must prove themselves as worthy and deserving. The narrative they repeat is the script most readily accessible in popular media: hard workers who contribute to society should have access to resources, and others who are lazy, criminal, on welfare, and do not contribute to society should not, or at the very least, are undeserving of the rights that they possess. Instead of challenging the social structures that award few (often Whites) as worthy of full participation in society and others (mostly Latinos, Blacks, and the poor) as unworthy, the students we interviewed are often boxed into deploying this very same strategy to defend their right for citizenship. While this strategy is individually useful to those who can prove their worth, in a national landscape where access to rights in the public sphere continues to erode and civil death is the public pathway of too many of our brothers and sisters, coalition building across differences is required to build a just democracy.

The dynamic at play is one that persists in the U.S. cultural imagination and has clear implications for both public policy and the racial justice movement. If hard-working youths who are not gangbangers merit citizenship, youths who fail in school or use drugs do not. This logic extends beyond immigration. If we have innocent men (and women) trapped behind bars, we clearly also have guilty or culpable individuals at large who need to be put behind bars. If children are exempt from incarceration, perhaps adults who are culpable are not. Innocence is a safe strategy that can be mobilized for policy and justice ends, but is often too narrow. A plan that forges access to civil rights for all will benefit the undocumented student as well as his brothers and sisters.

References

Amato, P. (2009, April 24). Illegal aliens cost Florida hospitals $100 million. *First Coast News*. Retrieved from www.firstcoastnews.com/news/news-article.aspx?storyid=136591

Davis, A. (2000). From the convict lease system to the super-max prison. *States of confinement: Policing, detention, and prison*. New York: St. Martin's Press.

Espiritu, Y. L. (1992). *Asian American panethnicity: Bridging institutions and identities*. Philadelphia: Temple University Press.

Evans, L. (2005). Playing global cop: U.S. militarism and the prison industrial complex. In J. Sudbury (Ed.), *Global lockdown; Race, gender, and the prison-industrial complex* (215–230). New York: Routledge.

Farrell, M. B. (2009, August 19). Immigrant detention deaths increase pressure for reform. *Christian Science Monitor*. Retrieved from www.csmonitor.com/USA/2009/0819/p02s13-usgn.html

Ferguson, J. (1994). *The anti-politics machine: "Development," depoliticization, and bureaucratic power in Lesotho*. Minneapolis: University of Minnesota Press.

Frosch, D. (2007, March 4). Inmates will replace wary migrants in Colorado fields. *New York Times*. Retrieved from http://query.nytimes.com/gst/fullpage.html?res= 9902E0D81731F937A35750C0A9619C8B63

Gilmore, R. W. (2002). Race and globalization. In R. J. Johnston, P. J. Taylor, & M. J. Watts (Eds.), *Geographies of global change: Remapping the world* (2nd ed.) (261–274). Oxford: Blackwell.

Gilmore, R. W. (2007). *Golden gulag: Prisons, surplus, crisis, and opposition in globalizing California*. Berkeley: University of California Press.

Hsu, S., & Moreno, S. (2007, February 2). Border policy's success strains resources: Tent city in Texas among immigrant holding sites drawing criticism. *Washington Post*, p. A01. Retrieved from www.washingtonpost.com/wp-dyn/content/article/2007/02/01/AR2007020102238_pf.html

Illinois State Board of Higher Education (2002). *Changing demographics/changing education needs: Report to the Illinois General Assembly on house resolution no. 982*. Retrieved from www.ibhe.state.il.us/board/Agendas/2002/December/Item 8Report.pdf

Lopez, M. H., & Light, M. T. (2009, February 18). A rising share: Hispanics and federal crime. *Pew Hispanic Center*. Retrieved from http://pewhispanic.org/files/reports/104.pdf

Martinez, R., Jr. (2006). Coming to America. In R. Martinez & A. Valenzuela (Eds.), *Immigration and crime: Race, ethnicity, and violence* (1–19). New York: New York University Press.

Mauer, M. (1999). *Race to incarcerate*. New York: New Press.

Mauer, M., & Chesney-Lind, M. (Eds.). (2003). *Invisible punishment: The collateral consequences of mass imprisonment*. New York: New Press.

Mehta, C., & Ali, A. (2003). *Education for all: Chicago's undocumented immigrants and their access to higher education*. Chicago: UIC Center for Urban Economic Development. Retrieved from www.urbaneconomy.org/node/53

Molina, N. (2006). *Fit to be citizens: Public health and race in Los Angeles*. Berkeley: University of California Press.

Montalvo, D., & Torres, J. (2009). NAHJ urges news media to stop using dehumanizing terms when covering immigration. *National Association of Hispanic Journalists*. Retrieved from www.nahj.org/nahjnews/articles/2006/March/immigrationcoverage.shtml

Ngai, M. M. (2004). *Impossible subjects: Illegal aliens and the making of modern America*. Princeton: Princeton University Press.

Noguera, P. A. (2008). *The trouble with black boys . . . and other reflections on race, equity, and the future of public education*. San Francisco: Jossey-Bass.

Norrid-Lacey, B., & Spencer, D. A. (1999). *Dreams I wanted to be reality: Experiences of Hispanic immigrant students at an urban high school*. ERIC Document Reproduction Service, no. ED 434 527.

Ogden, S. (2005). The prison-industrial complex in indigenous California. In J. Sudbury (Ed.), *Global lockdown: Race, gender and the prison-industrial complex* (57–66). New York: Routledge.

Passel, J. S. (2005). Estimates of the size and characteristics of the undocumented population. *Pew Hispanic Center*. Retrieved from http://pewhispanic.org/reports/report.php?ReportID=44

Patterson, O. (1982). *Slavery and social death: A comparative study*. Cambridge: Harvard University Press.

Pew Center on the States. (2008, February 28). *One in 100: Behind bars in America*. Retrieved from www.pewcenteronthestates.org/uploadedFiles/One%20in%20100.pdf

Rodriquez, D. (2008). I would wish death on you: Race, gender, and immigration in the globality of the U.S. prison regime. *Scholar & Feminist Online*, 6(3). Retrieved from www.barnard.edu/sfonline/immigration/drodriguez_01.htm

Suarez-Orozco, M., and Suarez-Orozco, C. (2001). *Children of immigration*. Cambridge: Harvard University Press.

The Sentencing Project (2007). *Felony disenfranchisement laws in the United States*. Retrieved from http://sentencingproject.org/doc/publications/fd_bs_fdlawsinusMarch2010.pdf

UCLA Center for Labor Research and Education (2007). Undocumented students, unfulfilled dreams. Retrieved from www.labor.ucla.edu/publications/reports/Undocumented-Students.pdf

U.S. Immigration and Customs Enforcement (2008). *ICE fiscal year 2008 annual report: Protecting national security and upholding public safety*. Retrieved from www.ice.gov/doclib/pi/reports/ice_annual_report/pdf/ice08ar_final.pdf

Vaugh, J. (2009, April 23). Illegal aliens with fake documents caught at border. *Yuma Sun News*. Retrieved from www.yumasun.com/news/border_49591___article.html/port_documents.html

Westheimer, J., & Kahane, J. (2004). What kind of citizen? The politics of education for democracy. *American Educational Research Journal*, 41(2), 237–269.

11

CLAIMING QUEER CULTURAL CITIZENSHIP

Gay Latino (Im)Migrant Acts in San Francisco[1]

Horacio N. Roque Ramírez

> WOMAN II, in a marked Uruguayan accent: Good evening. (Alejandro and Woman I exchange glances.)
> WOMAN I: Sit down. You're crossing, too? Where do you come from?
> WOMAN II: From Uruguay.
> ALEJANDRO: What are you doing so far from home?
> WOMAN II: I wanted to come to the United States with my son, but they wouldn't give us a visa. But then I saw on television that people cross running from Mexico to the United States, so I got tickets to Mexico and to Tijuana, and I told myself, we're going to run like any other Mexican. (Alejandro and Woman I laugh.)
> WOMAN I: Welcome, then.
> ALEJANDRO: Welcome to the adventure.
>
> (As quoted in the film *Del otro lado*)

By the time viewers see and hear the above border-crossing sequence in the 1999 independent, Spanish-language film *Del otro lado* (On/from the other side), they have already followed Alejandro's own "adventures" in Mexico City. Finding himself among strangers while weighing the risks for crossing the U.S.-Mexico border, after the *coyote*, or people smuggler, has deserted them in an isolated mountain in the middle of the night, Alejandro already carries multiple losses during his trip. He has left behind his biological family, his gay male lover, and his tight circle of gay friends in Mexico. Certainly a dangerous adventure for all, Alejandro's own crossing involves leaving queer networks behind—he is "*del otro lado*," after all, a playful, coded way to suggest being from "the other side," that is, gay, related to the Mexican historical phrase *"de los otros"*—"of the other kind." While Alejandro becomes just another immigrant in flight, his own trek involves the additional burden of negotiating his sexuality as a gay Latino who is HIV positive and in search of medical care and support to deal with his infection.

Alejandro indeed has these "invisible" life issues to address in *Del otro lado,* but his character also personifies the economic, social, and cultural dislocation of hundreds of thousands of Latinos in the United States—brown bodies disconnected from blood kinships and cultural ties in search of the promise of a better future in the United States. For these immigrants, California since the 1990s literally and figuratively has become a land of selective inclusion: immigrants fill the underpaid labor needs of the state, but are made invisible in the cultural life of its citizenry—politically, linguistically, and otherwise (Chavez, 2001; Santa Ana, 2002).

Scholars have taken up the question of citizenship and specifically that of cultural citizenship to address Latinos' political claims for inclusion in the United States. This idea of cultural citizenship speaks to claims for excluding and for belonging. Rather than encompassing a notion of citizenship solely as that quality of *legally* and *officially* belonging to the nation, cultural citizenship speaks to what Renato Rosaldo referred to as the "uneven field of structural inequalities" (Rosaldo, 1997, p. 276). In this field, domination and marginalization structure society, making some subjects "less equal" than others. But also in this field, those deemed lesser subjects aspire to eliminate such hierarchies and to redefine the meaning of citizenship for everyone. "Cultural citizenship," William V. Flores and Rina Benmayor (1997) argued, offers an opportunity to consider everyday forms for seeking entitlement in the United States:

> [W]hat makes cultural citizenship so exciting is that it offers us an alternative perspective to better comprehend cultural processes that result in community building and in political claims raised by marginalized groups on the broader society. Unlike assimilation, which emphasizes absorption into the dominant white, Anglo-European society, or cultural pluralism, which conceives of retention of minority cultural traits and traditions within U.S. society, but nonetheless privileges white European culture and history and assumes retention of existing class and racial [and gender] hierarchies under the pretense of political equality, cultural citizenship allows for the potential of opposition, of restructuring and reordering society.
>
> (Flores & Benmayor, 1997, p. 15)

Cultural citizenship thus allows for an exploration of alternatives to the dominant model of citizenship based on assimilation, for new possibilities for Latinos—immigrant and U.S. born—to make public communities and claim space and rights as full members of society. Cultural productions like *Del otro lado* become key sites for understanding how contestations over cultural citizenship operate—not only do they represent such contestations symbolically, but they also provide a literal means to intervene into these issues. Similarly, Lisa Lowe (1996) has discussed culture as a critical space for engaging the national discourse of citizenship:

> [C]ultural productions emerging out of the contradictions of immigrant marginality displace the fiction of reconciliation, disrupt the myth of national identity by revealing its gaps and fissures, and intervene in the narrative of national development that would illegitimately locate the "immigrant" before history or exempt the "immigrant" from history.
>
> (Lowe, 1996, p. 9)

As direct responses to the exclusionary political and cultural representations of the nation, Lowe continues, Asian Americans generate critical *acts*: "the *acts* of labor, resistance, memory, and survival, as well as the politicized cultural work that emerged from dislocation and disidentification" (ibid, p. 9, emphasis in original).

Building on these scholars' notions of cultural citizenship and politicized cultural work, I explore in this essay two instances of gay Latino (im)migrant cultural productions in San Francisco. Based on oral history field research and existing archives, I look at the social history and significance of two productions. The first one, the 1984 play *El Corazón nunca me ha mentido* (My heart has never lied to me), was an adaptation of Salvadoran novelist Manlio Argueta's *Un día en la vida* (*One Day of Life*, 1980; English translation, 1983). Set in 1970s El Salvador, both the testimonial novel and the play related the political and social dislocations in the country that decade. Written and produced in San Francisco by two gay Chicanos from Texas, the play drew attention not only for its sociopolitical engagement, but also for its homoerotic critique of patriarchy. The second cultural production I explore is the film *Del otro lado* (1999). Written in the mid-1990s in San Francisco by two gay Mexican immigrants, the film follows the challenges of a gay male couple in Mexico City and the decision of one of the partners to migrate to the United States as a result of his HIV positive diagnosis. Exploring the processes of departure, arrival, and exodus for gay Mexican immigrants in the context of AIDS and of economic dislocation in Mexico and the United States, *Del otro lado* is a cultural text of queer social membership and cultural citizenship. Together, these two cultural productions reveal how cultural works provide the means to renegotiate citizenship materially and the importance of reconceiving the very meaning of citizenship itself.

Sexiled Bodies and Their Cultures

Since the 1960s, queer Latinas and Latinos have been part of queer migrations settling in San Francisco (Cora, 2000; Rodríguez, 2003; Roque Ramírez, 2003, 2005, 2007, 2008, 2010; Rosales, 2001). Many have been regional migrants, while others have traveled farther, across international borders. Since the organizing days of the Gay Latino Alliance in San Francisco in the 1970s (one of the first gay Latino organizations in the country), local, national, and international politics have intersected in the lives of queer Latina and Latino activists in the Bay Area. For many of these (im)migrants, their lives in San Francisco have revolved around maintaining old networks of support while establishing new ones in the city's heterogeneous queer communities. These are the sexual migrants Manuel Guzmán (1997) has referred to as "sexiles," those queer migrants leaving home/nation as a result of their sexuality.

Queer Latino immigrants have had to contend with exclusionary politics around their immigration status in the country. But they have also had to negotiate their membership in the local queer body, specifically the queer Latina/o community. Despite some of the local rhetoric of diversity and openness, San Francisco has not been an altogether welcoming place for immigrants (Brook et al., 1998; Roque Ramírez, 2001). Queer and Latino non-profit service agencies themselves have often informally demarcated services and alliances around immigrant/non-immigrant social memberships. Although not formalized, these demarcations in practice speak to the limits of "community" and citizenship for queers marked as immigrants, and for immigrants marked as queer. The negotiations and relations between immigrant and non-immigrant Latino queers have taken place on broad social fields: political, cultural, and erotic/sexual. Their efforts to mark identity, visibility, space, and desire on these fields speak precisely to the notion of cultural citizenship—in a queer male Latino context—of collective membership always in contestation.

Given the role organizing has played for many gay Latino immigrants, their public cultural work is an excellent space for examining their negotiation of citizenship and social membership in the national and local body. "Culture" in their work speaks to the productions themselves, but also to the depiction and experience of social and community life. To employ Raymond Williams's (1977) observation about the social experience of "culture" as a lived present, their productions represent "structures of feeling," "affective elements of consciousness and relationships: not feelings against thought, but thought as felt and feeling as thought" (p. 132).

Feeling and thinking about culture and political change were at the center of the lives of the four gay cultural workers producing *El corazón nunca me ha mentido* and *Del otro lado*. All of them had (im)migration histories leading to their work in San Francisco, histories that in turn impacted the content and direction of their work as *gay* (im)migrants. In 1988, Gustavo Martin Cravioto, one of the writers and producers of *Del otro lado*, fled the economic deterioration of Mexico City and arrived in California at the age of 22, originally moving into the city of Novato, north of San Francisco. Eventually he helped about fifteen other friends and relatives, gay and straight, to immigrate to the United States. In this regard, his extensive immigration network, extending from Mexico to the United States (and back) was similar to that of many other Latin American immigrants (gay and non-gay). Specifically for gay-, or bisexually identified *mexicano* immigrants, however, as the important ethnographic work of the late gay Chicano sociologist Lionel Cantú, Jr. (2009) was demonstrating in diverse publications before his untimely death, the fact that they had to navigate the long and complicated border between the U.S. and Mexico—with all of the challenges and opportunities that this signifies—meant that through their immigrant lives, in all their social, political, sexual, familial, economic, and all other ways, they had to create new meanings, identities, spaces, and communities both on the border and on either side of it.

By the time Gustavo moved to San Francisco, an AIDS service industry had already developed in the Mission District, the city's historically Latino neighborhood.[2] Gustavo joined these efforts, volunteering in these and mainstream (White) services responding to the on-going AIDS crisis. While the epidemic was beginning to level off for White gays, it continued to impact disproportionately gays of Color, including a large immigrant class. As Gustavo's volunteering efforts turned into paid positions as an outreach worker, he came into close contact with immigrant and non-immigrant HIV clients. An immigrant himself, this segment in the city's Latino population needing HIV education and services would remain his priority.

Mario Callitzin, the other writer of *Del otro lado*, was also a Mexican immigrant when he landed in the Bay Area, although with a different family history than Gustavo's. The son of two professionals in Mexico City, Mario moved from this Mexican metropolis to a small town in South Texas in the late 1970s. Immersing into his studies to escape the culture shock and racism in the United States, and the "terror" he describes following him since childhood as a result of being harassed as a "sissy," Mario attended Stanford University in the mid-1980s. There, feminist, race theory, and anti-apartheid study groups fueled him with more purpose, leading to the birth of what he referred to as "Mario the activist."[3] Although Mario returned to Mexico briefly and joined the gay movements there, he moved back to the Bay Area with his lover, finding the economic challenges in Mexico too overwhelming. By the early 1990s, he had joined several San Francisco gay Latino organizations, usually in close connection to the work taking place elsewhere in Latin America and especially in Mexico.

Compared to Gustavo and Mario, Juan Pablo Gutiérrez and Rodrigo Reyes, the producers of *El corazón nunca me ha mentido*, were a different type of migrant when they landed in San Francisco. They were sexiles too, given the intimate connections between their gay selves and the work they sought to carry out in San Francisco. The son of migrant workers from the small Texas town of Weslaco, Rodrigo moved permanently to San Francisco in the early 1970s, part of the large gay migration to the city in that decade. Migrant work had taken Rodrigo and his family throughout the Midwest. With the financial support of one of his White high school teachers, Rodrigo attended Ohio State University, giving him an opportunity to dabble in acting and theater. This first theater experience was the foundation for his experiments one decade later in San Francisco's Mission District as an openly gay Chicano cultural worker. It was not until he got to San Francisco, Rodrigo recalled decades later, that he felt "at home," as a gay Chicano organizing around racial and gay consciousness—simultaneously.

Juan Pablo Gutiérrez, too, was a Texan transplant in San Francisco's Mission District. He arrived in the midst of the AIDS epidemic in the city, in 1985, one decade after the large gay migration had brought tens of thousands of newcomers to the city. A different kind of large migration into the city was taking place in the 1980s, one visible in the Mission District. As revolutionary struggles had triumphed in Nicaragua under the sandinistas, and on-going guerrilla warfare challenged U.S.-backed right-wing dictatorships in Guatemala and El Salvador, Central America was sending hundreds of thousands of its citizens to the United States, a visible portion of them to San Francisco's Mission District.

The very trip taking Juan Pablo from Texas to what he would eventually carry out in the Bay Area revolved precisely around Central American and particularly Salvadoran reality. Picking up the English translation of Manlio Argueta's testimonial novel *One day of life*, he read it on his way to San Francisco and began to make plans for a possible theatrical adaptation once he landed. Bringing with him a history of gay Chicano activism in Texas and other cultural work throughout the Southwest, Juan Pablo had a politicized theatrical sensibility grounded on Chicano experiences. Upon reading *One day of life*, his interest turned to the on-going conditions left behind by thousands of refugees escaping political repression and social deterioration in El Salvador. As part of a long tradition of cultural and community organizing in the Mission District, Juan Pablo, Rodrigo, Mario, and Gustavo brought to their respective cultural stages (im)migration experiences and the politics of their specific (gay) exodus. How they engaged gender and sexuality in these politicized cultural creations was itself a manifestation of the coalescence of gay and immigrant histories.

El corazón nunca me ha mentido: *Bodies and Nations at War*

AIDS and the specter of death enveloped a great deal of gay and lesbian culture and activism in San Francisco in the 1980s. While the 1970s had been a decade for sexual liberation and celebration, the 1980s was a different, less festive one. But many, like Juan Pablo, still came, especially those connected to earlier sexiles. For some gay Latinos, the cultural framing of AIDS as White and gay offered a convenient though counterproductive source of denial—a "gay white disease" would not affect them. As soon as gay Latinos began to get ill in visible numbers, however, community-based health agencies could not avoid responding to the growing crisis.

One challenge in this AIDS crisis involved educating Latino men who had sex with men yet identified themselves only as heterosexual. Vesting themselves

FIGURE 11.1 Flyer for Rodrigo Reyes and Juan Pablo Gutiérrez's *El corazón nunca me ha mentido*

Courtesy of Luis Alberto de la Garza C. and Archivo Rodrigo Reyes

with gender and sexual capital framed in heteronormativity, these men never-theless had sex with other men, often while maintaining sexual relations with women partners and, many health workers feared, without consistent safer sex practices. That a large portion of these men were undocumented added yet more complexity to the educational response: it required a simultaneous consideration of the men's sexual identity and agency, the necessity of taking an HIV antibody test to ensure that they were negative in order to qualify for residency status, and the community's response (or lack thereof) when many found out about their HIV positive status as undocumented immigrants. Thus, the fight against AIDS among Latinos in San Francisco involved not only those who openly identified as gay or bisexual, but also a large segment of the community of Latino men holding on to a public heterosexual sense of self, and thus engaged in a larger community debate around gender and sexuality, sexual consciousness and secrecy, and immigrant rights and needs.

Juan Pablo's and Rodrigo's theatrical adaptation of *One day of life* addressed questions of gender and sexuality directly relevant to this community dialogue. Framing El Salvador's political and armed struggles of the 1970s, the novel narrates the stories of rural poor Salvadorans caught in battle zones: between younger, progressive Catholic priests speaking on behalf of the poor and the military repressive forces targeting any activity deemed subversive; between the need to subsist on an everyday basis and the anger and desire to join the armed struggle against the government. Rodrigo and Juan Pablo's adapted play addressed these personal, political, and emotional battles. Directed by Rodrigo, the play represented the first time in San Francisco Chicanos theatrically addressed the revolutionary period in El Salvador, despite the fact that their presence in the Mission had been felt strongly long before. Although Chicanos co-wrote the play, the production team was an amalgamation of nationalities and (im)migrant histories in the Mission, with gay and non-gay, Salvadoran, Spanish, Mexican, and Nicaraguan actors. One of Rodrigo's lovers, a Salvadoran ex-soldier, helped develop the dialogue to reflect more closely Salvadoran vernacular Spanish. According to Juan Pablo, the then-exiled Salvadoran Argueta in Costa Rica reviewed the adapted script and made no corrections, and the project moved to bring local political attention to an on-going international crisis.

The play entered several cultural fields of contestation. First, the play represented the first time the long tradition of Chicano *teatro* (theater) in the city concerned itself with Central American immigrants. Second, the explorations of male gender and sexuality brought up immigrant *and* nonimmigrant homosocial visibility. A complex and, for some, controversial text, the play became an inter-section for local, national, and transnational representations. Running for five weekends in the Mission District's small Capp Street Playhouse from late June through early August 1985, *El corazón* was a cultural product produced by two openly gay Chicano cultural workers wanting to have the local Latino community engage grassroots political struggle in Central America as well as questions of gender and sexuality there and locally.

Culeros y Cultura

The play followed the general plotline of the novel, but a great deal of the tension in *El corazón* revolved around violence, shame, and stigma on the body. The everyday violence of poverty was present, but so were the gendered ways through which the state and its forces of repression instilled fear in the general population. Both women's and men's bodies were the focus of perceived or real violence in the civil war, but it was the violence on men's masculinity, enacted through the literal and figurative violation of their anus, that became contentious in the play's run in the Mission. Specifically, it was through the repetitive, excessive invocation of the *culero*, or "faggot," (its root word in Spanish being "*culo*" or "ass hole")—El Salvador's most popular derogatory term for the man presumed to be penetrated while having sex with another man—that the play drew attention to the strict policing and punishment of "weak" male gender. The recurrent references by members of the repressive National Guard to *culeros* and any perceived *culero*-like behavior often became comedic. But their use realistically linked patriarchal codes of masculinity to forms of violence in and out of war believed necessary for enforcing a national order. Culturally, the term *culero* suggests that which presumably all honorable, masculine men will not allow to have touched, much less penetrated: their *culo* or anus. *Culero* thus singularly and violently infers a fear of penetration, which is to mark all *culeros* and/or gay/ homosexual men, specifically the "passive" (penetrated) kind.[4]

In one of the scenes exploring this gender matrix of masculinity, propriety, and the need to defend the nation from "weak" ideas, *El corazón* depicted the encounter between two guards and a young priest. In the scene, just as a young couple leaves a store for fear of what the approaching guards might do to them, the guards make not-so-veiled threats against the priest about to enter the store:

> GUARD II (to the store clerk): Give me two sodas. (He takes them and moves away without paying for them. He sits next to the other guard at a table.) Hey look, I think these culeros are beginning to respect us. Ah, that's right, you're from here. You must be a culero too.
>
> GUARD I (as priest enters): Hey, if you want a real culero; one just came in.
>
> PRIEST II: Good afternoon, Don Sebastián. Can you please give me two colones worth of candy.
>
> DON SEBASTIAN: My pleasure, Padre. Anything else?
>
> PRIEST II: No, that's all this time. Thank you.
>
> (Reyes & Gutíerrez, 1984, p. 18)

Soon after this exchange, in a dramatic turn, repression comes alive as the guards apprehend the priest illegally; following a direct verbal confrontation, they take him out of the store to a nearby river. The store clerk witnesses the kidnapping and decides to inform local residents. The homophobic "playfulness" with which the guards greeted the priest earlier turns to actual violence. While *culero* had been staged only as a derogatory remark in the beginning, the guards turn the stigmatic label into an actual act of violence. After taking him to the secluded area and killing him, they follow with a final symbolic act of sticking a wooden stake in his anus.

Finding the priest's bloodied body proves to be the final blow for Chepe, a local *campesino*, and his family; they decide to take action despite fears of yet more reprisal. With other neighbors, Justino and Adolfina, they begin to look for the guards. Armed with wooden sticks and an old rifle, they find the guards back at the same small store. The neighbors carefully move in on them, threatening to give the guards a taste of their own medicine:

> JUSTINO: Hold it there, fuckers, or I'll send you to the other world right now. *(At this moment the others enter.)*
>
> CHEPE: Sons of a bitch! Damn you!
>
> JUSTINO: Get out, fuckers, get out. Now we're going to see how courageous you are. *(All of them push the guards out and head with them toward the same place where they found the priest. They form a circle around the guards, threatening them with sticks and machetes.)*
>
> CHEPE: Take your pants off! Take them off, didn't you hear?!
>
> NEIGHBOR: Now we're gonna do to you what you did to the priest!
>
> GUARD I: No, not that! Anything except that!
>
> ADOLFINA: Ah, you don't like it, right? Shitty monsters! Why do you like to do it to others?
>
> GUARD II: Not that, please, not that! Kill us, but please don't do that to us! *(They all form a circle around the guards while they force them to undress.)*
>
> (Reyes & Gutíerrez, 1984, pp. 21–22)

Ridiculing the guards who remain naked, the neighbors begin to laugh, their anger subdued through this collective act for justice. They walk away from the scene with the guards' clothes and firearms, leaving them exposed and never carrying out their threats of violence on their bodies.

This comedic effect on stage serves as an entry point for a critique of repressive, military heteronormativity. The fact that the neighbors only threaten but never carry out the act of violating the guards demonstrates the power of this particular threat. In a metaphoric sense, the extreme fear the guards express when presented with the possibility that they too will become victims of this form of gendered violence on their masculine bodies is a fear of turning into *culeros*, the penetration of the anus singly responsible for emasculating them.

More broadly, the play's depiction of this encounter between the neighbors and the guards affords the audience an opportunity to consider shame, gender, and sexual violence on multiple levels. The guards fear the actual act, but it is an act socially and culturally experienced and thus vested with more power than the violence alone. Bodily pain but also psychic and social shame would be made real on at least three levels: being penetrated as men in their anus, experiencing this shaming of their gender while in the company of other men, and experiencing this traumatic event while "exposed" before an audience of women and men (the neighbors, but also the audience watching the play).

The play's third act presents the audience once again with Guard I and Guard II. This time the guards are analyzing their situation as U.S.-trained Salvadoran soldiers, comparing the benefits and drawbacks of their new, "improved" diets, the military foodstuffs coming from the United States. Again, masculinity and sexuality around insult and honor play center stage in the dialogue the guards develop while taking a shower together following their day's military training. Appearing completely naked on stage, the guards make sure they reinforce their code of masculinity in the context of the closely erotic homosociality built into the shower scene:

> GUARD II: There's nothing like these gringos, man. These people do know what they're doing. Here one becomes a man because the special forces are not for *culeros*.
>
> GUARD I: Fuck, yeah. This is fucking paradise. Although at the beginning I didn't like the food . . .
>
> . . .
>
> GUARD II: You know what I didn't like? That thing they call mashed potatoes. That damned thing looks like shit and smells like cum. And that other shit, what they call yogurt, if the potatoes smell like cum, that is the actual cum.
>
> GUARD I: And you've tasted it already? If you're still hungry, I have some more here, if you want it.
>
> GUARD II: That one you can keep for your mother, you son of a bitch!
>
> (Reyes & Gutíerrez, 1984, p. 26)

This scene concludes with their getting dressed, finishing their political analysis of "traitor" priests and some of their own family members involved in the country's leftist movement. Seemingly unscathed by their mutual playful insults while showering together, they conclude by putting on their Rayban sunglasses. Cleansed and appropriately dressed, they prepare for the day's adventures.

Their washing and simultaneous reassurance of heteronormative positions are diametrically opposed to the two social bodies placed outside the national membership in times of revolutionary war, the symbolic *culero*, and the priest.

There is a close association between these two non-manly archetypes in *El corazón:* the *culero* who by definition loses his manliness through penetration, and the priest for willingly not being a man actively seeking to conquer women sexually (and thus also suspect for being a *culero*). Standing naked and next to one another, the guards, as the defenders of the state, could only playfully challenge and downplay each other's virility to keep their own manliness as intact as possible and as far away from these "fallen" archetypes of maleness.

The Significance of Bodies

The theatrical acts of resistance Juan Pablo and Rodrigo placed on stage went beyond the Salvadoran military struggle. The two were conscious about writing, seeking funding for, and producing a play about a displaced immigrant/refugee Latino community in San Francisco, in Spanish, about a national body at war with itself. In a sense, the play was on behalf of a *national* body, but also of the specific bodies in that national war.

The undressing and dressing of the guards in the scene above held great significance for the playwrights. In their memories about audience reactions to the scene, both Rodrigo and Juan Pablo reflected about the role of the cultural worker in community dialogue and representation. In one of his last interviews, months before his death from AIDS, Rodrigo discussed what he felt were the most important challenges in his career, including his observations of the lasting, unchanging patriarchal roles Latinos practiced among themselves as men and in relation to Latinas, and his cultural work and the goals behind his productions in the Mission District. Asked about some of the controversy *El corazón* raised among community members, Rodrigo explained what he felt were the links between particular audience members' anxieties and criticism of the work, and broader issues of sexuality and the body. The scene where the guards take a shower together and appear naked on stage without their military uniforms caused a strong recollection in Rodrigo's memory:

> I was aware there were uptight phonies, who anytime they're faced with the human body, will become moral arbiters and judges. . . . And I believe that under their own hang-ups, they missed the whole point of that scene, which was that under the trapping of a uniform, of any form of drag or uniform, we are all human beings. And I was trying to give these guys, who represented the National Guard in El Salvador, who represented monsters, [we] wanted to make them more human beings. Because if you represent them as bad guys, they become two-dimensional, cartoonish. Once they're naked, they become like little boys . . . they talk about food as something strange and wonderful. In other words, [we] showed them as boys by stripping them of all these power symbols. . . . And gradually, as

they finish their showers, and they're putting on their uniforms, they become more and more aggressive, so that at the end when they're fully dressed, and they have their M16s again, they are ready to kill their own families. That was the purpose of that scene. And if all people saw was their dicks hanging out, and they didn't even hear anything, that's where they're at.

(Reyes & Marquez, 1991)

In Rodrigo's words, the challenge was to bring questions of the body in the context of war to the stage. But it was not just the male homoeroticism built into the theatrical scene that audience members most resisted. Some found male gender and sexuality not only not central for addressing militarized violence and national repression, but also largely irrelevant.

The exploration of gender, sexuality, and nationhood in *El corazón's* treatment of homosocial space and of the *culero* happened onstage as well as off. In a tradition that continues to this day, cultural productions continue after the curtain falls. Following each presentation of *El corazón*, audience members had the opportunity to comment and to question the cast and production team. The last performances were no exception, coinciding with the historic International Theatre Festival in San Francisco. Bringing together Bay Area Chicano and Latino production teams with those of several Latin American countries, the festival was important for facilitating transnational dialogue among cultural workers. The collaborations that occurred through the festival were hardly smooth ones; gender and sexuality became some of the most contentious matters in debate and controversy.

Among the theater groups at the international festival was the Mexico City-based Los Mascarones.[5] According to Juan Pablo, the last evening's performance brought to the surface some of the specific tensions he and Rodrigo wanted to highlight:

> And from the back, the director of Teatro Mascarones raises his hand and says, "Well, in terms of a suggestion, I would suggest that you take out of the play the scene where you have the two guards naked." Because the fuckers came out naked. [Showing] dick! They were bathing in the showers. . . . He was suggesting that we remove that because it did not help in any way the development of the play. Now, our purpose in showing that naked scene was to place the guards in a naked situation. To have them in a naked state, completely, from their philosophical theory to their patriarchal theory to everything. And to show them precisely how they were.
>
> (Gutíerrez & Roque Ramírez, 2001)

Following the director's comments, Juan Pablo recalled, a Salvadoran lady voiced concerns that de-emphasized the male nudity on the stage and moved the discussion instead to the more commonplace form of sexual violence in war—that on the bodies of women.

A Salvadoran lady gets up, about seventy years old, raises her hand. And the lady says, "Well, I cannot speak like that gentleman, because I am not educated. And first I want to thank you young men because you're carrying out a very important task of showing people here how we the Salvadoran people really feel. And I want that gentleman to please excuse me, but I want to ask him a question. Why did he feel so offended seeing those two men naked, and did not feel offended when one of those naked men raped the young girl?"

(Gutíerrez & Roque Ramírez, 2001)

The exchange exemplified the multiple audiences in *El corazón* and that Chicano/Latino *teatro* has had to contend with the communities it engages through its material and audience participation, and the aesthetic concerns and interest of its critics. The respective commentaries disclosed some of the structures of feeling produced in the experience of the acts: anxieties about homosociality and concerns for violence against women.

El corazón and the ensuing community dialogue it generated spoke to community memory and history. The refusal to acknowledge the body, gender, and sexuality as fundamental ingredients to the writing and performance of community history point toward what Aída Hurtado (1998) has referred to as the politics of sexuality and gender subordination. In Chicano theatrical productions, Hurtado has noted, the goal originally had been to represent a "collective social vision of Chicanos and to represent all that is valued in these communities," subordinating the varied experiences of Chicanas and reducing them to a static virgin/whore dichotomy (p. 85). But in *El corazón*, the body and its experiences of violence are present as pivotal landscapes on which history and memory take meaning. That both male and female bodies were "exposed" to community reflection in the play afforded those audiences in the Mission District an opportunity to reconsider the violence of Central American revolutionary history and struggle through the lenses of gender and sexuality in more varied ways.

Such exposures of bodies, sexualities, and genders on stage are no simple entertainment. The gendered politics of sexuality function through multiple silences and silencing strategies that implicate both community members seeking (in)visibility and those enforcing dominant relations of power. *El corazón* contested such silences by expanding the expected narrative of warfare and human suffering (cast in heteronormative form) to make visible the pivotal role of male homosociality in militarized nationalist culture. The use of soldiers as strong embodiments of manliness and national culture also made male homosociality in war visible. Tactically, this narrative move spoke to some of the tensions that Ramón A. Gutiérrez (1993) has found in the interplay of the liberationist politics of nationalism in the Chicano movement of the 1970s. In these conflicted processes of racial ethnic pride, young radical Chicano men responded to their social emasculation and cultural negation as minority men by reasserting, if not exaggerating, their virility, thus reaffirming a rigid heteronormativity.

Del otro lado: Gay Immigrant Crossings

Like *El corazón nunca me ha mentido*, the production of the film *Del otro lado*, depicting the struggles of being a gay Mexican immigrant with AIDS, was a product of cultural and political crossings. Several years before filming it, Gustavo had written a short play version titled *Soy tu madre* (I am your mother) as a window into gay Latino immigrant lives. The city and state's context at this time around immigration mattered significantly, culminating in 1994 when California voters passed Proposition 187, seeking to deny social services to undocumented immigrants in the state, a measure later found unconstitutional. San Francisco was the only city where the measure was defeated, but the anti-immigrant discourse in the state made Latino immigrants (undocumented and not) the scapegoats for the economic downturn. In this period of racialized challenges to immigrant populations, gay immigrants like Gustavo used cultural productions to challenge public discourses of criminalization, of "aliens" invading the land of rightful (white) citizens (Ono & Sloop, 2002).

Gustavo's melodrama *Soy tu madre* centered on a heterosexual couple; the husband infects his wife with HIV, and both of them eventually die. The husband's mother is left to consider how different the consequences could have been had the family been more aware of forms of infection. *Soy tu madre* was his way of bringing AIDS awareness to a heterosexual Latino community in the Mission, a segment he felt knew even less about HIV and safer sex practices than did gay Latinos. For him, efforts culminating in *Soy tu madre* and *Del otro lado* originated in his public life as a gay Latino immigrant. Striving for such queer Latino cultural citizenship had its particular moments of personal meaning, when culture and politics came alive at once. These individual and collective actions for visibility and space connected the social space of the gay Latino bar, a common destination for many gay Latino immigrants in the city, to HIV and AIDS social service organizations where Latinos also struggled to have visibility as people of Color in mainstream White organizations. As Gustavo recalled, public visibility, gay and Latino pride, all came hand in hand:

> One of my most beautiful experiences, speaking of the city of San Francisco as an activist, was during a gay parade in 1991, when we marched for the first time as part of Shanti. And it was the first time we had a huge Mexican flag in a gay parade, with eight people holding on to it. That's when the whole idea of spirit comes out, of doing activism. Imagine the significance of marching, of crossing the entire city, that people see your face and that people say, "That one going there is gay," or, "I know him, I didn't think

he was." That's where spirit begins. "Yes, I am, so what!" That was one of the most incredible experiences.

(Cravioto and Roque Ramírez, 1995)

As a gay Latino immigrant, Gustavo highlights the incredible "spirit," in fact, the birth of spirit that comes through the creation of a gay Latino political visibility. It is a visible culture of opposition on multiple levels: a huge national emblem, a Mexican flag, in the middle of an overwhelmingly White and Anglo-centric queer moment; a flag held by *mexicanos/latinos*, somewhat foreshadowing the immigrant and nativist struggles around Proposition 187 that were to come three years later. It is simultaneously a culture of opposition in placing Latino bodies in public space to mark "gay" and for Latinos on the sidelines (and all others) to recognize that gay/queer citizenship can indeed take bodily presence in this racial ethnic group.

Gustavo's own transnational travels were intertwined with these new products of his creativity, using all possible opportunities to carry his vision. *Soy tu madre* premiered at the Mission Cultural Center in 1992 for the annual June Latino/a Gay, Lesbian, Bisexual, and Transgender Performance Art Festival produced by the late Chicano gay activist and cultural worker Hank Tavera (1944–2000). In 1993, the Mission Neighborhood Health Center (MNHC) sponsored a production of it for International AIDS Day in San Francisco. In 1994, also for International AIDS Day, the play was produced in Mexico City, in collaboration with Consejo Nacional para la Prevención del SIDA (CONASIDA), Mexico's National Council for AIDS Prevention. Returning from Mexico City in 1996 after networking with cultural and health workers there, Gustavo approached his close friend Mario Callitzin to write a play about the relationship between gay immigration and AIDS. Following positive response in Mexico to their play *Soy tu madre*, Gustavo returned to the United States reinvigorated, this time approaching Mario to make the film version. To fund it, they established the non-profit venture of *Dos Espíritus* (Two Spirits), raising funds in the United States but deciding to produce the film more affordably in Mexico. Three years in the making, with an international crew of queer and non-queer, Mexican and non-Mexican, *Del otro lado* became part of the very process of border crossings both Mario and Gustavo had experienced.

Del otro lado has drawn attention because of its focus on a gay Mexican couple, Alejandro and Beto. Alejandro's HIV-positive status and his dwindling T-cell count present a series of problems for the couple, most critical being Alejandro's inability to obtain adequate treatment in Mexico City. Without informing Beto of his plans, Alejandro applies for a visa to travel to the United States to seek medical help. Once the visa request is denied, however, Alejandro weighs the consequences of staying or seeking help, and decides to cross the border illegally. Alejandro's impending trek to the United States precipitates a series of reactions and possibilities on both sides of the border. In Mexico, his departure signals many losses; his move causes panic in Beto and his own emotional losses around family; it causes fear in his parents, who have been supportive of his relationship with Beto but disagree about his move; and it signals a separation between Alejandro and his extended network of lesbian and gay friends supporting his gay relationship. Seeking medical care in the United States by crossing illegally offers no security either: Alejandro faces the real (and eventual) possibility of getting caught while trying to cross, of facing exploitation along the way, and of encountering racism and discrimination, all alluded to in the film.

Del otro lado presents a transnational gay portrait that cannot be reduced to repression in the south—Mexico—and freedom in the north—the United States. The film depicts a thriving community of lesbians and gays in Mexico and does not present easy solutions of finding "progress" upon arrival in the United States. Literally having to choose between the potential for health care in the United States versus staying with his family and lover in Mexico, Alejandro embodies the tensions of many queer immigrants in their negotiations of nation and home, blood and queer kinships there, and health and immigrant identity while in the Bay Area and elsewhere in the United States. These ironies addressed in the film speak to the broader social dislocation and marginalization of queer immigrants— as queers *and* as immigrants—but specifically in the "gay Mecca" of San Francisco. That one of the actors herself, male-to-female transgender health worker and artist

FIGURE 11.2 Image taken from *Del otro lado* with Alejandro and Beto together in Mexico before Alejandro's failed and tragic attempt to cross the border

Courtesy of Mario Callitzin and Gustavo Martin Cravioto

Carla Clynes, encountered immigration problems before filming *Del otro lado* speaks to the trials queer immigrant productions must face in the making of culture (Clynes & Roque Ramírez, 2000).

According to Mario, legal and financial dynamics in their transnational production were overwhelming yet, once they overcame them, liberating:

> Carla Clynes was denied a Mexican passport, wanted a passport as a woman, the identity of a woman, and yet her birth certificate [has] a male name. And she made a scene at the consulate [in San Francisco], from what I hear, demanding that she be given a passport, demanding her rights to be able to travel to Mexico to do this. And eventually she was given a passport, and some letter that said that the Mexican government wasn't responsible for defining the gender of this person [laughter]. . . . "The Mexican government does not do gender."
>
> (Callitzin and Roque Ramírez, 1999)

Taking on a transnational film production, Mario notes, was as much about political border crossing as it was about bridge making—racially, nationally, and sexually. And it involved cultural and political border crossings by queer immigrants who were actually crossing back into the nation they first left for the United States. As Mario describes it, community was an active process of incorporating multiple identity vectors, a momentary emotional ride focused on this one binational cultural product.

The ability for gay immigrants to travel "back" to their own countries and carry out work linking two homes presents multiple challenges, some legal and financial, such as those that transgender Carla Clynes experienced, but others that have more to do with the everyday meanings of sexuality, race, and gender. The everyday life of transnational queers is shaped by seemingly banal practices that do in fact reveal the constant negotiation of "home" as a matter of "here," "there," and "in between." In the United States, this negotiation is neither to suggest a birthright nor to romanticize dissidence, as Martin F. Manalansan IV (2003) has explored in relation to gay Filipino men. But, I would argue, the dynamics of negotiating "here" and "there" are not always a successful process of seeking cultural citizenship in part because visibility and recognition as queer racial (im)migrant subjects take place in uneven contexts of domination and marginalization.

The challenges that transnational queers find in the everyday, including undocumented immigration, gay life, and HIV and AIDS, were present, too, in the making of *Del otro lado*. According to Mario, that the two leading actors and producers were gay Mexican immigrants themselves added to the volatility in their queer moves across borders:

> [That] it was an openly gay production also created certain dynamics, stirred up certain things—not so much the actors, but the crew, because we had

to work with them everyday. And I think it went all over the place, from playful teasing to lack of belief in the project. "No es gente seria [These are not serious people]," that kind of thing. To a certain level of contempt when things went wrong, and we had to put our feet down and say, "No! You're gonna have to do it this way. Period!" Which we had to do many times. Racism towards [African American lesbian film director] Crystal. Racism mixed with homophobia. And eventually in the midst of so many emotions, what ended up happening is that at one point it kind of sank in that this was a very serious project, that we were extremely committed, that it was very personal to us, that we were giving it our best.

(Callitzin and Roque Ramírez, 1999)

Completing *Del otro lado* was not a smooth production process and required struggles for authorial voice and decision making among bodies that were differently positioned by race, gender, sexuality, and nation.

Shown in the Bay Area, Southern California, New York, Mexico, and Ireland, *Del otro lado* explores communities made marginal in the context of migration, queer politics, and AIDS. Depicting the saga of undocumented gay immigration to the United States and the struggles for health care for people with AIDS, the film was neither a romance nor a comedy. As the central character, Alejandro serves as the vehicle for tracking an alternative narrative of migration, identity, and community health, culminating in his tragic death after being attacked on the U.S. side, a most violent "welcome" to the journey he must undertake. In making these writing and filmic choices, Mario argued, their production had a different context for considering merits and criticisms. For him, the effect the film has had on particular audience members who experienced and felt social marginalizations similar to those depicted in the film matters most:

The film is not this commercial [venture]. It's an unabashedly queer Film . . . and it scares people and stirs them up. People sometimes don't know how to react to it. We have seen so many different reactions. . . . I think the more interesting reactions have occurred in Mexico because Mexico is a country where art gets looked at differently. It's not seen in such a utilitarian manner as here. Just outside the United States, I think art gets looked at in a different way; I think that people are more willing to look at the themes, to look at the social context, to look at what is being said, rather than was it technically perfect. . . . This was a very low-budget thing. . . . The way people reacted [in Mexico], people were stirred up—angry, especially in Tijuana. [They said], "The things that we have to do to get people across the border. This is not fair!" And it just like sparked this big debate and set of responses that were very passionate for people. The film is a tragedy!

(Callitzin and Roque Ramírez, 1999)

The film's ending dedication speaks to the impetus for its creation: the AIDS crisis, specifically the social networks created and destroyed through the epidemic in Mexico, in the United States, and in between. "We dedicate this film" Mario and Gustavo wrote, "to all our brothers and sisters who have died of AIDS/to those who live with AIDS/and to all those people who work with honesty and respect in the struggle against AIDS" (Griffith et al., 1999).

Conclusion: Transnational Queer Latino Bodies and Cultures

The gay Latino cultural workers conceptualizing and producing *El corazón nunca me ha mentido* in the mid-1980s and *Del otro lado* in the late 1990s in San Francisco had in mind the notions related to what Williams (1977) described as structures of feeling: the making and experience of culture as feeling and as thought. With varying insider/outsider positions to the United States, Gustavo, Mario, Juan Pablo, and Rodrigo engaged public audiences with subjects the nation-state has marginalized or has made outright illegal. The impact of their work as visual (im)migrant acts were certainly felt *and* thought about by audiences interested in the performances and showings. The play and the film spoke to historical conditions very real to their makers and those around them: military repression and economic exploitation linked to Central American refugee histories in the San Francisco Bay Area, gay Mexican immigration, and the crises of AIDS and xenophobia (Rodríguez, 2003). The histories and politics performed and retold engaged discussions of membership, identity, and community where gender and sexuality did not play second fiddle to race, class, and nation. Enacting historical struggles for cultural citizenship, these gay (im)migrant acts were hardly simple forms for artistic expression; they required community participation and reflection. The queer moves these gay Latinos made through language, geography, and culture represented on-going contestations for what it means to be simultaneously queer and (im)migrant even in presumably open cities like San Francisco.

Because cultural citizenship takes meaning precisely in nonjuridical realms, we should note one critical intervention in both *El corazón* and *Del otro lado*—the social space of language. Written and produced overwhelmingly in Spanish, the productions represented the spatiality of (im)migrant lives in linguistic movement across geopolitics. For both productions, narrating bodies, desires, and violence took place in what is considered a "minoritarian" discourse in California and the United States, though this is hardly an accurate description for the lives of millions working, living, playing, and surviving in Spanish. As Lionel Cantú, Jr (2000) argued, the spatial dimensions of queer Latino immigrant lives cannot be reduced to desire, but rather incorporate larger economic and political conditions. In this larger sociopolitical context, language is a tool of resistance to the state's discourses, a form of solidarity for claiming space. Reyes and Gutíerrez's production centered the action through Salvadoran Spanish vernacular, a language that is very present in the Mission, but largely marginal in Latino cultural productions. Similarly, Callitzin and Cravioto chose the language of the migration process itself, the language that on a daily basis narrates border crossings most intimately. In privileging Spanish as the medium for a political and cultural literacy, they also privileged their audiences: Spanish speakers, those in refuge, exile, and/or migration in the United States, and those still in their own countries but well connected through transnational ties.

Cultural productions can be sites of resistance, alternative ways to engage the ideological state apparatus's forms of exclusion and marginalization. In making themselves visible, queer Latinos in San Francisco have claimed space through poetry readings, writing workshops, films and videos, artistic performances, and pre- and post-production dialogues to strengthen works in progress. As political interventions, *El corazón* and *Del otro lado* have had multiple effects on their audiences and broader political discourses. Often these effects run parallel to changes in public debate and policy. In 1985, as part of a larger citywide debate on Central American refugees, *El Corazón* took a direct stance in their favor. On December 23, 1985, four months after its first performance, the San Francisco Board of Supervisors, with an eight to three vote, passed a "Resolution to Declare San Francisco a City of Refuge for Guatemalan and Salvadoran Refugees" (*El Tecolote*, 1986). This San Francisco decision was part of the large transnational movement to support these refugees. Rodrigo and Juan Pablo's production, as a (gay) immigrant act, was part of it. *Del otro lado* is literally a narrative of queer immigrant crossings from the vantage point of queer immigrants themselves. The film ventured into the intersections of sexuality and immigration, offering no easy solutions to on-going crises built into a globalizing economy. As outsiders in the city's body politic, immigrant gay Latinos occupy a "gay Latino" space filled with cultural and political contestations that involve both the cultural representations of each and their position in the local political economy.

Hardly a static and predictable response to systems of marginalization and exploitation, cultural work travels with its makers. Queers move with their cultures, reinventing in their migrations the forms and meanings with which they invest their products. As cultural productions, they open spaces for dialogue and reflection. As audience members exit theaters, health agencies, and other venues for viewing and experiencing these productions collectively, they engage each other and themselves with the images and the words, considering technical questions along with content, intent, and impact. In this regard, cultural productions construct social space and facilitate further opportunities for creative interplay—feelings, thought, and social action thus intersected. In this tradition, *El corazón nunca me ha mentido* and *Del otro lado* were critical interventions into notions of the state, of citizenship broadly defined, and of queer bodies in transit between local and global histories.

Notes

1   Horacio N. Roque Ramírez acknowledges the kind permission from the University of Minnesota Press to reprint an updated, revised edition of this essay from its original publication in the volume edited by Eithne Luibhéid and Lionel Cantú, Jr., (2005) *Queer migrations: Sexuality, U.S. citizenship, and border crossings.*

The research and writing for this essay were supported by a University of California, Berkeley Humanities Diversity Dissertation Grant, a University of California MEXUS (Institute for Mexico and the U.S.) Dissertation Completion Grant, and a University of California President's Postdoctoral Fellowship.

2   Cindy Patton describes the "AIDS service industry" as "the private-sector non-profit organizations devoted exclusively to AIDS work . . . [implying] a set of social relations based on shared norms and styles of organizational behavior institutionalized through patterned power relations, rather than a collusion of the powerful who maintain an 'establishment' by coercion or conscious exclusion, or act purely as a conduit for government monies to communities" (Patton, 1990, p. 13).

3   All quotes come directly from the oral history interviews I carried out, with the exception of Rodrigo Reyes's interview that Richard Marquez conducted and that is now part of the Archivo Rodrigo Reyes in Oakland, California, in the possession of Luis Alberto Campos de la Garza (2001). Interviews took place in Spanish, English, and/or both, but space limitations prevent me from quoting several passages that took place originally in Spanish and are translated here and presented only in English. It is important to recognize this bi-, translingual exchange in the research process itself, for it speaks directly to the creation and narration of Latino and Chicano cultural production in multilingual contexts.

4   Foreigners' anthropological discussions of same-sex male cultures and practices "south of the border" have often reduced these to a monolithic binary of *pasivo/activo,* the passive or penetrated partner seemingly always already marked as the only shamed or stigmatized male *(culero* in El Salvador, *joto* in Mexico, for example), and the active or penetrating man never losing his masculine status. As more and more research and writing, especially from Latin Americans themselves, are showing, same-sex sexual and gender practices among men have historically found greater expressions and meanings than those framed in this rigid *pasivo/activo* paradigm (Bustos-Aguilar, 1995; Carrillo, 2000; Green, 1999).

5   According to Jorge Huerta (2000), Los Mascarones had been part of a transnational network of Chicano, Latino, and Latin American theater companies, first coming together at the 1970 Chicano Theater Festival in Fresno, California, sponsored by the Teatro Campesino.

References

Brook, J., Carlsson, C., & Peters, N. J. (Eds.) (1998). *Reclaiming San Francisco: History, politics, culture.* San Francisco: City Lights Books.

Bustos-Aguilar, P. (1995). Mister don't touch the banana: Notes on the popularity of the ethnosexed body south of the border. *Critique of Anthropology,* 15(2), 149–170.

Callitzin, M. interview by Roque Ramírez, H. N. (1999). Audiotape recording, San Francisco, CA.

Cantú, Jr., L. (2000). Borderlands: The socio-political dimensions of gay Latino community formation in greater Los Angeles. Working paper 29, Chicano/Latino Research Center. University of California, Santa Cruz, August 2000.

Cantú, Jr. L. (posthumously) & Naples, N., & Vidal-Ortiz, S. (Eds.). (2009). *The sexuality of migration: Border crossings and Mexican immigrant men.* New York: New York University Press.

Carrillo, H. (2000). *The night is young: Sexuality in Mexico in the time of AIDS.* Chicago: University of Chicago Press.

Chavez, L. R. (2001). *Covering immigration: Popular images and the politics of the nation.* Berkeley: University of California Press.

Clynes, C. interview by Roque Ramírez, H. N. (2000). Audiotape recording, San Francisco, CA.

Cora, M. (2000). *Nuestras auto-definiciones*/Our self-definitions: Management of stigma and identity by Puerto Rican lesbians. (Master's field study report, San Francisco State University).

Cravioto, M. G. interview by Roque Ramírez, H. N. (1995). Audiotape recording, San Francisco, CA.

El Tecolote (1986, January). Resolution to declare San Francisco a city of refuge for Guatemalan and Salvadoran refugees. 4, 1.

Flores, W. V. & Benmayor, R. (1997). Introduction: Constructing cultural citizenship. In W. V. Flores & R. Benmayor, (Eds.), *Latino cultural citizenship: Claiming identity, space, and rights* (1–26). Boston: Beacon Press.

Green, J. N. (1999). *Beyond Carnival: Male homosexuality in twentieth-century Brazil.* Chicago: University of Chicago Press.

Griffith, C. A., Cravioto, G. M., Callitzin, M., & Foley, F. (Producers), Callitzin, M., & Cravioto, G. M. (Screenwriters), & Griffith, C. A. (Director) (1999). *Del otro lado* [Motion Picture]. San Francisco, CA.

Gutíerrez, J. P. interview by Roque Ramírez, H. N. (2001). Audiotape recording, Berkeley, California.

Gutíerrez, R. A. (March 1993). Community, patriarchy, and individualism: The politics of Chicano history and the dream of equality, *American Quarterly* 45(1), 44–72.

Guzmán, M. (1997). "Pa' la escuelita con mucho cuida'o y por la orillita": A journey through the contested terrains of the nation and sexual orientation. In F. Negrón-Muntaner and R. Grosfoguel (Eds.), *Puerto Rican jam: Rethinking colonialism and nationalism* (209–228). Minneapolis: University of Minnesota Press.

Huerta, J. (2000). *Chicano drama: Performance, society, and myth.* Cambridge: Cambridge University Press.

Hurtado, A. (1998). The politics of sexuality in the gender subordination of Chicanas. In Carla Trujillo (Ed.), *Living Chicana Theory*, Berkeley: Third Woman Press.

Lowe, L. (1996). *Immigrant acts: On Asian American cultural politics.* Durham, NC: Duke University Press.

Luibhéid, E. & Cantú, Jr. L. (Eds.) (2005). *Queer migrations: sexuality, U.S. citizenship, and border crossings.* Minneapolis: University of Minnesota Press.

Manalansan IV, M. F. (2003). *Global divas: Filipino gay men in the diaspora.* Durham: Duke University Press.

Ono, K. A. & Sloop, J. M. (Eds.) (2002). *Shifting borders: Rhetoric, immigration, and California's proposition 187.* Philadelphia: Temple University Press.

Patton, C. (1990). *Inventing AIDS.* New York: Routledge.

Reyes, R. & Gutíerrez, J. P. (1984). *El corazón nunca me ha mentido.* San Francisco, CA: Unpublished typescript, in author's possession.

Reyes, R., interview by R. Marquez, (1991, June 16 and July 5). Videotape recording, San Francisco, Archivo Rodrigo Reyes, with permission of Luis Alberto Campos de la Garza.

Rodríguez, J. M. (2003). *Queer latinidad: Identity practices, discursive spaces*. New York: New York University Press.

Roque Ramírez, H. N. (2001). San Francisco. In J. Ciment (Ed.), *Encyclopedia of American Immigration* (964–973). Armonk, NY: M. E. Sharpe.

Roque Ramírez, H. N. (2003, April). "That's my place": Negotiating gender, racial, and sexual politics in San Francisco's Gay Latino Alliance (GALA), 1975–1983. *Journal of the History of Sexuality*, 12(3), 224–258.

Roque Ramírez, H. N. (2005). The living evidence of desire: Teresita la Campesina and the embodiment of queer Latino community histories. In A. Burton (Ed.), *Archive stories: Facts, fictions, and the writing of history* (111–135). Durham, NC: Duke University Press.

Roque Ramírez, H. N. (Spring 2007). "*¡Mira, yo soy boricua y estoy aquí!*": Rafa Negrón's *Pan Dulce* and the queer sonic *Latinaje* of San Francisco. *CENTRO: Journal for the Center of Puerto Rican Studies*, 18(2), 274–313.

Roque Ramírez, H. N. (2008). Memory and mourning: Living oral history with queer Latinos in San Francisco. In P. Hamilton & L. Shopes (Eds.), *Oral history and public memories* (165–186). Philadelphia: Temple University Press.

Roque Ramírez, H. N. (2010). Gay Latino histories/Dying to be remembered: AIDS obituaries, public memory, and the gay Latino archive. In G. M. Pérez, F. A. Guridy, & A. Burgos, Jr (Eds.), *Beyond el barrio: Everyday life in Latina/o America* (103–128). New York: New York University Press.

Rosaldo, R. (1997). Cultural citizenship, inequality, and multiculturalism. In W. V. Flores and R. Benmayor, (Eds.), *Latino cultural citizenship: Claiming identity, space, and rights.* (27–38). Boston: Beacon Press.

Rosales, K. E. (2001). Papis, dykes, daddies: A study of Chicana and Latina self-identified butch lesbians. (Master's thesis, San Francisco State University).

Santa Ana, O. (2002). *Brown tide rising: Metaphors of Latinos in contemporary American public discourse*. Austin: University of Texas Press.

Williams, R. (1977). *Marxism and literature*. New York: Oxford University Press.

PART 3

Race, Gender, and Skin Color in Constructing Identification

12

DOES RACE AND NATIONAL ORIGIN INFLUENCE THE HOURLY WAGES THAT LATINO MALES RECEIVE?

Clara E. Rodríguez
Grigoris Argeros
Michael H. Miyawaki

In the process of writing this chapter, law SB 1070 was passed by the state of Arizona, which requires that police determine the immigrant status of people they stop and suspect are in the country illegally. Some referred to this as sanctioning racial profiling. The passage of this law raised the importance of "race" and brought new attention to the way individuals are identified by others, in particular by people in positions of political or hiring authority. How people are identified by others can substantially impact what happens to them in everyday life and in the labor market. In the case of Latinos, there is extensive literature on the impact of race, skin color, and phenotype on their life chances and socioeconomic outcomes (see, for example, Arce et al., 1987; Cotton, 1993; Darity et al., 2002; Espino & Franz, 2002; Frank et al., 2010; Gomez, 2000; Logan, 2004; Murguia & Telles, 1996; Rodríguez, 1990, 1991; Tafoya, 2004; Telles & Murguia, 1990). It is, however, only recently that this issue has moved to a more public and political arena, where it has been tied to the contested issue of undocumented immigration. Indeed, replicating the results of earlier studies on all Latinos, Frank and colleagues' (2010) study of immigrants who were granted legal permanent residency in 2003 found that darker-skinned Latinos earned less than their lighter-skinned counterparts.

The research undertaken in this chapter seeks to examine whether the self-reported race of Latino males is related to the hourly wages they receive. Additionally, this study investigates the influence of national origin on the hourly wages of Latino males. We examine these questions within the context of the intersectionality of race, national origins, and other variables (i.e., educational attainment, English language proficiency, occupation, nativity status, length of time in the United States, region of employment, and employment status). We also proceed from the perspective that race is a social construction and that it exists as a part of other interlocking systems of oppression. We recognize that these systems affect individuals differently depending on where they stand at the intersections of race, class, gender, ethnicity, sexuality, and, we might add, color. Their location or positioning at these intersections influences not just the way in which they come to view themselves and to perform their roles, but also how they are viewed and regarded by others (Collins, 2004).

We seek to determine whether (holding constant variables known to affect labor market outcomes) race and national origin exercise independent effects on hourly wages. By examining the hourly wages of Latino men within the context of the intersection of race, national origin, and other variables, we look to address the following questions: What is the effect of race and national origin on the hourly wages of Latino males? Do White Latino males have higher hourly wages than Black Latino males? Is being of Mexican origin a positive or a negative when it comes to hourly wages? Finally, do Latina females differ from Latino males with regards to these questions? To answer the questions, we turn to data gathered from the 2000 U.S. Census.

Race, National Origin, and Socioeconomic Outcomes of Latinos

It is perhaps belaboring the point to say that race has been and continues to be strongly associated with advantages and disadvantages in the United States. The literature on this subject is extensive, and more recent studies continue to find disparities based on race. Over the years, studies have documented the impact of race on the life chances and socioeconomic outcomes of Latinos. Researchers have found significant racial differences within the Latino community in terms of education, employment, occupation, earnings, household income, and poverty (Cotton, 1993; Darity et al., 2002; Logan, 2004; Rodríguez, 1990, 1991; Tafoya, 2004). In brief, findings from these studies indicate that White Latinos are often associated with a higher socioeconomic standing, whereas Black Latinos and Latinos who report "[some] other race" are associated with lower socioeconomic positions.

With respect to earnings and hourly wages, research demonstrates that race does affect how much Latinos make in the labor market. For example, using data from the 1980 U.S. Census, Rodríguez (1991) examined the hourly wages of Puerto Ricans living in New York City. Findings revealed that even after controlling for variables known to influence earnings, Puerto Rican males who reported that they were White had higher hourly wages than those who reported that they were "[some] other race." There were no statistically significant differences between the hourly wages of Puerto Rican males who reported being White and those who reported being Black. Furthermore, race was not a significant predictor of hourly wages for Puerto Rican females, thereby suggesting that women faced different labor market dynamics than men at the time. Research by Cotton (1993), using data from the Current Population Surveys (CPS) from 1976 to 1984, noted that White Latino males with less than average schooling and work experience earned higher wages than Black Latinos. In a different study using the 1980 and 1990 Censuses, Darity et al. (2002) found that Black Latino males, regardless of their national origin, had lower earnings than their non-Black Latino counterparts. Findings for Latina females were less consistent across national origins. However, Borrell and Rodríguez (2010), using income and education data from the 2000 to 2003 National Health Interview Surveys (NHIS), found that Black Latinos (both men and women) were more educated and had higher incomes than White Latinos and "some other race" Latinos. These discrepant findings could be a reflection of sampling selection, and it is also possible that the sample used by NHIS is not representative of the income distribution for the Latino population in the United States.

Research also indicates that there are national origin differences among Latinos with regards to socioeconomic outcomes including hourly wages (Melendez et al., 1991; Saenz, 2004). As such, national origin may also matter in the life chances of Latino males. Moreover, due to the increasing numbers of Dominicans and Salvadorans in the United States, this study was expanded beyond an analysis of Mexican, Puerto Rican, and Cuban males to include Dominican and Salvadoran males. In doing so, we assess how race, national origin, and other elements known to affect labor market outcomes influence the hourly wages of Latino males. Throughout our analysis, relevant comparisons to Latinas are made.

Data and Method

Data for this study comes from the 5 percent public use microdata sample of the 2000 Census, extracted from the Integrated Public Use Microdata Series (IPUMS) (Ruggles et al., 2010). The IPUMS, housed at the University of Minnesota's Population Center, provides researchers with a rich, detailed set of individual-level data on the sociodemographic, economic, and housing characteristics of various racial and ethnic groups, unlike the aggregate-level data from the decennial censuses. There are approximately 5,663,214 household records in the 5 percent IPUMS sample of the 2000 Census. For the purpose of this study, the sample is restricted to the 18- to 65-year-old Latino population who reported positive income and selected "White," "Black," or "some other race" on the race question. This results in an unweighted sample of 541,240.

The present analysis predicts racial and national origin differences of Latino male earnings from their individual-level characteristics using ordinary least squares (OLS) regression. The dependent variable, hourly wages, is computed using the total wage/salary earnings in 1999, divided by the product of total weeks worked and usual hours worked in 1999. Furthermore, due to the non-linear distribution of income, the dependent variable is transformed to its natural logarithm. The independent variables in this study are race and national origin. Race is categorized into outcomes of White (reference), Black, and "some other race." National origin is constructed into categories of Mexican, Puerto Rican, Cuban, Dominican, Salvadoran, and other (reference).

In addition to race and national origin as independent variables predicting hourly wages of Latino men, we introduce several control variables known to affect labor market outcomes for Latinos. These include age, nativity, years in the United States, English language proficiency, education, employment status, occupation, and region of employment. In this analysis, age is treated as a continuous variable. Nativity is introduced as a dummy variable (1 = Native-born, 0 = Foreign-born). As for years in the country, the variable is constructed as continuous. English language proficiency is categorized as: Does not speak English, Speaks English not well, Speaks English well, Speaks English very well, and Speaks only English (reference). Educational attainment is divided into categories of less than high school (reference), high school, some college, and college or more. Dummy variables for employment status (1 = Employed, 0 = Unemployed) and occupation (1 = Managerial and professional, 0 = Non-managerial and professional) are created. Finally, region is divided into Northeast (reference), Midwest, South, and West.

Results

Table 12.1 presents results for the OLS regression predicting the hourly wages of Latino males. As expected, Latino males who were native-born had higher hourly wages than those who were foreign-born. Among the foreign-born, the number of years in the United States was positively and significantly correlated with higher hourly wage rates. Findings on English language proficiency indicate that those who were more proficient in English received higher hourly wages. For example, those who did not speak English experienced a 22 percent decrease in hourly wages compared to less than 2 percent for those who spoke English well. As for education, the higher the educational attainment of Latino males, the higher their hourly wage rates. It is worth mentioning that those with a college degree or more experience a 46 percent increase compared to just 11 percent for those with a high school diploma. Latino males who were gainfully employed had higher hourly wages than those who were unemployed. Moreover, Latino males with managerial and professional occupations also received higher hourly wages than those who had non-managerial and non-professional positions. Lastly, relative to those in the Northeast, Latino males from the Midwest had higher hourly wage rates, while Latino males from the South and West had lower hourly wage rates. These findings were consistent with the results for Latinas, with the exception of Latinas from the Midwest, who had lower hourly wages than those from the Northeast.

TABLE 12.1 Hourly Wage Equation, Latino Males and Females

	MALE White, Black, SOR sample		FEMALE White, Black, SOR sample	
	coef	std error	coef	std error
Age squared	.155	.001	.111	.002
Education (ref.=Less than High School)				
High School	.112	.003	.121	.004
Some College	.227	.003	.254	.004
College or more	.450	.005	.531	.005
Race (ref.=White)				
Black	−.033	.009	.018	.010
SOR	−.015	.002	−.018	.003
English language proficiency (ref.=Speaks only English)				
Does not speak English	−.222	.005	−.188	.007
Speaks English very well	−.018	.003	−.018	.004
Speaks English well	−.049	.004	−.086	.005
Speaks English not well	−.145	.005	−.149	.006
Employment Status (ref.=Unemployed)				
Employed	.096	.005	.081	.005
Occupation (ref.=Non-managerial & Professional)				
Managerial & Professional	.235	.004	.206	.004
Nativity Status (ref.=Foreign-Born)				
Native-Born	.088	.004	.080	.005
Years in United States	.004	.000	.004	.000
Region (ref.=Northeast)				
Midwest	.026	.005	−.058	.006
West	−.024	.004	−.053	.005
South	−.103	.004	−.162	.005
Latino Ethnic Group (ref.=other)				
Mexican	−.014	.003	**−.003**	**.003**
PR	.017	.005	.057	.005
Cuban	.050	.006	**.097**	**.007**
Dominican	−.024	.009	**−.004**	**.009**
Salvadoran	.021	.007	.029	.009
Constant	1.289		1.382	
N	317195		224045	
Adjusted r-square	0.195235		0.188219	
Standard Error	0.62		0.62	

a) The dependent variable, the natural log of hourly wages, is computed by dividing the total wage/salary earnings in 1999 by the product of total weeks worked and usual hours worked in 1999
b) Figures in bold are not significant

Source: Data for this study comes from the 5% public use microdata sample (PUMS) of the 2000 Census, extracted from the Integrated Public Use Microdata Series (IPUMS)

In terms of the effect of race on the hourly wages of Latino males, results reveal that both Black Latinos and those who reported "some other race" had lower hourly wages than White Latinos. Compared to White Latino males, Black Latino males and "some other race" Latino males incurred a 3.3 percent penalty and a 1.5 percent penalty, respectively, in their hourly wage rate. Interestingly, in the case of Latina females, only "some other race" Latinas had a lower hourly wage (1.8 percent penalty) than White Latinas. Though moderately significant, findings indicate that Black Latinas, on the other hand, had a higher hourly wage rate (1.8 percent premium) than White Latinas. The difference in the influence of race on the hourly wages of Latino males and Latina females suggests that race may operate differently for Latinos and Latinas in the labor market. It may also be that Black Latinas are relatively better off but that they also engender greater health costs.

With regards to national origin, Mexican and Dominican males had *lower* hourly wages, while Puerto Rican, Cuban, and Salvadoran males had *higher* hourly wages when compared to all other Latino national origin groups. Whereas Mexican males incurred a 1.4 percent and Dominican males a 2.4 percent disadvantage with regard to hourly wages, Cuban, Puerto Rican, and Salvadoran males received hourly wage advantages of 5.0 percent, 1.7 percent, and 2.1 percent, respectively. Results for the hourly wages of Latinas differed somewhat. Although the directionality of the coefficients was consistent with those of Latino males, only the hourly wage rates of Puerto Rican and Salvadoran females were significant and positive. These results are curious. Although previous research has shown that Cubans generally earn higher hourly wages, Puerto Ricans, for example, have higher poverty rates than Mexicans (Saenz, 2004, p. 22). In addition, our descriptive data analysis also shows that Salvadoran males and females have higher mean personal and salary incomes. Further research is needed to ascertain, for example, whether Puerto Rican citizenship influences hourly wages so that Latino males who are citizens may be able to command higher wages, or whether Salvadorans have more skewed income distributions and/or are more concentrated in higher wage labor markets.

Summary

The purpose of this investigation was to examine the effect of race and national origin on the hourly wages of Latino males. Using data from the 2000 Census, we uncovered that both race and national origin are related to how much Latino males make in the labor market. Even after controlling for variables known to affect earnings, Latino males who reported being Black or "some other race" were associated with lower hourly wages relative to those who reported being White. Consistent with much of the literature on the role of race on the socioeconomic outcomes of Latinos, we might conclude that White Latino males are advantaged relative to non-White Latinos in the labor market. Whether this is because they are generally perceived by others to be "White" requires further research, however. Research has shown that the way in which Latinos classify themselves does not always correspond with how they are classified by others (Itzigsohn et al., 2005; Rodríguez & Cordero-Guzman, 1992; Roth, 2010). In addition, given that many Latinos self-report "some other race" in the race question, it is difficult to ascertain how they might be racially classified by others, including their employers. What we can conclude from this analysis is that racial self-classification did make a difference in the hourly wages of Latino males.

In addition to the influence of race, national origin yielded some significant differences in the hourly wage rates of Latino males. While Mexican and Dominican males received lower hourly wages, Puerto Rican, Cuban, and Salvadoran males enjoyed wage premiums relative to all other Latino national origin groups. Although these findings point to the significance of national origin in the hourly wages and perhaps life chances of Latino males, we conclude that more research is needed to better understand the complexities of the Latino male population in terms of national origin.

Implications

Race and National Origin

What are the broader implications of this work for future research? Given these results, we need to investigate to what extent race is a structural factor affecting the economic, health, and criminal justice experience of Latino men. Race is clearly embedded in the historical-political structures of the United States and we have observed that historically it has had economic, political, and social consequences for both men and women. It has played an essential role in determining who is included and who is excluded from participation in all realms of the society. It has also been a factor determining the boundaries, both physical and social-cultural, of distinct communities; and clearly, it has been at the base of community and familial networks for the greater part of the country's existence. We need to further investigate the nexus between Latino males' race, socioeconomic status (SES), and health outcomes. This will help us develop programmatic and community interventions, as well as a more targeted policy for Latino males.

We also need to better understand the complexities of the Latino male population in terms of national origin. Currently, much of the research on wage earnings analyzes the generic group of Hispanics/Latinos, focuses on Mexicans, or excludes Latinos altogether. Although Mexicans are the largest Latino group in the nation, they do not predominate in all areas of the country. For example, in New York City, the largest Latino groups are Puerto Ricans and Dominicans. The "Hispanic paradox" of low SES scores but good health may be seen quite differently when we examine disaggregated data, for most studies have focused mainly on the Mexican American population (Borrell & Rodríguez, 2010). We need to examine both race and national origin to see how these variables impact the health outcomes of Latino men.

Racial segregation has been proposed as a fundamental cause of educational, health, and other SES disparities for African-American men and women (Williams & Collins, 2001). The research on Hispanic residential segregation has found that Hispanics are often in buffer positions between Black and White neighborhoods; but some research has also found that Puerto Ricans are highly segregated from non-Hispanic Whites as a result of their African ancestry (Massey, 1979, 2001; Massey & Bitterman, 1985) and that there is little evidence to suggest that the segregation of Puerto Ricans from Whites declined with increasing socioeconomic status (Massey, 1979). Other scholars have found that Black Hispanics are more segregated than White Hispanics (Iceland & Nelson, 2008; Rosenbaum, 1996). It would be useful to examine the extent to which such segregation continues in those suburban areas that border large cities and whether increasing immigration influences housing patterns (Acosta-Belén & Santiago, 2006; Frey, 2010; Singer et al., 2008).

In addition, we need to address the question of whether Latinos' race plays a role in the criminal justice system. For example, do darker or more stereotypical-looking male Latinos have a higher probability of being arrested, arraigned, and sent to prison? Does the health experience of institutionalized Latino males vary by race? It is important to separate out Latinos by national origin and race and to make researchers aware of how not doing so may influence results and policy. This is particularly important in some institutionalized populations, where the proportion of Latino males is increasing. For example, in the criminal justice system, racial designations are generally determined by others and the question of whether an inmate is classified as "White," "Black," or "Hispanic" may vary from institution to institution. It may also differ from how the inmates classify themselves.

Media and Public Perception

We need to also consider how Latinos are perceived by others and how the media may contribute to the public perception of Latinos and Latino males in particular. There is still a relative absence of Latino male actors and characters both on television and in film (Hoffman & Noriega, 2004; Rodríguez, 2004). There are also few Latinos represented on network news coverage (Montalvo & Torres, 2006). Their invisibility, for example, on Sunday morning news programs, which influence decision makers, is particularly glaring. However, stereotypical depictions of Latino males on both the small and large screens are commonplace. Research finds that Latino male characters have tended to be more associated with violence and crime (Lichter & Amundson, 1994; Navarrete & Kamasaki, 1994; Ramirez-Berg, 1997; Rodríguez, 1997). Some authors argue that these persistent and stereotypical images could result in "a belief in the authenticity of these characterizations" and that they may "serve as indicators of norms of treatment in real-world intergroup contexts" (Mastro and Behm-Morawitz, 2005, p. 126; see also ChildrenNow, 1998, 2004; Cortés, 2000).

How does the general public view Latino males? Entman (2006) examined the 2000 National Opinion Research Center (NORC) General Social Survey and found that respondents observed a racial/ethnic hierarchy with regard to whether members of particular groups tended to be violence-prone, hardworking, or intelligent. At the bottom of the hierarchy were Blacks, followed by Latinos, and at the top, Asians equaled or surpassed Whites. The figures are striking—37.4 percent of those sampled said that Latinos were violence-prone, 23.9 percent said they were unintelligent, and 21.9 percent said they were lazy. Entman (2006) added that, given the tendency of people to hide their racial/ethnic biases, "the prevalence of negative stereotyping is almost certainly greater than suggested" (p. 7).

In essence, research has indicated that we have continuing under-representation and misrepresentation of Latinos on both the entertainment side and the news side, and substantial proportions of the general public that admit that they see Latinos as violence-prone (37.4 percent), unintelligent (23.9 percent), and lazy (21.9 percent) (Entman, 2006). Given the stereotypical depictions of Latino males in the media and the negative perceptions of Latinos by the general public, how are Latinos affected by such images and expectations? In other words, what is the influence of the media and public perception on the life chances (and consequently, hourly wages) of Latinos? With the recent passage of law SB 1070 in Arizona and the increased media attention on the currently contested issue of undocumented immigration, stereotypical depictions of Latino males could very well impact their economic, health, and social outcomes.

In conclusion, Roberto Lovato (2007) recently pointed to the limited options that many Latino males face—the military, law enforcement, or jail. We need to investigate why these options are so narrow. Why do so many Latinos choose, or end up in, these situations? How do the media limit the consideration of other options? What role do media portrayals play in channeling Latino males in these directions? How do the stereotyping, brief appearance, and/or constant marginalization of characters (in plots or in character development) influence Latino males? How does the association of Latino characters with crime influence growing children? An offshoot of "Dora, the Explorer" was a similar animated program featuring her cousin, Diego. What has been the impact of this show on growing Latino boys? All of these areas are worthy of further research, but we see few calls to study them or their effects.

References

Acosta-Belén, E., and Santiago. C. E. (2006). *Puerto Ricans in the United States: A contemporary portrait.* Boulder, CO: Lynne Rienner.

Arce, C. H., Murguia, E., and Parker Frisbie, W. (1987). Phenotype and life chances among Chicanos. *Hispanic Journal of Behavioral Sciences*, 9(1), 19–32.

Borrell, L., and Rodríguez, C. E. (2010). *The implications and impact of race on the health of Hispanics or Latinos.* In M. Aguirre-Molina, L.N. Borrell, and W.Vega (Eds.), *Health Issues in Latino Males: A Social and Structural Approach* (32–52). New Brunswick, NJ: Rutgers University Press.

ChildrenNow. (1998). *A different world: Children's perceptions of race and class in the media.* Oakland, CA: Children Now.

ChildrenNow. (2004). Fall colors: 2003–04. Prime time diversity report. Oakland, CA: Children Now, 1–12.

Collins, P. H. (2004). *Black Sexual Politics: African Americans, Gender, and the New Racism.* New York: Routledge.

Cortés, C. E. (2000). *The children are watching: How the media teach about diversity.* New York: Teachers College Press.

Cotton, J. (1993). Color or culture?: Wage differences among non-Hispanic Black males, Hispanic Black males and Hispanic White males. *Review of Black Political Economy*, 21(4), 53–67.

Darity, W., Jr., Hamilton, D., and Dietrich, J. (2002). Passing on Blackness: Latinos, race, and earnings in the USA. *Applied Economics Letters*, 9, 847–853.

Entman, R. M. (2006). Young men of Color in the media: Images and impacts. Better health through stronger communities: Public policy reform to expand life paths of young men of Color (4–40). T. D. Commission. Washington, DC: Joint Center for Political and Economic Studies Health Policy Institute.

Espino, R., and Franz, M. M. (2002). Latino phenotypic discrimination revisited: The impact of skin color on occupational status. *Social Science Quarterly*, 83, 612–623.

Frank, R., Akresh, I. R., and Lu, B. (2010). Latino immigrants and the U.S. racial order: How and where do they fit in? *American Sociological Review*, 75(3), 378–401.

Frey, W. H. (2010). Race and ethnicity. In *The state of metropolitan America.* Brookings Institute. Retrieved from www.brookings.edu/metro/MetroAmericaChapters.aspx

Gomez, C. (2000). The continual significance of skin color: An exploratory study of Latinos in the Northeast. *Hispanic Journal of Behavioral Sciences*, 22(1), 94–103.

Hoffman, A. R., and Noriega, C. A. (2004). Looking for Latino regulars on prime-time television: the fall 2004 season (1–25). Los Angeles: University of California, Chicano Studies Research Center.

Iceland, J., and Nelson, K. A. (2008). Hispanic segregation in metropolitan America: Exploring the multiple forms of spatial assimilation. *American Sociological Review*, 73, 741–765.

Itzigsohn, J., Giorguli, S., and Vazquez, O. (2005). Immigrant incorporation and racial identity: Racial self-identification among Dominican immigrants. *Ethnic and Racial Studies*, 28(1), 50–78.

Lichter, R., and Amundson, D. R. (1994). *Distorted reality: Hispanic characters in TV entertainment.* Washington DC, Center for Media and Public Affairs.

Logan, J. R. (2004). How race counts for Hispanic Americans. *SAGE Race Relations Abstracts*, 29(1), 7–19.

Lovato, R. (2007). Becoming *Americano*: The ascent of the new Latino right. *The Public Eye Magazine*. Retrieved from web article. www.publiceye.org/magazine/v21n2/americano.html

Massey, D. S. (1979). Effects of socioeconomic-factors on the residential segregation of Blacks and Spanish-Americans in United-States urbanized areas. *American Sociological Review*, 44(6), 1015–1022.

Massey, D. S. (2001). Residential segregation and neighborhood conditions in US metropolitan areas. In N. Smelser, W. J. Wilson, and F. Mitchell (Eds.), *American becoming: Racial trends and their consequences* (391–434). Washington, DC: National Academy of Sciences Press.

Massey, D. S., and Bitterman, B. (1985). Explaining the paradox of Puerto-Rican segregation. *Social Forces*, 64(2), 306–331.

Mastro, D. E., and Behm-Morawitz, E. (2005). Latino representation on primetime television. *Journalism and Mass Communication Quarterly*, 82(1), 110–31.

Melendez, E., Rodríguez, C., and Figueroa, J. B. (Eds.). (1991). *Hispanics in the labor force: Issues and politics*. New York: Plenum Press.

Montalvo, D. A., and Torres, J. (2006). *Network Brownout Report*. National Association of Hispanic Journalists, 5–23.

Murguia, E., and Telles, E. E. (1996). Phenotype and schooling among Mexican Americans. *Sociology of Education*, 69, 276–289.

Navarrete, L., and Kamasaki, C. (1994). *Out of the picture, Hispanics in the media*. Washington, DC: Policy Analysis Center, Office of Research Advocacy and Legislation, National Council of La Raza.

Ramirez-Berg, C. (1997). Stereotyping in films in general and of the Hispanic in particular. In C. E. Rodríguez (Ed.), *Latin looks: Images of Latinas and Latinos in the U.S. media* (288). Boulder, CO: Westview Press.

Rodríguez, C. E. (1990). Racial classification among Puerto Rican men and women in New York City. *Hispanic Journal of Behavioral Sciences*, 12(4), 366–379.

Rodríguez, C. E. (1991). The effects of race on Puerto Rican wages. In E. Melendez, C. E. Rodríguez, and J. B. Figueroa (Eds.), *Hispanics in the labor force: Issues and politics* (77–98). New York: Plenum Press.

Rodríguez, C. E. (1997). Keeping it reel? Films of the 1980s and 1990s. In C. E. Rodríguez (Ed.), *Latin looks: images of Latinas and Latinos in the U.S. media*. Boulder, CO: Westview Press.

Rodríguez, C. E. (2004). Diversifying Hollywood: Hispanic representation in the media. Congressional testimony, U.S. House of Representatives forum report. 23–27, 49.

Rodríguez, C. E., and Cordero-Guzman, H. (1992). Place race in context. *Ethnic and Racial Studies*, 15(4), 523–542.

Rosenbaum, E. (1996). The influence of race on Hispanic housing choices: New York City, 1978–1987. *Urban Affairs Review*, 32, 217–243.

Roth, W. D. (2010). Racial mismatch: The divergence between form and function in data for monitoring racial discrimination of Hispanics. *Social Science Quarterly*, 91(5), 1288–1311.

Ruggles, S., Trent Alexander, J., Genadek, K., Goeken, R., Schroeder, M. B., and Sobek, M. (2010). *Integrated Public Use Microdata Series: Version 5.0* [Machine-readable database]. Minneapolis: University of Minnesota.

Saenz, R. (2004). *Latinos and the changing face of America*. New York/Washington, DC: Russell Sage Foundation/Population Reference Bureau.

Singer, A., Hardwick, S. W., and Brettell, C. B. (Eds.). (2008). *Twenty-first-century gateways immigrant incorporation in suburban America*. Washington, DC: Brookings Institution Press.

Tafoya, S. (2004). *Shades of belonging*. Washington, DC: Pew Hispanic Center.

Telles, E. E., and Murguia, E. (1990). Phenotypic discrimination and income differences among Mexican Americans. *Social Science Quarterly*, 71, 682–693.

Williams, D. R., and Collins, C. (2001). Racial residential segregation: A fundamental cause of racial disparities in health. *Public Health Report*, 116(5), 404–416.

13

THE RELEVANCE OF SKIN COLOR IN THE CONSTRUCTION OF AN ETHNIC IDENTIFICATION AMONG MEXICAN AND PUERTO RICAN BOYS

Edward Fergus

As much as Latino groups are an ever-present component of the educational discourse on academic variability, there is a predominant situating of the Latino population as a monolithic group. Yet recent data have documented the vast diversity within this population. According to Census 2000, over 35 million Latinos were living in the United States at that time. By mid-decade, this number rose to 42 million. The rapid and dramatic growth of the Latino population represented 51 percent of the change in racial/ethnic groups between 2000 and 2005 (Pew Hispanic Center, 2006). Given our shared border, the majority of the 42 million were Mexican (64 percent), followed by Puerto Ricans (9.1 percent), Cubans (3.5 percent), Salvadorans (3.0 percent), and Dominicans (1.7 percent). In Census 2000, over 900,000 Latinos (2.7 percent) self-identified as Black Hispanic and 17.6 million (47.9 percent) as White Hispanic; another 15 million (42.2 percent) identified as "some other race" (Logan, 2003). The descriptor of Black Hispanic as an identification marker was most prominent among Dominicans (12.7 percent), followed by Puerto Ricans (8.2 percent), Cubans (4.7 percent), and finally Central Americans (4.1 percent) (Logan, 2003). On the other hand, identification as White Hispanic was most prevalent among Cubans (85.4 percent), followed by South Americans (61.1 percent), Mexicans (49.3 percent), and Puerto Ricans (49 percent).

In 2007, these identification patterns changed; the American Community Survey estimated 677,000 (1.5 percent) self-identifying as Black Hispanic and 24 million (54.3 percent) as White Hispanic, with another 18 million (40 percent) self-identifying as "other race." These differences in race and ethnic identification between 2000 and 2007 could be signaling a migration pattern among Latino groups entering the United States or a shift in the identification patterns of Latino groups. Whatever the explanation for this shift may be, it is evident that Latino groups need to situate their identification as both a race and an ethnicity, as their social experiences involve the interplay of their racial and ethnic identification.

Educational research has established that the racial and ethnic identification process is not only a pertinent factor in child development, it also influences how racial/ethnic minority children make sense of their school experience and engagement. Specifically, the research on academic variability (i.e., why some minority students do well and others do not) has provided an analytical terrain in which students' interpretations of their racial/ethnic groups' sociohistory in the United States influences their perceptions of the relationship between schooling and social outcomes (Carter & Segura, 1979; O'Connor, 1997, 2001; Ogbu, 1978, 1991). Although this research points to a recognition of race/ethnicity, there are limited findings articulating how such notions of race and ethnicity apply to Latinos. For instance, what if the community and school context identified a student as White but he identifies as Puerto Rican? Recognizing that meaning is ascribed to racial/ethnic identifications, what do such identifications signal about social experiences? By disentangling how skin color is used as an external proxy for race and ethnicity, we can provide a lens through which to view a dimension of the schooling experiences and educational outcomes (as noted in Chapter 1) of boys from different Latino groups.

Cultural Ecological Explanations of School Experiences

The educational anthropologist John Ogbu (1978, 1991) attempted to address the limitations of previous research on academic variability among ethnic minority youth. He explored power differentials and how student subjectivity influences academic performance. Ogbu (1991) argued that cultural deprivation and difference models do not account for why some ethnic minority students perform better than other minority and White students. His contention is that ethnic minority students have different histories of entry into and subjugation within the United States, which embody experiences of racial discrimination and social mobility. These experiences, Ogbu argued, are reflected in the student's subjective interpretations of the relationship between school and social outcomes, which in turn inform the students' accommodation and/or resistance to school. This argument is referred to as the *cultural ecological model*.

Research on immigrant adaptation processes (e.g., Kao & Tienda, 1995; Rumbaut, 1994; Suárez-Orozco & Suárez-Orozco, 1995, 2008) and other academic variability research (Carter, 2005; Flores-González, 1999; O'Connor, 1997) have exposed two limitations of the cultural ecological model. First, although the model offers a substantive explanation for academic variability among ethnic minority students at a macro-level, little attention is given to its applicability at the micro-level —that is, the model is not able to fully explain academic variability within ethnic groups that have diverse ethnic identification, socioeconomic status, and involuntary and immigrant status. Thus, the cultural ecological model provides categories that can be used to generalize about an entire group, but by doing so the model overlooks micro-level variations that may greatly influence subjectivity.

The second limitation of the cultural ecological model is the way in which racial/ethnic identification is characterized within the model. The model operates on the implied assumption that racial/ethnic identification can be defined as an "essence" that is reflected in individual and group renderings of opportunity and academic orientation. This assumption defines collective identifications (e.g., Black, African American, White, Hispanic/Latino/a, West Indian) as having a set of core features commonly shared by members and not present in other groups. These features range from experiences of racism and discrimination to similar renderings of slavery, colonization, and cultural artifacts and symbols. In addition, essence invokes an implied biological construct by asserting that, in identifying as Black, African American, Latino/a, or Hispanic, the individual is read similarly by others. Thus, this assumption of essence implies that individuals and groups construct shared patterns of thoughts and beliefs that define their identification. Countering to this assumption, numerous recent studies have documented a vast variability in identification among adolescents (Dickar, 2008; Lundy, 2003; Lundy & Firebaugh, 2005). More specifically, these scholars have addressed variations in cultural artifacts and engagement that moderate the ways in which ethnic identity is articulated and experienced; they determined, for instance, the importance of social network participation (Flores-González, 1999; Stanton-Salazar, 1997); the relevance of caring adults in schools (Valenzuela, 1999); the valuable role of mothers and grandmothers (Garrett et al., 2010; Hidalgo, 2000; Rolon, 2000); and the nature of religiosity and church activities in constructing intergenerational networks (Sikkink & Hernández, 2003).

Such research suggests that essentializing of collective identifications within the cultural ecological model overlooks how identities and identifications are continuously manipulated by individual and external forces. More importantly, the cultural ecological model and subsequent perspectives minimize the significance of identity politics (Calhoun, 1995), in which issues of power relations complicate how an individual is able to view him- or herself. What is key in Calhoun's definition of identity politics is the significance of power and hierarchy in the formation of identification, particularly when considered in relation to racial hierarchies, which signal specific power relations. The construct of racial hierarchy is loosely defined as the stratification of racial categorization, with Whites at the top and Blacks at the bottom (Song, 2004). The placement of Whites at the top is based on social and economic-based privileges and institutionalized racism that have allowed for disproportionate wealth accumulation and other forms of social mobility (Bobo et al., 1997; Hacker, 1992). Although there is near-universal agreement in the existence of a racial hierarchy, there is less agreement as to which groups are most oppressed and, more importantly, whether this is a static hierarchy. Proponents of the Black-White binary model of racial hierarchy (e.g., Feagin, 2000; Hacker, 1992) have posited this framework as the basis of oppression for other non-White groups. Feagin (2000) argued that the oppression other groups experience (i.e., Arabs, Latinos, Asians) is based on an anti-Black framework. The question becomes, how do Latino groups fit into this racial hierarchy? Some scholars have argued that the presence of various groups and their racialization experiences expand our notions of the racial hierarchy beyond the Black-White model (Almaguer, 1994; Bashi & McDaniel, 1997; Bonilla-Silva, 2004). For example, religion (Arab-Americans), citizenship (Latinos), culture (Indians), and language (Latinos and Asian groups) disrupt the skin color-bound Black-White binary. Thus, there are social and political differences in whether the identification "comes from social groups within the category or if the pressure for boundary keeping and definitions come from without" (Bashi, 1998, p. 960).

In short, what is lacking in the cultural ecological perspective is an analytical exploration that considers the racial/ethnic identification process of Latino groups, which includes racial hierarchies involving power relations of being identified by others. Such an approach can provide a more robust understanding of how Latino students come to formulate their perceptions of opportunity and academic orientation as bound to racialization experiences.

Racial/Ethnic Identification Among Latino Students

This chapter situates how seven Mexican and Puerto Rican high school boys identify themselves and make sense of the external identifications that others use as their racial/ethnic identification. The findings discussed are based on an exploratory study of phenotypically distinct Mexican and Puerto Rican high school students living in Detroit, Michigan (1999–2000). The purpose of this qualitative study of twenty-six students was to understand how experiences of racialization moderate interpretation of societal structures of mobility (i.e., opportunity and the making-it process) and engagement in school.

Findings

The study's findings are organized around the semi-structured interview protocol,[1] which focused on how the students identified themselves, including self-identification and external identification. The internal identification findings indicate that these students use self-identification as a boundary for placement within the Mexican or Puerto Rican community. Meanwhile, culture is treated as "the stuff inside the boundary," which provides further context to why they construct specific boundaries. Although the students' discussions about their identification and culture highlight the degree of agency individuals employ in this process, discussing the construction of ethnicity as such "runs the risk of emphasizing agency at the expense of structure" (i.e., the external perceptions of identity and culture) (Nagel, 1994, p. xx). When discussing their external identifications, the students described the ways in which they made sense of these renderings as being based primarily on skin color. The responses point to the importance of recognizing ethnicity as a fluid construct that is either dependent on or takes context into consideration.

Internal Identification: What Am I?

Although the students invoked ethnic categories in asserting who they are, they also explained why they do not use racial categories. Such an action suggests that they intuitively infer a difference between ethnicity and race. In light of such differences, it is important to map the distinctions the students made between traditional definitions and their understanding of race and ethnicity. Students were asked a number of questions that targeted how they describe themselves (e.g., How would you describe yourself in terms of race or ethnicity? Do you describe yourself as Black or White? How about Hispanic or Latino/a?). There was consensus among the students that Black and White were not terms they used to identify themselves because of perceived cultural group identification. To them, "Black" means African American and "White" means White American. However, it is uncertain whether the categories Black and White referenced a biological construct: for example, as Alex, who has a brown complexion, stated, "I'm not Black," when asked if he identified himself as Black or White. In other words, his self-designation implies that he does not view himself as a member of the group, even though he may look like a member of that group. Alex's assertion may not be expected from a student with his complexion. However, this assertion of not being Black or White was also articulated by students with lighter complexions. How they described themselves established a model within which *their* use of categories like Black and White referred to a group identification rather than a biological construct, as seen with others (i.e., African American students and teachers) in the discussion below. More importantly, this model represents part of the distinction these students make between race and ethnicity and illustrates the interplay between these students' definitions of race and ethnicity and the definitions from their external context (which includes African American peers, teachers, and other Latino/a ethnic group members).

Instead of using racial labels, students opted to use ethnic terms, like Mexican, Chicano or Puerto Rican, Boricua, Detroit-Rican, and in some instances Hispanic. Although their use of ethnic terms provided a concrete idea of which groups they identified with, it offered no insight into the meanings they attached to these ethnic designations. Therefore, the students were additionally asked to discuss what it meant to be a member of the ethnic categories with which they affiliated. From this discussion, three main typologies of identification emerged: (1) a hyphenated, (2) an ancestral/national, and (3) a cultural. A hyphenated identification was a means of "representing" the multiple locales that comprise who the students considered themselves to be.[2] For example, John considers himself Mexican-American-Italian because of various ties, but he "feels" Mexican because of where he lives. As he stated, "Being Mexican is more important to me. I don't speak Italian. I've talked to Italians before and they are concerned about things that I'm not. . . . But living here in Mexicantown, it's all in my face."

Ancestral/national identification reflected a birth in Mexico or Puerto Rico or ancestral ties to Mexico or Puerto Rico. The terms are connected because it was implicit that the students' definition denoted a direct connection to Mexico or Puerto Rico, either through family or actual birth in the country. For example, Alex identifies as Puerto Rican because it is an inescapable identification and relates to the "races" he embodies: "Yeah, because like for me being Puerto Rican is like being mixed with two other races. Like me I'm mixed with Indian and Black. That's what makes me Puerto Rican."

Cultural identification reflects the students' actual use of the term "culture" in defining who they are. For example, Paul describes himself as "100 percent Mexican-blooded":

> Well, I describe myself as Chicano. I'm Mexican-American, Chicano I go with any one of them 'cause I'm 100 percent Mexican blooded but yet I was born in the United States. Like I was born in California. So I'm not from there, I'm an American citizen, I'm from here but I am full-blooded Mexican. I grew up with the identity like here what shaped my identity was this culture not Mexican I mean my Mexican tradition and culture through my parents but not like the outside world.

Even though the students may have articulated the meaning they attach to the term they use most often, these typologies were not mutually exclusive. Some students used two typologies to describe themselves, thus implying that the students' maintained multiple points of reference regarding their identification.

These typologies not only had specific meanings that defined who these students were, but they also emerged in relation to the students' immigrant generation. The third generation students mainly used a hyphenated identification, and second generation used cultural and/or ancestral/national identification. Such relationships are consistent with findings in immigration literature, which has argued that certain identifications are more prevalent in some generations than others (Portes, 1994; Rumbaut, 1994; Suárez-Orozco & Suárez-Orozco, 1995).

Overall, these three typologies—hyphenated, ancestral/national, and cultural—designate the meaning these students place on their self-identifications. In addition, various layers exist within each typology, which determine how that meaning is used to define the boundary of the identification. It is important to point out that operating across these hyphenating, ancestral/national, and cultural identifications is the individual's desire for recognition of their identification and the significance of their multiple worlds and identifications. However, these ethnic identifications do not provide complete renderings of how these students define themselves. As noted earlier, identity and culture are the basic building blocks of ethnicity and these two concepts assist in the boundary-making process of identification, which includes who we are, what we do, and what we think.

External Identifications: How Do Others Identify Me?

Over the course of interviewing these students, two competing narratives continued to surface. In the first narrative, the students described and defined themselves, and subsequently their social world, from a self-assertive perspective. In this instance, the emphasis was on how *they* defined their social locations. However, their self-definitions also operated, in part, on perceptions of external interpretations of racial/ethnic identification. This narrative involved the students being aware of how they perceived external forces and/or how other individuals define them and subsequently frame their social world. In essence, this second narrative elucidated those factors that constrained how the students could identify and who they could be.

These dynamics were based, in part, on external interpretations of their skin color. The high schools these Latino/a students attended were primarily comprised of African American students and/or teachers. Students who thought of and defined themselves as Detroit-Rican, Mexican-American, Boricua, and Puerto Rican simultaneously faced their African American peers and teachers who situated them into three discrete categories: White-looking, Mexican/Hispanic-looking, and Black/Biracial-looking. These students reported experiencing racial/ethnic designation based primarily on skin color. Their accounts raise substantive questions that not only challenge race/ethnicity as more than discrete categories but challenge the meanings attached to skin color and race/ethnicity.

These accounts provide us with one vantage point for assessing the racializing process that occurs in individuals operating within specific contexts. I borrow the concept of racializing from various researchers who have established it as a positioning process (Bashi, 1998; Omi & Winant, 1994), whereby individuals insert themselves and are inserted into existing racial hierarchies, especially the Black/White binary hierarchy. In accordance with the concept of racialization, the students reported that in addition to being situated within the traditional binary (i.e., Black versus White), they were also situated as Mexican/Hispanic. In light of this triad of racial/ethnic categories, we must reconsider the racialization process as not only who is in and who is out, but also what does that process look like from the perspective of the individual being positioned within the triad.

The group labels listed below are derived from the students' perceptions of how others situated them racially.[3] The placements, however, coincide with how I would have situated the students were I to rely on visual cues. These groupings are as follows:

White-looking: This grouping includes students who were identified as White and/or half White and half Hispanic. They generally had dark brown hair with green or brown eyes and a fair skin color.

Mexican/Hispanic-looking: This grouping includes students who were simultaneously identified as Arab or Indian and Mexican/Hispanic. They generally had dark hair, brown eyes, and an olive to reddish-brown skin color.

Black/Biracial-looking: This grouping includes students who were identified as Black and/or perceived as Biracial or having "some Black in them" (i.e., Black and White; Black and Hispanic; Black and Filipino). These students had what I consider a *trigueño* skin color, which ranged from an olive to brown skin color, along with brown eyes and curly black/brown hair.[4]

The analysis of the students' narratives follows along the lines of this phenotype. However, in reporting the data, I collapse the groups into two categories: White-looking and Mexican/Hispanic and/or Black/Biracial-looking. I do this because the latter two phenotype groups situating Hispanic and Black are described in similar ways.

White-looking Students

In 1995, Craig Calhoun asked us to observe identity as more than simply a self-discovery process that is held solely by the individual and matters only to the individual: "Rather, it is much harder for us to establish who we are and maintain this own identity satisfactorily in our lives and in the recognition of others" (p. 10). The chore of the self-discovery process for the students in this study was to learn how to maintain their identification even though others identified them differently. In addition, the process that I point to here focuses on the following questions: what do the students perceive the external voices are stating about their identification, and more importantly, what do they believe are the markers used to situate them into these racial/ethnic categories of identification?

The students answered various questions about how others viewed them (e.g., Do your teachers or friends see you as Mexican/Puerto Rican? Has someone ever assumed you were part of another ethnic or racial group?). The White-looking students responded to the latter question by discussing their experiences of others, mainly African Americans, who situated them as White based on their skin color. They were typically identified as White, Italian or, in some instances, a racial mixture that included White (e.g., White and Mexican; White and Japanese). Regardless of how they were situated, these students perceived themselves as being primarily viewed as White. Even during moments when they were "performing" their ethnic identification (explained later in the chapter), they continued to be seen as White. The students reported that this association with Whiteness sometimes signified only a physical congruence with Whites to these external others. Other times, however, the students registered that this Whiteness signified a racial affiliation with Whites to the external others. From the perspective of these others, *congruence* implied that the students had similar physical features as Whites, while *affiliation* signaled an identification with Whites. Such differentiation suggests that the students perceived African Americans made distinctions between Mexican and Puerto Rican students based on various markers including, but not limited to, skin color. It is important to point out that the process of racialization by others involved situating the students into already established racial categories, whether the categories were White or Biracial (e.g., White and Mexican/Japanese). Part of the external identification process, the students suggested, involved an assignment to the White category and maybe even Whiteness. In other words, their skin color raised questions with their peers as to their level of affiliation with Whites and others.

Edgard was situated as White-looking by his peers but such an identification referenced a racial affiliation and not congruence to Whites. As a Mexican student in a predominantly African American high school, Edgard generally felt that his teachers and friends viewed him as Mexican. However, he was also conscious that some people outside of his social circle situated him as White-looking. According to Edgard, he was perceived as having a racial congruence to Whites but not necessarily an affiliation. In other words, Edgard considered his external identification of White-looking as a function of his skin color and not because of interaction or behavior read by African Americans as an affiliation to Whites.

> *Interviewer:* Has someone ever assumed you were part of another ethnic or racial group?
>
> *Edgard:* Yeah, some people think that I'm half-White and half-Mexican.
>
> *Interviewer:* Can you describe that situation or what happened?
>
> *Edgard:* I think they thought I was half and half 'cause my skin wasn't that dark and I don't know, they just thought I was White, like half-White, half-Mexican.
>
> *Interviewer:* Did they tell you that or how did you find out that?
>
> *Edgard:* They told me they were like, are you Mexican or what? I was like, yeah, I'm Mexican. They were like I thought you were like White and Mexican. I was, like, no.

Edgard explained his external identification as marked by his light skin color. Such an identification is not in concert with how Edgard views himself, which is as "a Mexican with slicked black hair" that talks Spanglish (Spanish and English mixture) with other Mexican students. As far as Edgard is concerned, by invoking the attributes that he considers indicative of a Mexican identification, he is embodying a Mexican identification; his construct of identification operates around the idea of inescapability of a Mexican category. He is Mexican because he dresses, talks, and combs his hair like a Mexican: what else could he be and how else could he be seen? However, to his African American peers he was White-looking, based not on those attributes but on his skin color. Thus, Edgard and his African American peers operate under the same premise that identification is discrete. However, the use of different signifiers of that identification points to a fundamental disconnect that marked Edgard's experience and is possibly representative of experiences between in and out group members.

Paul's experiences around his identification have always maintained a gain-loss dynamism. Identification, as Hall and du Gray (1996) argued, is a process of gain and loss in which the individual and external forces make decisions about who can own an identification and how that is done. From this concept, I borrow the idea of power that lies behind an individual gaining or losing their identification. Paul's and other White-looking students' narratives point to identification as an endured process in which others assign racial/ethnic affiliation or congruence based on skin color. However, the latter only illustrates one dynamic of the gain-and-loss process of identification; power is also integrated into that process. In other words, there is a certain degree of power implicit in being able to gain or lose your identification with or without challenge from outsiders. In the following exchange with Paul, some of the power that lies in gaining and losing identification is evident.

> *Interviewer:* Have there been times when being Chicano has been more or less important?
>
> *Paul:* Oh yeah, when I was in middle school me and my sister we were the only Latinos in the whole school. You know, all my friends were White just because I assimilated myself with White folks because I had just moved out of my neighborhood and into a White neighborhood. You know I wanted to be like them. I started to lose my Spanish. . . . I really wanted to change my name, I just didn't want to be Mexican. You know, so my middle school years I really had a hard time because I wanted to assimilate my whole life to like White culture. But then as soon as I hit high school that changed cause there were so many Latinos, and so then I wanted to be more Chicano than ever. I lost my self-identity during my middle school.

Paul's account of being able to gain and lose his identification illustrates the unique power of moving in and of identifications. In other words, Paul was able to be White and possibly accepted as a White person because of his skin color, but he could also acquire a Chicano identification due to having White skin color and a Latino/a identification does not require hyphenation, unlike those who are Afro-Latino or Black Latino (Rodriguez, 2000). Basically, he can disown his White skin and be Chicano or vice versa. Either way such a shift in identification symbolizes the power and, to some degree, privilege that comes with White skin color. Thus, the White-looking students, as Paul's narrative above indicates, retain more flexibility in their identification process.

In sum, these illustrative cases of performance constitute unique occurrences that the White-looking students raised as relevant. As was made apparent, the performances may not have always been purposeful. However, these students were aware that others racialized specific artifacts or performances—that is, these performance signifiers were part of how their peers and African American teachers constructed/defined racial congruence and affiliation. Skin color, language, clothing, and festivals may have functioned as signifiers of racial affiliation. However, skin color ultimately appeared to have superseded these performance signifiers. In other words, although these students could be viewed as affiliated with a Mexican or Puerto Rican community, within a context in which skin color has specific meaning of who you are and how you are treated, the ultimate signifier of racial affiliation or congruence is skin color.

Mexican/Hispanic and Black/Biracial-looking Students

Skin color was also used to define the Mexican/Hispanic-looking and Black/Biracial-looking students. As in the case of the White-looking students, the Mexican/Hispanic-looking and Black/Biracial-looking students reported that external others made a distinction between those who affiliated with Mexicans or Blacks and those who solely had a physical congruence with Mexicans or Blacks. Each grouping signaled the general notion that non-White skin color symbolizes an affiliation or congruence with either Hispanics or Blacks. The Mexican/Hispanic grouping was based on African Americans using these terms interchangeably and simultaneously, implying a particular look. Several students described their African American peers and teachers identifying them as Hispanic, but they interpreted this to mean that African Americans have limited knowledge of other ethnic groups. In other words, Mexicans became the representative group for Hispanics. On the other hand, the Black/Biracial grouping was mainly comprised of Puerto Rican students, which implies that Puerto Ricans were viewed as having African features and/or looking Black.

The racializing process with these students appeared slightly different from that noticed with the White-looking students. The Mexican/Hispanic-looking students were positioned in a category that disrupts the historical racial binary of Black/White–Hispanic/Latino. More importantly, these students reported that African Americans racialized the Hispanic label to be synonymous with Mexican, that is, Hispanics look like Mexicans and vice versa. Meanwhile Puerto Ricans are racialized as looking like "they have some Black in them," which entails a racial congruence and at times a racial affiliation with Blacks. Such movement in the racialization process points to what Bashi (1998) considered a reconstitution of the existing racial hierarchy. The Black/White is transformed into a triad in which some are Black (i.e., "Black in you"), others White (i.e., look White or "have some White in you"), and yet others Hispanic (i.e., look Mexican). Thus, the narratives that follow tell the story of how external interpretations of skin color situated students with a Hispanic or Black racial affiliation/congruence. The students were asked how they perceived others view them and whether they have ever been identified as part of another ethnic or racial group. The accounts they provided involved them being situated as Hispanic, Mexican, Arab, and Black. Once again, these identifications were not always interpreted as racial affiliations, but sometimes conveyed a racial congruence.

Alex, a dark-brown student with hazel eyes, is an example of how racial congruence operated among the darker-skinned students versus the lighter-skinned students. Like other dark-skinned students, Alex was conscious of his skin color. He pointed out that his interactions with African Americans were positive because he looked like them.

> *Interviewer:* You indicated that you see yourself as a Puerto Rican, do your friends see you in this way or do they identify you in other ways?
>
> *Alex:* Sometimes, they mostly see me as Black. Some Blacks have my skin color so they get confused.
>
> *Interviewer:* Can you think of a time in your life when someone has assumed you were of another race or ethnic group?
>
> *Alex:* Just when my friends think of me as Black.

With Alex, skin color was not the only signifier used to identify him as Black; he also participated in this identification by talking like African Americans: "It's just when I am around full-blown Blacks I start talking like them." Alex could not explain why he tended to talk like "full-blown Blacks" but such behavior suggests that on some level Alex tried to develop a Black identification. In addition, his reference to African Americans as "full-blown Blacks" suggests that he views himself as distinct from African Americans but interprets himself as Black (i.e., it seems as if he is saying that he is less than full-blown Black). Such an interpretation implies a connection between self-identification and external identification— that is, Alex's definition of his ancestral/national identification as connected to an ancestral (i.e., Taino Indian and African) history suggests that the content of his self-identification parallels the external factors others use to identify him. This of course begs the question, does his self-identification respond to or take into consideration his lived experiences of others using skin color to identify him? It is difficult to predict any type of causality with identification, but in the cases of Alex and other Black/Biracial-looking students there appear to be consistencies in the content of their self-identification and the relevance of external factors in how others situate them racially/ethnically.

Even though these students did not seem frustrated by the fact that they were situated as Hispanic or Black, they ultimately wanted to be seen as belonging to their Mexican or Puerto Rican community. The racializing experiences of these students took on a distinctly different tone from the White-looking students. The positioning process involved being affiliated with Mexicans or Blacks. Some students were even identified based in part on a perceived performance of a Black identification, while others became Hispanic (aka Mexican) based on indigenous features and with whom they were seen. Such a racializing process purports that there are aspects of these students' identification that are constantly being interpreted based on the definitions of others.

Conclusion and Further Considerations

The construction of ethnicity and identification is a process that simultaneously involves self-defined notions of what ethnicity and race are and a process engendered by external notions of what ethnicity and race are. Thus, how these students thought of themselves and what identification they used sometimes took into consideration how they were being read by others. These students could not simply be Mexican, Chicano, Boricua, or Puerto Rican. They were simultaneously White-looking, Black/Biracial-looking, or Mexican/Hispanic-looking.

The White-looking students were positioned according to their skin color and behavior. They were situated into a White-looking identification either through congruence or affiliation. Being affiliated with or having features that were congruent with that of Whites placed these students in situations in which they were either treated as White or made to feel as though they did not readily belong to a Mexican or Puerto Rican community. To offset their light skin color, some of the students performed a Mexican or Puerto Rican identification. These performances represented the students' effort to position themselves within the racializing process. However, this self-positioning did not supersede the external interpretations of skin color. Thus, what emerged was a story of racializing that involved others positioning these students as either affiliated with or congruent with Whites, and the students challenging such racializing by positioning themselves in a Mexican or Puerto Rican category through artifacts and cultural events.

On the other hand, the Mexican/Hispanic-looking and Black/Biracial-looking students were situated into racial and ethnic groups that were somewhat connected to their ethnic identification. The Mexican/Hispanic-looking students were situated as racially affiliated with Mexicans. The Black/Biracial students were racially congruent with Blacks but not necessarily deemed as affiliated with Blacks. The Mexican/Hispanic-looking students contended with being situated as part of a collective term that others used as a code for Mexican. Such coding not only implied that African American students and teachers have little knowledge regarding the geographic, social and political differences between Mexicans and Puerto Ricans but also that this coding reflects the historical experience that African Americans have had with Latino/a groups in Detroit. Since the Latino/a group that has had a significant presence in Detroit is Mexican, that group has probably become the image of Hispanic.

The Black/Biracial-looking students experienced a similar kind of racializing. The students identified as such were Puerto Rican. Thus, it was plausible for these students to stretch their Puerto Rican identification to include Black because, as many of them stated, part of Puerto Rico's cultural history includes a significant African presence. However, by being positioned as Black/Biracial-looking in predominantly African American high schools, these students either donned a Black persona or were perceived as having a Black persona. This impression of a Black persona solidified their affiliation with Blacks. Overall, neither category allowed for the students to be Mexican or Puerto Rican. Many of the students incorporated these labels into their repertoire of identities, but they could not be absent of such identities.

In short, the narratives of these students illustrate that their lived experiences are complicated by how others situate them. More importantly, the construction of ethnicity is not only a self-ascriptive process but also bound to how others engage in this process through the racializing of individuals. These students were not only conscious that their identification could change depending on context; they also understood that skin color would be the primary factor that would initiate that change. As the foregoing discussion demonstrates, these students operate from the standpoint that who they are and how they are viewed by others is significant in how they navigate in their day-to-day lived experiences. This suggests that their experiences as students and how they perceive and orient themselves in their social world operates from and/or takes into consideration these myriad encounters as White-looking, Black/Biracial-looking, or Mexican/Hispanic-looking Mexicans or Puerto Ricans.

Although the patterns described in this chapter reflect a small sample of Mexican and Puerto Rican boys, they indicate that a monolithic view cannot be used to conduct research among this population. And given the findings of educational and social outcomes that are outlined in Chapter 1, matters of race and ethnicity identification are issues implicated in the academic engagement of Latinos. In other words, future research and policy on child development, community context, school climate, curriculum and instruction, student academic engagement, and other salient variables in educational attainment should consider the ways in which the identifications used by Latino boys contain an interplay of internal and external ascription.

Notes

1 Students were interviewed at three data points over the course of a school year using an open and close-ended interview protocol. Each interview lasted one to two hours.
2 "Represent" is used by various ethnic minority groups—mainly younger individuals—to imply that an individual should demonstrate who they are and what they have allegiance to.

3   I borrow from Cornell and Hartmann's (1998) analytical distinction between race and ethnicity. The authors explain that race is a classification that is typically assigned or externally imposed, while ethnicity is internally asserted. Such an explanation allows us to explore the difference in power positions of having an identification imposed versus constructing one for yourself.

4   The description of the groupings' appearances is only to provide a general picture of what these students looked like from the perspective of the investigator and what features others may have used to situate these students as White-looking, Mexican/Hispanic-looking, and Black/Biracial-looking.

References

Almaguer, T. (1994). *Racial fault lines*. Berkeley: University of California Press.

Bashi, V. (1998). Racial categories matter because racial hierarchies matter: a commentary. *Ethnic and Racial Studies*, 21, 959–968.

Bashi, V., & McDaniel, A. (1997). A theory of immigration and racial stratification. *Journal of Black Studies*, 27, 668–682.

Bobo, L., Kluegel, J. R., & Smith, R. A. (1997). Laissez faire racism: The crystallization of a "kinder, gentler" anti-Black ideology. In S. A. Tuch and J. Martin (Eds.), *Racial attitudes in the 1990s: Continuity and change* (15–44). Greenwood, CT: Praeger.

Bonilla-Silva, E. (2004). From bi-racial to tri-racial: Towards a new system of racial stratification in the USA. *Ethnic and Racial Studies*, 17, 931–950.

Calhoun, C. (Ed.). (1995). *Social theory and the politics of identity*. New York: Ballantine Books.

Carter, P. (2005). *Keepin' it real. School success beyond Black and White*. Oxford: Oxford University Press.

Carter, T. P., & Segura, R. (1979). *Mexican Americans in school: A decade of change*. New York: College Entrance Examination Board.

Dickar, M. (2008). *Corridor cultures: Mapping student resistance at an urban high school*. New York: New York University Press.

Feagin, M. (2000). *Racist America*. New York: Routledge.

Flores-González, N. (1999). Puerto Rican high achievers: An example of ethnic and academic identity compatibility. *Anthropology & Education Quarterly*, 30, 343–362.

Garrett, T., Antrop-González, R., & Vélez, W. (2010). Examining the success factors of high-achieving Puerto Rican male high-school students. *Roeper Review*, 32(2), 106–115.

Hacker, A. (1992). *Two nations: Black and white, separate, hostile, unequal*. New York: Scribner.

Hall, S., & du Gray, P. (Eds.). (1996). *Questions of Cultural Identity*. Thousand Oaks, CA: Sage.

Hidalgo, N. M. (2000). Puerto Rican mothering strategies: The role of mothers and grandmothers in promoting school success. In S. Nieto (Ed.), *Puerto Rican students in U.S. schools* (167–196). Mahwah, NJ: Lawrence Erlbaum.

Kao, G., & Tienda, M. (1995). Optimism and achievement: The educational performance of immigrant youth. *Social Science Quarterly*, 76, 1–19.

Logan, J. (2003). How race counts for Hispanic Americans. Unpublished manuscript. University at Albany: Mumford Center.

Lundy, G. F. (2003). The myth of oppositional culture. *Journal of Black Studies*, 33(4), 450–467.

Lundy, G. F., & Firebaugh, G. (2005). Peer relations and school resistance: Does oppositional culture apply to race or to gender? *The Journal of Negro Education*, 74(3), 233–245.

Nagel, J. (1994). Constructing ethnicity: Creating and recreating ethnic identity and culture. *Social Problems*, 41, 152–176.

O'Connor, C. (1997). Dispositions toward (collective) struggle and educational resilience in the inner city: A case analysis of six African American high school students. *American Educational Research Journal*, 34, 593–629.

O'Connor, C. (2001). Making sense of the complexity of social identity in relation to achievement: A sociological challenge in the new millennium. *Sociology of Education*, 74, 159–168.

Ogbu, J. (1978). *Minority education and caste: The American system in cross-cultural perspective*. New York: Academic Press.

Ogbu, J. (1991). Immigrant and involuntary minorities in comparative perspective. In M. Gibson & J. Ogbu (Eds.), *Minority status and schooling: A comparative study of immigrant and involuntary minorities*. New York: Garland Publishing.

Omi, M., & Winant, H. (1994). *Racial formation in the United States: From the 1960s to the 1990s*. New York: Routledge.

Pew Hispanic Center. (2006). Pew Hispanic Center tabulations of 2005 American community survey. Washington, DC: Pew Hispanic Center.

Portes, A. (1994). The new second generation. *International Migration Review*, 28, 1–10.

Portes, A., & Rumbaut, R. (1996). *Immigrant America*. Berkeley: University of California Press.

Rodriguez, C. (2000). *Changing race: Latinos, the census, and the history of ethnicity in the United States*. New York: New York University Press.

Rolon, C. A. (2000). Puerto Rican female narratives about self, school, and success. In S. Nieto (Ed.), *Puerto Rican students in U.S. schools* (141–166). Mahwah, NJ: Lawrence Erlbaum.

Rumbaut, R. G. (1994). The crucible within: Ethnic identity, self-esteem, and segmented assimilation among children of immigrants. *International Migration Review*, 28, 748–794.

Sikkink, D., & Hernández, E. I. (2003). Religion matters. Notre Dame, IN: University of Notre Dame Institute for Latino Studies Center for the Study of Latino Religion.

Song, M. (2004). Who's at the bottom? Examining claims about racial hierarchy. *Ethnic and Racial Studies*, 27, 859–877.

Stanton-Salazar, R. (1997). A social capital framework for understanding the socialization of racial minority children and youths. *Harvard Educational Review*, 67, 1–40.

Suárez-Orozco, C., & Suárez-Orozco, M. (1995) *Trans-formations: Migration, family life, and achievement motivation among Latino adolescents*. Stanford, CA: Stanford University Press.

Suárez-Orozco, M., & Suárez-Orozco, C. (2008). *Learning a new land*. Boston, MA: Harvard University Press.

Valenzuela, A. (1999). *Subtractive schooling: U.S.-Mexican youth and the politics of caring*. Albany: SUNY Press.

14

RACIALLY STIGMATIZED MASCULINITIES AND EMPOWERMENT

Conceptualizing and Nurturing Latino Males' Schooling in the United States

Nancy López

Curious about my presence in his math class at Southwest High School (SHS), a large public high school in New Mexico, Randy, a brown-skinned Latino young man in Ms. Anaya's ninth grade special education class, queried me: "Miss, are you a psychologist? Are you here to see how stupid we are?"[1] As a bilingual Afro-Dominicana who was born in the Lower East Side and raised in New York City public housing projects during the 1970s, I was pained by Randy's question; it echoed the profound sense of race-gender stigma felt by Latinos, particularly the microaggressions those of us who are dark-skinned experience regularly across a variety of social institutions in the United States (López, 2003). Randy's questions also allude to the presence of a double consciousness among Latino boys, whereby one is always looking at oneself through the eyes of a critical other (Du Bois, 1903). Donning baggy pants, a short crew cut, two large white faux diamond earring studs, and an oversized shirt, Randy physically embodied what I describe as one of the "racially" stigmatized masculinities that is disdained in contemporary society in the United States.

Why are Latino boys experiencing failure in U.S. schools? How do "racial" hierarchies and masculinities intersect in school settings? What is the cumulative lived experience of being Latino and male in U.S. schools and in the Southwest in particular? How can teachers, parents, and policy makers nurture the resilience and empowerment of Latino males? The purpose of this chapter is to outline key sociological conceptual tools for unraveling the education of "racially" stigmatized youth, specifically Latino males. Drawing on "racial" formation theory, theories of intersectionality, and critical "race" theory, I argue that the concept of "racially" stigmatized masculinities is a useful tool for understanding the schooling experiences of Latino males, as well as for working toward the empowerment of Latino males in U.S. schools. A fundamental assumption of this concept is that masculinities vary by "race," class, gender, sexual orientation, and ability status, and that all masculinities are not equal. Not all masculinities enjoy access to networks of power, are valued in society, or are represented in a positive light in the mass media or other social institutions; therefore it is important to examine how "racially" stigmatized masculinities are carved out in relation to racially privileged masculinities. Masculinities are relational, contextual, historically variable definitions, cultural scripts, and displays of what it means to be a man. "Racially" stigmatized masculinities refers to the cumulative lived masculinity of young men subjected to race-gender stigma in their everyday interactions in public spaces, classrooms, schools, and cultural institutions, such as the mass media. In keeping with theories of intersectionality and the nexus between social structures and agency, the concept of "racially" stigmatized masculinities acknowledges that the race-gender stigma attributed to these masculinities can serve as a site of simultaneous oppression and resistance, and may contain the seeds for empowerment.

In the first part of this chapter, I discuss "racial" projects, controlling images, White supremacy, and empowerment as key building blocks for the concept of "racially" stigmatized masculinities. In the second part, I present a snapshot of how "racial" hierarchies and masculinities intersect at SHS, a large public high school in a predominantly Latino area in New Mexico. I conclude with some policy implications for the theory and practice for improving the education of Latino males.

"Social Race," Masculinities, and Intersectionality

Before engaging in a meaningful discussion of "racial" inequality, it is imperative that we clarify two related but analytically distinct concepts: "race" and ethnicity. While most social scientists agree that both "race" and ethnicity are social constructions that have no biological meanings, there is considerable debate about whether to employ one term over another (American Anthropological Association, 1997, 1998; American Association of Physical Anthropologists, 1996; American Sociological Association, 2002; Human Genome Project, 2010). I argue that both analytical concepts are essential for understanding the enduring inequalities that persist over long periods of time for entire categories of people. Ethnic groups are distinguished by common cultural characteristics such as history, language, culture, and sometimes religion. For example, my ethnicity is Dominican; however in most social circumstances in the United States, I am racialized as Black. It is important to keep in mind that the experiences of a light-skinned Latino male may be qualitatively different from that of a darker-skinned Latino of so-called African phenotype or mestizo phenotype (Hunter, 2005; Murguia & Telles, 1996). This is not to say that lighter-skinned Latino males do not experience discrimination, particularly if they do not speak English or speak English with a so-called accent, or are low income, undocumented, or gay/ bisexual; rather it is important to account for how a pigmentocratic logic undergirds much of the race-gender stigma attributed to Latino communities (Vidal-Ortiz, 2004). In an effort to trouble commonsense understanding of race as a natural, essential biological reality and instead call attention to the fact that "race" has no biological meaning, in my writing I use quotation marks around the terms "race" and "social race," etc. and argue that examination of racial stratification is the first step to unraveling inequalities in education (Gillborn, 1995; López, 2003; Wagley, 1968).

Racial Formation Theory

In their groundbreaking book, *Racial Formation in the United States: From the 1960s to the 1990s*, Omi and Winant (1986, 1994) provided us with compelling conceptual tools for understanding "race" as a fundamental organizing principle in the United States. Whereas the United States was once a racial dictatorship, contemporary racial inequality is maintained via hegemony, whereby dominant legitimating ideologies are eventually incorporated by societal members as "common sense," which in turn justifies racial inequality.

> "Racial" formation is the synthesis of multiple "racial" projects, large and small, that we are all subjected to on a daily basis. "Racial" projects are definitions, interpretations, and representations of "racial" dynamics and simultaneous attempts to redistribute (both social and material) resources along "racial" lines.
>
> (Omi & Winant, 1994, p. 56)

They are constitutive of social institutions and occur at both the macro-level of policies, social movements, laws, representations in the mass media, and collective identities, as well as at the micro-level of individual identity, social interaction, lived experiences, psyche, and cognition.

Omi and Winant (1994) identified the state as the most important site of "racial" formation:

> Every state institution is a "racial" institution, but not every institution operates in the same way. . . . Through policies which are explicitly or implicitly racial, state institutions organize and enforce the "racial" politics of everyday life.
>
> (p. 83 [quotation marks not in original])

Under "racial" formation theory, "race" is not just a macro-level phenomenon at the level of social structure, culture, and representation, or a micro-level phenomenon at the lived experience or identity; rather "race" is all of these social realities simultaneously. "Racial" profiling (or what I call "race-gender profiling") in policing is an example of a "racist racial" project because it reproduces structures of domination based on essentialist definitions of "race." Affirmative action programs are examples of "an anti-racist racial" project because such programs aim to dismantle structural discrimination.

Racialized Social Systems, White Supremacy, and Critical "Race" Theory

In *White Supremacy in the Post-Civil Rights Era*, Bonilla-Silva (2001) extended "racial" formation theory by specifically linking "racial" inequality to racialized social systems:

> Societies in which economic, political, social and ideological levels are partially structured by the placement of actors in "racial" categories or "races" . . . the selection of some human traits to designate a "racial" group is always socially rather than biologically based . . . In all racialized social systems the placement of actors in "racial" categories involves some form of hierarchy that produces definite social relations among the "races."
> (Bonilla-Silva, 2001, p. 37 [quotation marks not in original])

The racialized social system framework examines how differential economic, political, social, and psychological rewards and disadvantages are allocated to groups along "racial" lines. Accordingly, one of the central tasks of the researcher is to unravel the specific mechanisms that shape White supremacy and on-going "racial" inequality in our society. Bonilla-Silva (2003) argued that "racial" inequality and specifically White supremacy are maintained through the adherence of the ideology of colorblindness to one or more of the following common frames: (1) abstract liberalism—meritocratic discourse; (2) naturalizing "racial" inequality as normal—people want to be with others like them; (3) cultural racism—lack of family values; and (4) minimizing the reality of "racial" inequality—it's just class.[2]

Critical "race" theorists examine the ways in which "racial" inequality in schools is anchored in White supremacy (Gómez, 2007; Ladson-Billings & Tate, 1995; Leonardo, 2005). The intra-school resource gap present in many schools is part of what Gloria Ladson-Billings (2006) referred to as the "education debt" owed to members of "racial" minority groups. A growing body of work in schooling inequality challenges the assimilation framework for understanding school failure and instead focuses on the racialization processes in schooling (Ferguson, 2001; Fine & Weis, 1998; Lewis, 2003; López, 2003; Pizarro, 1999; Staiger, 2005). I am inspired by the critical "race" theorists' insistence on the irreducibly political nature of the social science enterprise and their critique of the so-called objective and value-free social sciences (Dei & Sefa, 2005; Delgado, 1995).

Insights from Theories of Intersectionality

> Intersectionality refers to particular forms of intersecting oppressions, for example, intersections of "race" and gender, or of sexuality and nation. Intersectional paradigms remind us that oppression cannot be reduced to one fundamental type, and that oppressions work together in producing injustice.
>
> (Collins, 2000, p. 18)

Highlighting how "race" is gendered and gender is racialized, Collins' (2000) matrix of domination framework widened our analytical lens by focusing on the overall organization of hierarchical power relations as rooted in intersecting and shifting domains of power and regions of hegemony such as race, gender, class, nationality, and sexual identity, among others. Each of these domains of power has a structural, disciplinary, hegemonic, and inter-personal component. Collins' (2000) key concept of "controlling images" illustrates how Black women in schools, the media, and government agencies are objectified and framed as "Others," thereby providing ideological justification of race, gender, sexuality, and class oppression. The image of Black women as welfare queens is one such controlling image (Crenshaw, 1991; Roberts, 1997).

What are the controlling images of Latino masculinity, particularly in the Southwest? From 2006–2009, Lou Dobbs, former news anchor for a CNN national news program, was a key agent in promoting racist representations of undocumented Mexican immigrants as drug dealers, criminals, and potential terrorists. While Dobbs' rantings on the news channel painted the U.S.-Mexican border as an easy entry point for terrorists, rarely if ever is the U.S.-Canadian border mentioned. These discourses are important because they frame the ways in which Latino communities and Latino men, in particular, are seen in the United States. These controlling images become part and parcel of the "racial" common sense and "racial" hegemony that subject Latino males to "racial" and gender oppression in public spaces, schools, and the workplace. SB 1070 in Arizona as well as Albuquerque Police Department policy (adopted 5/18/10) that interrogates the immigration status of every arrestee with Immigration Customs and Enforcement (ICE), are only two recent examples of the racist policies and practices that are anchored in disdain for Latino males in particular.

Another powerful conceptual tool for addressing the schooling of "racially" stigmatized youth is Collins' notion of empowerment (2000; see also Freire, 1993, on the pedagogy of the oppressed). Collins' concept of empowerment underscores the agency of social actors in any oppressive situation:

> When it comes to knowledge, Black women's empowerment involves rejecting the dimensions of knowledge that perpetuate objectification, commodification, and exploitation. African American women and others

like us become empowered when we understand and use the dimensions of our individual, group and formal educational ways of knowing that foster our humanity. When Black women value our self-definitions, view the skills gained in schools as part of a focused education for Black community development, and invoke Black feminist epistemologies as central to our worldviews, we empower ourselves.

(Collins, 2000, p. 289)

Oppositional knowledge, developed by and for and/or in defense of an oppressed group's interest, fosters the group's self-definition and self-determination. Collins reminded us that hegemony is always incomplete and that oppressive cumulative lived experiences can be transformed into empowerment. This understanding of hegemony and resistance is key for the empowerment of Latino males, as well as other "racially" stigmatized youth, particularly in the school setting (Pizarro, 1999, 2005).

Eschewing the old eyeglasses that compartmentalized race, class, gender, and disability as discrete arenas, additive arenas of difference allow us to try on new lenses that examine how these differences are socially constructed in relation to one another. "Intersectional lenses" allow us to "see" how masculinities and femininities are relational, contextual, and permeated by multiple and intersecting inequalities such as race, ethnicity, class, sexuality, citizenship, and disability, as well as the simultaneity and dialectical relationship between social structure/agency, oppression/resistance, in addition to culture, structure, and lived experience.

Conceptualizing Gender and Masculinities via Lived Experience

The starting point for boys' work . . . must be through a critical assessment of lived masculinity—and through a thoughtful and informed consideration of how schooling and masculinity intersect . . . such a critical assessment cannot dodge how masculinity will be played out in diverse ways—as it is experienced differently by boys from different locations, families and communities, and through different sexual, cultural and class orientations.

(Gilbert & Gilbert, 1998, p. 25)

Men are not born; they are made. And men make themselves, actively constructing their masculinities within a social and historical context.

(Kimmel & Messner, 1992, p. 8)

Firmly anchored in a social constructionist perspective, Kimmel and Messner (1992), in their co-edited book *Men's lives*, theorized about the sociohistorical origins and consequences of discourses and social organizations of diverse masculinities; they argued that masculinities vary and are best unraveled by tracing the life course of masculinity as a fluid and ever-changing definition of what it means to be a man. The key point here is that gender can also be under-stood as a macro- and micro-level *process* instead of as an essential unchanging trait. Gender is accomplished in interaction within existing social structures; as a social construction, gender has macro- and micro-level dimensions. Just as all institutions are racialized and classed, so are they gendered (West & Zimmerman, 1987).

Another concept that is important for understanding the schooling of Latino males is the concept of stigma (Goffman, 1963; Link & Phelan, 2001). Goffman (1963) defined the stigmatized person as "a blemished person, ritually polluted, to be avoided, especially in public spaces" (p. 1). He distinguished between the discredited, those whose stigma is visible, and the discreditable, those whose stigma is hidden. Those who are discredited include those subjected to "the tribal stigma of race, nation, and religion, these being stigma that can be transmitted through lineages and equally contaminate all members of family" (p. 4). Goffman (1963) concluded that, "we believe that a person with a stigma is not quite human" (p. 5). Acknowledging the class, sexuality, and racial hierarchies among diverse masculinities, Goffman trumpeted a definition of hegemonic masculinity:

> There is only one complete unblushing male in America: a young, married, white, urban, northern, heterosexual, Protestant father of college educa-tion, fully employed, of good complexion . . . any male who fails to qualify . . . is likely to view himself . . . as . . . inferior.
>
> (Goffman, 1963, p. 128)

What is important here is that young men, and particularly young men from "racially" stigmatized communities, are bound to have to negotiate their identities and interactions against the backdrop of racialized hegemonic masculinities. These are all valuable concepts that can help us unravel the experience of Latino males in U.S. schools.

From Marginalized and Subordinated Masculinities to "Racially" Stigmatized Masculinities

In order to more accurately theorize the lived experience of Latino males (along with other young men subjected to "racial" stigma), we must extend the concepts of subordinated or marginalized masculinities and use the concept of "racially" stigmatized masculinities to more fully capture the lived masculinities of Latino males in U.S. schools. "Racially" stigmatized masculinities refers to the spectrum of cultural scripts, performances, and embodiments of what it means to be a man that are accorded "racial" stigma. Randy, the ninth grader I mentioned in the introduction, was the embodiment of race-gender stigma: dark skin, diamond earrings, baggy clothes. "Racially" privileged masculinities refers to the cumulative lived experience and social, material, and economic advantages that are accorded to those young men racialized as White; it also refers to the spectrum of cultural scripts and performances of what it means to be a man that is accorded "racial" privilege.

It is important to highlight that "racially" stigmatized masculinities can only be understood as relational rather than as essential static or innate characteristics. They are articulated in relation to "racially" privileged masculinities, as well as "racially" stigmatized and "racially" privileged femininities. For example, the bohemian masculinities displayed by some of the young White men at SHS were not seen as problematic. In contrast, the displays of masculinities displayed by some brown-skinned young men at SHS were widely interpreted by some teachers and staff as threatening.

Researchers should always clarify the conceptual basis of their investigations of masculinities. To this end, I operationalize "racially" stigmatized masculinities as a multi-dimensional concept, that is comprised of multiple facets, including but not limited to: (1) social "race"—in other words, how other people usually classify you in most social circumstances; (2) one's own racial self identity; (3) cultural and ethnic identity; (4) gender display and performance; (5) sexuality; and (6) embodiment—the cumulative lived experiences over the life course. The cumulative nature of race-gender experiences and specifically race-gender stigma, can be witnessed in a variety of social domains including, but not limited to, public spaces, schools, workplaces, formal and informal disciplinary practices in schools, the criminal justices system (e.g., race-gender profiling), popular culture and the media, etc. Although race, class, gender, sexuality, disability status, and other systems of oppression are all present at any given point, race-gender status and identity operate as master statuses, whereby in most social circumstances they overpower all other social statuses and identities, including social class (Collins, 2000; Crenshaw, 1991). However, it is important to note that hegemony is never complete. "Racially" stigmatized masculinities can be simultaneously a site of oppression, double consciousness, and reflection that could contain the seeds of resistance to negative controlling images about Latinos and other young men of color.

Colorblind Racism: The Paradox of "Racial" Stratification in a "Multicultural" State

Before describing the ways in which "racial" hierarchies and hegemonic and "racially" privileged masculinities are co-produced at Southwest High School, I provide a snapshot of the school district, the city of Santiago, and the state of New Mexico. In 2005, Governor Bill Richardson proclaimed New Mexico a "multicultural" state. Indeed, New Mexico has the largest percentage of Hispanics in the Union: 43 percent Hispanic; 30 percent White/White; 10 percent American Indian. The following year, Governor Richardson declared his candidacy for the presidential office and, along with Governor Janet Napolitano of Arizona, declared a state of emergency at the U.S.-Mexican border. Maria Hinojosa (2006), host of the National Public Radio program "Latino USA," pressed Governor Richardson about his motive for the declaration and questioned his use of the term "illegal alien." Governor Richardson, son of a

Mexican-born mother, responded by saying that he used this term out of frustration with the level of criminal activity on the border.[3] In the Southwest border states of New Mexico, Arizona, California, and Texas, the controlling image of Latino and Mexican masculinity, in particular, as violent, drug dealer, and "illegal alien" has become part and parcel of the racial common sense used to oppress dark-skinned Latino males.

In 2003, two brown-skinned Mexican-born high school students were singled out for interrogation in the school's parking lot in the city of Santiago. Although the youth were exchanging car keys, school safety officers automatically assumed that they were drug dealers. In violation of Santiago School District policy, school safety officers summoned federal immigration agents when they suspected that the youth were "illegal aliens" with false papers. A lifelong Latina educator commented that it was unlikely that school security officers would have assumed that the youth were drug dealers if they had been White. Indeed the deportation of the young men was ordered because even though they had lived in the United States since they were toddlers, they were undocumented. The deportation was stalled through the efforts of the Mexican American Legal Defense and Education Fund. This incident sent a chilling message to many Latinos living in the Southwest, as even those who are legal immigrants or are U.S.-born children of immigrants may be questioned and asked to present proof of citizenship at any time. The Arizona SB 1070 is one of the most recent iterations of racist anti-immigrant legislation. The recently elected mayor of Santiago campaigned on the premise that city law enforcement be allowed to inquire about the legal status of any person stopped by a police officer. In April 2010, the mayor authorized the Police Department to refer every arrestee to the Immigration Customs and Enforcement Agents stationed at the central booking office.

In a 7–2 vote, the Santiago District school board approved a controversial policy to arm school police during school hours. Prior to fall 2007, school police officers were required to keep their guns locked during school hours; only city police officers placed at some of the Santiago public schools were able to wear their guns during school hours. The Santiago School District is seeking approval from the state legislature to create an independent police department for the district. Again, the ideological justification for arming police officers is that there is a growing gang and drug trafficking problem fueled by "illegal aliens" from Mexico. This controlling image has also led to repeated racist incidents targeting Latino/Mexican-focused student services at The University of New Mexico, including the destruction of a Mexican flag on campus and the intimidation of staff via hate mail and defacement of property.

Southwest High School is located in the city of Santiago, which is one of the largest cities in New Mexico and home to over half a million residents. The campus consists of a one-story main building built in the 1970s; multiple additions mark the expansions of the school. About half a dozen temporary trailer classrooms occupy part of the parking lot. English language learners and students with behavior problems are housed there. The maze-like hallways are quite sterile; beige cinderblocks do not convey any sense of place. Sporadic artwork dots some of the school walls, but with the exception of the lunchroom space, which features a colorful mural, artwork is sparse. Southwest High School is a closed campus. The only time students have a fleeting respite from the wall-to-wall windowless classrooms is during their lunch break when students can escape to an inner court-yard. This is particularly ironic because with 300 days of sunshine and breath-taking views of blue skies and mountains, Santiago, New Mexico, is perhaps one of the sunniest places in the country. Students joke that this school is modeled after a prison. By the end of the day, it certainly feels like one.

Close to two-thirds of SHS students identify as Hispanic and about a third identify as White. About a third of students qualify for free school lunch. This figure may be an undercount because of the stigma associated with receiving free lunches. During the time of my fieldwork academic year, three-quarters of the out-of-school suspensions were Hispanic students; two-thirds involved males; one-quarter were special education students. Half of the suspensions involved ninth graders. It is telling that numbers on the teaching force are not readily available or included in the school demographics of the school, but the sole Latino and bilingual assistant principal shared an office with the armed police officer assigned to the school.

The four-year cohort graduation rate at SHS during my fieldwork was lower than the district-wide average (44 percent versus 50 percent). The district reports that fewer than half of Hispanics and Blacks and only a third of Native American students graduate after four years compared to close to three-quarters of White and Asian students. In accordance with district policy, no official statistics on the immigrant status of students is recorded; however, the principal estimated that close to one-third of Latino/a students at SHS are immigrants themselves or the children of immigrants, mostly from Mexico.

Although the official school discourse touts the numerical diversity at SHS, de facto "racial" hierarchies are lived by students vis-à-vis resource gaps, extracurricular activities, and student governance. White students comprise a minority; however, they are over-represented in Advanced Placement (64 percent White versus 30 percent Hispanic), Gifted, and Honors classes, as well as elite extracurricular activities, such as drama club, band, the school newspaper, and student government. In contrast, Latino boys are over-represented in special education classes, in-school and out-of-school suspension, wrestling, and other sports. Nevertheless, local papers and the SHS paper paint SHS as a "diverse" school.

At a combined school board and Parent Teacher Association meeting, Brad, the SHS class president, boasted that he chose to go to SHS because of its diversity: "We are so diverse; everyone gets along; there are no cliques . . ." After a brief pause, Brad, who donned torn bell-bottom jeans and wrinkled shirt and had matted, unkempt hair, exemplifying the bohemian, racially privileged masculinity of many of the White youth at the school, chuckled, "Well, maybe there are cliques but we all get along." This limited understanding of diversity as simple numerical diversity and cultural differences ignores the unequal distribution of material and non-material rewards in the school vis-à-vis power, prestige, status, social networks, schooling outcomes, and school staff. This minimization of "racial" inequality is one of the most prevalent frames and ideologies that upholds colorblind racism at SHS (Bonilla-Silva, 2003). When a SHS teacher was fired for using a "racial" epithet in casual conversation with a student, although the local city paper covered the incident, the school paper never once addressed the issue. The only response from the school was to provide counseling for the students who were specifically exposed to the epithet.

A review of the controversial 2001 No Child Left Behind (NCLB) benchmarks paints a different picture of "diversity," namely, the limits of numerical diversity. Southwest High School was among the schools that did not meet adequate yearly progress. This was due largely to the wide "achievement gaps" (read, resource gaps) measured in the State Assessment Tests. While over three-quarters of White students were proficient in reading, less than a third of Hispanic students were. The gap in mathematics was even wider (71 percent versus 15 percent). Students with a disability and students identified as English language learners, followed by those who enrolled in the free or reduced lunch program, had the biggest achievement gaps[4] (See Table 14.1).

Alarmed by the statistics that denoted SHS a failing school, Principal Johnson explained that all efforts were being made to have Southwest High School make adequate progress next year.[5] Southwest High School is among the few schools in the city that offer a dual-language program and bilingual certification for students who successfully complete a sequence of bilingual classes and examination; however the performance of students in dual-language programs are not captured

TABLE 14.1 Standard Based Assessments Examination Scores for Southwest High School

	% Proficient in Mathematics	% Proficient in Reading
White	Over two-thirds	Over three-quarters
African American	Less than one-fifth	Less than one-third
Hispanic	Less than one-sixth	Less than one-third
Asian	N/A	N/A
Native American	Less than one-fifth	Less than one-third
English language learners	Less than one-tenth	Less than one-sixth
Students with disabilities	Less than one-tenth	Less than one-tenth
Free/reduced lunch program	Less than one-sixth	Less than one-quarter
Overall school average	Less than one-third	Over one-third

Source: New Mexico Public Education Department

by the No Child Left Behind benchmarks. When I showed Ms. Rivera, a dual language teacher, the New Mexico Standard Based Assessment results, she was visibly upset: "Why don't they include the performance of dual language classrooms? Research has shown that English Language Learners (ELLs) in dual language programs outperform their monolingual peers." Ms. Rivera critiqued how different racial, ethnic and language groups framed in snapshot data that compares last year's ninth grades to this year's ninth grades is inherently flawed and methodologically unsound.

"Racially" Stigmatized Masculinities Under Surveillance and "Racially" Privileged Masculinities at the Country Club

> Schools do not merely inherit or manage "racial" and ethnic identities; they create and enforce "racial" meanings. Schools as contested spaces, structure the conditions for the embodiment, performance, and/or interruption of sustained and inequitable "racial" formations.
>
> (Fine, 2004, p. 246)

One of the most alarming trends affecting Latino males as well as other racially stigmatized youth is the growing school-to-prison pipeline (Ferguson, 2001; Morris, 2005; Noguera & Wing, 2006; Pizarro, 2005). When I asked the armed city police assigned to SHS to explain how school disciplinary procedures connect to the juvenile justice system, Officer Washington reported:

> It's the officer's discretion. Technically you are supposed to witness the fight before you can arrest them. What I have done with my supervisor is that if I get the teacher to write me a detailed report or statement then we arrest them and we take them down to the D home. Nine times out of ten we never have a repeat.

Off tape, Officer Washington said that he sees the importance of showing Latino and Black kids the hard lesson of what jail is like because they do not have parents or family support at home; White kids did have parental support and would not require the "lesson." For Officer Washington, a police officer of Color who described himself as growing up under similar circumstances as the youth, handcuffing and processing Black and Latino young men who had been engaged in a school scuffle would help them "straighten up." Disciplinary discretion is exercised in such a way that "racially" stigmatized masculinities are seen as more problematic than "racially" privileged masculinities.

Participant observations in the special education and gifted classes reveal how "racially" stigmatized masculinities are carved in relation to "racially" privileged masculinities at SHS. Because both of these classes fell under the rubric of special education, they had relatively smaller class sizes (N = 15; of these only 3 were girls); however, their similarities ended there.

The resource gap between these two groups of students was striking. All of the students in the special education math class for students with specific learning disabilities were dark-skinned Latino/a or Black and they were housed in a small, windowless classroom. The room was barren with minimal student work. There was only one computer available for the entire class. Throughout the semester, monotonous worksheets represented the main learning activity. So that she could better keep an eye on "her little boneheads" and "*mojados*" (wetbacks), Ms. Anaya, a veteran Latina teacher, placed her desk at the back of the classroom where she spent most of the class time watching her students. This created the effect of constant surveillance while students toiled on their worksheets or checkbooks. Going to the bathroom or getting a drink of water involved much social control, and the bulk of the class time was spent interrogating and reprimanding students for socializing. Young men who goofed off, engaged in banter, or left to get a drink of water or use the bathroom without permission were regularly verbally sanctioned and/or sent to in-school suspension.

During the entire semester the only math learning activity that took place was balancing a checkbook. Ms. Anaya justified her minimal teaching activities in terms of the dysfunctional families her students came from: "I don't assign homework because when they get home, they don't have anyone to help them with it." To relieve the boredom, boys would take turns listening to music via headphones at the sole computer located in the corner of the classroom. Others would pass the time by getting up to sharpen their pencils and making small talk with Ms. Anaya and their classmates.

Ms. Anaya regularly referred to the young men (not the girls) as "gang-affiliated." Short crew cuts and diamond earrings donned by most of the boys in the classroom were read as threatening to the classroom social order. As embodied "racially" stigmatized masculinities, these young men's displays of masculinity were read as anti-academic, oppositional, and potentially violent by school staff and teachers (Bettie, 2003; Morris, 2005). These observations echo previous work on "racially" stigmatized masculinities and schooling (Ferguson, 2005; Gilbert & Gilbert, 1998; López, 2003; Morris, 2005; Noguera & Wing, 2006). In both urban and rural school contexts, race, gender, and class intersect to produce what I call the surveillance and "hyper-disciplining" of brown-skinned masculinities (i.e., Black, Latino, and Native American male bodies).

Ms. Anaya was a caring teacher who generally had cordial relationships with her students as demonstrated by her numerous attempts to befriend students, make small talk, and inquire about their personal lives. Ms. Anaya celebrated all of her students' birthdays in an end-of-year birthday ice cream party. Indeed Ms. Anaya had connected with some of her students, as evidenced by visits from students during lunchtime. However, the fact that she did not expect much from them in the way of work and that she would affectionately refer to her male students as "boneheads" or "*mojados*" only served to reinforce race-gender stigma among her students.

In contrast, students in the gifted class, all of whom were racialized as White, had a very spacious and inviting classroom with numerous windows, origami hanging from the ceiling, a kitchen with sink, and plenty of snacks. There was a couch located at one end of the classroom. Students were free to move around the classroom, and warm up a cup of hot chocolate or a cup of macaroni and cheese if they so desired. This room functioned more as a country club than a high school classroom.

Ms. Smith's teaching techniques exemplified engaged pedagogy, replete with research projects, films, unlimited Internet access, oral presentations, and guest speakers, as well as trips to local museums and performances. I never once saw a worksheet and Ms. Smith seldom lectured. Instead, all students had access to any of the 20 computers in the classroom and worked on projects they selected. Students who brought in extra supplies for the class earned extra credits.

The majority of the young men donned dirty blond locks and bohemian attire, reflecting the masculinity that the class president Brad embodied. Like the young men in Ms. Anaya's class, the young men in Ms. Smith's class also engaged in horseplay and goofing off. These young men were quite tall and potentially intimidating to Ms. Smith, a petite White teacher in her twenties; however, they were not read as defiant or threatening because they represented the embodiment of "racially" privileged masculinity (Fine, 2004; Fine & Weis, 1998). Ms. Smith would tell the young men to settle down; however, not once did she threaten them with in-school suspension. Tom, a male student who had a specific learning disability and regularly got up and made jokes during class, was referred to as "twice exceptional" instead of disciplined. According to Ms. Smith, "These students are smarter than me."

These observations point to the importance of exploring disparities in the ways that hegemonic and "racially" stigmatized masculinities are co-produced in the school context. They also point to the disconnect between the official school discourse of respect for diversity, multiculturalism, and equal opportunity for all students as professed in the student handbook and public meetings and the de facto intra-school resource gap and "racial" hierarchies that go unquestioned under the hegemonic ideologies of colorblindness and meritocracy. However, hegemony is never complete. There were some teachers who did question this glaring disconnect.

Ms. Perez, a former SHS graduate who was working as a substitute teacher at SHS, explained that she only now realized the existence of the resource gap: "I was in the Honors classes when I was a student here and I never realized how different the classrooms were." The fact that one attends a school for so many years and never sees the intra-resource gap speaks to the way in which hegemonic ideologies of meritocracy, multiculturalism, colorblindness, and "racial" inequalities co-exist under one roof.

On April 10, 2006, over a hundred SHS students walked out of class chanting the empowering words of the late Civil Rights leader César Chavez: "*Sí, se Puede! Sí, se Puede!* (Yes we can! Yes we can!)" This student action was part of the national marches and coordinated student walkouts that took place across the county during the National Day of Action. However, the SHS school paper, which is staffed primarily by White students, failed to include a single reference to the youth action. Instead, the principal threatened to suspend students who walked out. Latino men, in particular, reported being threatened with suspension if they walked out. After the intervention of some of the teachers who advocated for the rights of students to engage in peaceful protest, the principal reached a compromise. Students who had written permission from their parents would not be punished.

Ms. Rivera, the bilingual/dual language math teacher, provided counter hegemonic discourse when she articulated her unapologetic solidarity with the National Day of Action:

> Yesterday was a very important day for Hispanics. We are over 40 million and we are a large part of the United States economy. We want a migration accord for those who are living on the border. We had a great impact yesterday even if they don't want to admit it. That is how Martin Luther King won Civil Rights for us. Boycotts. We are no longer afraid. We are not invaders. We want to be a part of this country. Our soldiers have died in war.
>
> (López, 2008, p. 4)

Ms. Rivera's counter hegemonic and unabashedly antiracist discourse provided the building block for the potential empowerment of Latino students, their families, and their communities.

Ms. Connors, a young White teacher who also engaged in antiracist pedagogy, incorporated art, poetry, and video that challenged controlling images of Latino youth as "problems," all working toward the empowerment of "racially" stigmatized Latino males (López, 2008). Indeed many of the young men who were withdrawn and unengaged or seen as problems in Ms. Anaya's class were some of the most engaged students in Ms. Connor's class. Part of the reason Ms. Connors was so successful with Latino young men was that she allowed them to engage in critical thinking and drew upon their interest in popular culture and music to connect to the literature and English assignments she discussed in class. Ms. Connors had students work on group projects, always taught her class in a semicircle, had students engage with each other, and provided multiple avenues for students to access the content of the work she had assigned them, including using artwork, debates, poetry, and performance. Far from being intimidated by Latino young men, Ms. Connors welcomed and accepted their masculinities and articulated her solidarity with immigrant rights as part and parcel of her English lessons and the books she assigned.

Implications for Theory and Practice

What would schooling, pedagogy, and school policies look like if educators anchored their work with Latino males in an understanding of "racially" stigmatized masculinities as a site of oppression and empowerment? What else can be done? Below I discuss a few crucial policy implications for eliminating the race–gender achievement gap for Latino males.

Anti-racist Pedagogy and Curriculum

Perhaps the most important and immediate policy implication is the need for teachers, principals, and school administrators to receive on-going training and workshops on antiracism. This training could take place on staff development days, as well as in weekly departmental meetings. Conversations on social justice and antiracism should include explicit values and learning outcomes for students, staff, teachers, administrators, and community on an on-going basis. Multicultural celebrations in the absence of a discussion of power and inequality may reproduce the status quo.

The resilience of "racially" stigmatized youth can be nurtured by equipping students with critical consciousness and empowerment as learning outcomes. Lessons should be given not only about oppression, but also on how social movements contribute to the empowerment of oppressed groups. Oppressed groups, particularly "racially" stigmatized youth, need to be able to name and change unjust situations. All classes—whether science, math, social studies, or Spanish—are well suited to include explicit lessons on the social construction of social inequalities and ways in which to dismantle these inequalities. Meaningful engagement and participation of "racially" stigmatized youth should be a pillar of antiracist pedagogy (Freire, 1993; Gillborn, 1995; Kailin, 2002; Leonardo, 2005; Valenzuela, 1999; Wiedeman, 2002; Yosso, 2005). This can be accomplished by creating smaller schools and classrooms and restructuring the school day from five to eight classes to three to four. In this way K–12 teachers can be valued as professionals who are given the opportunity to engage in peer-to-peer mentoring and the creation of professional learning communities that aim to open dialogue to taboo subjects like racial inequality. Smaller community schools with fewer than sixteen students per class can also help students get to know their fellow students better so that they can work toward community-based research projects that are driven by student interests.

Meaningful Accountability and Paradigm Shift in Conceptualizing "Race" as a Process

To achieve meaningful accountability, we need to track equity measures, such as graduation rates by race, class, and gender, and create a universal identification that can be used to track individual and cohort student outcomes (e.g., graduation, standardized assessments) for all students. This universal identification would never be tied to a student's immigration status or citizenship, but it would allow us to track enrollment in K-20 and beyond in U.S. schools. No Child Left Behind Measures should incorporate a developmental model that traces progress for individual students over time.

We also need a paradigm shift in the way that researchers in the academy and in school districts conceptualize race. In most reports or scholarly articles, race is seen as an individual-level characteristic. Instead, we need to problematize race as a process, a sociohistorically variable process. This would require that we use mixed methods, including statistics and qualitative data such as participant observations, in-depth interviews, focus groups, photographs, videos, and ethnography. Part of this paradigm shift can occur when researchers employ concepts such as racialization process. This type of data may allow policy makers and community members to understand that race, class, and gender are not static essences, but rather contextually produced social constructions.

Youth-Led and Community-Based Action Research

Public social science that engages community members, advocates, and non-academic audiences as meaningful co-researchers is one key way in which we can begin to contribute to the empowerment of Latino communities. Institutional review boards (IRB) consistently approve studies about youth from oppressed communities without involving the youth and members from those communities in the research process from start to finish. Indeed The University of New Mexico IRB, as well as the review boards at some of the public schools that my colleagues and I have tried to collaborate with, have objected to youth being included in the study as co-researchers because of concerns over privacy and confidentiality of study participants. (Even when we explicitly said that we will train youth in standard IRB regulations, and of course secure parental consent, IRB objected to including youth in our discipline study group.)

When sociologists and other social scientists work alongside community members, teachers, and students, we can promote higher quality research as well as school- and community-based mini-social movements that could lead to the empowerment of Latino males and the dismantling of race, gender, class, and other intersecting oppressions. I envision that some day research about youth and under-represented communities without the inclusion of a critical mass of community members would be seen as ethically immoral. Instead, youth and community-based action research will become the norm. Perhaps the next time a young Latino boy like Randy approaches me or another social scientist about whether she/he is the school psychologist, we will be able to invite Randy to be part of our research team and he will receive high school credit for his participation. The potential for unleashing the creativity and genius of our Latino young men as well as other oppressed groups would be harnessed by hands-on involvement in doing research and action on the recalcitrant social problems that have become a normal state of affairs in many oppressed communities. My vision is that through youth-led participatory action research, Latino males will be able to produce posters, artwork, films, dance, rap, and hip-hop performances as well as science, architectural projects, and documentaries that affirm their masculinities and contribute to their personal empowerment as well as that of the community (Cammarota & Fine, 2008).

Notes

1 Please note that the names of participants, schools, districts, and cities have been changed.
2 Frameworks that minimize the intersection of racialization process and class miss how power, social networks, and social esteem are all racialized in society (see, for example, Portes and Zhou (1993), segmented assimilation theory).
3 In 2010 Governor Richardson changed his discourse by strongly opposing the anti-immigrant legislation SB 1070 in Arizona.
4 NCLB tallies the achievement scores for students designated as English language learners, but not students in dual-language program.
5 One of the criticisms of the NCLB legislation is that it only captures snapshot data versus a growth model, which would examine gains across time.

References

American Anthropological Association (1997). AAA response to OMB Directive 15: Race and ethnic standards for federal statistics and administrative reporting. Retrieved from www.aaanet.org/gvt/ombdraft.htm
American Anthropological Association (1998). AAA statement on "race." Retrieved from www.aaanet.org/stmts/racepp.htm
American Association of Physical Anthropologists (1996). AAPA statement on biological aspects of race. *American Journal of Physical Anthropology*, 101, 569–570.
American Sociological Association (2002). Statement of the American Sociological Association on the importance of collecting data and doing social scientific research on race. Retrieved from www.asanet.org/page.ww?section=Issue+Statements&name=Collecting+Data+on+Race
Bettie, J. (2003). *Women without class: Girls, race and identity*. Berkeley, CA: University of California Press.
Bonilla-Silva, E. (2001). *White supremacy in the post-Civil Rights era*. Boulder, CO: Lynne Reinner.
Bonilla-Silva, E. (2003). *Racism without racists: Colorblind racism and the persistence of racial inequality in the United States*. New York: Rowman and Littlefield.
Bonilla-Silva, E. (2004). From bi-racial to tri-racial. *Ethnic and Racial Studies*, 27(6), 931–950.
Cammarota, J., & Fine, M. (2008). *Youth participatory action research*. New York: Routledge.
Carter, P. (2005). *Keepin' it real: School success beyond black and white*. Oxford: Oxford University Press.
Collins, P. H. (2000). *Black feminist thought: Knowledge, consciousness, and the politics of empowerment,* 2nd edition. New York: Routledge.

Crenshaw, K. (1991). Mapping the margins: Intersectionality, identity politics, and violence against women of Color. *Stanford Law Review*, 43(6), 1241–1299.

Dei, G., & Sefa, J. (2005). Critical issues in anti-racist research methodologies. In G. J. Sefa Dei and G. Singh Hohal (Eds.), *Anti-racist research methodologies* (1–27). New York: Peter Lang.

Delgado, R. (Ed.). (1995). *Critical race theory: The cutting edge*. Philadelphia: Temple University Press.

Du Bois, W. E. B. (1903). *Souls of the black folk*. New York: W. W. Norton.

Ferguson, A. (2001). *Bad boys: Public schools in the making of black masculinity*. Ann Arbor: University of Michigan Press.

Ferguson, R. (2005, October 28). Who gets accused of acting white, and why? Some new evidence. Keynote address presented at the Second Annual Youth and Race Conference: Acting White, Revisiting Ogbu and Fordhams's Hypothesis. Sonja Haynes Stone Center for Black Culture and History, University of North Carolina-Chapel Hill.

Fine, M. (2004). Witnessing whiteness/gathering intelligence. In M. Fine, L. Weis, M. L. P. Pruitt, and A. Burn (Eds.), *Off-white: Readings on power, privilege, and resistance* (245–256). New York: Routledge.

Fine, M., & Weis, L. (1998). *The unknown city: Lives of poor and working class young adults*. Boston: Beacon Press.

Freire, P. (1993). *Pedagogy of the oppressed*. New York: Continuum.

Gilbert, R., & Gilbert, P. (1998). *Masculinity goes to school*. London and New York: Routledge.

Gillborn, D. (1995). *Racism and antiracism in real schools*. Bristol, PA: Open University Press.

Goffman, E. (1963). *Stigma: Notes on management of spoiled identity*. New York: Simon & Schuster.

Gómez, L. (2007). *Manifest destinies: The making of the Mexican-American race*. New York: New York University Press.

Hinojosa, M. (Host). (2006, June 23). Interview with New Mexico Governor Richardson. Latino USA: The radio journal of news and culture. Washington, D.C.: National Public Radio.

Human Genome Project. (2010). Human Genome Project information. Retrieved from www.ornl.gov/sci/techresources/Human_Genome/elsi/humanmigration.shtml#7

Hunter, M. (2005). *Race, gender, and the politics of skin tone*. New York: Routledge.

Kailin, J. (2002). *Antiracist education: From theory to practice*. Oxford: Rowman & Littlefield.

Kimmel, M., & Messner, M. (1992). *Men's lives*, 2nd edition. New York: Macmillan.

Ladson-Billings, G. (2006). From the achievement gap to the education debt: Understanding achievement in U.S. schools. *Educational Researcher*, 35(7), 3–12.

Ladson-Billings, G., & Tate, W. (1995). Toward a critical race theory of education. *Teachers College Record*, 97, 47–68.

Leonardo, Z. (2005). *Critical pedagogy and race*. Boston: Blackwell Publishing.

Lewis, A. E. (2003). *Race in the schoolyard: Negotiating the color line in classrooms and communities*. New Brunswick, NJ: Rutgers University Press.

Link, B., & Phelan, J. (2001). Conceptualizing stigma. *Annual Review of Sociology*, 27, 365–385.

López, N. (2003). *Hopeful girls, troubled boys: Race and gender disparity in urban education*. New York: Routledge (2nd edition forthcoming).

López, N. (2008). Antiracist pedagogy and empowerment in a bilingual classroom in the U.S., circa 2006. *Theory Into Practice*, 47(1), 43–50.

Morris, E. (2005). "Tuck in that shirt?" Race, class, gender in an urban school. *Sociological Perspectives*, 48(1), 25–48.

Murguia, E., and Telles, E. (1996). Phenotype and schooling among Mexican Americans. *Sociology of Education*, 69(4), 276–289.

Noguera, P. (2008). *The trouble with black boys: And other reflections on race, equity, and the future of public education*. San Francisco: Jossey-Bass.

Noguera, P., & Yonemura Wing, J. (Eds.) (2006). *Unfinished business: Closing the racial achievement gap in our schools*. San Francisco: Jossey-Bass.

Omi, M., & Winant, H. (1994). *Racial formation in the United States: From 1960s to 1990s*, 2nd edition (1st edition, 1986). New York: Routledge.

Pizarro, M. (1999). Racial formation and Chicano identity: Lessons from the Rasquache. In P. Wong (Ed.), *Race, ethnicity and nation*. New York: Westview Press.

Pizarro, M. (2005). *Chicanas and Chicanos in school: Racial profiling, identity battles and empowerment*. Austin: University of Texas Press.

Portes, A., & Zhou, M. (1993). The new second generation: Segmented assimilation and its variants. *The Annals of the American Academy of Political and Social Science*, 530, 74–96.

Roberts, Dorothy. (1997). *Killing the black body: Race, reproduction, and the meaning of liberty*. New York: Pantheon.

Staiger, A. (2005). Whiteness as giftedness: Racial formation at an urban school. *Social Problems*, 51(2), 161–181.

Valenzuela, A. (1999). *Subtractive schooling: U.S.-Mexican youth and the politics of caring*. Albany: State University of New York Press.

Vidal-Ortiz, S. (2004). On being a White person of Color: Using autoethnography to understand Puerto Ricans racialization. *Qualitative Sociology*, 27(2), 179–203.

Wagley, C. (1968). The concept of social race in the Americas. In *The Latin American Tradition* (155–178). New York: Columbia University Press.

West, C., & Zimmerman, D. (1987). Doing gender. *Gender & Society*, 1(2), 125–151.

Wiedeman, C. R. (2002). Teacher preparation, social justice, and equity: A review of the literature. *Equity and Excellence*, 35(3), 200–211.

Yasso, T. (2005). Whose culture has capital? A critical race theory discussion of community cultural wealth. *Race, Ethnicity and Education*, 8(1), 69–91.

15

"SOMETIMES YOU NEED TO SPILL YOUR HEART OUT TO SOMEBODY"

Close Friendships Among Latino Adolescent Boys[1]

Niobe Way
Carlos Santos
Alexandra Cordero

Introduction

It is the middle of June and the New York City heat is on full blast, making it even hotter in the empty high school classroom where 15-year-old Justin and his interviewer José sit in the late afternoon. Justin, whose mother is Puerto Rican and father is Irish and Italian American, is being interviewed for our school-based research project on boys' social and emotional development. There is neither an air conditioner nor a fan in the classroom so Justin, dressed in baggy jeans and t-shirt, pulls out a notebook from his backpack and fans himself as José begins the interview protocol. This meeting is the second of four annual interviews. The first set of protocol questions is about Justin's friends in general, and he responds by discussing his network of peers in school. Turning to the topic of close friendships, he says:

> [My best friend and I] love each other . . . that's it . . . you have this thing that is deep, so deep, it's within you, you can't explain it. It's just a thing that you know that that person is that person . . . and that is all that should be important in our friendship . . . I guess in life, sometimes two people can really, really understand each other and really have a trust, respect, and love for each other. It just happens, it's human nature.

Listening to boys, particularly during early and middle adolescence, speak about their male friendships is like reading an old-fashioned romance novel in which the female protagonist describes her passionate feelings for her man. At the edge of manhood when pressures to conform to gender expectations intensify (Hill & Lynch, 1983), boys tell us, in great detail and with tremendous affect, about their best friends with whom they share their deepest secrets and without whom they would "feel lost."

While this theme of emotional intimacy in friendships has been echoed by most of the hundreds of boys in our studies over the past two decades, it has been particularly evident among the Latinos. Set against an American culture that perceives males in general to be emotionally stoic, autonomous, and physically tough, and Latino males, in particular, to be "macho" or "hypermasculine" (Gutmann, 1996), these stories of wanting and having emotionally intimate (i.e., self-disclosing) male friendships are surprising. Our studies suggest that boys, particularly Latino boys, value their male friendships greatly and see them as critical to their mental health not because their friends are worthy opponents in the competition for manhood but because they are able to share their thoughts and feelings—their deepest secrets—with these friends.

Yet when one looks at the research literature on adolescent boys or on Latino youth more specifically, discussions of close friendships are almost entirely absent. Although these friendships have long been considered crucial for social, emotional, academic, and behavioral adjustment (Erdley et al., 2001; Nangle & Erdley, 2001; Sullivan, 1953; Vitaro et al., 2009), they are remarkably under-explored among boys. This pattern is particularly evident in the research on ethnic minority youth. which is focused on high-risk behavior and, more recently, academic achievement, identity development, and family relationships (Decker & Van Winkle, 1996; Padilla, 1992). The lack of attention to friendships among ethnic minority youth implicitly suggests that such relationships are not important to these youths. Yet the small but existing research on this topic underscores the critical role of friendships for the emotional and social well-being of Latino, Black, Asian American, and White youth (Azmitia et al., 2006; Falicov, 1998; Santos, 2010; Way, 2011). Falicov (1998), a family therapist for Latino families, writes: "Relationships with same-sex peers, whether relatives or friends, are so important for Latinos that it's not unusual for them to be implicated in the presenting problem of an individual or family" (p. 167). Friendships are not only important for White middle-class children and adolescents, they are also important for children and adolescents from ethnically diverse contexts and cultures. In this chapter, we present findings from our Latino subsample of boys' social and emotional development from early to late adolescence and reveal the importance of emotionally intimate friendships for these boys.

Theory and Research on Friendships

Harry Stack Sullivan (1953) argued that during preadolescence (9–12 years of age) a need for intimacy arises that he defined as "that type of situation involving two people which permits validation of all components of personal worth" (p. 246). In response to this intimacy need, preadolescent boys develop extremely close relationships with a male peer. This relationship "represents the beginning of very much like full-blown, psychiatrically defined, love" (p. 245). During this period, "a child begins to develop a real sensitivity to what matters to another person" (p. 245), which represents a significant developmental milestone. These "love" relationships are essential, according to Sullivan, for the development of self-worth and the acquisition of the social skills necessary for engagement in future romantic relationships.

Drawing from Sullivan's theories, research has investigated friendship development and has found that the sharing of intimate thoughts and feelings do increase from childhood to adolescence (Azmitia et al., 2006; Berndt, 1981; Bigelow & La Gaipa, 1980; Furman & Bierman, 1984) and that such relationships provide a wide array of social, emotional, academic, and cognitive benefits for children and adolescents (see Rubin et al., 2009 for a review). Intimate and supportive friendships have been found, for example, to be associated with lower levels of depressive symptoms (Oldenburg & Kerns, 1997; Pelkonen et al., 2003; Vernberg, 1990) and higher levels of self-esteem (Bishop & Inderbitzen, 1995; Nangle & Erdley, 2001). A lack of close friendships is also associated with high levels of depressive symptoms, internalizing problems, and peer victimization (Ladd & Troop-Gordon, 2003). In one study, researchers found that a lack of close friends at age 16 predicted depressive symptoms at age 22 that were over and above previous levels of depressed mood (Pelkonen et al., 2003). Gender differences have been reported in the association between mental health and friendship quality, with the quality of best friendships being more strongly related to loneliness and depression for boys than for girls (Erdley et al., 2001).

A major limitation of the body of research on friendships has been that most studies have focused on American, White, middle-class adolescents or young adults. The exceptions to this pattern, however, reveal few ethnic/racial differences in the quality (e.g., emotional or social support) or importance of friendships (Azmitia & Cooper, 2001; Azmitia et al., 2006; Levitt et al., 1993; Way & Chen, 2000; Way, 2011) or in the link between friendship quality and psychological adjustment (Azmitia et al., 2006; Santos, 2010; Way & Robinson, 2003). Emotionally supportive friendships appear to be beneficial for the mental health of *all* youth regardless of their cultural or ethnic backgrounds. Yet, studies have found ethnic variation in the extent to which friendships are valued over family relationships, with later-generation Latino immigrants being more likely to value their friendships over family relationships than more-recent Latino immigrants (Azmitia & Cooper, 2001).

Another limitation in the research on friendships is the almost exclusive reliance on survey methodology to assess the quality of friendships. While examining the frequency of a predetermined set of dimensions of friendship quality is important, it reveals information only about the "quantity" of the friendships.

While it may be true that adolescent boys, for example, are less likely than girls to have intimate friendships, it is not clear how boys experience the quality of their friendships. When qualitative research has been conducted, such research has consistently suggested that boys have emotionally intimate male friendships and that they tend to speak about their friendships in similar terms as girls (Azmitia et al., 1998; Radmacher & Azmitia, 2006; Way, 2011). Furthermore, without knowing the quality of such friendships, the interpretation of the quantity is often misleading.

A third limitation in the study of friendships is the acontextual nature of it. Even with the heavy ecological emphasis in most psychological research, studies of the influence of micro and macro environments on friendships are almost entirely absent. Developmental research has suggested for decades that adolescent development is shaped by parents, peers, schools, neighborhoods, and larger political, social, and economic forces (Bowlby, 1969/1982; Bronfenbrenner, 1979; Eccles & Roeser, 1999; Spencer, 2006; Vitaro et al., 2009). Adolescent friendships are also influenced by such relationships and contexts (Bowlby, 1969/1982; Bronfenbrenner, 1979; Chen et al., 2006; Way, 2011). Boys, for example, are shaped by the beliefs and practices of their parents and peers and by an American culture that tells boys that emotionally intimate friendships are for girls or for gay youth (Kimmel, 2008; Way, 2011). Examining friendships in the micro contexts of families, peers, and schools as well as in the larger macro contexts of American gender expectations and stereotypes is essential if we are to advance our understanding of the development of friendships.

In response to these gaps, we have been exploring the experience of friendships among ethnic minority and majority youth for nearly two decades. We have also explored how these experiences vary by ethnicity and race and change from early to late adolescence. We have also examined the impact of families, schools, and the conventions of masculinity on boys' experiences of friendships.[2] This chapter focuses on our findings with respect to the Latino boys in our studies.

Methods

Participants

This paper presents findings from forty-eight Latino adolescent boys (avg. age at time one, 14.1; twenty-eight Puerto Rican, fifteen Dominican, and five boys from other Latin American countries) who participated in one of our longitudinal studies of social and emotional development. The Puerto Rican students were almost exclusively born in the United States; while six of the Dominican students were born in the Dominican Republic. The remaining five Latino students were born outside of the United States. Participants were purposively drawn from larger studies conducted in various public urban high schools in New York City and

Boston (Way, 2011). All of the Latino boys in our studies who participated in at least two years of data collection were included in the analysis. The schools in which we conducted our research catered to students from low-income families from the neighborhood with typically 60 percent or more of the students being eligible for the free or reduced lunch program.

Procedure

Students were recruited during their freshman or sophomore year from three high schools located in either New York City or Boston and were followed for a period of four to five years. We recruited these students from mainstream English classes to ensure that the study participants were fluent in English as the interviews were conducted in English and analyzed by a mix of Spanish and non-Spanish speakers. The interviews, which took place each year and lasted approximately 90 minutes, were held during the school day in an office in which confidentiality could be assured. The interviews were conducted by an ethnically diverse group of graduate students in psychology who had extensive training in interviewing techniques. All interviews were audiotaped and transcribed for analysis. The semi-structured interviews asked the participants to discuss a range of topics (e.g., family, school, peers), including their friendships. The interview protocol included questions such as: "How would you describe your relationship with your best friend?" and "What kinds of things do you talk about with your best friend? Give an example?" Although each interview included a standard set of questions, follow-up questions varied across interviews to capture the adolescents' own way of describing their friendships.

Data analysis

We used a process of open coding (Strauss & Corbin, 1990) to generate themes from the interview data. The research team first read through the transcripts and created narrative summaries that condensed the interview material while retaining the essence of the stories told by the adolescents (Miller, 1991). Following this step, team members read each narrative summary independently, looking for themes in the summaries. In any one year of the study, a theme retained for further analysis had to be identified as a theme independently by at least two team members. Once themes were generated and agreed on, each team member returned to the original interviews and noted the year and point in the interview where these themes emerged. They also noted if and how the themes changed during other years of the study (Way, 2011).

Friendships During Adolescence

In our longitudinal studies, two sets of themes have consistently emerged (Way, 2011). The first is that the boys have emotionally intimate male friendships, especially during early and middle adolescence. Furthermore, these friendships were perceived by the boys themselves as critical for their mental health. In addition, these patterns of intimacy were evident particularly among the Latino boys. While approximately 75 percent of the boys in our studies had such friendships, 90 percent of the Latino boys revealed such themes. In stark contrast to stereotypes held about boys, particularly those from ethnic minority families, Latino boys discussed "sharing secrets" in their friendships and believed that these secrets formed the foundation of their close male friendships. They also said that they couldn't "live without" these close relationships and if they did not have anyone to talk to about their "deepest secrets," they would go "wacko."

The second set of themes was that the boys, including the Latinos, found it increasingly difficult to maintain these emotionally intimate friendships as they reached late adolescence. This pattern was evident despite the fact that they continued to desire such friendships and reported feelings of depression over this loss. The boys were also less willing to express themselves emotionally as they grew older and were increasingly distrustful of others. They explicitly made the connection between their loss of friendships and their growing sense of distrust and feelings of loneliness and sadness. At 15 and 16 years old, when the nationwide suicide rate for boys rises to four times that of girls (Sax, 2007; Tyre, 2008), boys speak about losing their male friendships, becoming more distrustful of others, and feeling alone.

Shared Secrets

At the edge of adolescence, Latino boys—the same boys the media claim are obsessed with girls, gangs, and pumped-up cars—speak about "circles of love," "spilling your heart out to somebody," "sharing deep secrets," and "feeling lost" without their male best friends. Benny, a 15-year-old Puerto Rican boy said, "I trust my friends. Like if I have a deep secret I don't want to tell anybody, I tell one of my friends that I know won't tell anybody else unless I give them permission to tell somebody else." When asked what he *likes* about his friend, Marcus, a Puerto Rican freshman, replied, "We share secrets that we don't talk about in the open." When asked to explain why he felt close to his male friends, he stated, "If I'm having problems at home, they'll like counsel me. I just trust them with anything, like deep secrets, anything." Eddie, a Puerto Rican sophomore said, "It's like a bond. We keep secrets, like if there is something that's important to me like I could tell him and he won't go and make fun of it. Like if my family is having problems or something." He said that he knows he can trust his best friend because "when we were like younger it's like a lot of things that I told him that he didn't tell anybody. Like it's like a lot of things he told me that I didn't tell anybody."

Boys, furthermore, indicated that the intimacy or sharing of secrets in their friendships is what they *liked most* about their friendships. Ken, a Dominican

American sophomore, said, "We always tell each other everything. And um like, if something happens and I save it for [my best friend]." In his junior year, he said:

> [What I like most about my best friendship] is the connection. It's like, you know how you know somebody for so long you could talk about anything and you won't even think, I mean you won't even think about how 'oh what are they thinking?' You just talk.

The content of the boys' secrets varied considerably and the term "secrets" was often used interchangeably with "problems." "Problems" were always "secrets" but secrets weren't necessarily problems. Andy, a Puerto Rican student, made distinctions between secrets when talking about the friends whom he did not trust in his sophomore year:

> I mean I can like joke around with them and like if I'm like having trouble in my classes, like if somebody knows the subject better than me, like I'll ask them. Like yeah, it's pretty much like that, not too deep though. . . . I wouldn't tell them like my too secretest things, not too secretive. Yeah. Like maybe I would tell them about a girl or something. I mean that's the deepest, nothing deeper than that though.

The content of "regular" or "not too deep" secrets included crushes on girls or other girl-related topics. "Really, really big secrets" or "secretest things" were almost always about conflicts in the home or, on rare occasions, coping with disabilities or drug abuse of a family member. Paul, a Dominican American student, said that he shares secrets with his best friend "all the time" and admits that it is good to have a best friend because "sometimes, like you don't want to tell your family members because it's probably about them and you just tell your friend and they'll keep a secret and help you." Family-related problems or secrets were often considered the deepest secrets of all.

Such open discussions of thoughts and feelings, however, were not simply what boys did. They believed sharing secrets was necessary for their emotional health. Justin, a 15-year-old half Puerto Rican–half European American boy, said, "My ideal best friend is a close, close friend who I could say anything to. . . . 'Cause sometimes you need to spill your heart out to somebody and if there's nobody there, then you gonna keep it inside, then you will have anger. So you need somebody to talk to always." Boys consistently believed throughout adolescence that there were dire consequences to keeping their emotions "bottled up inside" and thus they sought a close friend or friends with whom they could "share everything."

Expressing Vulnerability

As Felix, a Puerto Rican student, reflected on his best friendship with Devin during his sophomore year, he said, "My best friend thinks physical pain is worse than emotional pain and I don't think that's true, 'cause physical pain could last but for so long, but when it's in the mind, it doesn't go away." Acutely attuned to the nuances of the emotional world, Felix is typical of the Latino boys during their freshman and sophomore years. Nick, a Puerto Rican boy, says:

> I don't give—I don't give my heart out to too many people, you know, especially when it could get broken or hurt easily. I've been through too many times of that. So it's like I don't have any room—I have to recuperate from my heart broken. There's been death in my family, girlfriends, you know, guy friends. I don't have any more for my heart to get stepped on. So I've picked myself up for awhile. I'm walking. But you know, you never know when you fall down again. So I'm trying to just keep my eye out.

Nick vividly expressed the wariness that comes after experiencing a broken heart. And in this conversation, he reveals that his heart is not simply broken over a girl or a family member but also by a "guy friend." Feelings for family members, girl friends, and guy friends blended together in a seamless discussion of having his "heart stepped on."

When considering whether he would like to be closer to his male friends, Justin said in his freshman year:

> I think so. But I don't really know if they're gonna stay here for four years. So I feel like I can't get too attached 'cause then if they leave, I still get attached to them even though 'cause a friend, he, he could come and go even though I really don't want it to happen. But it could come and go. I could make new friends or whatever. So it doesn't matter if I get attached to them or not. I don't know . . . I don't want to [become attached] because if they leave I really don't, I never really got emotional for a guy before but I don't know if I would or if I wouldn't.

Justin's struggle was palpable as he expressed both his desire for closeness and his fear that if he allows himself to feel "attached" he will get hurt. He attempted to assert the masculine convention ("doesn't matter if I get attached to them or not") but then recognized that it was not truly what he felt. By the end of the passage, he posed a question to which he already knew the answer.

The boys' vulnerability in their stories was often evident when they were asked what they liked and did not like about their friendships. Describing what he liked about his best friend, Devin, a Dominican American sophomore, said:

> I think our relationship is wonderful. Because we like, I can't explain. The feelings that I have for him if something would happen to him, I probably won't feel right. . . . Like when he was sick and I hadn't seen him for like a week and I went to his um house and I, and I asked his grandmother what was wrong with him and he was in the room like he couldn't move. So I went in there. I sat in his house for the whole day talking to him. And like the next day he got up and he felt better.

Devin's response reveals that he was acutely attuned to his own vulnerability ("I probably won't feel right") and to his friend's. He also knows, like so many of his male peers, that talking ("I sat in his house for the whole day talking to him") is good for his health ("and like the next day he got up and he felt better").

Being direct and open about his feeling of vulnerability, Paul, a Puerto Rican student in his junior year, said:

> Yeah 'cause [my best friend] is like a second person you could speak to. . . . It's like see how the kids carry a little teddy bear or whatever and when they cry, they'll hold it and stuff. So when like you get upset or something, you just walk over to them and they'll loosen, they'll loosen up whatever. They'll be like yeah it's alright, even though it's not.

Paul recognized both the safety that a friend (or teddy bear) provides but also the expectation to smooth over and make assurances that boys know are not true ("They'll be like yeah, it's alright, even though it's not"). In the context of gender stereotypes, Paul's sensitivity and emotional sophistication are surprising. In the context of our studies, it is not.

While some boys were consistently willing to express vulnerability, others peppered their responses with masculine norms, only to reveal their more vulnerable sides at other points in their interviews. When an interviewer asked one of the boys, Milo, how it felt when he was teased by his best friend, he said, "I know he's playing so it doesn't really, it doesn't feel bad, but if I didn't know he was playing, he probably would be able to hurt somebody. He would get somebody mad enough to do something, you know." Milo's switch from the first person (i.e., "I") to the second person (i.e. "somebody") at the moment in his response when his vulnerability was made explicit underscores the danger or sense of risk boys feel when expressing vulnerability. Yet the Latino boys in our studies often expressed such vulnerability anyway.

Expressions of vulnerability, care, and empathy were evident not only when boys discussed the details of their friendships but also when they spoke more abstractly about the importance of friendships. During his freshman year, Carlos, a Dominican American student, said this about his best friend: "Like we could express our feelings or whatever. And tell each other how we feel. Like if I feel bad one day, I tell him why." He described his best friend as a brother and used language such as "we show each other love" to describe the depth of this friendship. "I know the kid inside of him, inside of him. 'Cause I . . . I grew up with that kid." While the Latino boys in our studies occasionally couched their discussions of friendships in more masculine language, they were more willing than the non-Latino boys to reveal another story—a story of vulnerability, love, emotional connection, and desire for emotionally intimate friendships with other boys.

Becoming Distrustful and Alone

A simple question asked by an interviewer provokes a simple response that reveals everything about how friendships change as boys reach late adolescence. The question: "How have your friendships changed since you were a freshman in high school?" The responses given by two Latino boys in late adolescence were:

> I don't know, maybe, not a lot, but I guess that best friends become close friends. So that's basically the only thing that changed. It's like best friends become close friends, close friends become general friends and then general friends become acquaintances. So they just . . . If there's distance whether it's, I don't know, natural or whatever. You can say that but it just happens that way.

> Like my friendship with my best friend is fading. . . . So I mean, it's still there 'cause we still do stuff together, but only once in a while. It's sad 'cause he lives only one block away from me and I get to do stuff with him less than I get to do stuff with people who are way further so I'm like, yo. . . . It's like a DJ used his cross fader and started fading it slowly and slowly, and now I'm like halfway through the cross fade.

At the age of 16 or 17, as their bodies are almost fully grown and their minds are increasingly attuned to cultural messages about manhood, boys, including Latino boys, begin to distance themselves from their intimate relationships with other boys and lose connection with their emotionally sensitive selves. "Best friends become close friends, close friends . . . general friends" as one of the boys said expressing what the conventions of masculinity expects of him.

Homophobia was one of the key reasons boys gave, both directly and indirectly, for becoming more emotionally reserved and finding it difficult to maintain their emotionally intimate male friendships. In an American culture in which vulnerable emotions are frequently characterized as "gay" or "girlish" and "intimacy" is most often associated with sexual relations, this finding is not surprising. By late adolescence, boys turned our questions about close male friendships into questions about their sexual orientation. A common response when we asked about their close male friendships during late adolescence was:

"I'm not gay." Despite their strong desires for intimate male friendships evident throughout adolescence, the boys' need not to be perceived as gay or girlish consumed their interviews in late adolescence and prevented them from maintaining the very friendships they valued dearly. "No homo" became a commonly expressed phrase following intimate statements of how they felt about their current or former close male friends.

When Fernando was asked in his junior year what he likes about his best friend, whom he had already stated is not as close to him as before, he said, "everything, the way that we just relate, *no homo*, just the way we talk to each other." According to Urban Dictionary (n.d.), "no homo" is a "slang phrase used after one inadvertently says something that sounds gay." During late adolescence, Latino boys believed that questions about close friendships, the very relationships they had actively desired, sounded gay.

Addressing the question of good friends during his freshman year interview, Carlos said, "Like we could express our feelings or whatever. And tell each other how we feel. Like if I feel bad one day, I tell them why." He uses language such as "we show each other love" to describe the bond he feels with his close friends. Asked how he knew he could trust his best friend, he said, "'Cause I know the kid inside of him. 'Cause I grew up with that kid, you understand? I know who he really is." By his sophomore year, however, something had shifted. When asked what he likes about his best friend, he said, "It's cool, man. We could do anything. We joke around whatever. 'Cause I don't want to have a serious friend. That's boring, yo. Like I want a friend that I could joke around with. If I mess up he won't, you know, just laugh or I don't know." By mirroring ideals of masculinity that encourage boys to be strong and "make it on their own" ("'cause I don't want a serious friend") but then undercutting it with a more sensitive view ("If I mess up he won't, you know, just laugh"), Carlos revealed a central conflict for boys during late adolescence. Boys want to have an "understanding" friendship but they also want to be perceived as a heterosexual man.

By his junior year, Carlos' fears were directly stated as he repeated "no homo" every time he said something intimate about his best friend. In response to a question about what he does with his close friends, Carlos told the interviewer, "that question sounded homo, that sounded homo." When the interviewer expressed confusion as to how her question sounded "homo," he laughed and said, "we just do whatever, man, we like, we do whatever we can do. If we don't have money, we stay in his house, watch TV." No longer are Carlos and his friends "expressing feelings" as he indicated in his freshman year; they now do "whatever we can do." When asked about his best friend during his senior-year interview, a friend whom he rarely sees now but whom he still considers his best friend, he said, "The relationship, I mean it's a good relationship. It's um it's a tight bond whatever. Um, I can trust him. I don't know how to explain it. Somebody you feel chemistry. No homo." His qualification of "no homo" on the heels of expressing closeness (in traditional romantic terms), as well as his response of "it's a tight bond, *whatever*" suggests a discomfort with his feelings, but a continued willingness to have a close male friendship.

Other boys, however, were not so lucky. Guillermo, a Bolivian American student who was interviewed for the first time in his junior year, said when asked if he has a best friend this year:

> Not really. I think myself. The friend I had, I lost it. . . . That was the only person that I could trust and we talked about everything. When I was down, he used to help me feel better. The same I did to him. So I feel pretty lonely and sometimes depressed. Because I don't have no one to go out with, no one to speak on the phone, no one to tell my secrets, no one for me to solve my problems. . . . I think that it will never be the same, you know. I think that when you have a real friend and you lost him, I don't think you find another one like him. That's the point of view that I have. . . . I tried to look for a person, you know, but it's not that easy.

The yearning specifically for an intimate male friendship is evident in Guillermo's response, as is his sense of loss and feeling of inevitability associated with that loss. The boys' responses suggested a sensitivity that is similar to their response to betrayal. Once they lose a best friend, they find it difficult, if not impossible, to find a replacement. In addition, as evident in Guillermo's response, references to psychological well-being were evident throughout the boys' descriptions of the loss of their closest male friends. Guillermo's open admission of feeling "lonely" and "depressed" underscores the psychological costs these boys experience as a result of this loss.

While Guillermo's interviews explicitly deal with the sadness he feels surrounding the loss of his best friend, other boys described their frustration and anger with their growing inability to trust their male peers. Fitting with the masculine expectation that was articulated directly by Nick, a Puerto Rican boy who said, "I'm not gonna get mad because you dissed me, I'm gonna get mad 'cause I miss you, but I'll probably show it to you like I'm gonna get mad because you dissed me," anger and frustration were often the way the boys expressed their sadness. When Joseph, a Dominican student who had had a best friend for ten years, is asked whether he has a best friend in his junior year, he said, "No I don't trust nobody. . . . Can't trust nobody these days." He says that the reason for this lack of trust is that his former best friend got him in trouble for "breaking the elevator" in the school.

Although the degree of distrust varied, the boys in our studies were angry at "being dissed" by their friends; as a consequence, they often chose to retreat from their male peers entirely. Boys expressed anger at their friends for spreading their secrets, "lying" to them, "stealing" their girlfriends, or talking about them "behind their backs," and these experiences led them not to trust their peers. Milo, who early on referred to the "circles of love" among him and his two best friends, said by his third year of high school that he had been betrayed by his friends too many times to trust them any longer. Stories of being teased by his best friends for his beliefs (e.g., he goes to church) and of his friends "not being there" for him were the basis for Milo feeling angry and betrayed. Instead of finding new friends to replace the old, Milo said he does not have any "real" best friends any longer.

When Albert, a Puerto Rican student in his senior year, was asked why he still does not have a best friend (he has not had a best friend since early adolescence), he said,

> You know, I can't trust—I don't trust 'em too much. I had a friend and he [tried to steal my tapes and my girlfriend] and you know I can't trust nobody else. [I have] a kind of friend, you know but to have another best friend, that would be pretty hard now. Can't trust nobody else no more. . . . Can't trust people no more.

When asked in his junior year if he wanted a best friend, Mateo, a Puerto Rican boy, said:

> I really, it really doesn't matter to me no more. 'Cause when now-a-days like you can't really have a best friend. It's like the person who you think would never do something to you, out of nowhere something happens. And I don't. . . . I ain't gonna be crying because something happens to me, or I feel like so badly through my inside and I ain't tryin' to you know feel like that.

Like most of the boys in our studies, Mateo was trying to find ways "not to . . . feel like that."

Justin, the emotionally expressive boy from whom we have heard throughout this chapter, said during his junior year:

> I don't tell nobody my business so it's not like, it's not a trust thing. It's just something that I don't do. So with money—of course if my friend needs it, I give him. He'll give it back or whatever so it's not really a big thing. So with feelings though, I don't tell nobody. So it's not basically a trust thing, it's my personal reason not to tell nobody nothing.

Latino boys, who have been portrayed as macho gangsters and rap star wannabes, spoke to us about "breaking apart" or suffering when other boys got "inside" of their heads.

Patterns of Desire

When asked whether he has a best friend, Victor, a boy from Ecuador, said in his junior year:

> I wouldn't say . . . I don't say I would 'cause I feel that a friend is going to be there for you and they'll support you and stuff like that. Whether they're good and bad times, you can share with them, you could share your feelings with them, your true feelings. That's why I don't think I have any real close friends. I mean, things can travel around in a school and things would go around, and the story would change from person to person. Yeah. Basically, I hate it, I hate it, 'cause you know I wouldn't mind talking to somebody my age that I can relate to 'em on a different basis.

As with the route toward manhood, the expressed desire for intimate male friendships, heard so often in boys' interviews during late adolescence, took different forms. For some such as Victor, it was direct ("I hate it, I hate it . . . ") and for others, it was more reserved: "Well, no, I don't really wish I had a best friend, but if I had one, I wouldn't mind."

Francisco, a Dominican American student, said in his fourth year interview that he would like a friend who is "sensitive like me. . . . Like understanding like me . . . but um that's about it. . . . Like I see movies, in the theater, I start to cry and stuff . . . No, none of my friends is like that." Boys explicitly desired, even into late adolescence, "sensitive" friends with whom they could "talk about everything" and who were loyal and trusting. They wanted a friend with whom, as Lorenzo put it, "when you need a shoulder to cry on, inside, you need an arm to punch when you are mad and things like that."

The desire for a close male friendship was revealed in the boys' responses to different types of questions. Asked to articulate why his friendships are so important, Jorge, a Puerto Rican student in his junior year, said:

> 'Cause you always need somebody there for you. That's the way I see it. I always need somebody there. Someone that I could count on to talk to whenever I need anything. So I, I think they are really important, friendships. I don't, I mean if you're going to grow up being lonely like always, there's going to be something wrong. Either you're going to be mean to people, lonely, you're going to feel lonely all the time.

Asked what type of friendship he would like to have, Jorge said:

> The best of all? Well, I kind of have it now, but even better. But I would like it to get even tighter. I would like it—you know. I like . . . with the person, I can trust them with anything. But like—deeper, deeper than it is now would be cool.

Boys such as Jorge yearned for the "deeper" friendships that were so common during early and middle adolescence. Like Sullivan (1953) noted about boys from very different socioeconomic and cultural backgrounds, the Latino boys in our studies wanted "chums" with whom to share their secrets and who would "be there" for them in times of need. And they were well aware of the consequences to their mental health of not having such friends.

The Context of Friendships

The obvious questions after listening to the interviews of Latino boys during adolescence are how are these boys able to be so emotionally expressive when they live in such a rigidly gendered context where the "cool pose" (Majors & Billson, 1992) dominates and where ethnic and racial stereotypes about hypermasculinity are rigidly enforced? How is it possible that Latino boys are able to discuss their intense feelings for their male friends in a culture that often equates such talk with being gay, feminine, or immature? And why were these patterns of emotional expression particularly evident among the Latino boys? Our qualitative data suggest that the answers to these questions lie in the home, in the school, and in the ethnic context.

Our qualitative interviews suggested that the boys who were most passionate and expressive about their male best friends were often those who had the closest relationships with their mothers. Close friendships did not compensate for poor parent–child relationships but seemed to be enhanced by intimate relationships with mothers. In his junior year, Ricky, a Puerto Rican young man, said, "My best friend? I would like to say that I only have one friend—one best friend and that is my mother." His mother is the person with whom he shared his thoughts and feelings even though he also had numerous friendships with boys from his school. He trusted his mother to "be there" in times of need and to keep his secrets. Although fathers were occasionally mentioned, close relationships with mothers were more often evident among the boys with very close male friendships.

Theorists in developmental psychology have long contended that mother–child (as well as father–child) relationships help promote children's friendships (Bowlby, 1969/1982). A secure relationship with the primary caretaker provides the child with an "internal working model" (Bowlby, 1969/1982) that promotes the child's sense of self-worth and thus his or her ability to seek out and provide emotional support to others outside the family. In an analysis of African American, Latino, European American, and Asian American boys in six public middle schools,[3] Santos (2010) found that the boys who reported higher self-esteem and more supportive relationships with mothers were more likely to have emotionally intimate friendships than those who reported lower self-esteem and poorer relationships with their mothers. Furthermore, reports of high levels of mother support in sixth grade predicted an increase in boys' reports of having emotionally intimate friendships from sixth to eighth grade.

In addition to mothers, our qualitative observational data suggested that the social dynamics at school also supported (or constrained) boys' ability to have intimate male friendships. The boys, including the Latino boys, who discussed their vulnerabilities and desire for close friendships freely and expansively were those with the most social power among their peers in school. Social power among peers was acquired through numerous routes, including the familiar ones for boys such as being athletic, tall, conventionally good looking, and having a great sense of humor (Brown et al., 2009). Having these attributes resulted in greater social power, which, in turn, appeared to give boys the freedom to have the relationships they wanted without fear of being labeled girlish or gay (Way, 2011). Felix, for example, was one of the boys in our studies who was extremely popular, funny, and confident in his ability to attract girls, as well as in his ability to express vulnerability without being perceived as a "wuss." Psychologist Lyn Mikel Brown and her colleagues (2009) have noted a similar pattern in their book, *Packaging boyhood*: "The good news for parents is that being successful at sports not only protects a boy from being called gay but also gives him permission to do well academically, show sensitivity, and stick up for kids who are bullied" (p. 222). Boys who succeeded in sports and/or who appeared "manly" did not seem to feel as much pressure as the other boys to prove their masculinity or their heterosexuality.

Our data also indicated that "looking the part" in and out of school is contingent on race, ethnicity, immigrant status, and, of course, sexual orientation of the boys themselves and the stereotypes associated with these social categories. In American culture, being African American is perceived to be more masculine than being Chinese American. Looking American (e.g., wearing a baseball cap, untucked shirt, untied athletic shoes) is perceived to be more masculine than looking like an immigrant (e.g., button-up shirts, tucked in shirt, tied shoes). Similarly, looking "straight" (e.g., baseball cap, untucked shirt, untied athletic shoes), which is the same as looking "American," is perceived to be more masculine than looking gay (e.g., skinny jeans and tight shirts). The look of masculinity, which is based on a set of stereotypes about race, ethnicity, social class, nationality, and sexual orientation, is part of the same embedded set of masculine conventions that equates emotional stoicism, physical toughness, autonomy, and heterosexuality with being a man.

Within the context of our studies, the boys who had the desired look of masculinity, according to their peers, were the Puerto Rican boys.[4] These were the boys who the non-Puerto Rican teens—particularly the non-Puerto Rican Latinos in our studies—wanted to be like because of their "between" skin tone ("between White and Black'), their hair (which is neither stereotypically Black nor White), and their general hip and urban personal style (Way et al., 2008). The Puerto Rican students were also idealized by their immigrant peers because they were American citizens. In schools where being "an immigrant" is a racial slur, adolescents sought identities that were clearly American (ibid).

The Puerto Ricans were also the boys most likely among the Latinos to openly resist the conventions of masculinity by talking with great passion about their love for their male best friends. Although most Latino boys spoke with warmth and affection about their closest male friends, it was the Puerto Rican boys who were the most poetic in their language and fierce in their determination to maintain emotionally intimate male friendships. Our qualitative data suggest that these patterns of "resistance" were fostered by their high social status in school, as such status allows boys to challenge gender stereotypes without the risk of being ostracized by their peers (Brown et al., 2009). The Puerto Rican boys knew, in other words, that they could get away with it without being teased.

In addition to these family and school factors, being Latino also likely enhanced the boys' abilities to have intimate male friendships. From the literature of Gabriel Garcia Marquez or Junot Diaz to the poetry of Pablo Neruda, emotional expression clearly plays a central role in the construction of Latin American identity and culture. Research has repeatedly found that Latino families, including Latino males, strongly value the open expression of emotions and inter-personal relationships more generally (Azmitia et al., 2006; Falicov, 1998; Gloria et al., 2009; López et al., 2009).

Yet the variations found among Latino boys, with the Puerto Rican boys being more likely than the other Latino boys to be emotionally expressive, suggest that the family, school, and ethnic contexts weave together to create various possibilities and constraints. None of these factors in isolation determines boys' experiences of their friendships. The very fact that the boys who reported having poor relationships with their mothers and being verbally harassed by their peers were the least likely among the Latinos to have emotionally intimate friendships and to speak in emotional terms about their friendships suggests that the proximal context (i.e., family and school) makes a difference as does the distal context of sociocultural values and beliefs.

Yet this pattern of emotional expressiveness among all of the boys, including the Latinos, diminished significantly by late adolescence. As the boys reached late adolescence, they grew increasingly suspicious of their male peers and were less willing to speak in emotional terms about their male friendships. Strikingly, however, these boys continued to express a desire for intimate friendships and of increased sadness, depression, and isolation. These patterns of loss, distrust, and sadness among the boys are likely the product of an American culture of masculinity that does not value intimacy among males. As Latino boys become men in American culture, they experience the pressures that all boys in the United States experience—the pressures to be a heterosexual man in all of its stereotyped meaning.

The loss of close friendships was not what the Latino boys in our studies wanted and was clearly not good for their mental health. Although mainstream culture has framed such losses as a product of "maturity" as boys grow increasingly interested in girls, the boys themselves did not see these losses as positive. The boys' stories indicate, as do the research findings from decades of social science research, that supporting boys' desires for emotionally intimate male friendships will significantly enhance their health over the long term. The research on adults suggests that those without strong social networks, including close friendships, are more at risk for numerous mental and physical health problems (Adams & Allan, 1998). Studies have even found that close friendships are more important than a close spousal relationship for various health-related problems (Orth-Gomer et al., 1993). The challenge is to find ways to support the bonds these boys experience and wish to maintain in the midst of an American culture that believes that such relationships are only for girls and gay boys.

While our research studies present contextually rich evidence of the importance of friendships for Latino boys, our findings are specific to Latinos in a particular context and may not generalize to Latinos elsewhere. In addition, the themes of loss may have been heightened by the low-income status of the families in our studies who typically experience more residential transition than middle- and upper-class families (Putnam, 2000). However, our studies do reveal that poor and working-class Puerto Rican and Dominican American boys from urban contexts are having and seeking close friendships and that these friendships are a core component of their mental health throughout adolescence. Supporting such relationships seems to be the critical next step toward improving their well-being.

Notes

1   This chapter has appeared in part in *Latina/o Adolescent Psychology and Mental Health, Vol 2: Adolescent Development,* edited by H. Fitzgerald, N. Cabrera, and F. Villarruel and published by Praeger Press; and will also appear in the forthcoming book by N. Way entitled *Deep Secrets: Boys' Friendships and The Crisis of Connection,* to be published by Harvard University Press.
2   For a more detailed discussion of these studies on friendships, see Way (2011).
3   This study was part of the Center for Culture, Development and Education at New York University. The P.I.'s for the adolescent cohort are Niobe Way and Diane Hughes.
4   A study done in the Midwest also reported on this phenomenon of "wannabe" Puerto Ricans among White youth (Wilkins, 2004).

References

Adams, R., & Allan, G. (1998). *Placing friendship in context.* Cambridge: Cambridge University Press.

Azmitia, M., & Cooper, C. (2001). Good or bad? Peer influences on Latino and European American adolescents' pathways through school. *Journal of Education for Students Placed at Risk,* 6(1–2), 45–71.

Azmitia, M., Ittel, A., & Brenk, C. (2006). Latino-heritage adolescents' friendships. In X. Chen, D. French, & B. Schneider (Eds.), *Peer relationships in cultural context* (426–451). New York: Cambridge University Press.

Azmitia, M., Kamprath, N., & Linnet, J. (1998). Intimacy and conflict: The dynamics of boys' and girls' friendships during middle childhood and early adolescence. In L. H. Meyer, H. Park, M. Grenot-Scheyerm, I. S. Schwartz, & B. Harry (Eds.), *Making friends: The influences of culture and development* (171–187). Baltimore: Paul H. Brookes.

Berndt, T. (1981). Relations between social cognition, nonsocial cognition, and social behavior: The case of friendship. In J. Flavell & L. Ross (Eds.), *Social cognitive development* (176–189). New York: Cambridge University Press.

Bigelow, B., & La Gaipa, J. (1980). The development of friendship, values and choice. In H. Foot, A. Chapman, & J. Smith (Eds.), *Friendship and social relations in children* (15–44). Chichester, United Kingdom: Wiley.

Bishop, J., & Inderbitzen, H. (1995). Peer acceptance and friendship: An investigation of their relation to self-esteem. *Adolescence,* 15(4), 476–489.

Bowlby, J. (1969/1982). *Attachment and loss: Volume 1, Attachment.* New York: Basic Books.

Bronfenbrenner, U. (1979). *The ecology of human development.* Cambridge: Harvard University Press.

Brown, L. M., Lamb, S., & Tappan, M. (2009). *Packaging boyhood: Saving our sons from superheroes, slackers and other media stereotypes.* New York: St. Martin's Press.

Chen, X., French, D., & Schneider, B. (2006). *Peer relationships in cultural context.* New York: Cambridge University Press.

Decker, S. H., & Van Winkle, B. (1996). *Life in the gang: Family, friends, and violence.* New York: Cambridge University Press.

Eccles, J. S., & Roeser, R. W. (1999). School and community influences on human development. In M. H. Bornstein & M. E. Lamb (Eds.), *Developmental psychology: An advanced textbook* (503–554). Hillsdale, NJ: Erlbaum.

Erdley, C., Nangle, D., Newman, J., & Carpenter, E. (2001). Children's friendship experiences and psychological adjustment: Theory and research. In D. Nangle and C. Erdley (Eds.), *The role of friendship in psychological adjustment* (5–24). San Francisco: Jossey-Bass.

Falicov, C. (1998). *Latino families in therapy: A guide to multicultural practice.* New York: Guilford Press.

Furman, W., & Bierman, K. (1984). Children's conceptions of friendship: A multimethod study of developmental changes. *Developmental Psychology,* 20, 925–933.

Gloria, A. M., Castellanos, J., Scull, N. C., & Villegas, F. J. (2009). Psychological coping and well-being of male Latino undergraduates: Sobreviviendo la Universidad. *Hispanic Journal of Behavioral Sciences,* 31, 317–338.

Gutmann, M. C. (1996). *The meanings of macho: Being a man in Mexico City.* Berkeley: University of California Press.

Hill, J., & Lynch, M. (1983). The intensification of gender-related role expectations during early adolescence. In J. Brooks-Gunn & A. Peterson (Eds.), *Girls at puberty: Biological and psychosocial perspectives* (201–228). New York: Plenum.

Kimmel, M. (2008). *Guyland: The perilous world where boys become men.* New York: HarperCollins.

Ladd, G. W., & Troop-Gordon, W. (2003). The role of chronic peer difficulties in the development of children's psychological adjustment problems. *Child Development,* 74(5), 1344–1367.

Levitt, M., Guacci-Franco, N., & Levitt, J. (1993). Convoys of social support in childhood and early adolescence: Structure and function. *Developmental Psychology,* 29(5), 811–818.

López, S., García. J. I. R., Ullman, J. B., Kopelowicz, A., Jenkins, J., Breitborde, N. J. K., & Placencia, P. (2009). Cultural variability in the manifestation of expressed emotion. *Family Process,* 48(2), 179–194.

Majors, R. G., & Billson, J. (1992). *Cool pose: The dilemmas of black manhood in America.* New York: Lexington Books (Macmillan).

Miller, B. (1991). Adolescents' relationships with their friends. Unpublished doctoral dissertation. Cambridge: Harvard University.

Nangle, D. W., & Erdley, C. A. (Eds.). (2001). *New directions for child and adolescent development: The role of friendship in psychological adjustment.* San Francisco: Jossey-Bass.

Oldenburg, C., & Kerns, K. (1997). Associations between peer relationships and depressive symptoms: Testing moderator effects of gender and age. *Journal of Early Adolescence,* 17, 319–337.

Orth-Gomer, K., Rosengren, A., & Wilhelmsen, L. (1993). Lack of social support and incidence of coronary heart disease in middle-aged Swedish men. *Psychosomatic Medicine,* 55, 37–43.

Padilla, F. M. (1992). *The gang as an American enterprise.* New Brunswick, NJ: Rutgers University Press.

Pelkonen, M., Marttunen, M., & Aro, H. (2003). Risk for depression: A 6-year follow-up of Finnish adolescents. *Journal of Affective Disorders,* 77(1), 41–51.

Putnam, R. D. (2000). *Bowling alone: The collapse and revival of American community.* New York: Simon & Schuster.

Radmacher, K., & Azmitia, M. (2006). Are there gendered pathways to intimacy in early adolescents' and emerging adults' friendships? *Journal of Adolescent Research,* 21(4), 415–448.

Rubin, K. H., Bukowski, W. M., & Laursen, B. (Eds.). (2009). *Handbook of peer interactions, relationships, and groups.* New York: Guilford Press.

Santos, C. E. (2010). The missing story: Resistance to ideals of masculinity in the friendships of middle school boys. Unpublished doctoral dissertation. New York: New York University.

Sax, L. (2007). *Boys adrift: The five factors driving the growing epidemic of unmotivated boys and underachieving young men.* New York: Basic Books.

Spencer, M. B. (2006). Phenomenology and ecological systems theory: Development of diverse groups. In W. Damon & R. Lerner (Eds.), *Handbook of child psychology* (829–893). New York: Wiley.

Strauss, A., & Corbin, J. (1990). *Basics of qualitative research: Grounded theory procedures and techniques.* Thousand Oaks, CA: Sage.

Sullivan, H. S. (1953). *The interpersonal theory of psychiatry.* New York: Norton.

Tyre, P. (2008). *The trouble with boys: A surprising report card on our sons, their problems at school and what parents and educators must do.* New York: Crown Publishing.

Urban Dictionary: No Homo. (n.d.). In *Urban Dictionary.* Retrieved from www.urban dictionary.com/define.php?term=no+homo

Vernberg, E. (1990). Experiences with peers following relocation during early adolescence. *American Journal of Orthopsychiatry,* 60, 466–472.

Vitaro, F., Boivin, M., & Bukowski, W. M. (2009). The role of friendship in child and adolescent psychosocial development. In K. H. Rubin, W. M. Bukowski, & B. Laursen (Eds.), *Handbook of peer interactions, relationships, and groups* (568–585). New York: Guilford Press.

Way, N. (2011). *Deep secrets: Boys' friendships and the crisis of connection.* Cambridge: Harvard University Press.

Way, N., & Chen, L. (2000). Close and general friendships among African American, Latino, and Asian American adolescents from low-income families. *Journal of Adolescent Research,* 15, 274–301.

Way, N., & Robinson, M. G. (2003). A longitudinal study of the effects of family, friends, and school experiences on the psychological adjustment of ethnic minority, low-SES adolescents. *Journal of Adolescent Research,* 18, 324–346.

Way, N., Santos, C., Niwa, E., & Kim-Gervey, C. (2008). To be or not to be: An exploration of ethnic identity development in context. In M. Azmitia, M. Syed, & K. Radmacher (Eds.), *The intersections of personal and social identities: New directions for child and adolescent development* (61–79). San Francisco: Jossey-Bass.

Wilkins, A. (2004). Puerto Rican wannabes: Sexual spectacle and the marking of race, class, and gender boundaries. *Gender & Society*, 18(1), 103–121.

PART 4

Environmental Factors and Violence

16

STREET SOCIALIZATION AND THE PSYCHOSOCIAL MORATORIUM

James Diego Vigil

Introduction

Among the many experiences that gang members undergo, none is more crucial than the adolescent psychosocial moratorium. According to developmental psychologist Erik Erikson (1956, 1963, 1968), the psychosocial moratorium is the marginal status crisis in the passage from childhood to adulthood. Street-socialized males in low-income neighborhoods are especially affected by this transition. During this phase, the boys become tentative and confused about their age and gender identity while learning to cope within an often violent, male-dominated street culture. The personal psychological struggle that occurs in this context is sometimes overwhelming. This "storm and stress" situation triggers many attitudinal and behavioral shifts in individuals, irrespective of environment, that render them unpredictable and ambivalent. Being raised in the streets can make this human development phase even more difficult and problematic, twisting and skewing options and opportunities in detrimental ways.

Street Socialization and Human Development

The streets generate—through the process of street socialization (Vigil, 1988a, 2002)—a need to seek out the gang in order to survive. There are certainly precursors to street socialization, such as households characterized by stressful family life, crowded living conditions, and personal emotional problems that I have referred to as "multiple marginality" (Vigil, 1988a, 2002), which reflect the poverty and stressed neighborhoods of mostly Latino communities. It is in these households mainly that children find themselves bereft of supervision and seek attention and adventure in the streets. Mostly, poor immigrant families and their second-generation offspring are the ones likely to experience such adaptation problems (Vigil, 2007).

In gang-ridden neighborhoods, the street gang has become a competitor to traditional sources of identity formation, often replacing family, school, and other conventional influences. Since their inception more than six decades ago, Chicano street gangs have been made up primarily of groups of male adolescents and youths who have grown up together as children, usually as cohorts in a low-income neighborhood of a city. In Los Angeles today, about 100,000 gang members are spread throughout the metropolitan area, most of them concentrated in Latino neighborhoods. However, only about 10 to 15 percent of youth in most of these neighborhoods join gangs (Esbensen & Winfree, 2001; Short, 1996; Vigil, 1988a), and of this number about 70 percent eventually "mature out" (Vigil, 2007). Those who do join participate in both conventional and anti-social behavior (Thornberry, 2001). The anti-social behavior, of course, attracts the attention of authorities as well as the general public (Decker & Van Winkle, 1996).

Gang Families and Non-gang Families

Gang families can be distinguished from families whose young members are not drawn into gang activities along a number of dimensions. Youths in some families are more vulnerable to gang membership (Vigil, 2002), in other words. Generally, social control influences (families, schools, and law enforcement) tend to break down in a stressful, low-income community. Of the many larger social and cultural forces at work in such neighborhoods, those that stand out are: chronic unemployment, residents' lack of adequate employment skills, a high incidence of drug use and sales, and a pervasive street gang presence that affects all residents. Research in these neighborhoods (Moore, 1978, 1991; Moore & Vigil, 1987, 1993) has shown differences in family dynamics; these variations account for why some children in the same neighborhoods undergo street socialization early and become gang members and why others are able to pursue a more conventional lifestyle.

Poor home socialization leads inexorably to street socialization. This means that not only are children prone to getting caught up in delinquent behavior, but they are also socialized by their peers on the street. Researchers (e.g., Cartwright et al., 1975; Klein, 1971) have noted that the absence of parental and home-based influences, combined with limited schooling and teacher interaction, leaves little to attract youngsters to more positive socialization patterns. In such an environment the children inevitably encounter gang members who alternate between hurling threats and offering protection to youngsters. Additionally, in the absence of other conventional sources, gang members show obvious emotional support for one another. The gang is a multiple-age peer group that has readily available values and norms of its own. All of these factors make the gang extraordinarily attractive to many young people.

In one Los Angeles housing development where we conducted a community study, Latinos made up 85 percent of the residents in the project. This number would have been significantly larger if "an unknown, but undoubtedly significant, number of individuals and families with non-legal immigration status" (Housing Authority, 1990, pp. 3–4) were included. The principal source of income for over one-third of the projects' households was AFDC payments. Despite the fact that many of the households derived their incomes from employment, most jobholders worked in low-paying, low-status service and manufacturing jobs that have largely replaced the unionized, high-paying jobs previously available to East Los Angeles residents (Moore & Vigil, 1993). In the Pico Gardens housing project, for example, the average reported annual income per household in the 1990s was $10,932 (Vigil, 1988a). One survey of Pico Gardens households indicated that the families with one or two youths who were active in the local street gang were poorer and had less support from extended relatives than other families in this generally low-income neighborhood, and were much more likely to be headed by a single-parent mother (Vigil, 2007).

The pervasive poverty in Pico Gardens meant that many families had few options available to them that would enable them to leave the environment. Furstenberg (1993) has found that the communities where families live have a major influence on children's development. He wrote that, "the interplay between neighborhood and parenting process probably affects . . . children's success in averting serious problems and finding pathways out of poverty" (p. 234). The potential harm that ensues, however, by staying in neighborhoods with resident gangs is that younger relatives are inclined to emulate the older gang members in their families.

Family networks, especially in Latino culture, are the primary source of early socialization and enculturation for children. Bronfenbrenner (1979) and Garbarino et al. (1986) have noted ways that wider social forces are linked to the dynamics of family life. Parker et al. (1988) suggested that children are shaped by the "dynamic interplay between the environment and the child" (p. 3), and Schorr (1988) has found that "the interplay between constitution and environment is far more decisive in shaping an individual than either alone" (p. 25). Moore (1991) found that barrio family life was mediated by economic opportunities that are determined by larger, macro forces. In a previous study by Moore and Vigil (1987), we noted that four family types exist in many barrios: (1) the underclass, (2) the conventional/controlled, (3) the unconventional/controlled, and (4) the conventional/uncontrolled.

In the underclass family, family members often become involved in deviant behavior and are just as influential (if not more so) as gang peers in affecting youngsters' lives. These families are ineffective at controlling family members who are often involved in the gang/criminal subculture. The polar opposite to this family type is the second variant, the conventional or controlled family, which resembles the kind of family that is often found in stable, working-class communities. These families usually consist of two parents, although they sometimes are headed by a single parent; the family heads are exemplary role models for their children and effectively maintain control over them. The third type of family, the unconventional/controlled family, is comprised of adult members who may be involved in gangs and some deviant activities, such as drug sales, but are able to maintain the façade of conventionality and conceal their deviance from the rest of the family. These adults are still able to provide guidance and leadership to the children. Finally, the fourth type of family, the conventional/uncontrolled family, is simply ineffectual. There are many different variants within this category.

A large body of literature argues that single-parent households adversely affect children by thwarting and undermining their integration and involvement in society (Loeber & Stouthamer-Loeber, 1986; McLanahan & Sandefur, 1994). Generally, the most serious difficulties that children in single- and female-headed families encounter emerge during the adolescence crisis occurring during the developmental passage between childhood and adulthood (Erikson, 1968; Loeber & Stouthamer-Loeber, 1986). Children at this age often suffer from the far-reaching negative effects that poverty has on them and their families. Specifically, living in poverty is closely linked with a number of other risk factors (Whitehead, 1993). For instance, Whitehead stated that, "Single-mother families are vulnerable to not just poverty but to a particularly debilitating form of poverty: welfare dependence" (p. 16).

The Psychosocial Moratorium

The gang, in fulfilling many of the personal needs related to the problems, pressures, and strivings of street socialized youth, has perpetuated itself and has extended its influence over marginally troubled youth. These young males temporarily or sporadically seek the gang as a source of support and identity, especially during junior high school years. It is at this age of 13 or 14 when males in particular undergo the psychosocial moratorium posited by Erikson (1956), during the status crisis from childhood to adulthood when ambiguity and ambivalence reign. It is no coincidence that most aggressive gang behavior is committed by male youths between 14 and 18 years of age (Hirschi & Gottfredson, 1983).

The psychosocial moratorium is a period of human development during which teens face their new social and sexual identities and roles with uncertainty. As a result, they increasingly rely on peers and slightly older male role models as guides. According to cross-cultural researchers (Bloch & Neiderhoffer, 1958; Burton & Whiting, 1961), it is common during this developmental phase to seek older male role models and undergo some sort of initiation ceremony into all-male organizations. In Chicano street gangs, this initiation takes the form of "jumping in," a quasi-ritualized beating that tests the mettle and fighting skills of the initiate. This rite of passage serves to accentuate the youths' masculine qualities as they break away from female influences, mainly the mother-centered families in which so many of them were reared (Vigil, 1996).

The status crisis of puberty is accompanied and strongly affected by bodily changes and hormonal adjustments and imbalances. Ambiguity and confusion characterize self-identification pathways that affect developmental dynamics (Erikson, 1968; Vigil 1988a, 1988b, 2002). Becoming more self-conscious of these developments in the context of street life, where the pressures and demands can sometimes be overwhelming, generates a heightened sense of internal conflict in these youths during this passage. This is especially the case because there is developmental tension between early household socialization, often dominated by females, and the new street socialization under the aegis of the male multiple-aged peer group.

Ego formation, group affiliation, and adoption of role behavior dominate during this time. It is no accident that the misshapen ego finds solace in the group; together with other similarly fragile egos, like pieces of a puzzle, they find a wholeness and completeness to aid their survival and a feeling of security that they have seldom experienced. What else to do but accept the role gestalt that the group has fashioned over the years for similarly disaffected and unaffiliated youth? In short, to understand the developmental processes of gang affiliation and identification, one must examine how the ego, group, and role psychologies are intertwined, producing connections and interactions backing up to their past lives in order to understand their present street ones.

Seeking friends that like you and relying on them almost exclusively for guidance and direction can also play havoc on the cognitive level of a gang member. There are many physical and mental incongruities exhibited by gang members that reflect this tendency: trying to act tough when one is not; over-dressing in the street style; not carrying school books home; playing to the gang audience; and faking defiance of authorities. In keeping with this variable behavior, some gang members follow a more extreme Jekyl-and-Hyde character change, reflecting the chameleon identity of the gang life.

Much of what was stated earlier about the emotional state of mind during puberty applies to the physical changes of human development as well. While the interior of a person is undergoing mostly masked changes, it is more obvious when the physical appearance exposes a tell-tale statement about ambiguity and uncertainty. The voice changes, the height increases, the bodily alterations remake the person, and the control and management of ones self-image is under siege. Added to this uneven development is the need to show mastery by achieving or shining in some capacity. However, in contrast to dominant-society teenagers that are socialized in conventional areas of accomplishment, the streets dictate a different arena. Showing "toughness" is a particularly important characteristic for street children, and a few are actually very tough, even "out of control": they can dish it out and they can take it. A street world molds a protective physical appearance, a posturing that often deters potential aggressors—a street camouflage, so to speak.

Significant parties of the multiple-aged peer group are the *veteranos* (veterans, or original gangsters [OGs]) who are the street power brokers. Everyone must contend with these seasoned street toughs, including the many youths who are not gang members. The *veteranos* are both feared as potential predators and respected as potential protectors. Much of the gang behavior of youths on the streets stems from this fear, with youths tending to emulate those they fear most, while simultaneously seeking protection from them. Thus, left to the world of the streets, who do you think you want to have like you?

Locura: Requisite for Street Survival and for Assuaging the Psychosocial Moratorium

One role and role performance especially instrumental in the context of street reality is *locura* (literally, madness). It is both essential for street survival and for assuaging fear and ambiguity born of the psychosocial moratorium. In street culture, *locura* is a state of mind where various quasi-controlled actions of craziness or wildness occur. A person who is a *loco* demonstrates this state of mind by alternately displaying fearlessness, toughness, daring, and other unpredictable forms of destructive behavior, such as getting "loco" on drugs and alcohol or excelling in gangbanging. Such traits are, more or less, considered gang ideals. Some are confirmed *vato locos*, as loco actors can easily and authoritatively manage this role, while others only rise to the occasion when peer pressure or situational circumstances dictate a loco act. This difference reflects the distinction made by Edgerton (1978) between deviant persons and deviant acts.

The *locura* psychosocial role has become a requisite for street survival and a behavioral standard for identification and emulation, in addition to a quick fix for managing this difficult developmental phase. A person who is loco, either situationally or regularly, adds an important dimension to the group. This is especially the case when the barrio is beleaguered by other barrio gangs and must show a strong force of resistance to outside challenges and pressures. The loco one is a prized member of the group for he can sometimes serve as a deterrent to stave off confrontations. In many other instances, however, the loco can be a hindrance to the group when his unbridled actions cause unnecessary and unwanted trouble.

Factors that can be traced directly to the streets are especially important in helping one comprehend the stressors and pressure of street gangs. One is how a person early on in life has been socialized in the streets—the socialization of last resort when home, school, and other caretakers have failed—thus taking on this crazy persona as an actor. The other one is more nuanced, unpredictable, and variable. When a person enters the streets later in life, often only temporarily, that person must learn to act like a street person, including acting crazy; that is one reason why drugs and alcohol are used, to ease the performance. In brief, there is a tremendous range of *locura* behavior among individuals within a barrio and between barrios.

In short, early painful experiences and/or early street socialization are more likely to result in the development of a crazy actor, while late street socialization is apt to turn out individuals who periodically perform crazy acts. Police most often care little about these distinctions and care more about who crosses the line rather than why or how often the line is traversed. However, Klein (1971, 1995) and others (Cartwright et al., 1975) have noted a hard-core and fringe dichotomy of gang membership, and Klein has even developed a typology of gangs (Klein, 1995), as have we, in distinguishing gang members as regular, peripheral, temporary, and situational. Such typologies reflect differing intensities and durations of gang membership and attachment (Vigil, 1988a).

Although these situations and conditions generally affect most gang members, it is the experienced role models, the ones with tarnished early lives and street experiences, who most influence the fringe gang members. The dress, talk, walk, and a whole set of other gestures and demeanors of these street models are the standards for members to emulate and effuse with an aura of masculinity. Because of conflict between Mexican immigrant and American culture, the second generation of urban Mexican American youth worked out a syncretic style that blends the cultures, often referred to as *cholo* (i.e., a cultural marginal). These street styles began in the 1940s during the Zoot Suit period, and over the decades, as street socialization routines and rhythms have shifted, the styles have varied widely.

Policy Issues

This chapter describes how poverty and marginalization lead to "street socialization" (i.e., being raised in the streets) and the emergence of street gangs and gang members. Street socialization, in turn, undermines and transforms the otherwise normal course of human development in ways that institutionalize a street subculture. Before we can develop prevention, intervention, and suppression strategies, we must look to these gang roots by examining the historical and cultural experiences of ethnic minority youth. Establishing the realities of time, place, and people will inform the formulation and implementation of remedial strategies (Vigil, 2010).

Los Angeles, for example, is both a model of urban diversity—a place full of different languages and cultural traditions—and also a city filled with ethnic and racial tensions that threaten to erupt at any moment. Its history is one of rapid, uneven change that transformed a small Mexican pueblo practically overnight into a major American and global metropolis. During this time, both internal migration (from small towns and various regions of the country) and large-scale immigration from foreign countries increased exponentially, eventually pushing White working- and middle-class residents into the suburbs. These dramatic social transformations strained the city's infrastructure and institutional support systems. Finding affordable housing became a problem for many, first in low-income areas like Watts and much later in older, once prosperous neighborhoods like

Pico-Union, where Central Americans made their home. Both homes and schools were filled beyond capacity. Schools built for several hundred students were expected to hold twice that number. For decades, as Black and Chicano leaders railed against unfair and unequal treatment of the residents in the mostly low-income communities they represented, police–community relations also took a turn for the worse.

Los Angeles is therefore more than a model of the mega-city; it is the prototypical mega-city with multiple, intertwining problems, the same sorts of problems that to some degree are also afflicting other major urban centers worldwide such as Rio de Janeiro and Paris. These cities have generated or are in the process of generating mega-gangs, mostly within their poor communities. This subcultural process unfolds in like manner from place to place, although, as it does, the unique history and culture of each place leaves its stamp.

What has emerged in this brief outline of the roots and traditions of the gang street lifestyle is that the facts of time, place, and people can serve as a template for developing a balanced strategy (Vigil, 2010). A balanced strategy to combat gangs would emphasize prevention and intervention. This concerted effort would fill a major void by adding rewards to the punishments. For example, a more inclusive approach to improving community health focusing on youth at risk would also address human developmental processes (social, emotional, cognitive, and physical). Our society must address the problems associated with gang families and re-equip parents with coping strategies to guide their children. Although our schools are under siege, we must undertake a serious effort to remediate the educational problems of children at risk.

Prevention of street socialization must begin in the early childhood years and continue up to age 8 or 9. Communities and agencies must take a pro-active approach in addressing the primary problems of the general population in low-income areas and factor in secondary prevention for specific at-risk youths and any related issues. Interventions are aimed at the crucial preteen years, from age 9 to 12 or 13, and should involve treatment and work with youths who are close to but not yet deeply connected to the streets. Dissuading youth early on from the attitudes and behavior that clearly lead to delinquent and criminal paths opens the possibility of a return to more pro-social activities.

Lacking in many of these youths' lives are the pre-employment experiences that assist human growth and development, such as beliefs and behavioral traits reflecting discipline, obedience, punctuality, responsibility, and value and honor in work. It is for this reason that many observers and writers have emphasized that economic concerns (e.g., training, work, and jobs) matter most in getting youth off the streets by engaging them in productive, conventional activities and grounding them in the skills, knowledge, and attitudes that will stay with them for life. This will give them a stake in society. But even before that can be accomplished, consideration must be given to how to "steal time" and when to reorder time spent in the streets by involving youth in conventional activities.

Conclusion

As a result of street socialization and the status crisis of the psychosocial moratorium, street gang violence in Los Angeles has become a central concern of law enforcement authorities. There are many ways to analyze and address gang violence; most important to an assessment are the social situations and conditions that engender a violent tendency and the personal experiences and motivations that create and mold individuals to carry out these acts.

What needs to be fathomed is that most caretakers have failed these youths—families and schools primarily—and that, in the void left by these institutions, street socialization has taken over and created a basis for a new set of values and norms. For some individuals in the most marginalized and impoverished communities, a series of personal traumatic experiences and influences have generated a sense of rage and aggression such that lashing out violently becomes a predictable type of behavior. In this context of social determinants and psychological propensities, street gangs have become a street-created medium and vehicle to encourage and vent this aggression.

References

Bloch, H. A., & Neiderhoffer, A. (1958). *The gang: A study in adolescent behavior.* New York, NY: Philosophical Library.

Bronfenbrenner, U. (1979). *The ecology of human development: Experiments by nature and design.* Cambridge, MA: Harvard University Press.

Burton, R. V., & Whiting, J. W. (1961). The absent father cross-sex identity. *Merrill-Palmer Quarterly, 7,* 85–95.

Cartwright, D. S., Thompson, B., & Schwartz, H. (Eds.) (1975). *Gang delinquency.* Monterey, CA: Brooks/Cole Publishing.

Decker, S. H., & Van Winkle, B. (1996). *Life in the gang: Family, friends, and violence.* New York, NY: Cambridge University Press.

Edgerton, R. (1978). The study of deviance—Marginal man or everyman? In G. Spindler (Ed.), *The making of psychological anthropology* (442–476). Los Angeles, CA: University of California Press.

Erikson, E. H. (1956). Ego identity and the psychosocial moratorium. In H. L. Witmer & R. Kotinsky (Eds.). *New perspectives for research on juvenile delinquency* (1–23). Washington, DC: U.S. Children's Bureau, publication #356.

Erikson, E. H. (1963). *Childhood and society.* New York: W. W. Norton.

Erikson, E. H. (1968). Psychosocial identity. In D. Sills (Ed.), *International encyclopedia of the social sciences* (Vol. 7) (61–65). New York, NY: Macmillan and Free Press.

Esbensen, F., & Winfree, L. T., Jr. (2001). Race and gender differences between gang and nongang youths. In J. Miller, C. L. Maxson, & M. W. Klein (Eds.), *The modern gang reader* (2nd ed.) (106–120). Los Angeles, CA: Roxbury Publishing.

Furstenberg, F. (1993). How families manage risk and opportunity in dangerous neighborhoods. In W. J. Wilson (Ed.), *Sociology in the public agenda.* Newbury Park, CA: Sage Publications.

Garbarino, J., Schellenback, C. J., & Seber, J. M. (1986). *Troubled youth, troubled families: Understanding families at-risk for adolescent maltreatment.* New York, NY: Aldine.

Hirschi, T., & Gottfredson, M. (1983). Age and the explanation of crime. *American Journal of Sociology*, 89(3), 552–584.

Housing Authority of the City of Los Angeles (1990). Public housing drug elimination grant application: Public Housing Drug Elimination Program. Application submitted to HUD, Los Angeles, CA.

Klein, M. (1971). *Street gangs and street workers*. Englewood Cliffs, NJ: Prentice-Hall.

Klein, M. (1995). *The American street gang*. New York, MY: Oxford University Press.

Loeber, R., & Stouthamer-Loeber, M. (1986). Family factors as correlates and predictors of juveniles conduct problems and delinquency. In M. Tonry & N. Morris (Eds.), *Crime and justice: An annual review of research* (Vol. 7) (29–149). Chicago, IL: University of Chicago Press.

McLanahan, S., & Sandefur, G. (1994). *Growing up with a single parent: What hurts, what helps*. Cambridge, MA: Harvard University Press.

Moore, J. W. (1978). *Homeboys*. Philadelphia: Temple University Press.

Moore, J. W. (1991). *Going down to the barrio*. Philadelphia: Temple University Press.

Moore, J. W., & Vigil, J. D. (1987). Chicano gangs: Group norms and individual factors related to adult criminality. *Aztlan*, 18(2), 27–44.

Moore, J. W., & Vigil, J. D. (1993). Barrios in transition. In J. W. Moore & R. Pinderhughes (Eds.), *In the barrios: Latinos and the underclass debate*. New York, NY: Russell Sage Publications.

Parker, S., Greer, S., & Zuckerman, B. (1988). Double jeopardy: The impact of poverty on early child development. *Pediatric Clinics of North America*, 35(6), 1227–1240.

Schorr, L. (1988). *Within our reach: Breaking the cycle of disadvantage*. New York, NY: Anchor Press/Doubleday.

Short, J. (1996). Personal, gang, and community careers. In C. R. Huff (Ed.), *Gangs in America* (2nd ed.) (3–11). Thousand Oaks, CA: Sage Publications.

Thornberry, T. P. (2001). Risk factors for gang membership. In J. Miller, C. L. Maxson, & M. W. Klein (Eds.), *The modern gang reader* (2nd ed.) (32–43). Los Angeles, CA: Roxbury Publications.

Vigil, J. D. (1988a). *Barrio gangs: Street life and identity in Southern California*. Austin, TX: University of Texas Press.

Vigil, J. D. (1988b). Group processes and street identity: Adolescent Chicano gang members. *Ethos*, 16(4), 421–445.

Vigil, J. D. (1996). Street baptism: Chicano gang initiation. *Human Organization*, 55(2), 149–153.

Vigil, J. D. (2002). *A rainbow of gangs: Street cultures in the mega-city*. Austin, TX: University of Texas Press.

Vigil, J. D. (2007). *The projects: Gang and non-gang families in East Los Angeles*. Austin, TX: University of Texas Press.

Vigil, J. D. (2010). *Gang redux: A balanced anti-gang strategy*. Long Grove, IL: Waveland Press.

Whitehead, B. (1993, April). Dan Quayle was right. *The Atlantic Monthly*, 46–54.

17

LATINO MALE VIOLENCE IN THE UNITED STATES

Ramiro Martinez, Jr.
Jacob I. Stowell

Introduction

There are considerable race/ethnic and gender disparities in violence across the nation. Previous public health data illustrated that Latino males were three times *more* likely than non-Latino White males to be a victim of homicide but almost three times *less* likely than Black males to be killed (Keppel et al., 2002). More recent national crime victimization surveys have indicated that Latino and Black males were victims of robbery at similarly high rates, but Latinos were victims of aggravated assault at a level comparable to that of Whites and Blacks (Catalano, 2006). These differences, which are affected to a large extent by structural influences including economic well-being, remind us that social science research on gender/racial/ethnic variations in crime must incorporate Latino males and consider variations within Latino groups in order to fully understand group differences in criminal and delinquent behavior.

Indeed, research on Latino males and violent crime in general has lagged behind that of Black or White violent crime. This neglect holds even in the face of long-held beliefs and stereotypes about crime-prone Latinos by some politicians and the mass media (Martinez, 2002, 2006). A recent search of citations in *Social Science Full Text* produced 80 journal articles on Latinos/Hispanics and crime; in contrast, there were almost 700 journal articles on African Americans/Blacks and crime over the 1990 to 2006 period. This is important to note as the lack of research on Latino male violence limits our understanding of the sources of racial and ethnic disparities in violent crime, and how culture and social structure intersect in shaping Latino violent crime (Morenoff, 2005; Peterson & Krivo, 2005).

In this chapter, the key findings on Latino male violence in the United States are reviewed. The chapter begins by outlining the shape of ethnic disparities in violent crime—that is, Latino criminal victimization relative to White and Black males from a major self-report survey of victimization. This is done by drawing from some of the most extensive national sources of crime and directing attention to Latino males. The survey discussion is followed by a discussion of the quantitative analyses that have focused on Latino or ethnic group comparisons. Most of the work on race/ethnicity and violent crime direct attention to the impact of structural influences, especially economic disadvantage (economic stress), at the city or community level rather than on individual level outcomes (Peterson & Krivo, 2005). While qualitative and ethnographic studies are insightful, particularly regarding issues facing Latino males (i.e., masculinity research), they remain limited in number relative to quantitative studies on Latinos and crime (for exceptions, see Dohan, 2003; Kil & Menjívar, 2006). The final section of the chapter considers some initial results from an on-going analysis of male homicide victimization that situates this question in a national context. We close by highlighting the importance of policy and addressing issues for future research.

National Victimization Survey

The primary source of crime victimization data in the United States is the National Crime Victimization Survey (NCVS), a nationally representative study of person and household victimization administered by the United States Census Bureau. The NCVS, unlike most data reported to the police, records the race (White, Black, or Other) and "Hispanic" origin of the victim (Hispanic or non-Hispanic). The incorporation of ethnicity in the NCVS permits estimates of both racial and ethnic differences in crime or criminal victimization, which elevates this survey to the leading source of Hispanic/Latino crime across the United States.

In Table 17.1, we see that African American (Black) males are more likely than White males to be victims of violent crimes in urban areas. This disparity varies by type of crime and race/ethnicity/gender. For example, there are also some similarities between Black and Latino male robbery rates. The Black male robbery victim rate (11.2 Black male robberies per 1000 Black males) is much higher than the White male robbery victim rate (6.7 White robberies per 1000 Whites) but is closer to the Hispanic/Latino robbery rate (9.0 Hispanic robberies per 1000 Hispanics). Put another way, Latino males are 1.3 times and Black males

TABLE 17.1 NCVS Rates of Violent Crime Among Males by Race and Ethnicity in Urban America, 2005

| | Victim race/ethnicity | | |
	Non-Latino White	Non-Latino Black	Hispanic/Latino
All areas	3.3	7.3	5.6
Robbery	6.7	11.2	9.0
All assaults	27.3	33.5	27.0
Aggravated assault	7.1	11.8	8.3
Simple assault	20.2	21.7	18.8

1.7 times more likely to be victims of robbery than are non-Hispanic White males. Racial differences in the NCVS victimization rates are greatest for robbery, followed by aggravated assault. In fact, aggravated assault differences among racial/ ethnic group members are usually minor and Latino males usually fall between White and Black male rates.

The NCVS has also collected race and ethnicity information for decades, which allows for the examination of changes over time in violent crime victimization. The overall violent victimization rate among Latinos has declined dramatically, in fact by almost 55 percent, between 1993 and 2005 (see Catalano, 2006). This decline, however, was consistent across all racial/ethnic and gender groups— overall non-Hispanics declined by 58.4 percent, and more specifically Whites declined by 58 percent, Blacks by 59.9 percent, and other race respondents by 65.1 percent. Thus, Latinos appear equally likely to have experienced similar declines in violent crime victimization as other racial/ethnic group members. This finding is important because it counters the arguments offered by immigrant opponents in the popular media who contend that immigrants have "contributed" to crime rates in their local areas. It goes without saying that these assumptions are counterfactual and, by extension, that the notions regarding high crime rates among Latino immigrants are similarly flawed. Putting legal status aside, Latinos as a whole have long experienced similar levels of violent victimization as other racial and ethnic groups, as evidenced by the fact that rates of victimization have declined among all groups, even in an era of intense immigration (Martinez, 2002, 2006).

Taken together, the comparison of racial/ethnic differences using national victimization data illustrates that the differences in violent crime victimization among Black, White, and Latino males appear sizeable in the case of robbery and modest in other types of violent crime. Perhaps the most important outcome of this analysis is that while reliable Latino crime data are scarce, existing sources confirm that the specific consideration of Latino males is important to study racial and ethnic disparities in crime rates. Regardless of the findings or the surveys, it is clear that researchers can no longer focus on the racial dichotomies of Black and White when considering racial/ethnic disparities in male crime.

Macro-level Studies

Much of the recent research on race/ethnicity and crime has been conducted at the macro-level census tract, city, or nation with official crime data (Morenoff, 2005; Peterson & Krivo, 2005; Sampson & Bean, 2006). This literature does not examine individual variations in criminal offending; instead it considers variations in violent crime victimization or offending across larger areal units (Morenoff, 2005). Research on crime and violence also draws attention to the relationship between race/ethnicity and place (i.e., cities, metropolitan areas, neighborhoods) and proposes that racial disparities are linked to the varying social contexts in which population groups reside. A consistent finding in this literature is that violent crime rates, measured as both rates of offending and victimization, are higher in places with greater proportions of Blacks or African Americans, and that this finding persists over time (Morenoff, 2005; Sampson & Bean, 2006). A majority of these studies use homicide or violent crime rates or counts of racial/ethnic-specific violence as the outcome measure because lethal violence is both detected and reported to the police more frequently than are less serious forms of violence. It is common practice among these studies, however, to focus exclusively on broad Black or White crime differences, which again ignores important and growing segments of the American population.

These macro-level studies have been valuable because they demonstrate the need to consider racial disparities in crime more broadly, and in some cases encourage scholars to include the Latino composition in crime studies (Peterson & Krivo, 2005). Unfortunately, this literature has rarely considered the level of Latino male crime or compared Latinos to other ethnic minority groups, largely due to official crime data limitations (for a more detailed description of "place-based" disparities, see Morenoff, 2005, p. 152). This omission in part has led some researchers to revisit (and raise questions) regarding long-standing assertions advanced in research on communities and crime, an academic tradition that dates back to the founding of American criminology (Sampson & Bean, 2006; for an historical perspective, see Bursik, 2006).

Early criminologists studied the consequences of movement of Black migrants and immigrants into urban areas. Indeed most pioneering ethnicity and crime studies focused on European immigrants in Chicago. A notable exception to this pattern is the publication of *Mexican Labor in the United States, Volume II,* which documents perhaps the earliest quantitative study on Mexican immigration to the United States. In this study, Paul S. Taylor ([1932] 1970) described the labor market, education, criminal justice, and fertility experiences of Mexican-origin persons in Chicago. By explicitly linking arrest statistics for felonies and misdemeanors and comparing them to local population sizes and community characteristics, Taylor was able to gauge the criminal activities of White and Mexican residents. While Mexican males were over-represented in these data, arrested at a percentage two to three times their population size, most of the arrests were not related to violence. Rather, the arrests were disproportionately for property and alcohol-related offenses, a finding that Taylor attributed to the demographic characteristics of this population. Regarding violence, Taylor ([1932] 1970) noted that "the offenses of Mexicans are concentrated much more than average in these two groups of charges, probably mainly because of the very abnormal age and sex composition of the Mexican population in Chicago" (p. 147). These findings are important to highlight because they suggest that patterns of criminal involvement are shaped by cultural and structural factors, including poverty, age, and sex distributions of the Mexican immigrant population, not the inherent criminality of immigrants.

Few of the early scholars, however, acknowledged the presence of Latino or non-European immigrants. This was likely due to the passage of anti-immigrant quota laws in the 1920s and assimilation campaigns that gradually rendered the study of the European immigrant experience obsolete and forced scholars to focus on race or "Black versus White" crime. Some scholars have recently begun examining violent crime counts across census tracts within a city with varying levels of racial and ethnic composition. Some of the existing research compares and contrasts the characteristics of Black, White, and Latino homicides in Chicago, Houston, Los Angeles, and Miami (Martinez, 2003; Reidel, 2003; Titterington & Damphousse, 2003). Other research efforts control for social and economic determinants of crime thought to influence racial/ethnic disparities across neighborhoods (Lee et al., 2001; Morenoff & Sampson, 1997). None have found evidence suggesting that increased immigration is associated with higher levels of Latino lethal violence (Martinez, 2002, 2006). This body of work is important because there is a strong relationship between economic well-being and violent crime, and this connection has received a great deal of attention given the racial/ethnic differences in the strength of the association between crime and socioeconomic context.

Latinos and Immigration

A review of contemporary research on racial/ethnic differences in crime also highlights the fact that studies with a focus on Latino experiences with crime and victimization are in short supply. For example, in the notable research by Sampson and Wilson (1995), the emphasis was on explaining crime differences between Blacks and Whites, leaving unexamined questions regarding whether and to what degree the explanations could be generalized and applied to Latinos. This approach was entirely consistent with the existing research because the majority of the analyses on race and violence focused on deep-rooted social and economic divisions between Blacks and Whites in urban America, especially in areas where the loss of manufacturing jobs devastated the local economy.

However, historically high peaks in immigration have transformed the ethnic composition across the nation, and Latinos have emerged as the largest ethnic minority group in the United States (Sampson & Bean, 2006). Latinos now comprise about 14 percent of the population, with many members of this population having migrated from Spanish-speaking Latin American countries. Some scholars have started to address the compelling issues that impact Latino violence, advancing the research beyond the traditional reliance on a comparison of Black and White crime.

In general, researchers have evaluated whether the cultural and structural conditions relevant to Black and White violence also apply to Latinos (Peterson & Krivo, 2005). Martinez and colleagues have been at the vanguard of recent ecological analyses of Latino violence and have provided results that lay the groundwork for future research by suggesting the predictors of Latino violence or homicide are unique (Peterson & Krivo, 2005). Using homicide or violent crime data gathered directly from police departments and linked to census tracts (widely used as proxies for communities), Martinez and colleagues (Lee et al., 2001; Martinez, 1996; Martinez & Lee, 2000; Martinez et al., 2008; Stowell & Martinez, 2009) analyzed Latino-specific homicide either alone or in comparison with models for native-born Blacks and Whites, and sometimes immigrant Haitians, Jamaicans, or Latino subpopulations (e.g., Mariel Cubans). This body of research noted that Latino males usually follow the familiar pattern seen with Black and White males in terms of the all-encompassing effect of concentrated disadvantage or lack of economic well-being, even though some predictors of Latino homicide are distinct. Thus, being disadvantaged predicts levels of lethal violence for African Americans, Haitians, and Latinos in the city of Miami, and similar findings hold for Blacks and Latinos in other places, such as the cities of San Diego and El Paso.

One issue influencing Latinos, much more so than Whites or Blacks, is the impact of immigration (for a discussion of race/immigration nexus, see Nielsen & Martinez, 2006). Some scholars have written about the "Latino paradox," where Latinos and immigrants do much better on certain health indicators, including violence, than Blacks and in some cases than Whites, given relatively high levels of disadvantage (Sampson & Bean, 2006; Stowell et al., 2009). Thus, Latinos record high levels of poverty but lower levels of homicide or violence than expected, given the power of economic disadvantage (or deprivation). The impact of recent immigration (i.e., the percentage of the foreign-born who have lived in the United States for fewer than ten years) and the role of immigrant concentration suggest that it may not be appropriate to conceive of an area's nativity composition as a proxy for more violence in the same way that the racial concentration of African Americans is described in the race and crime literature (Sampson & Bean, 2006; for more detailed discussions, see Martinez & Lee, 2000; Mears, 2001).

Martinez and colleagues have also been at the forefront of research debunking the popular notion that higher levels of immigration or percentage of immigrants leads to increased violence, directly challenging the belief that more immigrants necessarily means higher levels of homicide (Peterson & Krivo, 2005; Sampson & Bean, 2006). In fact, immigration generally has no systematic effect on violence in the manner anticipated by criminological theory, a notion that dates back to the turn of the last century—namely, that an influx of immigrants disrupts communities, creates neighborhood instability, and contributes to violent crime (Bursik, 2006). If immigration increases violent crime it should do so among Latinos and in Latino communities, as movement from abroad is heavily concentrated in Spanish-speaking countries. Instead, immigration policy makers should heed the research showing that more immigrant Latinos usually means *less* violent crime. The causal mechanisms behind this finding are not entirely clear, but scholars have speculated about several possible factors. Culturally, immigrant males might vary from the native born by selection issues, attachment to work, or ability to avoid authorities. Structurally, immigrants are poor, but are working, and have low levels of criminal activity. Thus, future researchers should pay closer attention to potential variations across and within various immigrant and ethnic groups including Latinos (Mears, 2001; Stowell, 2007; Stowell & Martinez, 2009).

One consistent finding in the empirical research literature is that there is little evidence that immigration promotes higher levels of lethal violence. Time and again studies show that average levels of neighborhood violence are higher, for example, in Miami than in Houston, which is largely attributable to the differences in the social structural contexts between these two cities. In Miami neighborhoods, not only are immigrants a larger share of the overall neighborhood populations, but they also tend to be more economically distressed (Stowell, 2007). With the inclusion of ethnic-specific measures of immigration, the findings yield a combination of negative and null effects of the presence of foreign-born ethnic groups on violent crime. In other words, more immigrants in Houston or Miami neighborhoods mean either less violent crime or no impact on violent crime, contrary to the popular impression that immigrant communities are crime-prone (Martinez 2002, 2006; Stowell, 2007; Stowell & Martinez, 2009).

Together the findings discussed above offer a consistent picture of the impact of immigration and other cultural and structural outcomes on violence across an array of Latino-dominated cities, yet there is a relative scarcity of studies examining this question in a national context. A number of recently published articles do take seriously the notion that the arrival of largely Latino and predominantly male immigrants may be systematically associated with national temporal patterns of violence (Ousey & Kubrin, 2009; Stowell et al., 2009; Wadsworth, 2010). The results from this series of studies document that the large increase in immigration over the past two decades is not associated with higher levels of crime, but rather that the level of criminal deviance is lower in the areas (i.e., cities, metropolitan areas) that experienced increases in the size of the foreign-born population.

Although these studies are able to frame the immigration/crime debate in a national context, they are limited by the fact that they are not able to disaggregate their measures of crime in order to quantify the degree to which cultural and structural factors may impact levels of crime or victimization for different racial/ethnic groups. Furthermore, studies that provide estimates regarding the connection between immigration and race/ethnic-specific *and* gender-specific criminal outcomes are even more uncommon. As mentioned above, we recognize that the lack of scholarly attention to questions on Latino male homicide risk is owing to a dearth of available data. However, we also submit that this is an important issue for which little empirical information is available. The absence of research on this narrow, yet substantively important subject is surprising given the attention that the purported relationship between immigration and crime receives in the popular press (for an exception, see Unz, 2010).

In an effort to address this gap in the research literature, we conducted an analysis using a national sample of counties that permits the separation of homicide victims by the race/ethnicity and sex of the victim (Table 17.2). In this analysis, we examined four male-specific dependent variables—total number of male homicide victims, Latino male victims, non-Latino White males, and non-Latino Black males (Martinez et al., 2010; for a discussion of the estimation procedure, see Stowell, 2007). The homicide data were provided by the National Center for Health Statistics through the Centers for Disease Control (CDC). Following previous research, in the regression models we also included a series of control variables, including indicators of socioeconomic distress in counties, as well as other factors such as age, occupation, and nativity compositions—information that was gathered from U.S. Census 2000 (Martinez et al., 2010; Reid et al., 2005; Sampson, 2008; Stowell, 2007; Stowell et al., 2009).

Turning to Table 17.2, a consistent picture emerges in the multivariate analysis with respect to the association between cultural and structural indicators and levels of male homicide. First, immigrant concentration, defined here as a combination of the percentage of the population who are foreign-born and the percentage of the population who are Hispanic/Latino, has a statistically significant and negative impact on all levels of male homicide victimization. Even after holding constant an array of indicators associated with levels of homicide, including economic disadvantage or economic stress, more immigration means lower levels of male homicide victimization for all groups including Latino males. This finding resonates with an emerging body of research literature that focuses on immigration and violence in a longitudinal context and identifies how increases in the foreign-born population contributed to the large reductions in violence observed over the past two decades (Martinez et al., 2010; Ousey & Kubrin, 2009; Stowell et al., 2009; Wadsworth, 2010). In sum, we find continued empirical support for the notion that greater economic disadvantage and fewer immigrants mean more male homicide, and that this effect holds even for the population most likely to experience violent victimization—that is, Latino males (Martinez, 2006; Sampson, 2008).

Conclusion

Overall, this chapter yields at least one clear conclusion: violent crime studies should include Latinos and Latino males as separate entities (from each other and from Blacks and Whites) whenever possible while considering cultural and structural influences. The growth of the Latino population across broad sectors of U.S. society mandates a renewed focus on multiple racial/ethnic/immigrant groups when comparing levels of violence across a variety of communities and regions, some of which, until recently, rarely encountered Latinos (Martinez, 2002). The expanded research focus will help scholars of violent crime obtain a broader understanding of the race/ethnic and violent crime linkages and expand

TABLE 17.2 Negative Binomial Regressions for Total and Race/Ethnic-specific Male Homicide Victimization (n = 323)

	Total		Hispanic/Latino		Non-Latino White		Non-Latino Black	
	B	s.e.	B	s.e.	B	s.e.	B	s.e.
Disadvantage index	0.153	0.009***	0.062	0.012***	0.019	0.010*	0.091	0.010***
Stability index	0.004	0.029	0.039	0.037	0.013	0.029	−0.004	0.035
% Professional	−0.003	0.005	−0.013	0.007	−0.021	0.005***	−0.010	0.006
Immigrant concentration	−0.003	0.001*	−0.005	0.002**	−0.004	0.001**	−0.005	0.002**
Adult–child ratio	−2.737	0.545***	−1.148	0.668	−2.527	0.555***	−2.490	0.679***
% Young males (18–34 years)	0.012	0.013	0.017	0.018	0.006	0.015	−0.013	0.016
Intercept	−9.038	0.315***	−8.829	0.419***	−9.438	0.317***	−7.319	0.385***

*p < 0.05, **p < 0.01, ***p < 0.001

Note: Race/ethnic-specific male populations are included in models as regression exposure. For each of the regressions, the counties had at least 5,000 Latino males regardless of the sizes of the other race/ethnic groups

Source: Homicide Victimization Data provided by the Center for Disease Control (CDC) and Independent Variables taken from 2000 Census

our focus to include such topics as the resilience of Latino males, including immigrants, in the face of immigration hysteria and economic disadvantage.

Policy Recommendations and Implications

There are a number of important issues concerning the research of Latino violence that should be addressed in the future. More data collection is necessary before we can answer important questions on Latino male violence in addition to those examined at the national level in this chapter. For example, how does economic disadvantage operate to produce violence within and across Latino groups in structurally similar communities, including educational opportunities and economic well-being? Many Latino communities have high levels of working poor but more data should be collected to help us better understand complex neighborhood dynamics. As immigrant Latino males move into older, established Latino areas, should we expect more or less conflict in places with ethnic succession, such as in Miami where Cubans are replaced by Columbians or Nicaraguans? Does Latino male violence rise in cities like Los Angeles and Houston where a dominant Mexican-origin population (native and foreign-born alike) resides along with Salvadorans and other Latino group members? It is also possible that, as disadvantaged as conditions in U.S. barrios may be, with low levels of educational achievement and poor economic well-being, the resilience of immigrant Latino males is fortified as their sending countries experience even worse economic well-being and political violence (Portes & Rumbaut, 2001).

There is also a need to conduct more qualitative and ethnographic research to provide important insights on emerging populations and broaden the portrait of Latino violence. For example, the degree to which Latino violence is shaped by masculinity, gender, and particularly the experience of Latinas has been largely ignored in the social scientific literature. Researchers should explore a variety of issues related to this topic: little is known about the prevalence or conditions influencing levels of either Latina victimization or offending. For example, to what degree is Latina violence shaped by inter-personal relations at home, work, school, or in the streets; or does immigrant status influence patterns of crime reporting among Latinas? These suggestions could be extended to include comparisons of Latinas to females of other racial/ethnic groups, and across a variety of neighborhood settings, including extremely poor communities, ethnically mixed middle-class communities, heavily immigrant communities, and primarily native-born areas. Studies with such a focus would shed more light on the connection to crime and victimization experiences of Latinas. Future qualitative studies should help us understand why Latinas are less crime-prone than expected in various settings and fill in the gap in the Latina violence literature.

This chapter also serves as a reminder of the importance of sound immigration policy based on research, not political rhetoric. According to long-held "wisdom," the assumed influence of immigration on criminal activity is that Latino males have high rates of violence or that immigrant males are crime-prone predators (for recent examples, see Martinez, 2006). These are longstanding beliefs promoted by some self-styled populist commentators in the mass media or are stereotypes rooted in anecdotes or impressions perpetuated by some politicians. These opinions ignore the broad reductions in violence simultaneous with increased Latino immigration over the past decade, the protective mechanism of concentrated immigration, and other aspects of the unique Latino male experience articulated in this chapter and in this book. In the current rabid anti-immigration climate, it is no longer reasonable to assume that immigration and immigrant Latino males have a deleterious impact on violent crime in contemporary U.S. society or that singling out Latinos with legislation to deter the movement of undocumented workers into communities will decrease crime, as some advocate. In fact, the opposite could occur if Latinos are targeted for selective enforcement of immigration laws and removed from their communities, reducing neighborhood stability and possibly setting the stage for increased crime now and perhaps later among the children of immigrants stigmatized by mean-spirited legislation.

Lastly, scholars should examine changes in cultural and structural conditions for Latino men over time and compare these to other racial and ethnic group members during an era of intense isolation, segregation, and immigration. An historical perspective will enable researchers to compare periods of high crime to low crime and permit comparison in racially and ethnically diverse or homogenous communities. Given the growth of the Latino population and the corresponding increase in ethnic diversity across the country, it is important to not only ask more questions about Latino male violence but to answer them with more serious cutting-edge research studies on violence, crossing theoretical and methodological approaches, academic disciplines, and data sources. This chapter highlights many studies focusing on Latino males that serve as starting points for future research but much more work remains to help assess the protective role of immigration in Latino communities and provide more meaningful context to explanations of ethnicity and crime.

References

Bursik, R. (2006). Rethinking the Chicago school of criminology: A new era of immigration. In R. Martinez, Jr., & A. Valenzuela (Eds.), *Immigration and crime: Race, ethnicity, and violence* (20–35). New York: New York University Press.

Catalano, S. M. (2006). National crime victimization survey: Criminal victimization, 2005. Washington, DC: Bureau of Justice Statistics Bulletin.

Dohan, D. (2003). *The price of poverty: Money, work, and culture in the Mexican American barrio.* Berkeley, CA: University of California Press.

Keppel, K. G., Pearcy, J. N., & Wagenar, D. K. (2002). *Trends in racial and ethnic-specific rates for the health status indicators: United States, 1990–98.* Hyattsville, MD: National Center for Health Statistics.

Kil, S. H., & Menjívar, C. (2006). The "war on the border": Criminalizing immigrants and militarizing the U.S.-Mexico border. In R. Martinez, Jr., & A. Valenzuela (Eds.), *Immigration and crime: Race, ethnicity, and violence* (164–188). New York: New York University Press.

Lee, M. T., Martinez, R., Jr., & Rosenfeld, R. (2001). Does immigration increase homicide? Negative evidence from three border cities. *Sociological Quarterly*, 42(4), 559.

Martinez R., Jr. (1996). Latinos and lethal violence: The impact of poverty and inequality. *Social Problems*, 43, 131–146.

Martinez, R., Jr. (2002). *Latino homicide: Immigration, violence and community.* New York: Routledge.

Martinez, R., Jr. (2003). Moving beyond Black and White violence: African American, Haitian, and Latino homicides in Miami. In D. F. Hawkins (Ed.), *Violent crime: Assessing race and ethnic differences* (22–43). New York: Cambridge University Press.

Martinez, R., Jr. (2006). Coming to America: The impact of the new immigration on crime. In R. Martinez, Jr., & A. Valenzuela (Eds.), *Immigration and crime: Race, ethnicity, and violence* (1–19). New York: New York University Press.

Martinez, R., Jr., & Lee, M. T. (2000). On immigration and crime. In G. Lafree (Ed.), *Criminal justice 2000: The changing nature of crime, Vol. 1* (485–524). Washington, DC: National Institute of Justice.

Martinez, R., Jr., Stowell, J. I., & Cancino, J. M. (2008). A tale of two border cities: Community context, ethnicity, and homicide. *Social Science Quarterly*, 89(1), 1–16.

Martinez, R., Jr., Stowell, J. I., & Lee, M. T. (2010). Immigration and crime in an era of transformation: A longitudinal analysis of homicides in San Diego, 1980–2000. *Criminology*, 48(3), 797–830.

Mears, D. P. (2001). The immigration-crime nexus: Toward an analytic framework for assessing and guiding theory, research, and policy. *Sociological Perspectives*, 44(1), 1–19.

Morenoff, J. D. (2005). Racial and ethnic disparities in crime and delinquency in the United States. In M. Tienda & M. Rutter (Eds.), *Ethnicity and causal mechanisms* (139–173). New York: Cambridge University Press.

Morenoff, J. D., & Sampson, R. J. (1997). Violent crime and the spatial dynamics of neighborhood transition: Chicago, 1970–1990. *Social Forces*, 76(1), 31–64.

Nielsen, A. L., & Martinez, R., Jr. (2006). Multiple disadvantages and crime among Black immigrants: Exploring Haitian violence in Miami's communities. In R. Martinez, Jr., & A. Valenzuela (Eds.), *Immigration and crime: Race, ethnicity and violence* (212–234). New York: New York University Press.

Ousey, G. C., & Kubrin, C. E. (2009). Exploring the connection between immigration and violent crime rates in U.S. cities, 1980–2000. *Social Problems*, 56, 447–473.

Peterson, R. D., & Krivo, L. J. (2005). Macrostructural analyses of race, ethnicity, and violent crime: Recent lessons and new directions for research. *Annual Review of Sociology*, 31(1), 331–356.

Portes, A., & Rumbaut, R. G. (2001). *Legacies: The story of the immigrant second generation.* Berkeley: University of California Press.

Reid, L. W., Weiss, H. E., Adelman, R. M., & Jaret, C. (2005). The immigration-crime relationship: Evidence across US metropolitan areas. *Social Science Research*, 34(4), 757–780.

Reidel, M. (2003). Homicide in Los Angeles County: A study of Latino victimization. In D. F. Hawkins (Ed.), *Violent crime: Assessing race and ethnic differences* (44–66). New York: Cambridge University Press.

Sampson, R. J. (2008). Rethinking immigration and crime. *Contexts*, 7, 28–33.

Sampson, R. J., & Bean, L. (2006). Cultural mechanisms and killing fields: A revised theory of community-level racial inequality. In R. D. Peterson, L. J. Krivo, & J. Hagan (Eds.), *The many colors of crime: Inequalities of race, ethnicity and crime in America* (8–36). New York: New York University Press.

Sampson, R. J., & Wilson, W. J. (1995). Toward a theory of race, crime, and urban inequality. In J. Hagan & R. D. Peterson (Eds.), *Crime and inequality (*14–36*)*. Stanford, CA: Stanford University Press.

Stowell, J. I. (2007). *Immigration and crime: The effects of immigration on criminal behavior*. New York: LFB Scholarly Publishing.

Stowell, J. I., & Martinez, R., Jr. (2009). Incorporating ethnic-specific measures of immigration in the study of lethal violence. *Homicide Studies*, 13, 315–324.

Stowell, J. I., Messner, S. F., McGeever, K. F., & Raffalovich, L. E. (2009). Immigration and the recent violent crime drop in the U.S.: A pooled, cross-sectional time-series analysis of metropolitan areas. *Criminology*, 47(3), 889–928.

Taylor, P. S. ([1932] 1970). *Mexican labor in the United States*. New York: Arno Press/New York Times.

Titterington, V. E., & Damphousse, K. R. (2003). Economic correlates of racial and ethnic disparity in homicide: Houston, 1945–1994. In D. F. Hawkins (Ed.), *Violent crime: Assessing race and ethnic differences* (67–88). New York: Cambridge University Press.

Unz, R. (2010, March, 22–31). His-Panic: Talk TV sensationalists and axe-grinding ideologues have fallen for a myth of immigrant lawlessness. *The American Conservative*.

Wadsworth, T. (2010). Is immigration responsible for the crime drop? An assessment of the influence of immigration on changes in violent crime between 1990 and 2000. *Social Science Quarterly*, 91, 531–553.

18

WHAT WE HAVE LEARNED

The Role of Public Policy in Promoting
Macro- and Micro-levels of
Intervention in Response to the
Challenges Confronting Latino Men

Pedro A. Noguera
Aída Hurtado
Edward Fergus

The chapters in this book provide a launching pad from which a set of policy interventions and policy principles can be proposed. Our hope in offering these is that community activists, politicians, practitioners, and policy makers can utilize them to counter the marginalization of Latino men and boys in various arenas. In addition, the incisive scholarship presented in this volume points to the areas where further research is needed to sharpen an understanding of the issues confronting Latino men and boys.

The Changing Social Scene

As growing numbers of baby boomers slide into their senior years and the number of retirees rapidly expands, the United States finds itself in a precarious position: there is a growing imbalance in numbers between those who rely on social security and those who work to keep the coffers of social security flush. Gradually, a growing number (though still a minority) of policy makers have come to recognize that it is essential for all children, regardless of their race, language or immigration status, to be educated and trained so that they can contribute to the growth and prosperity of society. Our desire is that their contributions will also make it possible for them to share in the economic opportunities that are created. Of course, as the current debate over immigration reminds us—most notably the stalled effort to adopt the Dream Act—we are still a long way from the time when a recognition of the demographic imperative will lead to more enlightened public policy.

Many political pundits and researchers may resist targeted interventions because they regard race- or gender-based policies as unwarranted. Some go so far as to suggest that race-specific policies may even contribute to intergroup conflict (McWhorter, 2001). The on-going discourse over whether or not we have entered a "post-racial" society and the conservative backlash against affirmative action will undoubtedly serve as significant obstacles to enacting the types of policies that are needed. Nonetheless, we believe that a case can be made for targeted interventions that are rooted in a rigorous analysis of social problems and human needs.

Origins of the Book

In the fall of 2009, the three editors of this volume organized a meeting of policy makers, researchers and practitioners focused on ameliorating the obstacles confronting disenfranchised Latino men. With support from the Ford Foundation, we brought together policy makers from education, health, employment, and criminal justice. In addition, we invited practitioners from these four areas who lead successful intervention programs in various parts of the United States; and researchers who study how to replicate successful models of intervention. The goal of the meeting was to use "best practices" in programmatic interventions as the basis for developing public policy strategies at the local, state, and federal level. For example, we brought the leaders of a job-training program in Los Angeles that has been successful at reducing recidivism among previously incarcerated men together with the Director of Juvenile Corrections for the states of New York and New Jersey. The conversation was rich and encouraging as those present realized that policies could be changed to allow for the development of similar programs elsewhere, which could in turn lead to concrete changes in behavioral outcomes. However, during the course of our day together it became clear that without the support of elected officials to enact legislation that leads to new policy, not much would change. In other words, we were forced to recognize that even though there was clear evidence that certain types of interventions were effective, policy is more likely to be driven by politics than research. Nonetheless, we believe it is still important to begin developing policy interventions that are rooted in sound research.

Below we propose some possible policy and programmatic recommendations for restructuring social institutions and re-designing public policy. These are necessarily framed in fairly general terms because in order to be effective, they would have to be modified to meet the needs of particular communities and regions. Despite their obvious limitations, we offer these recommendations because it is essential that we recognize that actions can be taken now to address the needs of Latino men and boys.

Macro and Micro Social Processes in the Disenfranchisement of Latino Men and Boys

A unifying theme in all of the chapters in this volume is a recognition that the disenfranchisement of Latino men and boys must be conceptualized as a process, one that is influenced by both macro and micro social factors, and not a state of being. Many of the analyses presented in this volume go back and forth in recognizing the influence of macro factors—racial discrimination, political victimization, economic restructuring—on the behavior of Latino men. We believe that understanding the influence of social structure on human behavior is a powerful and effective theoretical frame that should also be used to inform the types of policy changes that are needed. At the same time, we recognize that individuals retain the potential for human agency. In many ways, agency is most clearly evident among recent immigrants who often demonstrate extraordinary resilience in finding ways to support themselves and their families in their native countries. Throughout history, ordinary people have been able to exercise the power to transform their environments in positive and unpredictable ways.

For example, in Detroit, one of America's most economically depressed cities, Mexican immigrants have created a thriving business community that generates employment for hundreds of people at a time when the city is still losing jobs and population. According to a May 20, 2010 report on National Public Radio:

> Despite the city's severe economic problems . . . the Hispanic business community is flourishing. . . . Detroit's Latino population has more than doubled in the past 10 years. Mexicans came in droves during the 1990s and continue to trickle in. There are roughly 400,000 Latinos in Michigan; half of them live in Detroit. Many work in construction, landscaping and the service industry. But hundreds have opened food-related businesses.

If this type of collective agency is possible in a depressed city like Detroit, certainly it would be a mistake to become overly deterministic or pessimistic in our thinking about the impact of the current political climate on Latinos or the influence of social structure on human behavior.

Principles for Policy Interventions

We begin by outlining a set of policy principles and overarching guidelines that the authors in this volume propose as important steps that can be taken to alleviate the disenfranchisement of Latino men and boys. We follow with an overview of the most important social spheres that should be addressed when developing policy interventions. The final section of this chapter discusses the sites we should focus on for future research. Rather than leaving readers with the sense that the problem of Latino men's position in society is without solutions, we hope this mapping provides guidance for the design and application of policy interventions and points to areas that require further research and attention.

Although the chapters in this volume cover a broad variety of topics there are general guiding principles for developing policy interventions that the chapters have in common. These include:

- Educational interventions should be implemented early. The longer the educational hardships experienced by Latino boys are ignored, the more difficult it is to eradicate them. Increasing access to quality early childhood programs, providing extended learning opportunities, cultivating literacy and bilingualism during the elementary years, are just some of the ideas that the authors in this volume have suggested. A substantial body of research has shown that early intervention programs are both more cost effective and have a greater long term impact than those that are implemented after a problem has become manifest and been allowed to fester. For example, any effort to reduce the dropout rate among Latino men and to increase college attendance must begin with a concerted effort to improve educational support for Latino boys during the early years of their education.

- Policy interventions should be holistic and integrated. In order to respond to the broad range of individual needs—economic, social, psychological, emotional—that influence individual development—it is essential for policy interventions to be designed in a comprehensive manner. For example, any effort to reduce recidivism among recently incarcerated youth must not only address the educational and employment needs of young men as they make the transition to life on the outside but must also provide psychological and social support. This is the type of approach taken by the most successful community-based programs, and it is the approach that should be supported by policy at the local, state, and federal level. These interventions should also involve efforts to transform the institutions that serve young men and boys so that they become more responsive to their needs. Similarly, serious efforts to increase college enrollment must focus both on the changes that individuals might need to make (i.e., improved study habits, more pro-active help-seeking, etc.) as well as changes that are needed in the structure and climate of educational institutions (i.e., greater access to counselors and mentors, access to campus jobs, etc.) In many schools, this may mean conducting part of an early intervention in English and Spanish because of the predominance of immigrants in several schools.

- Policy interventions must be evaluated regularly and modified to ensure effectiveness. Too often, local communities and school districts adopt programs aimed at addressing a social issue or problem (gang involvement, youth unemployment, etc.) but fail to carry out effective evaluations of these efforts. Similarly, foundations frequently launch funding initiatives in response to a pressing problem but fail to consider how such interventions can be sustained. Sporadic efforts that are not evaluated or assessed for their effectiveness are unlikely to succeed in addressing the complex challenges confronting Latino men and boys. Without a commitment to sustain and adjust intervention efforts as necessary, it is unlikely they will have a lasting impact.

- Policy interventions should be sensitive to ethnic and racial differences among different groups of Latino men and boys. Many of the authors of this volume brilliantly illustrate how different groups of Latino men, differentiated by national origin, class, geographical location, educational level and age, need different kinds of interventions to advance in all arenas. The most effective interventions will be based upon an intersectional approach that acknowledges the complex interaction between ethnicity, gender, social class, and sexuality. Rather than a "one size fits all" approach, special attention needs to be paid to social context and the ways in which social identities are shaped by the unique conditions in a particular milieu. As Noguera and Hurtado point out in chapter 1 in this volume:

> Put most obviously, middle class fourth generation Cubans in Miami are likely to have different experiences with gender relations and masculinity than recent Mexican immigrants working at the poultry farms in Iowa, or Salvadoran war refugees living in central Los Angeles.

- Policy interventions should be designed to construct environments that benefit multiple constituencies. In *La Clase Mágica*, an intervention developed in San Diego schools, immigrant parents and their children are trained to use computers in collaborative activities after school. Researchers use university resources to conduct research with participants in *La Clase Mágica* and hire undergraduates to engage them in research. This type of collaborative approach provides each participant with a framework for maximizing the benefits of their undergraduate education. Such an approach makes it possible for parents to obtain English lessons and to begin to understand their role in their children's educational experience. Such approaches can make it possible for researchers to test their models with diverse populations and begin to understand the model's advantages and disadvantages from an ethnically and racially diverse perspective (Vásquez, 1996).

- Policy interventions should consider both individual and institutional/system levels of change. A growing body of research has shown that the most successful interventions for supporting students focus on both school change strategies and provide additional support for individual students. Similarly, interventions that are designed to address social problems like unemployment and under-employment, domestic violence, gang violence, and HIV must focus on both individual behaviors and the need for system change. As several of the authors in this volume have shown, changes in social outcomes can only be achieved through structural change and changes in individual behavior.

• Policy interventions must include systems of social support that create a context for in-depth inter-personal interactions. Several of the authors in this volume have shown that changes in the attitudes and behavior of Latino men and boys are most likely to occur if they are carried out within a collective, community-based approach rather than one that focuses exclusively on the individual (de Jesús Acosta, 2007). A collaborative approach that occurs within the support of a community is more likely to result in the internalization of a new set of attitudes and behaviors. This is true for health and education-based interventions and it may also be true for other social issues.

We turn now to the social spheres where changes are needed, which this volume proposes as important for policy development.

Relational Spheres of Intervention

Rather than conceptualizing the disenfranchisement of Latino men and boys as an insoluble puzzle, our analysis of the different spheres that influence the success of Latino men has allowed us to develop a broad and encompassing focus that does not exclude any one sphere as an area of intervention (Hurtado & Gurin, 2004). Such an approach is aimed at facilitating the development of policy interventions that link changes in individual behavior to system and institutional level changes within social spheres that influence outcomes for Latino men. It is our contention that when all aspects of an issue are taken into account—the underlying causes at the individual, familial, community, and societal level—the interventions that emerge as potential solutions will do more than merely assign blame; they will offer a collaborative set of strategies rooted in reciprocal relationships that benefit not only Latino men and boys but women as well, and eventually society as a whole.

Incorporating Community and Parents

A salient change in the younger years would be the integration of Latino parents (including extended family members such as grandparents, uncles, aunts, and cousins) into the policy interventions designed to help Latino men and boys. The research by Hurtado and Sinha (2006) indicate that many young Latino men attributed their educational success to the help received from their parents and from extended family members. Single parents in particular relied on family members for child care and after-school care (Hurtado, 2003). The research shows that isolated individuals, single-parent households, and disconnected youth are significantly more vulnerable than those who have the support of an extended family, and an influential group of mentors. Finding ways to extend social support to isolated individuals and providing assistance to families that are mired in destructive conflicts may be one of the most effective ways to improve outcomes for Latino men. The familial sphere may be harder to reach as a site of intervention due to concerns about privacy, but it is one area ripe for policy and programmatic interventions.

The Use of Peer Networks

For many young Latino men, peer networks can be used as sources of information, inspiration, and mentoring. In many cases, peer support is provided within families by older siblings and relatives who have experienced educational success. Most often, peer influences on young men are represented as a source of negative influence in the research literature (Gordon et al., 2004). Several studies on gangs and educational under-achievement document that many young men have to fend off negative pressures from peers in poor neighborhoods who are engaged in anti-social activities. There is also considerable evidence that the development of new networks and friendships could potentially serve to help young men by re-directing their activities toward success in school and in life (Riegle-Crumb & Callahan, 2009). However, in most instances of positive mentoring (e.g., an older sibling helping a younger one to succeed educationally), there is no structural support or guidance for these activities (Hurtado, 2003). Institutions should be more pro-active in providing support for informal mentoring, creating study groups for students (Treisman, 2009), and organizing activities such as visits to colleges and universities to expose them to higher education.

Proactive Mentoring

Young Latino men would benefit significantly from increased mentoring accompanied by strategic scaffolding throughout the educational pipeline. From previously conducted research (Stanton-Salazar et al., 2001), it is apparent that many Latino males are less likely to develop relationships that support and nurture them throughout their educational trajectories. The social networks that they belong to typically do not provide access to the bridging social capital—individuals with links to jobs, internships, and higher education—that expand opportunity and provide a pathway to social mobility. Angela Valenzuela's (1999) research demonstrates that many young women, especially girlfriends, provide the academic support needed by young Latino men. It should be possible for institutional resources in secondary and post-secondary settings to reinforce and undergird these informal efforts. Furthermore, these supportive educational structures should exist throughout the educational system, as many Latino men come from households in which they are the first generation to attend institutions of higher education and where most family members will be predominantly Spanish speakers (Verdugo, 2006). Rather than waiting for Latino males to get into trouble, it would be far more effective if mentoring were provided pro-actively so that help-seeking behavior was nurtured and supported throughout the educational experience.

Restructuring Education

Institutions of higher education have to be restructured to attract new constituencies who have not had the benefit of a long history of attendance in universities. While the federal government and groups like the Gates Foundation have made increasing access to college a national priority, they have framed the issue as one of increasing the number of students who are "college ready." Missing from the policy discourse is what colleges and universities must do to be ready and prepared for a new generation of students. Student Affairs and Academic Affairs departments at colleges and universities should work in tandem to create microenvironments where students become part of academic communities. Scholars such as Claude Steele (1997) have shown that alienation and social isola-tion take a particularly heavy toll on students of Color, and available research suggests that this is especially true for young Latino men. Informal peer networks are typically insufficient to provide the academic and social support that Latino young men and other vulnerable students require to succeed in higher education.

Developing a Critical Men's Studies

From the research presented in this volume, it is apparent that there is also the need for a critical men's studies where the negative aspects of different masculinities are explored. Many of the microprocesses holding young Latinos back are a result of the narrow, traditional forms of socialization that reinforce misogyny and chauvinism as an integral aspect of Latino masculinities. To the degree that these identities impede authentic engagement in healthy social relationships with women and other men, they are also likely to hinder educational and employment pursuits. As stated at the start of this paper, the coupling of these microprocesses with the state-sponsored violence against men of Color produces a deadly combination that may turn valuable minds away from educational pursuits and toward the criminal justice system.

Critical Examination of the Criminal Justice System

Finally, an analysis of educational achievement among Latino men cannot be carried out independently from an analysis of its relationship to the criminal justice system. Increasingly, the educational pipeline for young Latinos is intimately tied to the prison pipeline (Smith, 2009), and an analysis of that interaction and how it might be disrupted is essential to improving the educational trajectories of young Latino men. As many have already noted, educational programs and the building of educational institutions have been severely restricted because large sums of the public budget have been allocated toward prison building and maintenance (Newell, 2010). Additionally, Latino boys are over-represented among students who are suspended and expelled from school (Wald & Losen, 2003). Racial disparities in discipline practices have been shown to contribute to the delinquency and the criminalization of disadvantaged youth (Nicholson-Crotty et al., 2009). Young Latino men are especially vulnerable to these dynamics; behavior that is ordinarily not criminalized among white middle-class youth is lethal for young Latinos (Fine et al., 2003). Added to this burden, many young Latino men come from families that lack the resources to rescue them from the criminal justice system once they are pegged as "troublesome" youth. Furthermore, once these young men are in the system or under custody, very little effort is made to ensure their success when they leave criminal justice institutions. These dynamics are especially detrimental during adolescence, a period when young people typically obtain the education and life skills that will help them succeed in life. Illiteracy is rampant in juvenile halls, jails, and prisons. Lacking minimal skills to re-enter educational institutions, the educational failure of young Latinos is assured.

There must be a concerted effort to establish strong educational programs (e.g. adult literacy, GED programs, college enrollment, etc.) within the prison system. A vast body of research has shown that individuals who are able to pursue their education while incarcerated are substantially less likely to return to prison than those who are denied educational opportunities (Vacca, 2004). Education, counseling and job training can also prepare Latino men to re-enter their communities as productive individuals who can contribute to the well-being of their families and break the cycle of crime and violence that plagues many poor communities.

This is only a partial listing of the many principles and research areas that can be derived from the chapters in this volume and other related research on successful policy interventions. We encourage our readers to expand upon these recommendations, to critique them, and to offer new ones based upon further experience and research.

References

de Jesús Acosta, F. (2007) *The history of Barrrios Unidos. Healing community violence*. Cultura es cura. Houston: Arte Público Press.

Fine, M., Freudenberg, N., Payne, Y., Perkins, Y., Smith, K, & Wanzer, K. (2003). Anything can happen with police around: Urban youth evaluate strategies of surveillance in public places. *Journal of Social Issues, 59*(1), 141–158.

Gordon, R. A., Lahey, B. B., Kawai, E., Loeber, R., Stouthamer-Loeber, M., & Farrington, D. P. (2004). Antisocial behavior and youth gang membership: Selection and socialization. *Criminology, 42*(1), 55–87.

Hurtado, A. (2003). *Voicing Chicana feminisms: Young women speak out on sexuality and identity*. New York: New York University Press.

Hurtado, A., & Gurin, P. (2004). *Chicana/o identity in a changing U.S. Society. ¿Quién soy? ¿Quiénes somos?* Tucson: The University of Arizona Press.

Hurtado, A., & Sinha, M. (2006). Differences and similarities: Latina and Latino doctoral students navigating the gender divide. In J. Castellanos, A. M. Gloria, & M. Kamimura (Eds.), *The Latina/o pathway to the Ph.D.: Abriendo Caminos* (149–168). Sterling, VA: Stylus.

McWhorter, J. (2001). *Losing the race: Self-sabotage in Black America*, 3rd edition. New York: Harper Perennial.

Newell, M. (2010, September). Dwindling public investment in higher education and growing funding for prisons. Sacramento, CA: California Postsecondary Education Commission. Retrieved from www.cpec.ca.gov/Agendas/Agenda1009/Chair_2.Pdf

Nicholson-Crotty, S., Birchmeier, Z., & Valentine, D. (2009). Exploring the impact of school discipline on racial disproportion in the juvenile justice system. *Social Science Quarterly*, 90(4), 1003–1018.

Riegle-Crumb, C., & Callahan, R. M. (2009). Exploring the academic benefits of friendship ties for Latino boys and girls. *Social Science Quarterly*, 90, 611–631.

Smith, C. D. (2009). Deconstructing the pipeline: Evaluating school-to-prison pipeline equal protection cases through a structural racism framework. *Fordham Urban Law Journal*, 36(5), 1009–1049.

Stanton-Salazar, R. D., Chavez, L. F., & Tai, R. H. (2001). The help-seeking orientations of Latino and non-Latino urban high school students: A critical-sociological investigation. *Social Psychology of Education*, 5(1), 49–82.

Steele, C. (1997). A threat in the air: How stereotypes shape intellectual identity and performance. *American Psychologist*, 69(5), 797–811.

Treisman, U. (2009, March). Carnegie perspectives: Assessing how students learn. *CIRTL Network*, Austin, TX.

Vacca, J. (2004). Educated prisoners are less likely to return to prison. *Journal of Correctional Education*, 55(4), 297–305.

Valenzuela, A. (1999). *Subtractive schooling: U.S. Mexican youth and the politics of caring*. Albany: State University of New York.

Vásquez, O. A. (1996). A model system of institutional linkages: Transforming the educational pipeline. In A. Hurtado, R. Figueroa, & E. Garcia (Eds.), *Strategic interventions in education: Expanding the Latina/Latino pipeline* (137–166). Santa Cruz, CA: Regents of the University of California.

Verdugo, R. (2006). *A report on the status of Hispanics in education: Overcoming a history of neglect*. Washington, DC: National Education Association.

Wald, J., & Losen, D. J. (2003). Defining and redirecting a school-to-prison pipeline. *New Directions for Youth Development,* 99, 9–15. Retrieved from http://onlinelibrary.wiley.com/doi/10.1002/yd.51/pdf

CONTRIBUTORS

Ian Ankney is currently a graduate student at the University of Denver earning a degree in sport performance and psychology. He played soccer at the University of the Incarnate Word where the program was ranked in the top 20 in the nation each year.

Grigoris Argeros is an Assistant Professor at Mississippi State University. His Ph.D. research at Fordham University investigated nativity, birthplace, and locational outcome differences among Black ethnic groups in the United States.

Megan Brodie is a graduate at the University of the Incarnate Word; her B.A. is in psychology.

Dolores Inés Casillas is an Assistant Professor of Chicana and Chicano Studies at the University of California, Santa Barbara. She researches and teaches on the topics of Latino media and language politics, as well as gender and immigration.

Alexandra Cordero is a Ph.D. candidate in Counseling Psychology at New York University's Steinhardt School of Culture, Education and Human Development.

Daysi Diaz-Strong received an M.A. in Educational Leadership from Northeastern Illinois University. She has been a community college administrator in Illinois for eight years.

María Félix-Ortiz is an Associate Professor of Psychology at the University of the Incarnate Word in San Antonio, and former columnist for the San Antonio Express-News. Her publications are in drug use, community psychology, and cultural identity.

Edward (Eduardo) Fergus is the Deputy Director of the Metropolitan Center for Urban Education at New York University. He holds a B.A. in Political Science from Beloit College and a Ph.D. in Social Foundations and Education Policy from the University of Michigan.

Christina Gómez is an Associate Professor of Sociology and Latino & Latin American Studies Program at Northeastern Illinois University in Chicago. Her research has concentrated on racial identity construction in the United States, discrimination, and immigration.

Craig W. Haney is a Professor of Psychology at the University of California, Santa Cruz. He has a doctorate in Psychology and a J.D. degree from Stanford University. His empirical research and scholarly writing are focused on the nature of crime, punishment, and injustice.

Aída Hurtado is Professor and Chair of the Chicana and Chicano Studies Department at the University of California, Santa Barbara, where she holds the Luis Leal Endowed Chair. Professor Hurtado received her B.A. in Psychology and Sociology from Pan American University, Edinburg, Texas, and her Ph.D. in Social Psychology from the University of Michigan. Her research focuses on feminism, education, and media representations of gender and race.

José Hurtado is a Child Welfare Worker for Alameda County. Hurtado received his B.A. in Community Studies from the University of California at Santa Cruz and his Master's degree in Social Work at San Jose State University.

Nancy López is Associate Professor of Sociology at the University of New Mexico and co-directs the Institute for the Study of "Race" & Social Justice, housed at the Robert Wood Johnson Foundation Center for Health Policy at UNM. Dr. López's research focuses on "race," ethnicity, education, and gender.

María E. Luna-Duarte is the Interim Director at Northeastern Illinois University-El Centro Campus. She is currently pursuing a Ph.D. in Policy Studies in Urban Education from the University of Illinois at Chicago. Her research interests include the access and retention of minority students in higher education.

Ramiro Martinez, Jr. is a Professor in the School of Criminology and Criminal Justice and the Department of Sociology and Anthropology at Northeastern University in Boston, Massachusetts. His research interests include exploring the determinants of race/ethnicity and crime, with a special focus on immigration population.

Erica R. Meiners, a Professor of Education and Women's Studies at Northeastern Illinois University, has written about her on-going labor and learning in justice movements in *Flaunt it! Queers organizing for public education and justice* (2009), *Right to be hostile: schools, prisons and the making of public enemies* (2007), and articles in *Radical Teacher, Meridians, AREA Chicago,* and *Social Justice.*

Michael H. Miyawaki is working on his dissertation in Sociology at Fordham University. His research focuses on the racial identity of the offspring of Latino intermarriages.

Miguel Muñoz-Laboy is an Associate Professor of Sociomedical Sciences at the Mailman School of Public Health at Columbia University. He is currently the principal investigator of two research studies funded by the National Institute of Health: Network determinants of sexual risk, marijuana, and alcohol use among formerly incarcerated Latino men; and Gender, power and HIV risk among Latino bisexual men.

Pedro Antonio Noguera is the Peter L. Agnew Professor of Education at New York University and the Executive Director of the Metropolitan Center for Urban Education.

Maria C. Olivares Pasillas is a Master's student in the Social Sciences and Comparative Education program in UCLA's Graduate School of Education and Information Studies. Her research interests include representation of Latina/o youth in television and radio commercials, critical media literacy, and Latina/o youth and media education.

Ashley Perry currently works as a researcher at the Center for Gender Sexuality and Health at Columbia University. Her studies focus on sociocultural and structural determinants of sexual and reproductive health, spatial analysis of risk and social vulnerabilities, and the development of multilevel intervention initiatives for improving Latino men's health. Prior to her current position, she conducted health services systems research, and assisted in the implementation of localized medical interventions across the United States.

Horacio N. Roque Ramírez is Associate Professor at the University of California Santa Barbara, and the author of two forthcoming books: the co-edited anthology *Bodies of evidence*, and his own *Queer Latino San Francisco.*

Catherine Ramsay Roberts is Assistant Professor of Psychiatry (Psychology) at the University of Texas Medical School. She has a long-time interest in life stress and mental health functioning and the mental health of adolescents, in particular depression, suicide, and insomnia.

Robert E. Roberts is Professor of Behavioral Sciences at the University of Texas School of Public Health. He has a long-time interest in the mental health and functioning of minorities, particularly Mexican Americans. His research focuses on depression, psychiatric disorders more generally, suicidality, and insomnia.

Harold Rodinsky is an Assistant Professor of Psychology at the University of the Incarnate Word, San Antonio, Texas. His research is in social cognition, teaching of psychology, and service learning.

Clara E. Rodríguez is Professor in the Sociology and Anthropology Department at Fordham University. Her research has focused on Latinas/os in the United States, and she is now examining race and ethnicity in globally comparative contexts. She is expanding her research from Latinas/os in the United States to international comparisons of race and ethnicity.

Carlos Santos is Assistant Research Professor at Arizona State University.

Phillip Serrato is Assistant Professor of English and Comparative Literature at San Diego State University, where he is on the faculty of the National Center for the Study of Children's Literature. His research and teaching interests include gender and sexuality in Chicano/a literature, film, and performance.

Jacob I. Stowell is an Assistant Professor at the University of Massachusetts Lowell. Currently, his research interests include immigration, immigrant mortality, and the temporal impacts of immigration on levels of violence.

Mellie Torres is a doctoral candidate at New York University researching the educational experiences of Latino males. She received a Master's degree in Public Policy from the University of Michigan and a Master's degree in Teaching from Montclair State University.

Niobe Way is Professor of Applied Psychology in the Department of Applied Psychology at New York University. She is also the Director of the Developmental Psychology program and the co-Director of the Center for Research on Culture, Development, and Education at New York University.

Abel Valenzuela Jr. is Professor and Chair of the César E. Chávez Department of Chicana/o Studies at the University of California, Los Angeles. He is also Professor in the Department of Urban Planning and Director of the Center for the Study of Urban Poverty. His research on labor market inequality among low skill immigrant workers has been widely published.

James Diego Vigil is Professor of Social Ecology at University of California, Irvine. His research interests include street youth and gangs, ethnohistory of Mexican Americans, and psychology and education of Mexican Americans.

INDEX

Please note that page references in *italics* refer to figures and tables. Page numbers followed by the letter 'n' refer to notes.